Plant Identification

PEOPLE AND PLANTS CONSERVATION SERIES

Series Editor
Martin Walters

Series Originator
Alan Hamilton

People and Plants is a joint initiative of WWF,
the United Nations Educational, Scientific
and Cultural Organization (UNESCO)
and the Royal Botanic Gardens, Kew

Plant Identification

Creating User-Friendly Field Guides
for Biodiversity Management

Anna Lawrence and William Hawthorne

London • Sterling, VA

First published by Earthscan in the UK and USA in 2006

This publication is an output from a research project funded by the United Kingdom Department for International Development (DFID) for the benefit of developing countries. The views expressed are not necessarily those of DFID. R7475 and R7367 Forestry Research Programme.

ISBN-10: 1-84407-079-4

ISBN-13: 978-1-84407-079-4

Typesetting by MapSet Ltd, Gateshead, UK
Cover design by Yvonne Booth
Index by Indexing Specialists (UK) Ltd

Printed and bound in the UK by Bath Press

For a full list of publications please contact:

Earthscan
8–12 Camden High Street
London, NW1 0JH, UK
Tel: +44 (0)20 7387 8558
Fax: +44 (0)20 7387 8998
Email: earthinfo@earthscan.co.uk
Web: **www.earthscan.co.uk**

22883 Quicksilver Drive, Sterling, VA 20166-2012, USA

Earthscan is an imprint of James and James (Science Publishers) Ltd and publishes in association with the International Institute for Environment and Development

Printed on elemental chlorine-free paper

Contents

10 Publishing the field guide
Anna Lawrence

List of plates, figures, tables and boxes

PLATES

The plate section is betwen pages 144 and 145

FIGURES

TABLES

BOXES

List of case studies

People and Plants Partners

WWF

The World Wide Fund for Nature (WWF), founded in 1961, is the world's largest private nature conservation organization. It consists of 29 national organizations and associates and works in more than 100 countries. The coordinating headquarters are in Gland, Switzerland. The WWF mission is to conserve biodiversity, to ensure that the use of renewable natural resources is sustainable and to promote actions to reduce pollution and wasteful consumption.

UNESCO

The United Nations Educational, Scientific and Cultural Organization (UNESCO) is the only UN agency with a mandate spanning the fields of science (including social sciences), education, culture and communication. UNESCO has over 40 years of experience in testing interdisciplinary approaches to solving environmental and development problems in programmes such as that on Man and the Biosphere (MAB). An international network of biosphere reserves provides sites for conservation of biological diversity, long-term ecological research and demonstrating approaches to the sustainable use of natural resources.

ROYAL BOTANIC GARDENS, KEW

The Royal Botanic Gardens (RBG), Kew, has 150 professional staff and associated researchers, and works with partners in over 42 countries. Research focuses on taxonomy, preparation of floras, economic botany, plant biochemistry and many other specialized fields. The Royal Botanic Gardens has one of the largest herbaria in the world and an excellent botanic library.

Acknowledgements

This book has been five years in the making, off and on, and was inspired by our diverse experiences of producing field guides before that, which led to the idea of a manual based on actual experience, tested and documented through a logical process with the users. It has been a collaboration between two research projects, and we thank John Palmer, manager of the Forestry Research Programme, for bringing us together, and Katelijne van Rothschild, senior administrator, who has constantly supported and encouraged us.

For encouragement and the opportunity to publish this within the People and Plants Initiative series, we thank Alan Hamilton, Anthony Cunningham and Susanne Schmitt, and for initial guidance and direction, we thank Steve Tilling (Field Studies Council), Sandra Knapp (Natural History Museum), Gwilym Lewis and Simon Mayo (both of the Royal Botanic Gardens, Kew).

Thanks from Anna Lawrence go in particular to Bob Allkin of the Royal Botanic Gardens, Kew (and based in Brazil during the time of the project), who helped to create the project and provided much energy and input to debates and team-building. Thanks, also, to Frans Pareyn of the Plantas do Nordeste Programme, Brazil; Carlos Eduardo Leite of Serviço de Assessoria às Organizações Populares Rurais (SASOP); Luciano Queiroz of the University of Feira de Santana; and Pierre Ibisch of the Fundación Amigos de la Naturaleza for their advice and support to the research teams in Brazil and Bolivia. The members of those research teams are co-authors of some of the chapters; but the whole process relies on their actions, reflections and communication, all of which have been part of a profound and rewarding learning experience for which I am particularly grateful. In the UK, Karen Jarvis helped to organize material at an early stage when it all seemed rather confusing, and Mark Temple contributed elegant translations as I sought to incorporate documents arriving in Spanish and Portuguese.

Acknowledgements from William Hawthorne: apart from our project staff, who are listed as authors of some chapters, thanks go to Stuart Cable, Rosemary Wise and, in particular, Colin Hughes, who was initially in charge of the project and worked briefly in Mexico with the Sociedad para el Estudio de Recursos Bióticos de Oaxaca (SERBO), before leaving to monograph lupins, whereupon William Hawthorne has since managed the project. Thanks also to Stephen Harris, curator of the Oxford University herbaria, and Alison Strugnell for keeping the herbarium in order. Our main collaborators in Grenada have been Alan Joseph (chief forest officer), and with the fieldwork and interviews, Dean Jules and Alban Clarke (forestry co-workers).

In Ghana, we were greatly assisted by Abu Juam Musah (Ministry of Lands Biodiversity Unit and Northern Savanna Biodiversity Project), Ntim Gyakari (curator of the Kumasi Forest Herbarium), Patrick Ekpe (curator of the Legon Herbarium), and Nana Adjoa, Agatha Rockson, Leititia Owusu and other field assistants. We are grateful to the Ghana Forestry Commission; Forestry Resource Management Service Centre, Kumasi; the Ghana Game and Wildlife Department, especially their European Union-supported Protected Areas Development Project; the Botany Department of the University of Ghana, Legon; and to Andreas Brede (manager of the Oda-Kotoamso Agroforestry Project, Ghana, and of Samartex Ltd, Samreboi). In Cameroon, our main collaborators have been the staff of Limbe Botanic Garden, and thanks go especially to Nouhou Ndam, Rita Lysinge and Elias Ndive. We also thank approximately 1500 respondents who took part in our interviews and field trials.

1

Identifying biodiversity: Why do we need field guides?

Anna Lawrence and William Hawthorne

INTRODUCTION

Plants and animals are the life support systems for all of us. People who farm, live in forests or depend upon fishing are particularly aware of this because they take produce directly from nature. Managing those resources has become the motto of the 21st century as the crowded planet struggles to accommodate all of us and our aspirations for a better life. Yet, it is not only our immediate use of nature for food, warmth, shelter and income that demands our attention; our climate, soil and water need these things to go on working together, functioning as a complete, healthy system. Scientists, and many others, now refer to this complete system and all of its constituent species, genes and habitats as 'biodiversity'.

Consideration of this wider concept – biodiversity rather than just the species we use on a daily basis – brings a host of further concerns, such as maintaining climate regulation, food security and medicinal discoveries in the future, and emphasizes the wealth of meaning that nature has for our planet's diverse cultures and religions. These concerns came to a head in 1992 when the world's nations met in Rio de Janeiro to labour over the details of the Convention on Biological Diversity (CBD). The 180 parties to the CBD have committed themselves, under international law, to 'the conservation of biological diversity, the sustainable use of its components and the fair and equitable sharing of the benefits arising out of the utilization of genetic resources'.

This question of fair and equitable sharing of benefits from biodiversity has been explicitly linked to rural communities in developing countries, who live among the greatest wealth of species on Earth and are often heirs to rich and unique knowledge about that biodiversity, yet who rarely benefit directly from conservation or scientific exploitation. There has been plenty of debate and some innovative laws and practices to link local people more closely with the benefits from conservation and sustainable use. This book is written in the belief that tools that enable more people to identify and know biodiversity can also contribute to rural livelihoods. They can do this by helping rural people to recognize and manage their biodiversity by linking with scientific knowledge, but in many less direct ways, as well. When eco-tourists buy guides that have been prepared by communities, or through science–community collaboration, they are helping to put money directly into the hands of the local communities without middle-men, while supporting some local pride in being able to show tourists how much the communities understand of the local biota. There is also a potentially beneficial role for the communities in being able to identify plants reliably, demonstrating their capacity for managing these resources when they are negotiating with government agencies about tenure and rights to manage biodiversity. Finally, of course, the national offices which are mandated to report as signatories of the United Nations Framework Convention on Biological Diversity, and the related planning and management of national, regional and local biodiversity, can enhance both natural biodiversity monitoring and local involve-ment (and employment) if they have the right tools to enable these tasks to be devolved to rural people.

So, there are both local and global pressures to take more care in our use of biodi-versity. To do this, we need to know biodiversity better. Knowing biodiversity achieves two things: it makes us better managers because we can observe what is there and measure the impact of our activities on biodiversity; and it motivates more of us to be managers, in the widest sense, by inspiring and educating us about the natural world.

There are different ways to know biodiversity: through direct exploration of the natural world; learning with experts; and studying and comparing our learning with what we observe. Both scientists and local people have valuable knowledge about plants. In order to manage, use and conserve plants we need to improve communication of useful information about plants. Central to this is the need for accurate identification of the plant – if we do not know which species we are talking about it is impossible to exchange information about it.

This book is about helping rural people, farmers, tourists, students, amateurs and a whole host of different kinds of people to engage with biodiversity by being better able to identify what it is they are looking at. Specifically, it is about producing tools to help people identify species, in a scientific way, while also recognizing the need for informa-tion to be presented in a culturally appropriate and relevant way, according to the requirements of the people who use those tools.

HOW DO WE 'KNOW' NATURE?
CLASSIFYING, NAMING AND RECOGNIZING

Sorting and classifying are fundamental human activities. Young children can be completely absorbed in sorting fallen leaves, accurately, into piles according to species. They are quick to pick up the 'feel' of the species and sort them precisely, without worry-ing about either the names of the trees or the purpose of sorting. A label or name remembered guarantees a slot in our mind reserved for the plant and its associations, and makes the noun concrete; for this reason, of course, names are inevitable whenever we become serious about managing or understanding a resource. For scientists, the naming of species – that is, inventing a name from scratch, rather than identifying – is at the centre of scientific taxonomy, and 'nomenclature' (the system for naming species) is controlled by strict rules. This is covered in Chapter 4.

Having classified and named a species, there remains the crucial step of recognizing it when you come across it again. People who are not familiar with plants, or who do not recognize them immediately, have various options: ask an expert; collect a specimen and take it to a herbarium for comparison with other, named, specimens; work through a flora or monograph which asks them a series of questions about the flowers and fruits of the plant, sometimes microscopic and difficult to observe; or use a field guide. All of these options can be slow and expensive, or require training; but well-designed field guides can provide the fastest answer. Field identification revolutionized and democratized natural history in Europe and North America in the past and can have equally dramatic impacts in other parts of the world now.

FIELD GUIDES

What is a field guide?

We discuss in Chapter 4 precisely what we mean by 'field guide' because the term should be understood in the context of the full range of publications that relate to how plants are identified.

By 'guide' we mean a source of information: a reference tool. We are not talking about people as guides – signposts in a national park are also excluded; but a poster on a tree in a national park telling us about the poisonous plants is close to the borderline of what we might include. If it explains how to distinguish various species of these poisonous plants, the poster would qualify.

By 'field' we are distinguishing guides that are intended to be carried into the wild, out of the lab or herbarium, out of the realm of microscopes and test tubes, but potentially still within the realm of pocket hand lenses and our taste buds and noses. The implication is that these are guides that people will carry along with them, as opposed to being intended primarily for the library reference shelves. A computer guide will only become a true field guide if the computer is to be carried and used in the field.

We don't, however, want to be too purist about the definition; so if a guide is primarily about identifying species in the wild, and yet is only available on the internet and is not easily printed out for outdoor use, we may nevertheless consider it in this book. However, the internet is not – in 2006, at least – an ideal medium for this purpose.

Most popular field guides are, in practice, books (or laminated cards) concerned with identification. Their main point is to tell you the generally accepted name(s) of something – an unknown animal, mineral or vegetable – that you have come across while outside. There is often also other information in existing field guides – perhaps about the uses or ecology of the species, snippets of interesting trivia or facts which might corroborate your tentative identification. There is a strong presumption of identification as the main purpose of the guide, and this generally affects the layout and sequence of the books.

Most field guides are aimed at the general public and rely heavily on pictures. This is in contrast to other sorts of scientific identification tools, which are aimed at experts, where illustration tends to be seen as less important than technical writing.

In this book, we do make some excursions in to the more general realm of 'plant guides', and under this heading we will include publications that encourage use of plants through disseminating local knowledge.

Field guides obviously did not suddenly spring into being as we see them today; for a start, the notion of 'the field' was very different when explorers were discovering new continents by ship. Such explorers might have taken a large guide book for identifying plants on their trips if it was kept mainly in their cabin and carried by servants. Illustrations of old plant books were often engraved, and the possibilities for high-resolution printing in a small book were limited. Development in field guide production in industrialized countries has been driven by demand and commercial decisions, and the availability of improved photographic and colour printing technology; but big developments have also been going on elsewhere. As biodiversity hit the international agenda, governments and scientists became anxious to monitor it – to know what is there and how it is changing. International tourists began to find it attractive and to pay for eco-tourism; and communities and development workers sought ways of conserving their traditional knowledge about plants and their uses, and of communicating methods of cultivating and using them. All of these people required ways of identifying the plants, or checking their names in order to find the information associated with them. New kinds of guides sprang up to meet these demands.

What can a field guide achieve?

If asked: 'What is the purpose of your field guide?', most authors would probably reply: 'To help people identify plants.' But what does this identification of plants achieve? Why is it that the authors have gone to the trouble of putting together a field guide in order to help people identify plants? Is it to improve conservation, educate the public, attract eco-tourists or help forest management? To find out, it is useful to look at existing guides and ask both their authors and their users about the effects of using the guide. Many users can say how they have used it, and authors can divulge what feedback they have received.

The World Bank has given considerable support to field guide production over the last decade, based on the philosophy that 'people will only protect what they love and can love only what they know'. In Indonesia, for example, the Indonesian Institute of Sciences commissioned or translated 15 field guides covering birds, amphibians, dragon-flies, snails, bamboos, orchids and wild bananas, among others. These guides make biodiversity information easily accessible to students, environmental assessment professionals and the broader public, and help to build a constituency for conservation.

We shall see throughout this book that guides in different circumstances can achieve some or all of the following:

- By enhancing general accuracy of identification of plants in the field, they can improve the precision of forest inventories, growth and yield studies, or pre-harvest stock maps (where one identification error can cost a timber company hundreds if not thousands of dollars).
- Secondary benefits of the above are, then, a greater probability of sustainable logging and more efficient selection between protection and production areas.
- By allowing local users of a forest to look up a scientific name, and by allowing scientists to validate a local name, a better link between global and local knowledge is likely. People can look up whether species are globally rare, locally used, toxic, dangerous to livestock, nutritious or self-fertile – the list is endless and the benefits unpredictable.

- By improving general knowledge of plants, local residents will have more to tell tourists and are more likely to earn money as tourist guides. Eco-tourists are more likely to enjoy themselves on a forest visit and recommend the place (and the guide) to their friends.
- Field guides, particularly less technical ones, are commodities in themselves even if they are not used for identification. People buy them as souvenirs, and people can profit by selling them to tourists.
- Situated in a library, or advertised or available on the internet, field guides are a beacon that say: these people value this forest; this forest must be of some interest. They put the ecosystem on the map for politicians, bankers, visitors and others to see.

Why do we need new field guides and a manual?

The authors of the *Global Biodiversity Assessment*, a mammoth work to establish the base-line of biodiversity assessment after the CBD in 1992, state: 'The range of available field guides, keys and other identifying aids is a major constraint to the assessment of biodiversity' (Heywood, 1995, p568).

Scientific work (biodiversity monitoring and ecological studies) is being held up by the lack of guides based on recent taxonomic revision, and especially by the lack of guides in local languages. Botanists may know the species well; but they often produce guides that are difficult to use (for example, because they do not know the users well). Conversely, local people and community workers may know the users well, but may produce guides that contain scientifically inaccurate information.

We intend this manual to be useful to all producers of plant guides by focusing on the process which they should follow in order to ensure that the guide will suit the objective of the author and users, and the needs and abilities of the user group for which it is intended. The manual also helps the producers of guides to work within the limits of available resources. The manual is supported by the Virtual Field Herbarium (VFH) website (see Box 1.1).

In this book, we focus on plant field guides for several reasons. First, the great majority of field guides are for birds (as many as 70 per cent, according to Stevenson et al, 2003). However, there are about 25 times more species of plants than of birds. Second, plants, as primary producers, often form the most significant part of the biomass and control climate. And, finally, we are botanists. Having said all of that, we believe that most of the main points in this manual will also apply to animal guides.

In writing this book, we worked with teams of researchers in five countries to explore more systematic and participatory ways of producing field guides that really work and that meet the needs for which they are produced. Our collaborators have produced a range of acclaimed guides (see Box 1.2) and their experiences have led them to write parts of this book. We accompany the development of these particular guides through the chapters that follow.

HOW TO USE THIS BOOK

This manual is structured around a core process that is outlined in Chapter 2. The text is supported by examples drawn from real experiences of producing a range of guides, as

---

Box 1.1 The Virtual Field Herbarium (VFH)

The Virtual Field Herbarium (VFH) is a website for tropical field botanists, available at http://herbaria.plants.ox.ac.uk/VFH/ (see Figure 1.1). It is closely linked to this book, supporting it with added detail and examples.

The VFH is maintained and will be further developed in the Oxford herbaria: it aims both to stimulate field guide production at national or more local levels around the tropics, and to help with tropical plant identification. The VFH has the following features:

- various 'how to write' tips – an extensive overview of this process, with historical, practical and other details;
- the ability to explore and understand images of various jargon terms, and how they relate to plants of various families in different countries (a glossary with notes emphasizes how various types of terms are appropriate for various types of users);
- an interactive bibliography of tropical plant field guides;
- images that can be downloaded free for use in local field guides (providing illustrations is often a daunting task for many prospective authors);

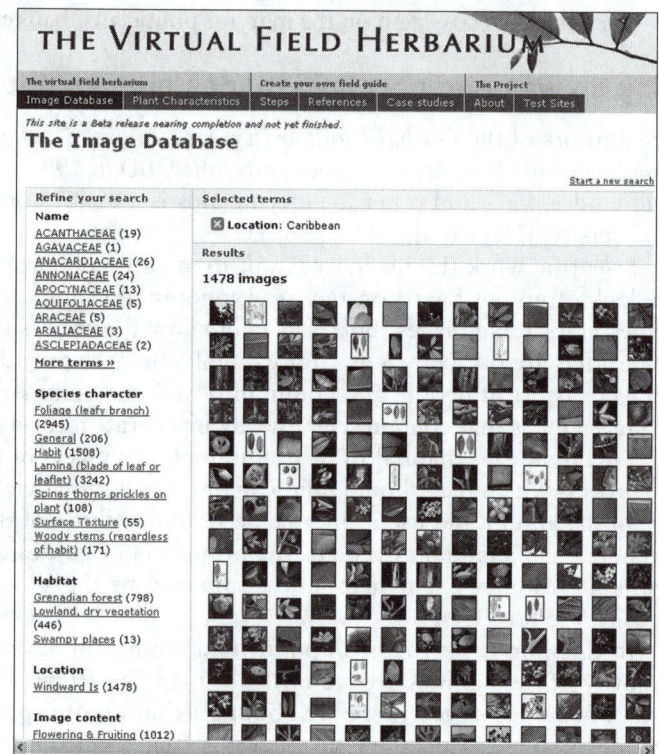

Figure 1.1 *A page from the Virtual Field Herbarium website*

- a VFH interactive image gallery, which behaves as an identification tool itself, filtering images by species characters;
- prepared field guides that can be downloaded for local printing – we will help users to make a simple type of pictorial guide directly from the site.

See Box 5.12 (page 112) on the concept of modular field guides for foresters to see how the the VFH might also help in making a usable modular guide.

well as by detailed methods to help achieve particular stages in the process. Each step in the process is described in detail in separate chapters (see Figure 2.1, page 16). However, the book is in no sense a linear description of a process. In order to plan a field guide (using the methods described in Chapter 3), readers will need to be familiar with the options and issues described in Chapters 4–8, which outline alternatives in format, types of illustration, information context and presentation, and the need for identification keys. Similarly, the latter stages of testing and publishing are described in Chapters 9 and 10 respectively, but it is essential to think about the costs and scope of these steps at the planning stage, and it will be valuable to read these chapters before starting out. Chapter 2 goes through the process in detail and will help you decide which chapters will be most useful to you. We hope that this book inspires and helps you to produce new and useful guides, and to bring the fields of botany and participatory development closer together.

BOX 1.2 LEARNING BY DOING: FIELD GUIDES IN FIVE COUNTRIES

To write this manual, we worked with scientists, non-governmental organizations (NGOs) and communities in five countries to produce field guides, tailored to particular uses and circumstances, or 'guidelets' – parts of a full field guide designed specifically for effectively testing their usability. This work was supported by the Forestry Research Programme (FRP) of the UK's Department for International Development (DFID), and enabled us to compare experiences and methods used across a wide range of case studies. Those case studies comprise the following.

Bolivia

RELEVANT CASE STUDIES: 3.1 (page 27); 3.4 (page 48); 3.7 (page 57); 9.2 (page 232); 10.1 (page 239); 10.2 (page 245)

The NGO Fundación Amigos de la Naturaleza (FAN) is contracted by the Government of Bolivia to manage the Noel Kempff Mercardo national park on the border with Brazil, which features exceptionally high biodiversity. Its approach involves the development of eco-tourism opportunities and close collaboration with the indigenous communities who live in the buffer zone and now manage large areas of forest. With support from the Centro Internacional de Agricultura Tropical, or CIAT (Bolivia's Centre for Tropical Agricultural Research), FAN collaborated with park staff and communities to produce two guides, one a loose-leaf folder of laminated pages for eco-tourists, easily taken into the humid muddy conditions of the park (Vargas and Jordán, 2002), and the other a more conventional book, rigorously researched and tested, with the villagers illustrating and recording their most used species and knowledge (Vargas and Jordán, 2003). The production of this book involved dozens of local people in order to make sure that everyone felt clear about why they were involved and what they might expect at the end, and featured complex political aspects. It was a hugely popular exercise that attracted new community members at each stage.

Brazil

RELEVANT CASE STUDIES: 3.2 (page 30); 3.5 (page 50); 3.8 (page 58); 7.1 (page 164); 7.3 (page 179); 9.1 (page 231)

Guides in northeast Brazil were prepared by a consortium led by the environmental NGO Serviço de Assessoria às Organizações Populares Rurais (SASOP), working with the University of Para and supported by Plantas do Nordeste, a network of organizations including the Royal Botanic Gardens (RBG), Kew. As in Bolivia, a comparative approach was taken – two guides were written in the same area (the Caatinga of Bahia), based on the same subset of plants (forage legumes), for different user groups. One (Costa et al, 2002), a short guide to 21 species selected for their usefulness to farmers, was produced with a local NGO; the other (de Queiroz et al, forthcoming), an ambitious guide to all 265 species in this category, was led by the University of Pará. As with the Bolivian community guide, the shorter Brazilian guide was a vast multi-stakeholder exercise with many planning and evaluation workshops to work out the most user-friendly options and to document the process for this manual.

Cameroon

RELEVANT CASE STUDY: 8.1 (page 184)

The genus *Cola* was the focus of field tests of various formats; there are at least 21 species in the forest near the Limbe Botanic Gardens around Mount Cameroon. This area is a hotspot of globally rare species, and there are several initiatives promoting local participation in biodiversity inventories, notably at the botanic gardens themselves. Unfortunately, very few people can name many of the rarer plant species in the area, and the demand for village-friendly, yet scientifically accurate, field guides is therefore high.

One of the principal issues was how different formats of minimal text, such as picture- or real plant-based guides, might help to identify individual species within a complex genus. Distinguishing infertile plants is notoriously difficult for some species; however, *Cola* are generally small trees, so leaves are usually easy to collect or inspect. Since the field tests concentrated on a small number of species, a wider variety of different formats was used than was possible in the other trials.

Ghana

RELEVANT CASE STUDIES: 3.3 (page 43); 4.2 (page 65); 8.1 (page 184)

Ghanaian forests are commercially important as a source of timber; yet farmers often do not know the names of large trees on their farms, even if they are relatively well known to botanists. Even the best technical tree-spotters cannot identify many non-timber species, and for many there is even confusion about timber tree names, causing problems in sawmills and for sustainable management plans. There is an increasing demand to diversify sustainable forest use for the benefit of the villagers surrounding the protected hotspot forests in the southwest corner of the forest zone. Many villagers around these hotspot forests are newcomers and know little of the local and often rare species. Eco-tourism and other initiatives related to this demand would therefore benefit from new field guides – forest shrubs and lianas are even less well known locally than trees. Initiatives for villagers to earn a local income from eco-tourist schemes will otherwise suffer due to limited knowledge.

Past experience has indicated that an earlier technical guide to Ghana's trees, based around line drawings and text, cannot be used accurately by people outside the original target of forestry technical staff. This is not surprising given the limited opportunities to read and understand technical English in the villages of the forest areas. It was therefore decided that a guide based on photographs of bark slash, alongside other images, would work best in helping identification (see Case study 8.1, page 184). A 'modular guide' approach was tried, capable of being expanded though time or reduced to specific local interests.

Grenada

RELEVANT CASE STUDIES: 3.3 (page 43); 8.1 (page 184)

Grenada is a small Caribbean island state, known locally as a Spice Island, yet ironically too small to justify any local botanical infrastructure. Grenada relies heavily on tourism (as well as nutmeg and other agroforestry products) and is covered by a variety of forest types. Nevertheless, very few Grenadines know many of their indigenous species. It was soon discovered that the flora is incompletely known to botanists globally, in spite of the recent completion of the *Flora of the Lesser Antilles* (Howard, 1974–1989). The main demand is for field guides that will 'unlock' the value, interest and appeal of the vegetation's biodiversity, facilitating poverty alleviation among tour guides; return visits from and sales to eco-tourists; and awareness of biodiversity among schoolchildren. There is also some demand for more detailed knowledge for those seeking to manage natural resources effectively. For instance, the recent and uncontested conversion of a national park to a golf course was facilitated by a complete lack of knowledge of Grenada's endemic or very rare plants.

Trials here (see Case study 8.1, page 184) cover a large cross-section of species on the island in a variety of habitats (around 100 of the 1000), including a wide variety of different species, but with some 'difficult' groups of similar species. Three of the most likely formats for illustrating an eco-tourist guide were tested – photographs, line drawings and paintings – making a set of 315 items (that is, 105 species in three guidelet sets). The material and lessons from these tests have subsequently been used in a full field guide to most of the flora.

2

Producing a successful guide:
Principles, purpose, people and process

Anna Lawrence and Patricia Norrish

WHAT MAKES A SUCCESSFUL GUIDE?

A successful guide is one that is used by those for whom it was produced, for the purpose for which it was produced. Of course, a guide needs to be accurate, attractive, relevant, affordable and available; but it also has to function well. To be genuinely successful, a guide must convey good quality information that actually improves the capabilities of the user. This means that it has to be usable – the person reading it can find, understand and apply the information that he or she needs. In order to achieve all of this, the authors need to involve a range of experts (who may include local experts with traditional knowledge), as well as the potential users, in planning and researching the guide. This may necessitate a consultative planning process and a collaborative team approach.

This chapter explores the principles of a good field guide and links them to the people and processes required to fit the guide to its purpose. Box 2.1, at the end of the chapter, gives some examples of these principles as demonstrated by real field guides produced in Brazil.

PURPOSE

It is surprising how many guides are produced without a clear aim. While the obvious primary function of a field guide is to help people identify plants, apart from professional biologists, most field guide users require more than the identification of an unknown plant. Instead, guides are often used to help confirm the identity of a plant in order to find further information about it. It is this information which may, in fact, comprise the purpose of the guide. For example, a guide to fuelwood species may be intended to encourage farmers to plant more trees for firewood – in which case, farmers are unlikely to have trouble with identifying trees, but may simply need reassurance that they are talking about the same species as is highlighted in the guide. They can then find information on how to cultivate the species. If the guide is to be sold, it is also important to be aware of the market. In some cases, the sale of the guide is itself the main purpose of the enterprise.

Having a clear idea of what the field guide is supposed to achieve will make producing the book much simpler, and will help in deciding how to apply the following principles and processes.

PRINCIPLES

Scientific accuracy

An accurate guide is one that contains correct information, including information on the characteristics and names of the plants, as well as supplementary information about their uses, ecology, cultivation and features of interest. Accuracy is achieved through sound research and information-gathering from reliable sources, and from careful production and cross-checking, avoiding mistakes in, for example, labelling pictures or spelling scientific names. Users of the guide can be reassured about the guide's accuracy by having sources and research procedures clearly identified.

There are different approaches to ensuring accuracy. In the case of scientific names, a standardized international procedure exists for linking plant specimens to their unique scientific name (see Chapter 4). Information about the uses, ecology and other qualities of the plant may come from books, the internet or notes found on herbarium specimens; in all of these cases, sources should be cited. Alternatively, new information from knowledgeable local people may be gathered, in which case it is important to use social science methods in order to ensure reliability (see Chapter 7).

Accuracy is time consuming and costly, involving hours of research and expertise. As a result, it is important to consider just how accurate you need to be and this depends upon the purpose of the guide. Cases where accurate identification is essential include medicinal plant guides and manuals for ecological monitoring where indicator species might affect conservation planning. These cases require the attention of botanical experts (see Chapters 4, 5 and 6). Cases where accuracy is less important might include guides for tourists who are interested in learning more about a species but where identification does not involve important conservation or scientific decisions. In such cases, there is less need to consult experts about the botanical identity of the guide's plants.

Relevance

The guide is only likely to be effective if it meets the needs of its readers and is relevant to their lives, jobs or hobbies. This is why it is so important to consult with the guide's users, or to have a good understanding of their needs, before engaging in the project in order to ensure that the following choices are relevant:

*   species included in the guide;
*   level of taxonomic detail;
*   relevant linked information (such as uses, cultivation methods and traditional knowledge).

Consultation will ensure that the right species are included in the guide and that descriptions of the plants, and their ecology and uses, are targeted appropriately to the level of the reader. While missing information can discourage people from using a guide, too much detail or irrelevant information can make the guide unwieldy and unaffordable. Chapter 3 discusses the consultation processes, and Chapter 9 explains how to check the guide's relevance by testing drafts with the target audience.

Availability

A guide also needs to be easily available to the people who want to use it. Factors to take into account are attractiveness (in order to gain people's attention in the first place), distribution (to ensure that it reaches potential buyers and users) and price (see Chapters 3 and 10). Involving potential users at an early stage in the project will provide a good indication of what people are prepared to pay for a guide that is relevant to their lives. In some cases, having a guide may be extremely important to a community who cannot afford to pay for it. In this case, it may be necessary to find funding that enables guides to be provided free.

Usability

The concept of 'usability' – which has been particularly developed for websites (Bevan, 1997) – refers to those qualities that a publication needs in order for users to benefit most from the guide. The criteria for usability are:

- effectiveness – meeting the goals of the user in finding the required information;
- efficiency – reducing the time and effort needed to find that information;
- satisfaction – enjoyment from using the guide.

In practice, this means ensuring that readers can find their way around the contents, understand the pictures and symbols, comprehend the terminology, feel confident that the information they find is correct, and use the guide under field conditions, which may include carrying it all day in the rain.

In order to achieve usability, therefore, it is important to identify the guide's potential users (see the section below on 'People' and Chapter 3) and to test the guide rigorously (see Chapter 9). In particular, the authors will need to consider the following:

- Why do the users want a guide and how and where do they want to use it? If they want to take a guide into the field with them, then it must be small enough to carry and robust enough to be used many times in conditions where it may become wet and dirty. If the guide is for use in a school or community centre, then it needs to be durable enough to withstand usage by many different people.
- What kind of presentation (verbal and visual) is needed to enable readers to find what they need? This includes considering three common aspects of a guide: the language which is used, the way in which it is illustrated, and the kinds of systems provided to enable users to find their way around the guide (for example, keys, indexes and contents pages).
- There are two issues to consider in relation to users' language needs. First, are readers happy for material to be in their national or official language, or is it of real

importance to them that it is in their local language? Second, to what extent is scientific language understood? There is little point in producing a guide using language suited to a fully trained scientist if it is not understood by the guide's readers (see Chapter 7).

- Levels of scientific knowledge and ease of use of scientific language also affect the way in which users prefer the information to be organized on the page and within the guide as a whole. Unless these preferences are known, it is difficult to make decisions about the order in which species are presented, the kinds of botanical keys to include, and the layout and level of detail of contents pages and indexes so that users can search the guide to find the information they need.

It is commonly said that a picture is worth a thousand words. However, it has to be remembered that pictorial recognition is complex, as is the use of symbols. Use of inaccurate colour; different scaling systems; showing parts rather than the whole; or diagrammatic representations rather than realistic images, and universal rather than local symbolic systems, all have an effect on the recognition and use of illustrations. Finding out what kinds of illustrations people prefer and can use, and the kinds of symbols that they understand, is a necessary part of the process of comprehending users' needs. Different types of illustrations and symbols for different groups may be required. And, as emphasized in Chapter 9, the results must be tested thoroughly in order to ensure that the target audience really does understand the guide's content.

PEOPLE

A decision to produce a guide may be taken by a variety of people. It may be the personal brainwave of one dedicated person; the result of a community discussion about loss of traditional knowledge; a requirement from donors in order to make a scientific project more community oriented; a suggestion from the tourist authority, responding to demand from tourists; or a project proposed by a non-governmental organization (NGO) to help a group of women in a village pass on their knowledge to their children. Most often, the idea comes from scientists who want to make their knowledge more accessible to other users and need to develop novel ways of doing that.

Whoever has the original idea, it is unlikely that the guide will be produced by them alone. Often, many people are involved, such as the authors or producers of the guide, and those who can supply information. Perhaps even more important, however, are the potential users. Surprisingly, they are often forgotten during the production process. However, if they are not involved in all stages of producing the guide, the end result is unlikely to satisfy their needs. Their involvement is essential in order to:

- ensure the relevance of the objectives and support for the project;
- test assumptions that this is the type of guide that is needed;
- identify existing relevant information; and
- test comprehension and usability of the various parts of the guide.

Sometimes the potential users are also the people who are providing the information or even writing the guide – although this is not common. It is important to establish who all the different people involved in the project are and to clearly define individual roles before embarking on production.

When trying to work out who should be involved in producing a guide, it can be useful to think in terms of stakeholders. Stakeholders are those individuals, groups or organizations who have an interest in a project – in this case, in the production of a guide. Chapter 3 provides more detail about identifying and involving stakeholders.

Stakeholder involvement helps to ensure that the guide is what the proposed users want, and that significant groups all feel proud of their achievement and help to promote the guide. Involving all stakeholder groups can become complicated: in Bahia, northeast Brazil, the NGOs and universities who were collaborating to produce two guides to forage legumes found themselves in a seemingly ever-expanding team of biologists, community extension workers, design experts and assistants. While this brought stimulating new ideas, it risked delays in publication. Management and diplomacy skills may therefore also be required in order to stay focused on the main objectives. Chapter 3 discusses these aspects in more detail.

There are several different approaches to involving potential users and other stakeholders in the production and design of a guide. The three most important are consultative, collaborative and participatory approaches:

- In a *consultative* process, authors will ask other stakeholders (especially a guide's users) for their opinions and preferences, which they will then take into account in writing the guide so that it is well suited to the needs of the target audience and therefore more likely to be used by them.
- In a *collaborative* process, different stakeholders will work together in order to produce the guide, perhaps in a multi-disciplinary team.
- In a *participatory* process, power and responsibility will be shared by authors, producers, users, sources of information, etc., and decisions will be taken together. Work may even be led by the potential users, as in the case where a community has chosen to produce a guide in order to protect or preserve its own knowledge.

Each process is valid within a particular context, depending upon:

- what the authors and other stakeholders want;
- how much time each has for participating; and
- how much capability they have in assembling and presenting
  the necessary information.

PROCESS

No matter who has made the initial decision to produce a guide, if it is to be successful, a logical process is required to ensure that all of the principles mentioned above are taken into account (see Figure 2.1). This process begins with planning and consultation, leading to the design of the various components. The 'design' of the guide refers to the way in which the information is put together and presented: what is the shape and size of the book; what type of paper is used; how is the book bound; what will be on the cover; how are the pages laid out; what size of illustrations should be used; and should

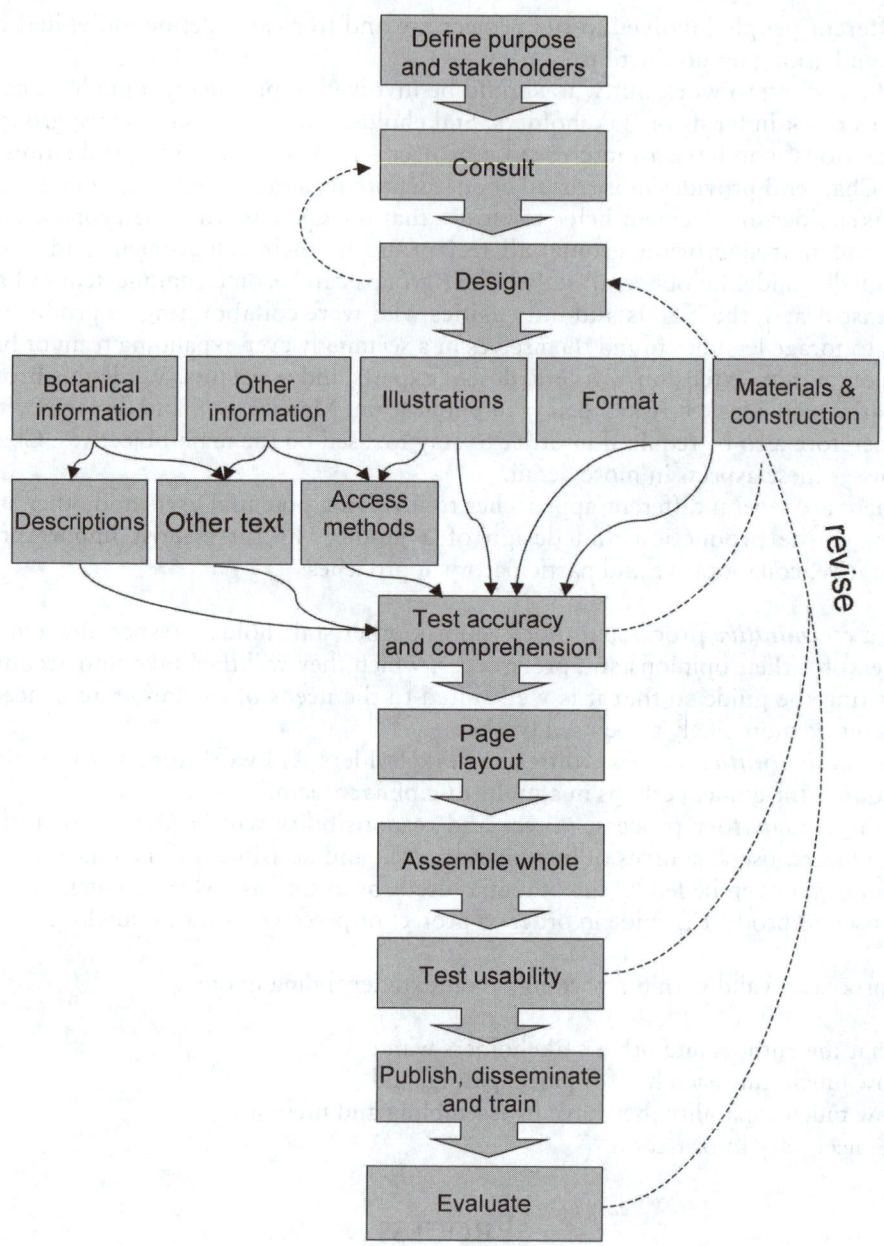

Figure 2.1 *The process of producing a field guide*

there be some symbols on the page to help users find their way around? As explained in Chapter 3, this is often best planned by leafing through a sample of existing field guides to stimulate ideas and seek reactions to particular designs. Each of these must be carefully costed and staff needs assessed (see Chapter 3).

Once an affordable plan is agreed by all stakeholders, each component (botanical content, text, illustrations and keys, or other access systems) must be researched in detail (Chapters 4–6 explain botanical aspects of a guide, while Chapter 7 deals with social research and writing; Chapter 8 describes the use of illustrations). All elements of the guide must then be tested for accuracy and accessibility before being revised and compiled into a first draft, which is again assessed before publication (see Chapter 9). The only way to ensure that a guide is usable is to test it thoroughly with representatives of potential users.

Both usability and information quality must be checked with users and contributors to the guide. It is unfortunate that many otherwise beautifully produced field guides, resulting from much hard work and investment, are not popular because readers cannot understand how to use the key, or find a mistake in the information given for one plant, and therefore distrust the rest of the information provided in the book. Good consultation at the outset should help to get things right; but there will always be unexpected details that need to be corrected. Do not wait to test the whole guide; test parts of the book as they are written and illustrated. Show descriptions to the kinds of people who may use the guide; ask them if they understand and if they think the information is correct; ask for their comments on how to improve the guide. Check whether people can recognize the species illustrated in the drawings or photos.

The penultimate step in the process is dissemination – ensuring that the guide reaches the people intended to use it. This may involve publication; advertising and distribution through networks of contacts; training; or holding a conference to launch the guide. Whatever method seems appropriate will again depend upon the target audience, the social context of the project and the information systems that the target audience uses. Ways of achieving this are explained in Chapter 10.

Finally, if you can find out how your guide has been used and what its impact has been this can provide useful information for people producing guides in the future. It can also help to identify any necessary changes for reprints. Some guidelines for evaluating field guides are given in Chapter 10.

BOX 2.1 ADAPTING PRODUCT TO PURPOSE AND PEOPLE: SOME EXAMPLES OF THE PRINCIPLES IN ACTION

This box presents four examples of field guides from Brazil, produced for a range of users and purposes. All of them followed broadly the process outlined earlier, and each has strengths in particular principles of guide production. Together, they respond to a range of needs, from highly technical to motivational.

Flora da Reserva Ducke (Ribeiro et al, 1999)

The most botanical of the four guides, this is a 799-page guide to 2250 plant species found in a 10 square kilometre non-flooded reserve in the Amazon forest. It relies on vegetative characters for identification, avoiding the traditional dependence on flowers and fruits, which according to the authors are only visible on 15 per cent of Amazonian species at any given time. Its publication in 1999 raised enormous interest, particularly among botanists, although it is intended for the 'non-botanical public'. The work, by 60 botanists over five years, is the only guide of its kind in the Amazon and has been bought by biologists thousands of kilometres from the reserve, where many of the same species occur; identification to genus level in the guide is invaluable. Another important factor is language – it is published in Portuguese, making it accessible to most native botanists of Latin America (botanical Portuguese is largely comprehensible to Spanish speakers).

In this paragon of field guides, the book's purpose and target audience were carefully considered, and careful use of botanical language makes it particularly accessible. In the process of preparing the guide, planning involved a lengthy search for funds. The detailed research is outstanding, as is the attention to involving relevant stakeholders. Furthermore, the innovative design ensures that an unprecedented number of species can be identified using a guide that has been designed for usability in the field.

In an interview, one author (Mike Hopkins) explained that compared with other tropical areas, the flora of the forests of the Amazon Basin is poorly known, and knowledge is limited by few collections. Furthermore, the distribution of the collections is extremely biased, concentrated close to urban centres and, only secondarily, along the rivers and roads. Large areas of the Amazon Basin remain botanically unknown. The prospect of having a reasonable knowledge of the size and composition of the regional flora remains distant; so the Reserva Ducke – a 10 square kilometre block of non-flooded rainforest situated on the outskirts of Manaus, Brazil – was chosen as the site for a local flora precisely because it is situated in an area with a high collection density, and it was assumed to be relatively well collected.

The initial idea was to provide a means for the 'ordinary' biologist to accurately identify plants in the field without having to be familiar with a vast specialized vocabulary. Taxonomic botanists rely heavily on fertile material to both describe species and identify plant specimens, and botanical keys typically concentrate on flower and fruit characters. Generally, in tropical forests only a small proportion of the flora is fertile at any time, and many species flower only once every several years. Identification of sterile specimens (collected without flowers or fruit) is particularly difficult, and less confidence can be placed in the identifications. The authors therefore felt that a guide catering to both immediate and accurate identification of flora would be a major contribution to Amazonian botany, and the original concept of the field guide was expanded to include the species of the entire flora, based exclusively on field characters.

The project was approved for funding by the UK government's foreign aid agency, the Department for International Development (DFID). As the project evolved, a move towards a broader, and more Latin American, set of specialists was both practical and political. Thirty-seven specialists visited the project, whereas only six were originally planned. A further 37 specialists provided identifications from material sent by mail. Involving researchers from within the country obviously reduces travel costs considerably, and it goes without saying that researchers in countries such as Brazil should be encouraged to study their own flora. Specialists were chosen based on their reputation in identifying their studied families in the Amazon region, giving preference, where possible, to botanists in Brazil, especially students. Botanical specialists visited for periods of between a few days and several months.

Several experienced *mateiros* (local tree-identification experts) were employed full time by the project; three eventually became co-authors of the field guide. A group of young Brazilian botanists and students also became co-authors of the guide. Their role was to integrate the knowledge of *mateiros* and specialists (or their own technical knowledge) and to design the eventual output in a user-friendly manner.

Project staff participated in all stages of the field guide production. The philosophy was to separate functions by the families selected, rather than the stage in production. As a result, all team members did their own fieldwork, database management, photography, image

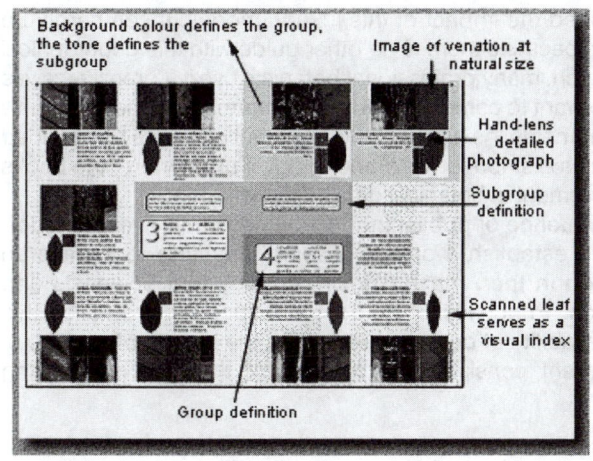

Source: Ribeiro et al (1999)

Figure 2.2 *Example of a botanical guide page layout*

enhancement, and guide design and production. The project leaders decided to spread tasks horizontally rather than vertically in order to allow all members of the team to participate in every aspect. This is perhaps less efficient than a vertical structure (specializing in certain tasks), and may lead to inconsistency.

The guide's page layout (see Figure 2.2) allows for quick comparison of species and for the presentation of several species per page.

A typical page contains around 20 images. The achievement of illustrating all vegetative characters (leaves, bark, slash, or inner bark, and venation) photographically for such a large number of species is extraordinary and was only possible due to the development of digital photography, as well as the payment of all research and production costs by the UK DFID. At 799 pages and 4cm thick, this is a heavy book; but with its plastic cover, it is still feasible to take it into the field.

Not surprisingly, such a large number of species presents enormous complexity in helping the user to find the relevant species, or group of species. Various glossaries, ingenious keys and colour coding point the reader's way around. Nevertheless, the biggest single criticism of the book is that it is hard to navigate around. The authors explain that this is inevitable, and have organized training courses to help users become familiar with the layout.

Source: Mike Hopkins interviewed by Anna Lawrence

Árvores Brasileiras (Lorenzi, 2002)

Another lavishly illustrated guide is the larger format and less portable book by Harri Lorenzi, typical of a series of expensive guides to Brazilian trees, palms, weeds and ornamental plants. *Árvores Brasileiras* (*Brazilian Trees*) is now in its fourth edition in Portuguese, and also features an English translation, both currently priced internationally at US$100 (in Brazil, the cost is approximately half).

The book features a clearly identified purpose: to sell the guide and create revenue to support further botanical research. While the author freely admits to a lack of consultation and testing in the production of the guide, he is not aiming at a tool that is usable in the field, but rather a book that provides accurate and reliable information. The guides are therefore very carefully designed and researched to the extent that every species page is identically formatted, and the author holds up publication until exactly the required illustrations are available. This degree of scientific accuracy has brought unexpected results for scientific research – users provide detailed feedback to Lorenzi and have filled in gaps in knowledge about the distribution and phenology of the trees illustrated. While the book is one of the most expensive available, it is suitable for its audience in Brazil and the US, and is widely distributed.

In an interview, Lorenzi explained the impact of this luxury 'model'. It can hardly be thought of as a field guide, and yet, because there is no other guide with this geographical range and quality of botanical research, many professional botanists use it. Lorenzi receives letters every week from people who want to correct or add to his information, and every new print run of the book includes amendments. As a result, new contributions have been added to the scientific knowledge of species distribution and phenology. Furthermore, the books have clearly stimulated public involvement in botanical data collection.

Another, less common, consequence of publishing this guide is the revenue generated, which has been sufficient to establish a private research institute, purchase an aeroplane for botanical exploration in the Amazon Basin, employ four scientists and conduct further botanical research. Principles of guide production illustrated by this example include the quality and reliability of botanical research; the benefit of a range of illustrations for different parts of a plant; consistency of format; and the value of providing mechanisms for feedback.

Source: Harri Lorenzi interviewed by Anna Lawrence

Frutíferas da Mata na Vida Amazônica (Shanley et al, 1998)
Receitas sem Palavras (Shanley et al, 1996)

These examples illustrate a very clear identification of purpose and an obvious sense of who the target users are. By carefully following through the later stages of the process, the authors have tested and ensured that their users, who do not read often, find the books easy to understand; they have also paid particular attention to dissemination and feedback so that the guides reach a wide audience, even on different continents.

Five rural communities in eastern Amazonia, Brazil, asked researchers to help them generate technical information on the ecology and comparative economics of the value of timber and non-timber forest products. They realized that although this technical input was critical, what was really needed was some way of presenting and collaboratively sharing information about the plants in order to catalyse new ways of thinking. The large size of the region meant that it was impossible to offer workshops to even a small percentage of the remote communities facing forest transformation. Therefore, in order to reach a wider area, the communities developed two illustrated booklets on the non-timber medicinal, fruit and game-attracting trees of local/regional value.

Ecological and economic data presented in workshops was transcribed onto paper in an illustrated form with a descriptive text. In order to make the book *Frutíferas da Mata na Vida Amazônica* (*Fruit Trees of the Forest in the Lives of Amazonians*) culturally appealing to a wide variety of literate and non-literate readers, data about the ecology and economics of trees is featured alongside illustrated songs, stories and lore. Primary data on the economics, density and production of fruit trees is featured next to a section on women's rights, tips for selling fruit, and recipes for shampoo and ice cream.

A second booklet, *Receitas sem Palavras: Plantas Medicinais da Amazônia* (*Recipes without Words: Medicinal Plants of Amazonia*), features illustrations depicting medicinal plant remedies. By providing data on the density, fruit production and economic value of native forest fruit trees, the book offers tools for families to estimate the timber versus the non-timber value of the forest tract. It also gives tips and techniques on planting and managing fruit trees and on value-added processing of medicinal oils and fruits. Information is designed to be used as a springboard for discussion, experimentation and new thinking about forest management and the use of forest resources. The guiding philosophy is stated on the first page: 'This is not a book to be read; it is a book to be used in practice.'

These two examples are clearly not field guides in the conventional sense; they are books that help barely literate people plan their management of forest trees. In order to do so, they need to link the information to the plant in question, and both books unambiguously help them to do this.

Readers have commented on the rural authenticity of the language, which enhances the accessibility of the guides to populations who frequently feel shut out by the formality of most written material. By presenting information in a culturally captivating form to communities, the authors made the unexpected discovery that knowledge presented in this way was also more accessible to policy analysts, conservation organizations and urban citizens. Because the learning materials were specifically designed to reach semi-literate persons, they are also understandable by non-Portuguese speaking populations. Requests for the books are being fielded from countries as diverse as Ecuador, Greece, Mexico, Sri Lanka and Malaysia. Discussions outside of Brazil reveal that the books can serve as templates for how to encourage new thinking, while giving back scientific data to local communities in an accessible form (Shanley and Gaia, 2002).

Source: abstracted from Shanley and Gaia (2002)

Flores Nativas da Chapada Diamantina (Harley and Giulietti, 2004)

The idea of producing field guides targeted at eco-tourists is becoming popular in some of Brazil's most accessible protected areas. Rio de Contas, an upmarket mountain retreat in Bahia, northeast Brazil, has tourists with time and money, and an unrequited interest in the flora. Professor Ray Harley of the Royal Botanic Gardens, Kew, has described his plans to address this demand in *Flores Nativas da Chapada Diamantina* (*Native Flowers of the Chapada Diamantina*).

He points out that eco-tourists are interested not only in identifying species, but in understanding their context. Such tourists are intelligent and highly educated readers with a curiosity about the natural world. Before the availability of a more accessible guide, tourists had relied upon the *Flora Pico das Almas* (a large technical botanical work, with few illustrations), which is in English, apart from an introduction in Portuguese. This guide is not suitable for most Brazilian users because it is too technical and is written in an unfamiliar language. The writing of *Flores Nativas da Chapada Diamantina* was nevertheless made much easier because the botanical information for the area already existed in this earlier work.

A group of botanists therefore saw the opportunity to provide something more tailored to eco-tourists. *Flores Nativas da Chapada Diamantina* is illustrated with plenty of line drawings and photos. The authors recognize that identification is not the most important point of the book; instead, it is intended to help visitors be informed about the plants and attracted to spending more time there. As a result, it contains a substantial introduction with a background on tropical plants, climate, seasons, the natural history of Brazil and a 'preview' of what might be seen in the area, and it is based on a description of a series of trails and plants within their vicinity.

The text is written in Portuguese on one side, English on the other, with small plates scattered among the pages. Local popular names are included so that tourists can discuss the plants with local people. Usability is ensured by reducing the size of the guide and toning down the technical language, while more illustrations than usual are included.

Source: Ray Harley interviewed by Anna Lawrence

3

Planning and budgeting

Anna Lawrence, Ana Paula Lopes Ferreira, Maria Theresa Stradmann, Israel Vargas, Claudia Jordán, Marcelino Lima, Patricia Norrish, Sarah Gillett and Teonildes Nunes

INTRODUCTION

Chapter 2 set out the characteristics of a successful guide and presented an overview of the steps involved in the production process. The aim of this chapter is to provide more detail about steps 1 to 3 of this process (see Figure 2.1, page 16) in order to help authors or project initiators arrive at an action plan.

One of the most common pitfalls when writing a field guide is to seriously underestimate the time and money needed to produce it. Most of us, given the choice, would want to include as many species as possible, with full details of identification, habitat and use, along with a range of high-quality colour photographs for each species. Most of us will also have to search for the funds for such a project. Before embarking on data collection and analysis (steps 4 to 10), it is therefore important to plan and budget in order to balance the needs of potential users and producers with the money, time and skills available.

The early stages are also important for deciding who will be involved in producing the guide. During this time, working roles and relationships are established, available resources (financial, human and information) are identified, and the kind of guide that can be produced within these resources is chosen. It is worth making the guide's objectives, activities and budget explicit by drawing up a project plan, and making the roles, activities, resources and deadlines clear by preparing an action plan and institutional agreements, where appropriate.

All of this is based, however, on an understanding of the needs of users. We advocate a participatory approach that emphasizes consultation with users and balances their requirements with scientific knowledge in order to ensure that the guide is accurate. Sound planning is also essential so that the guide may be produced within the limits of the available resources. One of the most common problems with such consultations is that the people who participate become enthusiastic and expect great results; it is therefore important to be clear about what is asked of them and why – and how this will be transformed into something that they can use.

STEP 1: IDENTIFY THE NEEDS AND PURPOSE OF THE GUIDE WITH THE STAKEHOLDERS

The consultation process will help to determine what is needed in terms of:

- the species to be included;
- the kinds of supporting information that users will need;
- the kinds of illustrations and symbols that will best suit users' needs;
- the format and design that will enable people to find the information they want easily.

Stakeholder analysis for preparing a guide

As explained in Chapter 2, stakeholder involvement helps to ensure that the guide is what the potential users want, and that significant groups all feel proud of their achievement and help to promote the guide. Making decisions on who should be involved in the production of a guide can best be done through a limited stakeholder analysis, which lists the stakeholders and their potential interest in, or contribution to, the guide. A team approach is likely to be more effective than an individual conducting the analysis alone, and is always the best way to carry out a brainstorming exercise. However, a first attempt can be made by the originator of the project.

Box 3.1 explains how to carry out a stakeholder analysis for a field guide, and Table 3.1 provides some examples of both primary and secondary stakeholders in field guides. Primary stakeholders are those with a direct interest and who are ultimately affected by the results: the target readers (users), the authors and people who may use the guide in other ways, such as local communities who may gain from sales of a field guide or from increased income from tourists visiting the area. Secondary stakeholders are those who can help to produce the guide (or, occasionally, who may wish to stop you from producing the guide if they feel that it competes with their interests). They include people who can provide information for the guide, funders, publishers and experts in particular aspects, such as communication or layout.

The results of the stakeholder analysis will help to carry out the remaining planning activities.

Define the purpose of the guide and users' needs

The best way to decide on the purpose of the guide, and to relate it to the needs of the users, is to work with representatives of the potential users, either through a workshop or group discussion, or by using a questionnaire to interview key individuals.

In carrying out this consultation, it is helpful to keep in mind that it is important to match up the goals of at least two sets of stakeholders – the users and the authors. Because the authors are very often the same people as those who carry out the consultation, they must be aware of their own goals and expectations, and not confuse them

BOX 3.1 IDENTIFYING THE STAKEHOLDERS

- *Objective*: identification of all stakeholders with an interest in the guide, or who would be helpful in its production.
- *Output*: list of stakeholders and their interest in the field guide, useful skills and willingness to contribute.
- *Staff*: authors, facilitator.
- *Participants*: discussions can occur in a small group of people who know the social context or in a larger workshop. If the project is a community guide, then it is best to gain social approval for the process through a workshop. Otherwise, identifying stakeholders will probably be more efficient in a small group of authors and colleagues.
- *Time*: two hours.
- *Equipment*: flip chart and markers/blackboard and chalk.
- *Method*:
  1 The best way to do this is to brainstorm (see Box 3.3, page 39). Think about both primary and secondary stakeholders, and use Table 3.1 to provide you with ideas to get started.
  2 Start by listing those people, organizations or groups who:
     - use the guide (be specific if you can – for example, women of village X who want to prepare medicines; women who want to sell medicinal plants; men who collect medicinal plants in village X);
     - can provide useful information for the guide (these people, who have specialist knowledge about plants, are known as *key informants*);
     - already use or regularly come into contact with the species in the guide;
     - might be useful in helping to make the guide user friendly, such as tourist guides who know the tourists' interests, or teachers who can advise on levels of comprehension among rural communities;
     - support or oppose the project.
     Among these, consider subdivisions among the users – for example:
     - Should men and women be considered as different user groups?
     - Should young and old people be considered as different user groups?
  3 Add these stakeholders to one column, then make further columns to show, to the best of your knowledge, what are their:
     - interests in the field guide (in what way will it be useful to them?); and
     - knowledge or skills.
     Furthermore, what is their willingness to:
     - be consulted;
     - collaborate;
     - make decisions?
  4 Finally, review the stakeholders and their interests, consider potential problems that you think might arise and that could affect the production of the guide, and note your strategy for ensuring that these problems will not affect you.

Source: adapted from ODA (1995)

with the goals and expectations of the users. There is a delicate balance to be achieved here. Participation means sharing knowledge and decision-making; it does not mean simply handing over all the responsibility to local people, without outside support – and it certainly does not mean ignoring the usefulness of scientific expertise. Users may have

Table 3.1 *Examples of stakeholders who may be involved in producing a field guide*

Primary stakeholders		Secondary stakeholders	
Users	*Authors*	*Sources of information*	*Others*
Agroforestry farmers	Local NGOs	Local users	Publishers
Tribal forest groups	Government	Herbalists	
Local communities – farming or indigenous groups	Foreign aid projects		Funding organizations
Extension workers		Farmers Hunters	
Eco-tourists	Local user groups		Printers
Botanists		Specialists	
Non-governmental organization (NGO) staff	Multinational companies	Botanists	Photographers
Village teachers			
Village schoolchildren	Herbaria staff	Herbaria	Governments
Local promoters			
University lecturers	Social scientists	Healers	
Forest guides			Government
Women	Scientists	Social scientists	
Men			NGOs
Children	Protected area staff	Scientists	
Adults			
Healers	Educational institutions	Forest guides	Private-sector organizations

Source: chapter authors

little or no experience of field guides. They may find it difficult to say what they need, which is why we recommend examining a range of examples with them.

Consulting with users can be like conducting a market study if your primary aim is to produce a guide that is going to sell well. But users will not be able to tell you what makes a guide accurate; you will be responsible for ensuring that the guide is more than an attractive cover or a compilation of attractive illustrations, and that it provides reliable and useful information.

CASE STUDY 3.1 DEFINING THE NEEDS OF USERS BY PROXY: A GUIDE FOR ECO-TOURISTS IN BOLIVIA

Fundación Amigos de la Naturaleza (FAN), a Bolivian conservation NGO, planned a guide (Vargas and Jordán, 2002) for eco-tourists visiting the Parque Nacional Noel Kempff Mercado (PNNKM) in the following way.

Stakeholders were identified as belonging to one of eight categories:

1   FAN scientific personnel, such as authors and consultants who provide botanical information;
2   FAN editorial personnel, who are developing expertise in publishing and are interested in expanding the NGO's range of quality publications;
3   FAN eco-tourism team: a group of individuals interested in attracting more tourists to the park;
4   FAN management, which is interested in maintaining the high reputation of FAN for scientific research and in expanding FAN's profile through publications;
5   tourists, who perceive PNNKM as remote, beautiful, highly diverse (with 21 per cent of the bird species found in South America), difficult to reach and lacking in information;
6   biology students, who perceive PNNKM as highly diverse and lacking in scientific study and information;
7   PNNKM park guards, who protect the park (in a remote and challenging border region) and guide tourists around it (these guards have a rich local knowledge about plants and animals);
8   community members in the buffer zone, who benefit little from eco-tourism (aware of the potential for increased revenue, they are nevertheless without practical experience).

The primary stakeholders were seen as 1 and 5 – authors and users – although stakeholders 6 and 7 were also likely to be users. Secondary stakeholders were primarily the other FAN staff and the park guards (2–4 and 7).

The objective of producing the guide is to attract more eco-tourists to a park that, while extremely attractive, currently receives few visitors; some imagination was required in consulting with them. Three tactics were used:

1   Questionnaires were prepared for tourists; but, in fact, the sample included mostly Bolivian biologists who work in the park. In this case, the questionnaires produced little useful information.
2   Staff of FAN, the NGO which manages the national park, held a workshop to discuss their perceptions of what would be most attractive to eco-tourists.
3   The authors of the guide held small group discussions with the park guards, who are the people who spend the most time with the tourists and have a strong idea of their interests and preferences. These guards also know the park very well and were able to suggest information that could be included in the guide.

At the staff workshop, staff pooled their ideas about what eco-tourists wanted and what it would be possible to provide. There were five factors that influenced their decisions:

1   Eco-tourists are interested in both animals and plants, and although the team was better able to offer information about plants at this stage, they wanted to be able to add information about animals at a later stage.

2   The habitat diversity of the park was a key feature that staff wanted to emphasize, and they felt that eco-tourists should understand the dynamic relations between plants, animals and their habitats. The information should therefore be organized according to habitat. This is quite different from the way in which the information was organized in the guide to useful plants (Vargas and Jordán, 2003) produced with the help of communities in the same area (see Case study 3.4, page 48).

3   Eco-tourists can afford to pay for a high-quality publication, and are much more likely to buy something that is visually attractive. It is therefore important to use plenty of high-quality illustrations.

4   Eco-tourists are mainly English speaking, some are Portuguese speaking, and other local visitors need information in Spanish.

5   The guide should be a practical tool that helps visitors to explore the park. It should be portable and resistant to wet weather conditions, common in the park.

It was therefore proposed that the guide for eco-tourists should be organized according to the diverse habitats found in the park in order to emphasize the area's biodiversity, and in a loose-leaf format of laminated pages to make it easier to add information about mammals, birds and other organisms later on.

At the workshop with the park guards, FAN scientists aimed to solicit the park guards' views on species which both typified the habitats, and which were of interest to the eco-tourists.

FAN scientists classified the park into seven habitats. However, in order to relate the guards' experiences to their own perceptions, they began by asking them to brainstorm about all of the different habitats they could think of. The facilitator asked the guards: 'What environments do you know in the park; which should be included in a guide?' The local name for each habitat was written on a card. Seven posters were then prepared, showing the names of each of the scientifically defined habitats, and the guards arranged the cards showing the local names on each poster. This exercise helped to show respect for the guards' local knowledge, to relate local names to scientific names, and to emphasize species diversity within each habitat.

Having established the kinds of habitat that are recognized both locally and scientifically, the group then went on to identify seven to ten plant species that are important in each habitat, as well as being visually attractive. These species form the basis of the guide.

Defining scope and scale: A first estimate of number of species to include in the guide

Once different stakeholders and their preferences or needs have been defined, it is important to have an idea of how many species will be included in the guide. This will be determined both by budget and by the purpose of the guide. There are several approaches to deciding which species should be included in a guide:

- Define a geographical area and then aim to include all of the species that occur in that area or a subset of the species, such as trees.
- Define a plant group (such as a family or genus) and aim to include all of the species of that group.
- More commonly, use a combination of the two preceding methods, such as the legumes of Bahia or the grasses of Bolivia.

- Focus on a particular user group and a subset of 'recommended' or 'useful' species for that group. These human-defined factors, such as 'medicinal plants', 'well-known fruit trees' or 'species suitable for cultivation', require a different approach to species selection since the decisions will be subjective.

Having decided whether the guide's criteria are biological, geographical or human, it is important to prepare a 'long list' from which the final list will be selected. This can be a surprisingly time-consuming activity, beginning by listing all of the known species in the group in the target area.

Listing the species according to natural criteria

If you are working in a relatively small area (for example, in one forest or one community) and you want to write a guide to all of the species, you may need to create a checklist (see Chapter 4) to find out how many species there are and whether it is feasible to incorporate them all within one guide. More likely, you will choose to write a guide to some biological group within that area – for example, the bromeliads of the Atlantic forest of Bahia or the leguminous trees of a forest in Bolivia. In this case, you will still need a checklist to ensure that you know how many species you are dealing with. If botanists do not already have this information, you may need to organize a rapid species assessment of the area in order to find out which species from your chosen group occur there. To ensure accuracy, you will have to either go with an expert who has complete confidence that he or she can tell you what the species are and whether any need further identification, or you will need to collect specimens (see Chapter 4) and take them to a herbarium for identification. This will give you an idea of how much work will be required: how many species you need to include in your guide and how many species require botanical identification or even further taxonomic work.

If you are covering a wider area, you will need to gather your information through other means. For guides covering biological or geographical groups, you will need to talk to botanical experts to find out how well the area is known, and where all the species in that area or group are listed. If you are unfamiliar with the procedures that botanists use for updating their knowledge of species, read Chapter 4 first. Then make sure that your guide is based on the most recent revision of the family or group of species that you are including. You may still have a very long list, and you may need to use other criteria to cut it down. For example, Case study 3.2 describes the process through which leguminous species were chosen to be included in a detailed guide of the Caatinga in Brazil.

At this stage, it is not advisable to list more detailed information; the aim is to provide an initial idea of how many species might be included in order to estimate, later, how much information is already known about them (see Chapters 4 and 7). Once you have found out how much work is necessary to include each species in the guide, a cut-off point can be given by estimating time and financial constraints, and assessing whether the number of species still needs to be reduced. If so, stricter criteria for including or excluding species must be defined.

Occasionally, guides are written as part of the process of finding out how many species occur in an area. For example, Box 2.1 (page 17) describes this process for the Ducke Reserve in the Brazilian Amazon. If the number of species is unknown at the beginning of the project, budget flexibility will be needed in order to assess species diversity.

CASE STUDY 3.2 SPECIES SELECTION IN THE CAATINGA, BRAZIL

Species selection is often a highly iterative process – in other words, the preliminary list is defined roughly, and is periodically reassessed after episodes of fieldwork or reflection. SASOP (Serviço de Assessoria às Organizações Populares Rurais), an environmental NGO based in Salvador, Bahia, Brazil, wanted to involve the farmers in the Caatinga in selecting 21 species to be included in a guide to forage legumes for use in more sustainable agricultural systems (Costa et al, 2002). In each community, the process involved:

1   A meeting with the farmers and the project team to explain the objectives of the project and to discuss what kind of fieldwork would be necessary in order to select and collect the plants.

2   A field walk so that:
   - the farmers could point out the plants which interest them and talk about their knowledge of each plant;
   - the team could collect the plants at the same time in order to take them to the herbarium.

3   Summarizing information in the table. This serves to highlight gaps in information and also allows surplus information (that is, not needed for the purpose of the guide) to be identified.

4   Returning to the communities to fill in the gaps in the table. For example, this approach might show that soil preferences were known for most species but lacking for one or two.

5   Developing a systematic format for each species.

6   Filling in a questionnaire (see Chapter 6) with the help of the community. Questionnaires assist in structuring questions, increasing the efficiency of information collection and promoting the recording of information in a structured way.

7   Selecting the final species list, taking into account both botanical knowledge and the farmers' knowledge.

8   Presenting the results to the community.

9   Asking farmers to prepare a definitive species list. This was achieved by going back to the plants in the table and arguing that not all of the species in the botanists' list would be used for forage. The farmers also considered other criteria, such as use as food during drought; use as food throughout the year; fast leaf production during the rainy season; leaves slow to decompose when they fall, thereby conserving dry forage; medicinal uses; human food; and concerns about the decline or disappearance of some species, whether through plagues, diseases or deforestation.

10 Repeating the process in other communities so that the final list incorporates the priorities of each. In communities consulted later in the process, much time was saved by proposing that the species should be selected immediately by applying the questionnaire.

It is important to be particularly careful when attempting to write a guide on all species in a given family (or a given forest, etc.). If a species is not included, users may assume that it is a different species. It must be clear from the outset whether the book covers a sample of species from that group or all species.

Listing the species according to subjective criteria

If the guide is about species that serve a particular purpose (for example, medicinal use or aesthetic beauty), or is simply about a sample of species within a particular group, species selection requires more subjective decision-making. In such cases, the stakeholders will not all be in agreement about which species to include. What is useful to one person may be quite unimportant to another. The authors and facilitators therefore need to think about:

- Who will decide which species to include?
- What criteria will be used to determine which species to include and exclude?

Participatory methods for prioritizing species are described in the section on 'Prioritizing species according to subjective criteria'.

The decision about who chooses the species to include in the guide is similar to the one about who decides the purpose of the guide. To some extent, the decision must be influenced by those who are expected to use the guide because they are the ones who know their needs. However, if the users knew all of the species, they probably would not need a guide; therefore, suggestions for species may come from other knowledgeable sources, such as local people and botanists. Finally, of course, the authors of the guide will have their own suggestions, and these will often complement those made by users or local people, based on the authors' insights into both the kinds of information that might be helpful and the species occurring in the area. So a balance is needed between these different views.

For example, the criteria for *Arboles y Arbustos para Sistemas Agroforestales en los Valles Interandinos de Santa Cruz, Bolivia* (Vargas et al, 2000) were that the species should be the most broadly distributed in the region of Santa Cruz, Bolivia, with the highest economic potential, service and subsistence value. Species were prioritized through a mini-survey in six communities of the Andean foothills. The authors interviewed farmers about their species preferences and found that:

- Priorities varied between different ecological zones.
- Fuelwood species were favoured in the highest zones.
- Fodder species were favoured in the driest zones.
- Timber species were favoured in the lower subtropical zone.
- Species priorities varied between men and women.
- Women prioritized fodder and medicinal species.
- Men prioritized fuel and timber species.

The authors then combined the priorities of farmers, both women and men, from all three ecological zones, with some lesser-known species recommended by biologists.

Four aspects of design

Apart from the species content, the overall design of the guide must be considered carefully at this early stage. Four broad aspects of design cover all of the factors that need to be taken into account:

1   text – descriptions of each species, as well as any other explanatory text, such as an introduction; factors to be considered include content, format and layout;
2   illustrations for each species, as well as illustrations to accompany the introduction, glossary, etc.;

Table 3.2 *Options for guides based on the four key aspects*

Aspect	Sub-aspect	Possibilities include	Further information in
Text	Information about each species	Scientific name Synonyms Common name(s) Botanical description Diagnostic characteristics Habitat Distribution Ecology Phenology Use; economic importance Conservation status Cultivation Management Harvest Similar species Folklore, etc.	Chapter 7

	Other written sections	Preface
		Acknowledgements
		Contents page
		Who and what this guide is for
		Geographic or botanical area covered
		Map
		How to use this guide
		How to identify plants in the field
		Key characteristics of the plant
		  group covered by the guide
		Introduction to encourage readers to
		  use the guide
		Glossary
			Chapter 7

	Language of written text	Language Style Use of technical terms	Chapter 7
	Formatting of written text	Font Size Spacing Number of columns Title; subtitles – number, format (bold, italics or underlined) and spacing Mixing text and illustrations	Chapter 7
Access systems	Navigating around the guide	Indexes Icons Names Order Page colour	Chapter 5
Illustrations	Format	Colour; black and white Photographs/drawings Silhouettes Illustrated glossaries	Chapter 8
Physical aspects	Materials	Paper Cover Binding Size	Chapter 3, Box 3.4 and Table 3.5

3 access systems – tools for finding information (these can include identification keys, indexes, coloured page margins and symbols to help the user navigate around the guide), as well as factors such as the order in which the species are presented;
4 physical attributes, such as size and durability.

Variables for each of these aspects are listed in Table 3.2 as a checklist of options to consider when planning the design; each aspect is described in greater detail throughout the rest of this book. The text, illustrations, access systems and physical attributes must be considered carefully and discussed with the relevant stakeholders in order to decide what is most relevant, accessible, informative, cost effective, usable and attractive. Table 3.2 serves as a reminder of the alternatives, but even more helpful would be to review a range of existing guides that demonstrate these different characteristics (for example, photographs or drawings; small or large pages; local names and/or scientific names).

As Table 3.2 demonstrates, the different aspects of guides are all related to each other. For example, in producing *A Field Guide to the Rattans of Lao PDR* (Evans, 2001), the text was kept to a minimum and was always closely related to pictures and photographs. Furthermore, the authors decided that for ease of comprehension, they would keep a uniform format for describing each species so that all characters were included for all species. This approach helped to develop consistency throughout the guide and appeared to make species identification easier; but it meant that decisions about content and format affected decisions about photographs and access systems.

In thinking about the physical aspects of design, authors need to consider all of the options, including posters, books, leaflets, CD-ROMs and loose-leaf folders. Some of the pros and cons of each are described in Table 3.3.

Table 3.3 *Comparing different physical designs of guides*

Guide format	Pros	Cons
Book	Easy to take into the field Can hold a lot of information Relatively hard wearing Familiar format	Users may not wish to take an expensive or heavy book into the field
Poster	Visually interesting Easily displayed in prominent places, thereby reaching a larger audience	Cannot take into the field Number of species and information on each very limited due to space
Leaflet	Easily taken into the field	Not hard wearing Number of species and information on each very limited due to space
CD-ROM	Accessible by many (as long as equipment is available) Can hold a lot of information Small and easily stored	Cannot take into the field Requires high-specification equipment and reasonable knowledge of computers
Loose-leaf folder	Can select pages that you wish to take into the field More hard wearing than leaflets Easy to add additional species later when more funds or knowledge become available	Pages may easily go missing

METHODS FOR CONSULTING

Given all the options outlined above, consultations with stakeholders are required to discuss the aim, species content and design of a guide. While separate planning activities can be held for each of these aspects, many of the same stakeholders and methods will be useful for each, and it may make sense to combine some of them in small workshops. Here we offer a range of approaches for helping stakeholders to contribute to the planning phase. We focus on the participatory approaches needed for working with communities or multiple institutions. Although a more top-down approach can be taken, this risks producing a guide that is less useful than it might have been.

In our combined experience of producing dozens of field guides, we have found that the best place to start is to examine a range of published examples. This is particularly helpful when consulting with rural people who may have little experience of field guides. By examining the type of paper, the kind and size of images, the arrangement of the photos throughout the text, the size and clarity of the font, and the level of language, you can help your stakeholders to think through the aspects that work for them.

Consultations with whom?

Obviously, the results of the consultation survey will depend upon whom you interview, so you need to choose your participants with care. The main point about choosing people to define user needs, whether through a questionnaire or through a workshop, is that you do not need a large number; but they must be representative of the users. It is not necessary or appropriate to carry out a detailed survey with statistical analysis of the results, although some indication of the 'convincingness' of the results (such as 'most people were able to identify plants with drawings') is useful, especially where the guide's readers are expected to be in the thousands. It is important to ensure that the informants either know the users well or include a wide range of people expected to use the guide (for example, both men and women, if community members).

It is not always possible to reach the users; in some cases, it may be necessary to work with intermediaries who have a good understanding of potential users instead. Case study 3.1 describes how staff of the Fundación Amigos de la Naturaleza (FAN) planned the format for the guide for visitors to the Noel Kempff Mercado national park in Bolivia. Their user group – eco-tourists – comprises an elusive and highly seasonal target for questionnaires; so the authors held a group discussion with the park guards who work with the tourists and who have come to know their expectations and interests.

Workshops, group discussions, interviews and questionnaires

There is no doubt that the best way to define all of these needs and preferences is to gather a sample group of the users, or their representatives, together for a group discussion or workshop in order to analyse their information needs, as well as their impressions of a range of existing guides, their preferences and their understanding of the guide's content. A well-planned and informative workshop will take a whole day; but this is a good investment. In groups, people stimulate each other's thoughts and help to build up a sense of consensus. Care must be taken when using this approach, however, as it can generate a lot of extra information – people enjoy the chance to air their views and in a group may interrupt one another or 'help one another out', or not take turns.

Box 3.2 describes one workshop format, based on an experience with farmers, environmental activists and local health workers in the state of Pará in northeast Brazil. Here, an environmental NGO had been working with the farming communities for several years, helping them to document knowledge of medicinal plants, cultivate them in nurseries, and test new combinations of native trees and crops in agroforestry systems. The workshop participants were therefore enthusiastic about documenting and sharing their knowledge of local plants, and had an excellent working relationship with the NGO. They were willing to spend a day reflecting on their experience and planning a new guide because of this positive experience. They had used a few guides themselves, which they brought to the workshop as examples, and analysed them together with a range of other guides brought by the facilitators to stimulate discussion.

The basic aims of the workshop were to:

- define a field guide and its purpose;
- review a range of field guides and comment on their positive and negative characteristics;
- test the usability of the field guides by searching for particular information;
- test the clarity of illustrations by checking recognition of local well-known species using only the drawings or photographs given in the guide;
- test the usability of the field guides by attempting to identify selected species in the field.

These exercises helped to stimulate discussion on the purpose and content of the proposed new guide, and helped the facilitators to find out what really worked, as well as what was appealing to users.

A helpful method to use with groups or individuals at the exploratory stage of planning is semi-structured interviewing. Unlike the questionnaire method, which follows a list of ready-made questions, semi-structured interviewing starts with more general questions or topics and allows the facilitator and the group to probe for details or to discuss issues. It is less formal and more fun than using a questionnaire, and can help participants to get to know the other stakeholders. The method is described in more detail in Chapter 7, but can be used in a group discussion to help plan the guide.

Where people have less time or inclination, the guide may have to be planned in a less participatory way by interviewing willing individuals. In this case, the best way to ensure that all of your questions are answered is to prepare a structured questionnaire (see Chapter 7 for further information on questionnaires). Informants should be carefully chosen, either as thoughtful, responsible members of the group for whom the guide is intended, or as key people who know them well. Again, it will help to ask informants to comment on a range of field guides, to describe their experience in using guides and to explain what they might use a new guide for.

Prioritizing species according to subjective criteria

If you can assemble a group who represents the interests of the users of your guide, then you can conduct a brainstorming exercise with them where everyone contributes ideas

Box 3.2 A workshop to plan a field guide with stakeholders

- *Objective*: this workshop is to help potential users define the reasons for producing a guide, select format and content, and plan the activities involved in producing it. The example described here aimed to help participants:
  - define a field guide and its purpose;
  - review a range of field guides and comment on their positive and negative characteristics;
  - test the usability of the field guides by searching for particular information;
  - test the comprehension of illustrations by checking recognition of local well-known species using only the drawing or photographs given in the guide;
  - test the usability of the field guides by attempting to identify selected species in the field.
- *Output*: a plan for the production of a user-friendly field guide.
- *Staff*: a facilitator.
- *Participants*: representatives from as many primary stakeholder groups as possible, representing a range of users.
- *Time*: one day.
- *Equipment*: a range of field guides; sufficient stationary such as flip charts, pens and forms for participants.
- *Rationale*: workshops are a good way of involving many stakeholders and promoting discussion between different user groups. The results from this workshop should give an indication of the type of guide that stakeholders would like. It should meet the needs discussed, and ideas for the format and layout can be gleaned from existing guides, taking strengths from each and avoiding weaknesses.

Before the workshop

- Think carefully about who to invite: include a representative range of users, rather than focusing on bringing together a predetermined number of participants.
- Locate a trained facilitator who has had experience of workshops before.
- Define the workshop's aims.
- Make sure that participants understand the aims of the workshop before they arrive.

The workshop

The dynamics of the workshop activities should vary to maintain interest and should include some group activities, some discussion in pairs and some evaluation of particular guides.

Step 1: Introduce the objectives of the guide

These will depend upon the stakeholder. For example, if a community-level guide is planned, objectives will be to:

- stimulate group/individual discussion about the characteristics and role of plant field guides in the user group;
- identify current user perceptions regarding the utility of plant guides;
- identify the present level of use of plant guides by the user group;
- identify the key user needs/priorities with respect to plant field guides;
- develop principles/criteria for developing an 'idealized' plant guide for the community.

In addition, are other types of guides required? Are there any general questions that could be listed here?

Step 2: Group discussion session

This step uses brainstorming to address key questions, the focus of the questions moving gradually from the general to the specific. The number and nature of the questions posed will be determined largely by specific user needs and their experiences in using guides. Key questions will include (but not be limited to):

- What is a field guide?
- What do you want a field guide to do for you?
- What are your priority topics for a new field guide?
- What guides do you currently use?
- What should a field guide include in order to identify a plant? This question stimulates discussion about the important characteristics needed to identify plants.
- What are the benefits of using guides in your work? This question stimulates discussion to help define the impact of field guides.

Occasionally, it helps to ask further questions, such as why do you need to know about the plants or know their scientific name?

Step 3: Collate and summarize participant responses

Attempt to identify patterns in the comments and statements regarding the requirements and characteristics of an ideal plant guide. Write these on a flip chart (or deliver them verbally), presenting them to the participants in a series of point-form summary statements. Ask the group for confirmation that the summaries are substantially correct. Amend if not.

Step 4: Participant reviews of plant guide types

The aim of this activity is to collect a range of factors that users want to see, and find practical, in a guide. Additionally, the four aspects of a guide (text, illustrations, access systems and physical attributes) should be analysed. Key information on the preferences of the participants can be revealed during their review of existing guides.

The participants' views on the usability of existing guides are fundamental to developing a plant guide tailored to addressing specific user needs. This phase of the workshop terminates with ranking the guides in order to summarize participants' criteria:

- The facilitators introduce the step, highlighting the objectives and emphasizing that participants must now decide what types of guide formats meet their needs. Users should have control of the process.
- The facilitators sort the plant guides into the types available – for instance according to user (guides for scientists and guides for communities) or according to objective (guides for plant identification, guides for management) etc. If the facilitators have an idea of what the participants' needs are, they will probably select the type of guide that the users prefer.
- The facilitators explain what is meant by the four aspects of field guides:
  - text: content (language, themes, accessibility of the information);
  - illustrations: drawings and photos;
  - access systems: resources that help to locate the information;

> – physical aspects (size, durability and quality of the materials).
> • Replace the definitions with those provided by the user group.
>
> ### Step 5: Evaluating guides
>
> • The facilitators ask the participants to choose the guides to be analysed. These can be selected from a range of guides brought to the workshop by the facilitators, or by the participants (one that they use), or both. The participants then work in pairs, each analysing a different guide.
> • The facilitators ask the pairs (or individuals) to analyse their guide according to the four aspects mentioned above (text, illustrations, access systems and physical aspects).
> • The facilitators write, on separate cards, positive and negative reactions to each of these aspects, ending up with eight cards in total (use different coloured cards for the different aspects).
>
> ### Step 6: Summary/categorization of working group evaluations
>
> A summary of key points from the evaluation exercise is presented on a flip chart, including strengths and weaknesses/good and bad points of each guide based on the four criteria (text, illustrations, access systems and physical aspects).
>
> ### Step 7: Ranking the guides (plenary)
>
> Each participant gives each guide a score, ranging from 1 (poor) to 5 (very good). The total or average scores show the overall group preference. Debate the results. Ask why some guides are better than others, and discuss whether any guide is ideal in all aspects or whether there are trade-offs.
>
> To conclude the workshop, results should be documented and the information used to help plan guides.

without feeling criticized or intimidated by anyone else's views, and where everyone's interests are covered. This will lead to a 'long list' of species that might be included, and that will need to be organized and prioritized.

Box 3.3 provides methods for how to sort and rank species. These methods, in addition to helping participants to prioritize species, help to elicit the criteria that people use when judging whether a species is important or not. This, in turn, provides useful information for the guide (see Chapter 7).

Nevertheless, participatory processes must combine the best of both local and scientific knowledge, and the final list cannot be decided upon without some expert input. Only specialists will be able to advise, for example, about:

• species that might be confused with the selected ones – this is particularly important in a guide to medicinal or edible species;
• how much is known about these species, and how feasible it is to obtain new information about these species.

By this stage you may be beginning to realize why the process is an iterative one: you cannot just plan your guide, collect the information and publish it. There will always be

Box 3.3 Participatory brainstorming methods
for species selection

- *Objective*: to quickly generate a broad range of ideas and then prioritize them with a group of stakeholders.
- *Output*: list of species/groups of species to include in the guide.
- *Staff*: experienced facilitator.
- *Participants*: representatives from all stakeholder groups.
- *Time*: two hours.
- *Equipment*: flip chart, markers, pens, cards, board and pins.

Brainstorming

Brainstorming is the name given to the exercise of gathering ideas in a spontaneous and rapid way. It is a useful tool in a group context since members of the group can be stimulated and provoked to formulate new ideas by other members' suggestions.

There are two ways of carrying out a participatory brainstorming exercise:

- The group openly shares suggestions, calling out ideas that the facilitator lists on a flip chart; this method can help to stimulate plenty of debate and to recall people's memories.
- Each person in the group writes or draws their suggestions on cards – one suggestion per card. This method helps to ensure that shy people are included, and that internal politics in the group does not prevent everyone from being heard.

It is the facilitator's job to ensure that the activity does not get bogged down in detailed discussion or debate. Everybody's ideas should be treated equally at this stage.

Sorting

This step allows some order to be given to the plethora of ideas that will emerge from the brainstorming exercise:

- All the suggestions should be read through by the group or a facilitator without comment or discussion.
- Participants can then be asked to organize their cards into groups based on similarities. This part of the exercise may indicate how participants would naturally order the species.
- Once all of the cards have been sorted, participants can be invited to comment on the different groups and the positioning of individual cards. This will elicit the *reasons* for putting cards in particular piles, which can be important in defining people's criteria for including species in the guide. At this stage, participants can change the position of their cards if they feel that they are in the wrong group.

Ranking or voting

Ranking or voting is a way of assigning importance or prioritizing species or groups.

Figure 3.1 *Indigenous villagers in Bajo Paraguá, Bolivian Amazon,
prioritize species to include in their* Guide to Useful Plants

Prioritization of different groups will define criteria for what types of species to include in the guide (for example, 'medicinal plants' or 'trees'), and ranking species will define criteria for which species to include within that group. It may also suggest an order for species to appear in the guide.

Ranking can be carried out in the following ways:

- Once groups have been established by the sorting exercise, participants can be invited to give their opinion on the level of importance for each group or species that may be included in the guide.
- If cards have been used and grouped, ranking can then be achieved by counting the number of cards in each group; the more cards in the group, the higher the ranking or priority of the group.
- Another way of ranking is to ask participants to vote on the different groups or species. There are two ways of doing this:
  1   By a show of hands – the facilitator can go through the different groups and ask the participants to raise their hands for the group that they think is the most impor-tant. The group with the most votes has the highest priority.
  2   By giving out stickers (for example, three per participant) – the facilitator can request that participants place the stickers by the groups that they think are most important. A count of the stickers, once they have all been added to the board, will provide the ranking for each group.

an element of adjusting and redefining the content and illustrative material. Biological, climatic, social and economic factors all need to be taken into account. How wide an area is the user group likely to visit? How feasible is it to produce a guide for a large area; is it uneconomic to produce one that is too local and, hence, has only a small user group? And – the big question – are the resources available to produce the guide you have planned?

STEP 2: REVIEW THE SCOPE IN RELATION TO AVAILABLE RESOURCES

Having carried out a stakeholder analysis and determined the purpose of the guide and what must go in it, you now need to assess whether you can do it with the resources available. These resources are existing information, time and money.

Available information

In order to fulfil the guide's purpose, based on the draft species list and the criteria specified by user groups, how much more information will be needed in addition to that which already exists? To answer this, you will need to identify all the existing sources of information, including: species that fit the selection criteria but are missing from the draft list; species identification and names; useful information, both scientific and local, about the species; illustrations; and keys, contents, introduction and indexes.

Chapter 7 gives further guidance on thinking through the sources of information; you may need to do a considerable amount of research at this stage to find out what herbarium and library resources exist. It will help to read Chapters 4 and 5, as well, before producing a guide with many species that have perhaps not been identified properly. Too many guides have been published in which incorrect scientific names are used. One of the biggest mistakes made is to simply repeat scientific names used elsewhere for what is apparently the same species. Specimens of every species must be collected and verified at herbaria in order to ensure correct identification.

Available time

With a clear idea of the information required, you can begin to estimate the time that you will need to produce the guide. How much time will it take to collect new information and assemble existing information; analyse and edit it; design the pages; test, modify and finalize the content and layout; and, finally, publish it? Examples given in Case study 3.3 and Table 3.4 will help you to think through these questions.

It is not just a matter of the total time required, but also the order of events and the way in which they are distributed throughout the year. Many of the activities involved in producing a guide are seasonally dependent because:

- Plant specimens need to be collected with flowers and fruits (see Chapter 4).
- Some stakeholders are more available at certain times of the year – eco-tourists visit during the dry season; farmers have more time for workshops and ethnobotanical research when they are not busy with sowing and harvesting.

If species need to be identified, specimens of both fruit and flowers may be required, and these can take a whole year to collect. If specimens must be sent off to a national or international herbarium for identification by a specialist, do not expect a reply by return post. Botanists are often busy doing fieldwork themselves; even if they are at home, the administrative work needed to process specimens and to return names can take another year, unless you have a close working relationship with the specialist in question. Case study 3.3 sets out an example of the time needed for different activities in Ghana and Grenada.

A timeline or calendar is an easy way of organizing events into chronological order and fitting activities to appropriate seasons. This can be used as a management tool throughout the project in order to assess progress. Table 3.4 shows a summary of the activities carried out in Bolivia to produce a guide (Vargas and Jordán, 2003) to 60 useful species in the indigenous communities around the Parque Nacional Noel Kempff Mercado (PNNKM); the guide took three years to produce. Of course, the authors had other work to do; but given the seasonal importance of access to the field sites, the time that the communities needed to think about their involvement and contributions, and the repeated visits that were required to check on species identification and fill in information gaps, it could not have been completed in less time. The calendar also helps to plan the activities in a logical order. Tips include:

- Talk to publishers at the start of the project.
- Begin illustrations early.
- Aim for a first draft halfway through the available time.

Estimating costs

With a good idea of the guide's information requirements and the time needed to complete the guide, you can estimate the amount of money necessary to produce it. First, who will do the work? Case study 3.8 describes the experience of the team in Brazil, and provides tips on deciding who should be included. Will you have to pay salaries or consultants' fees? How much will it cost to gather all of the information, including field visits to collect specimens and data; workshops with users and other stakeholders; and trips or postage to national or international herbaria in order to check specimen identities?

The real costs of preparing a guide, in time and money, are often much higher than the costs of printing; but it is the printing costs that are often harder to cover. This is because many people who decide to produce guides do not count the cost of their own time, either because they work in NGOs or government organizations where their salary is already paid, or because they are so enthusiastic and dedicated to the idea of the guide that they do not think about such practicalities. Nevertheless, collecting specimens and field data, including local knowledge, costs more than time – transport and materials must also be taken into consideration. Projects often cover these; but it is the costs of printing and distributing the guide that can be overlooked at the outset. A checklist of costs, which need to be considered and included in the project budget, can be found in Box 3.4, and examples of guide format options and costs are presented in Case study 3.5.

Once you have prepared your budget, the big question is, do you have this money, and if not, can you get it? If the time and money required are not available, you must go back and revise your ambitions for the guide. Almost every guide takes more time and money to produce than was envisioned at the beginning. Alternatively, if you have a fixed amount of time and money, you can work out how many species your guide can contain and what kind of illustrations you can afford to include. After doing this, you may need to return to your user group to revise the scope of the guide.

CASE STUDY 3.3 GUIDES IN GHANA AND GRENADA: TIME NEEDED FOR DIFFERENT ACTIVITIES

William Hawthorne

Every field guide is different. Different plants, habitats, available information, countries and cultures will all affect aspects of timing. This case study outlines examples from our projects that provide some estimation of timing in particular cases.

Producing a picture guide to trees in Ghana

Although, in principle, one can take 200 to 300 digital photographs a day, covering perhaps 10 to 30 species, fieldwork never turns out to be as efficient as this, averaged over a long time period and when making a field guide. On the Forestry Research Programme (FRP) trial guides project in Ghana, making a 128-species photo guide to Ghanaian trees took two experienced people about 60 days (120 person days) of fieldwork, including a lot of travelling to cover the forest types of Ghana and to find appropriate individual trees. Once photographed, only about 30 days of more work were required to produce the laminated guide book we tested (and which worked well); but because we were researching alternatives formats, layouts and various digital photo cataloguing devices, we needed a further 30 days.

A workable 'modular' field guide, therefore, can be completed by one author with approximately one to two days per species, approaching the shorter end of this estimate as one becomes more experienced. Complex keys, introductions and so on will increase the time required. Picture guides with additional text per species will obviously take longer, depending upon the research required for the content. At this rate, about 100 people could cover all plant species in the world in about eight years! Of course, not all circumstances are so favourable for rapid guide production as Ghana's trees.

The summary of time costs is as follows:

- Twenty to 30 species can be photographed per day in a best case scenario; in reality, around one species per day is achievable (remember to account for travel time).
- The 128-species guidebook took 30 days to format.
- It also took 30 days to test.
- In total, a 128-species guidebook took 120 + 30 + 30 person days = 180 person days.

Time taken for an illustrated guide, Grenada

Caribbean Spice Island Plants was a book with a difficult remit – decidedly non-technical – since it has to be usable, to some extent, by older schoolchildren and a broad range of eco-tourists. However, it also has to inform Grenadian forestry and ministry staff of endemic and other important plants. The first phase was not directly aimed at making a field guide, but at collecting illustrations for testing formats as a research exercise. The fieldwork of gathering specimens and creating illustrations of 100 Grenadian species involved collecting and photographing a larger set of about 300 species in order to allow a fair sample size within which to establish priorities. This took three people with almost no previous experience of the flora about 60 working days (equating to 180 person days; however, it might have been done in 75 hours by just two of us, i.e. 150 person days). Most species were collected more than once during different seasons. These plants were easier to collect and photograph than the Ghanaian trees because we were including common small forest plants. The island is much smaller than the forest zone of Ghana, and there was less need to hunt for plants in suitable lighting conditions and with a good display form.

Rosemary Wise, our artist, meanwhile, could draw around five fairly simple line drawings of specimens per day, or do two to three simple paintings. Note that artists vary considerably in productivity, and Rosemary is particularly quick. All 100 specimens could, in principle, be photographed or scanned in a day. The Grenadian species were illustrated only on A6 cards (the size of a postcard or a typical family photograph) for our tests, and an average formatting time would be equivalent to the Ghanaian example.

The summary of time costs for phase 1 (research to compare illustration usability) of the Grenada example is as follows:

- Collecting and photographing 100 species in three formats for testing took 180 person days (by inexperienced staff) over several seasons, making duplicate photographs.
- A faster than average illustrator could create four simple line drawings per day or two to three simple paintings.
- Formatting and testing took 60 person days for the main researcher, as well as the time of numerous 'almost-volunteer' testers and volunteers being tested. One test with two to four participants trying three formats and twenty species took about one invigilator an hour. Invigilator time is therefore about 100 hours for 300 tests, or 6000 plant trial identifications. If we added all of this time, as well as the time unaccounted for waiting for participants, good weather, etc, the total would approach three times this figure.
- In sum, production and testing (of about 300 people) of three formats of A6-size illustrations for 100 species took 180 + 25 + 50 + 60 person days = 315 person days, as well as at least 100 hours of casual labour, and more than 300 hours from volunteers.

Grenada phase 2

The time taken subsequently to format and publish a field guide using illustrations and lessons from phase 1 consisted of the following:

- Collecting, identifying and photographing extra plants (about 450 more species, using only photographic illustrations) by myself and a field assistant to bring the book to 740 species took 95 person days. Productivity was much more efficient due to experience, better knowledge of the flora, and the focus on taking photos for the guide book, not for 'format research'.
- Library research for textual information and historic illustrations, as well as adding species, editing and initial formatting of the basic text, keys, introduction and contents, for a circa 350-page book (primarily by one person) took 155 person days.
- Copyediting, final layout and other publication tasks took ten days.
- Printing took approximately one month.
- In sum, phase 2, minus printing took 260 person days.

The estimated total time to produce a circa 350-page 2000-picture field guide completely 'from scratch' (including training field assistants), in a country with no herbarium, to camera-ready copy ready for printing was 315 + 260 = 575 person days (that is, a team of two botanists, as well as one assistant or artist, working for a whole year). Phase 1 overestimates the essential time required since we were preoccupied with obtaining testing results for interest beyond the Grenadian guide. However, this was compensated for by the time taken (and not accounted for) identifying specimens. Note that this guide is explicitly a 'picture guide book with interesting notes'. Field guides to 750 species normally take much longer to produce.

Discussion

In terms of fieldwork costs, and not counting the time taken to arrive within the geographical area covered by the field guide, one can assume that averaged over 100 species or so, one should plan for an average of about one person day's fieldwork per species included in the guide if two people are working together and the guide is to be based on photos of fresh plants. It is always better to work in pairs, with one person collecting specimens and the other photographing, easily halving the total time taken. The incremental advantage of a third person is less marked, and a team of five or more definitely represents 'too many cooks'. So, assume an average of only two species per team day of work, averaged over many species – regardless of how many photographs you think you can snap in a day!

The big difference between the Grenada and Ghana guide preparation task was not so much fieldwork, although that is certainly easier in the tiny country of Grenada, but the greater time taken in Grenada to identify the species and come to grips with the flora, as none of us had any extensive botanical knowledge of the area. Some species could be identified in a matter of minutes with the *Flora of the Lesser Antilles*, mainly due to prior knowledge of families and genera, or occasionally by using a local name that was correctly listed in the Flora. However, the majority of species take much longer than a few minutes to identify, with perhaps 10 per cent taking more than two hours to identify, spread out over years (several specimens still remain unidentified). It may also be necessary to add the time taken for trips to distant herbaria. Often one can discount some of these time factors since specimen identification or a herbarium trip might have been part of the field guide author's normal work anyway.

Conclusion

Budget for an average of one to two species per day for a botanically minded person, as well as a field assistant and occasional help from an artist, to produce basic but usable field guides to hundreds of plant species with limited textual information for regions where the flora is reasonably well known, such as West Africa and the Caribbean. Add to this your own estimate for researching and writing the other textual information that is to be added to the guide, and about one month per 100 species at the end to convert a completed manuscript into a polished publication. Corners can be cut to produce reasonable picture-based guides at the rate of two to four species per person day. More detailed guides, requiring substantial research per species, might easily decline to a rate of one species per month; so consider the implications of incorporating additional data carefully.

Table 3.4 *An example of an activities calendar used by the Fundación Amigos de la Naturaleza (FAN) and the Centro Internacional de Agricultura Tropical (CIAT) in preparing a community field guide (Vargas and Jordán, 2003)*

Activity	Year 1 Q1	Q2	Q3	Q4	Year 2 Q1	Q2	Q3	Q4	Year 3 Q1	Q2	Q3	Q4
Planning the field guide												
Meetings to initiate planning of the guide	■	☐	☐	☐	☐	☐	☐	☐	☐	☐	☐	☐
Define the user groups and their needs	■	☐	☐	☐	☐	☐	☐	☐	☐	☐	☐	☐
Consult users and identify needs	☐	■	■	■	☐	☐	☐	☐	☐	☐	☐	☐
Establish agreements with local groups on documentation of local knowledge and production of the guide	☐	☐	■	■	☐	☐	☐	☐	☐	☐	☐	☐
Participatory selection and prioritization of species to include in the guide	☐	☐	■	■	■	☐	☐	☐	☐	☐	☐	☐
Define content of the guide (family, scientific name, common name, text, illustrations, etc.)	☐	☐	■	■	■	☐	☐	☐	☐	☐	☐	☐
Prepare an action plan with user groups and institutions	☐	☐	☐	☐	☐	☐	☐	☐	☐	☐	☐	☐
Coordinate activities with communities and other personnel	☐	☐	■	☐	■	☐	☐	☐	■	☐	■	☐
Preparing the field guide												
Analyse and organize existing information, the quality of botanical information and access to information	■	■	■	■	■	☐	☐	☐	☐	☐	☐	☐
Meeting to map and characterize the vegetation, and plan the transects with key informants from each community	☐	☐	■	☐	☐	☐	☐	☐	☐	☐	☐	☐
Review scientific names and additional information on selected species	☐	☐	☐	■	■	■	■	■	■	☐	☐	☐
Review the literature and other sources for additional information about selected plants	☐	☐	☐	■	■	■	■	■	■	☐	☐	☐
Collect botanical specimens and verify identification	☐	☐	■	■	■	■	■	■	■	☐	☐	☐
Field walks with key informants to identify species and start collecting information	☐	☐	☐	☐	☐	☐	■	■	☐	☐	☐	☐
Interviews to collect more detailed information about species from key informants in the community	☐	☐	■	■	☐	☐	☐	☐	☐	☐	☐	☐
Participatory identification of diagnostic characters for the selected species	☐	☐	■	■	☐	☐	☐	☐	☐	☐	☐	☐
Take photos of the whole plant and of parts of the plant to scan, and find existing illustrations for the field guide	☐	☐	■	■	■	■	■	■	☐	☐	☐	☐
Commission illustrations for initial testing with users	☐	☐	■	☐	☐	☐	☐	☐	☐	☐	☐	☐
Define distinct morphological descriptors, uses and management of selected species	☐	☐	■	■	■	☐	☐	☐	☐	☐	☐	☐
Define necessary indexes and other access methods with users	☐	☐	■	■	☐	☐	☐	☐	☐	☐	☐	☐
Define indicators for participatory evaluation of the field guide	☐	☐	☐	☐	☐	☐	☐	☐	☐	☐	☐	☐
Prepare descriptions and/or diagnostic characters for each species (seek the participation of local users)	☐	☐	☐	■	■	■	■	■	■	☐	☐	☐

Prepare preliminary draft of the field guide

Complete field information with key informants: ethnobotanical data, characteristics of the plants and ecosystems

Testing the field guide

Test different types of illustrations with users

Modify, and complete the illustrations based on feedback from field testing and availability of new illustrations

Define the required illustrations for the guide based on results and test the availability of existing illustrations

Modify activities according to the conclusions of evaluating the guide

Communicate the results of the validation exercises to the community

Modify the guide according to the conclusions of the validation exercise

Test the keys and tools with users

Communicate the results of the validation/evaluation exercises

Complete the list of scientific names of included species

Validation workshop to test usability and to evaluate the draft guide with user groups

Communicate the results of the validation/evaluation exercises

Write indexes, introduction and glossaries, if necessary

Prepare a second draft of the field guide

Evaluation workshop to test the whole guide

Communicate the results of the validation/evaluation exercises

Make the adjustments and changes requested

Publishing and disseminating the field guide

Define content of the text and the level of detail of the information for publication

Organize the content of the text, format and detailed information for publication

Layout the final guide

Publish final guide

Send copies of the field guide to tourist agencies, the national institute of tourism and community members

CASE STUDY 3.4 SELECTION OF SPECIES AND DISCUSSIONS ABOUT THE CONTENT FOR A GUIDE TO USEFUL PLANTS IN BAJO PARAGUÁ, BOLIVIA

This guide (Vargas and Jordán, 2003) was prepared in the same area as the guide for eco-tourists described in Case study 3.1, but instead of being targeted at tourists in the PArque Nacional Noel Kempff Mercado it was developed by the indigenous communities living around the national park, both to preserve their knowledge and to produce an attractive product that they could sell. The planning process was therefore much more participatory. It involved the following steps:

- The initial list of plants was drawn up during the first workshop.
- Information was then gathered about the plants from field trips and individual interviews with key informants.
- Based on this information, a list was transcribed onto cards of the plants that were named most frequently and that had the most important uses.

In participatory workshops in each community, we defined the species to be included. Before generating a list of plants, we talked about some criteria for their selection, which were:

- multiple-use species – in other words, those species that have several important uses;
- species that were mentioned most frequently as having one or more important use;
- species that are present in the community or in neighbouring zones, or that are currently used or valued (preference was given to these species);
- other species that are considered very important in medicine, nutrition or construction, even though their habitats are not close to the community.

During the workshop we asked participants to nominate the species that they considered most important for inclusion in the guide. As a result of this exercise we obtained a list of 25 to 30 plant species. Whenever we noticed that participants were having difficulty in remembering more names, we turned to the cards with the list of plants nominated most frequently in each community. On reading out the names, participants decided individually whether they accepted or rejected the plant, and so the initial list was duplicated, which resulted in an important collection of species covering a wide range of local uses.

Consultations about the content

Defining the content of the guide to useful plants was carried out after collecting the preliminary information for two reasons: to decide what information is available about each species and whether it should be included; and to improve our understanding of the guide's group of users and their needs.

An initial activity of the project was to show users examples of existing guides and books on various plant-related themes. This activity was very important because the users clearly preferred some of the books and relied on them to inform their decisions about format, size, content, keys and illustrations, in this way developing their own guide.

Based on the content of other guide books to nearby areas of Bolivia that the users had examined, we prepared a draft outline of our guide's subject matter. When defining and presenting the content to workshop participants, two key questions emerged:

1   What information do we want to include for each plant in the guide?
2   How should we organize this information and what order should we present it in?

In order to standardize the guide's format, it was necessary to focus on the aims of the guide, the seasons of the year, the way in which the vegetation is classified, the selected species and suitable illustrations.

First, the suggestion of arranging the species in order of common name was accepted. After presenting and discussing initial ideas about the content, we then made some adjustments, and participants agreed and accepted the following content for the description for each species:

- *Characteristics of the plant.* This refers to a description of the plant's form (herb, tree, shrub, palm, bamboo, etc.) and includes the size in metres or its behaviour. It then briefly describes the characteristics of the stem, bark, leaf, flower and fruit, highlighting characteristics that are important for identification in the field and noting if there are any similar plants that may be confused with it.
- *Where does the plant grow?* This describes the plant's preferred habitat and whether it is abundant or scarce within the area.
- *Season of flowering and fruiting.* This covers leaf form or reshooting (or whether it is evergreen).
- *Uses of the plant.* This briefly describes the uses of the plant according to categories – for example, medicinal, nutritional and timber (we tried to adopt a symbol for each of the principal categories).
- *The part used and the way in which it is used.* This mentions the use of the complete plant or its parts (root, stem, bark, leaf, flower, seeds and fruit) and the way in which the plant is prepared or exploited.
- *Additional information about the species.* This covers taxonomy, which refers to the taxonomic classification of the plant (scientific name and family); information about uses in other places; and complementary information from the international literature which is relevant to the zone.

BOX 3.4 CHECKLIST OF COSTS

Below is a list of costs that should be considered when drawing up a budget for your project:

- materials;
- time needed to collect information;
- time needed to collect and identify specimens;
- fuel/transport – the number of field trips required to collect information and specimens;
- computer, printers, software;
- illustrations: the number of species required to illustrate, multiplied by the cost per illustration;
- time needed to write, rearrange and edit the material;
- specialist services (layout, editing);
- time needed to test and correct errors;
- printing (pages, format, illustrations);
- distribution of finished guide.

CASE STUDY 3.5 FORMAT AND COST OPTIONS FOR A SMALL GUIDE DESIGNED FOR FARMERS IN NORTHEAST BRAZIL

This case study reports on the costs of different options for producing a colour guide to 21 forage legumes in Bahia, Brazil (Costa et al, 2002). The research into costs was conducted towards the end of the process; but it is good to be aware of the choices available and the cost implications near the beginning of the project in order to avoid nasty surprises, or to find that you cannot provide what your users require.

The following specifications were decided upon in consultations and tests with the target audience.

Guide specification

*   *Size:* 22.5 x 15cm.
*   *Binding:* spiral.
*   *Type of cover:* thick and durable; preferably waterproof.
*   *Cover:* laminated, gloss, white, with colour printing.
*   *Paper for the inner pages:* matt, white and durable (weight: 80g–150g).
*   *Number of pages (extent):* 116.

When researching the budget to print the guide and trying to lower the costs as much as possible, we had to make other decisions. For example, in deciding how many pages would be in colour, we had to prioritize those for which colour was necessary for identification. The main points we had to consider were:

*   type of paper – thickness/weight, colour, finish, durability;
*   total number of pages;
*   he number of pages in full colour; and
*   number of copies to be printed.

Table 3.5 shows the range of options available to us from a range printers who supplied quotes, showing also the different services they offered and their prices. Note that some printing companies do not accept orders to print fewer than 1000 copies. We also realized that there was substantial variation in the quality of printing materials and in the finish of the cover, and that it is extremely difficult to compare budgets for exactly the same product (material and finish and format) between printers as they all use different materials.

Tips to help with publication budgeting

*   It is much easier to get estimates of the costs for printing the guide once you have a final mock-up. With the final draft, it is possible to define the number of pages in the guide, the number of coloured and single-colour pages, and other details that are important and directly affect the final value of the guide.
*   It is also much more likely that the final printed product will be closer to what you expected if you can get the quotations on the final draft.
*   Table 3.5 demonstrates that when a larger number of copies are printed at the same time (in a single print run), it is possible to reduce the individual cost of each copy, which leads to savings in the overall cost.
*   Generally, we found that the quotations were valid for 30 days; so the value of the product is subject to changes if you experience delays in the printing.

Table 3.5 *Printing options and associated costs*

	Description	Cost (US$ equivalent*)	
		500 copies	1000 copies

Option 1	*Size:* 22.5x15cm
	Binding: spiral
	Extent: 116 pages
	Cover: 4 colour on 300gsm
	  cream card, laminated
	Inner pages: 4 colour throughout
	  on 150gsm matt cream paper
		2100	2826

Option 2	*Differences from option 1:* fewer
	  inner pages in colour (26 of 116);
	  inner pages paper 150gsm bright white
		1618	1958

Option 3	*Differences from option 1:* the number
	  of photographs was an element of the
	  cost; fewer inner pages in colour
	  (20 of 116); inner pages paper 95gsm
	  matt cream; cover 170gsm with flaps
		n/a†	3330

Option 4	*Differences from option 1:* fewer inner
	  pages in colour (26 of 116); inner
	  pages paper 150gsm bright white;
	  cover was hardback (very thick
	  cream card)
		n/a†	4198

Option 5	*Differences from option 1:* fewer inner
	  pages in colour (26 of 116); inner pages
	  paper higher quality 250gsm; cover
	  was hardback with dust jacket; text
		n/a†	3490

Option 6	*Differences from option 1:* fewer inner
	  pages in colour (26 of 116); inner pages
	  paper 350gsm; cover was printed both
	  sides, laminated and ultraviolet resistant
		3316	3682

Notes: * Original costs were in Brazilian reals; conversion rate US$1 = 5 reals.
†Printer does not print fewer than 1000 copies.

- When choosing a printer or a particular type of printing, be certain of the service you are contracting and of the material that will be used for the final product. Wherever possible, check a sample of materials with the printers themselves, and ask to see other types of guides that the printers have prepared in order to be sure of the overall quality.
- Some printers include in their quotations the printing of a proof copy – in other words, a complete printing of the product so that it can be checked and revised, and everyone can be sure that the final product is of a high quality. Printing errors or omissions can occasionally occur, such as photos in the wrong place, smudge marks on pages, changes in the font or size of the text, and text moved around by mistake. It is for this reason that it is very important to check the proofs and give your approval before the final copies of the guide are printed.
- The guide's editor and author should check the initial proof since this involves detailed and critical work by someone very familiar with the work.

Seeking funding for the field guide

Seeking funding may be the hardest part of writing a field guide. Donors change regularly, and money available for such activities can depend upon multiple factors, such as fashion, politics and national economy.

Potential sources of funding

Funding may be available from a range of sources, some of which are listed here – although the list is not exclusive. It is always worth approaching other sources with a written proposal if you have an idea that they might be willing to fund such a project.

The value of researching your potential donor's interests cannot be stressed enough. Proposals tailored to emphasize points that may catch their interest will be much more successful. When you apply for funds, check what the implications of funding will be – for example, you may have to put their logo on your cover. Never forget to acknowledge your donors.

With this in mind, different sources should be targeted depending upon the overall goals of your field guide. If conservation is a priority, then a good source of funding may be derived from conservation charities, trusts and foundations. Alternatively, if the guide's aim is to increase social capacity or benefits for the user groups, social development charities, trusts and foundations can be targeted. These types of organizations may have money available for innovative or worthwhile projects if they fit their organizational or funding criteria.

If the guide is aimed at eco-tourists or other people coming to the region on holiday, funding could be sought from local tourist agencies, with an emphasis on how useful the guide would be for them in stimulating further interest from tourists. These agencies could also be a good outlet for sales.

The national government may have funding available for projects, and relevant departments to approach could include ministries dealing with the environment, forests, agriculture or wildlife. An emphasis on relevance to the United Nations Convention on Biological Diversity or the National Biodiversity Strategy could be helpful (depending upon the country of origin).

There are also international donors, such as the World Bank. Case study 3.6 presents an example of the World Bank's criteria for field guide proposals, as well as generic advice on how to write them. These guidelines can be tailored to individual cases. Other people to approach might include wealthy individuals with an interest in a particular group of species, or wildlife in general. Industries and companies may also be interested in funding such a project as a means of improving their corporate image.

Another way of funding the field guide is to plan to sell the guide (and to borrow money depending upon sales forecasts) or to reinvest money from the sales of previous guides. However, if you are planning to make money from the field guide, don't forget that you will not receive the full cover cost of many of the guide's copies. If the guides are distributed to a bookshop, you will have to sell them at a substantial discount (sometimes at less than half the cover price). And you will usually end up giving away quite a few copies as samples or review copies.

How to apply for funding

Writing proposals can take a long time. However, this activity can be an extremely useful way of planning your project, and of clarifying all of the activities that need to be done. Often the proposal document is referred to throughout the project.

Key points are:

- Be concise. Donors do not want to read through a 100-page document; they want to be able to read it in ten minutes. They can always ask you for more information if necessary. An executive summary in which key points are covered is a good way of representing your project on one sheet.
- Demonstrate the need for the field guide. Donors are more willing to fund projects that will be of obvious and direct use to at least one specified user group. Activities that result in the users specifying what kind of guide is needed and why can provide strong evidence of user demand. It is always good to include statements of support from different stakeholder groups.
- Present the budget and time frame. Donors will need to know immediately how much money you are asking for. Some donors may have cut-off points, and these should be researched and noted before submitting the proposal. There is no point in submitting a proposal with a budget that exceeds the funding available. If you can contribute money or other resources, this may increase the chance of acceptance.
- Emphasize the interests of the donor. If the donor has any specific requirement for projects that it wishes to fund, make sure that your proposal mentions these and try to relate project activities and outputs to them.

Ensure that these details also go into your proposal:

- who you are;
- why you are doing this project;
- the purpose of the project itself;
- why it is needed (justification for the project);
- a description of your team members and their roles within the project;
- outputs or products;
- activities (what will be done to get to the outputs or products);
- lasting expectations of the project once financial support has been withdrawn;
- budget.

STEP 3: PREPARE AN ACTION PLAN AND AGREEMENTS WITH STAKEHOLDERS

Once the planning stage for the guide is nearing an end, an action plan must be prepared with stakeholders in order to clarify who does what, when and where. An action plan contains the following elements:

- activity;
- dates;
- person(s) responsible;
- resources needed.

CASE STUDY 3.6 WORLD BANK GUIDELINES
FOR FIELD GUIDE PROPOSALS

The World Bank, together with The Netherlands government, provided US$150,000 during 2001–2003 for writing field guides to Southeast Asia. The guidelines provided under this scheme are helpful when planning the stages of any guide and also indicate the kind of information that funders will be looking for.

Introduction

In reviewing proposals for field guides, particular attention will be given by the World Bank to the following factors:

- demonstrated need;
- the potential for using the field guides to encourage and support biodiversity conservation;
- procedures for ensuring scientific quality of the text and illustrations;
- procedures for ensuring local language quality (particularly in the case of translations);
- the availability of publication/republication/translation rights;
- cost;
- availability of co-financing.

Detail

Proposals should be no more than four pages long and should include the following information:

1 *Title of the proposal.*
2 *Background and justification.* This section should clearly demonstrate the need for the project and should contain a brief assessment of the current field guide situation in the concerned country or region.
3 *Objectives.* This section should briefly list two or three objectives that the project hopes to achieve as a result of publishing the proposed field guides.
4 *Description of the proposed field guide.* This section should, as far as possible, include the following information:
    - title of the field guide;
    - authors' language (local language only or dual);
    - thematic focus;
    - scope and coverage (all species or only those that are common);
    - description of contents (including any special features/additions of locally relevant information);
    - type and number of illustrations;
    - likely size (physical dimensions) and length (number of pages);
    - number of copies to be printed (recognizing that most people underestimate this).
5 *Production process.* This section should briefly describe the steps that will be taken to produce the guide and to ensure overall quality. The following questions should be addressed:
    - Will the field guide use new text or will it be based on the translation of existing text?

- Will the field guide use new illustrations or will it make use of existing illustrations?
- Will it be necessary to obtain translation/republication rights or letters of authorization? (If relevant, please contact the original publishers for an indication of terms and conditions. Some publishers are willing to be very generous for local language guides.)
- What steps are to be taken to ensure the scientific accuracy of the guides?
- What steps are to be taken to ensure the quality of the translation?
- Where – and by whom – will the guide be printed?
- Who is the likely publisher/distributor? This section should also describe any previous experience which the organization may have had with the production of books or printed materials.

6   *Dissemination and pricing strategies.* This is a key section, clearly describing the steps that will be taken to distribute and disseminate the field guide once it has been printed, and the ways in which the guide will be used to promote biodiversity conservation. It should also describe the way in which any proceeds from the guide will be ploughed back into reprints, etc. The intended audience for the guide should be clearly identified, as well as the approaches that will be used to reach different target groups. This section should also outline a proposed pricing strategy for the field guide. For example, how many copies will be provided free of charge? To whom? How many copies will be sold at subsidized prices, at cost price or at a profit? To whom? How will any proceeds be utilized?

7   *Administration and management.* This section should describe the administration and management arrangements for the proposed field guide. In particular, it should identify which organizations/staff will be responsible for overseeing the work, implementing activities, submitting progress reports and maintaining accounts. Finally, this section should identify a 'focal point' for future correspondence (including relevant contact details).

8   *Budget.* The budget should be presented in US dollars and include all costs associated with the production of the proposed field guide, including preparation, translation, review, editing and formatting of the text; preparation of illustrations; colour separation; printing; payment for use rights for text, illustrations and colour films from existing publications; dissemination; and management overheads (limited to a maximum of 10 per cent). We expect proposals to be between US$10,000–$20,000, and no proposals in excess of US$20,000 will be entertained. Co-financing arrangements are strongly encouraged.

9   *Work plan.* A short work plan should be included, indicating the timing of the different production steps.

Sources: Tony Whitten, senior biodiversity specialist; adapted from World Bank (2005)

If you have already prepared a calendar of activities (such as Table 3.4), a budget and a project proposal, you will already be well on the way to having these essential management tools.

Finally, where a range of stakeholders is involved, it can be desirable (and normal institutional practice) to formalize the project and the action plan through agreements. This helps to ensure that stakeholders' roles are defined and feasible, and that the institutional management structures can accommodate the work that each member of the team is expected to do.

Case studies 3.7 and 3.8 illustrate two contrasting approaches in projects in Bolivia and Brazil. In both cases, those involved were enthusiastic; but there were differences between the two experiences. In Bolivia (see Case study 3.7), there had long been a demand for field guides in the Noel Kempff Mercado national park, and park guards were keen to contribute. Nevertheless, the communities had no experience of producing a guide, and experience with participatory conservation projects shows that misunderstandings can arise when rural communities have great expectations of a project's outcome. Considerable care, therefore, was taken to discuss the objectives, who would participate and how, and how the outcomes would be shared. This became rather an extended political process, which respected the indigenous decision-making structures – but in the end, it was the process, rather than the formal agreement, that made everyone feel happy to participate.

In Brazil (see Case study 3.8), the issues were more inter-institutional. The initiative came from one NGO – the Serviço de Assessoria às Organizações Populares Rurais (SASOP) – and while the other NGO partners were interested, especially to learn about the participatory methods and to use them in their own extension materials, they were also concerned about their work plan. It was important, therefore, to clarify how SASOP would bear the burden of the work involved, but to ensure that the NGOs and farmers were available for key events, such as workshops for planning and testing the guides. SASOP's experience also demonstrates the importance of ensuring that the right staff are involved, with coordination and administration available as necessary.

SUMMARY: CHECKLIST OF QUESTIONS FOR THE PLANNING STAGE

- Who will use the field guide?
- What will it be used for?
- What should it ultimately achieve?
- Which species will be included?
- Why will they be included?
- What information should be included about each species?
- What other information should be incorporated within the guide?
- What illustrations should be included?
- How will the information and illustrations be formatted?
- How will it all fit together into a complete guide? What will be the medium? If a book, what will be the overall size, type of binding, paper thickness and cover quality?
- Above all, how can these decisions be tested to see if they really work for the users?
- Who will do all of this?
- How will they be paid?
- How will the field trips, the workshops and the materials be paid for?
- How will the printing be paid for?
- Who will print it?
- Who will publish it?
- Will the guide be sold commercially?
- How can project initiators ensure that it will reach the intended users?

CASE STUDY 3.7 DEVELOPING AGREEMENTS WITH INDIGENOUS COMMUNITIES IN BOLIVIA

Bajo Paraguá is an area of lowland Amazon forest in the buffer zone of the Parque Nacional Noel Kempff Mercado (PNNKM) in Bolivia. The conservation NGO Fundación Amigos de la Naturaleza (FAN) is working with the indigenous communities there to support community forest management. It was FAN who proposed the idea of making a field guide (Vargas and Jordán, 2003); but the decisions about what kind of guide was needed were made by the communities themselves. Researchers from FAN wanted to make sure that the communities would contribute and feel that the guide they were preparing was their own. They spent considerable time discussing the objectives and issues to ensure that they and the communities were aware of the difficulties which can arise when communities contribute their time and knowledge to a project of this kind, without being sure of the benefits that might arise. The researchers wanted to ensure that all of the participants who were involved were quite clear about who could contribute and in what way, at the same time as feeling free to make decisions about what type of information they wanted to include and publish in the guide.

These discussions are time-consuming but essential, in order to ensure that everyone is clear about the results. Bajo Paraguá is a remote area, and every trip from FAN's offices in the regional capital of Santa Cruz required four days' travel (two in each direction). A further two days was usually needed to travel between the various communities along the muddy and waterlogged tracks. Each community meeting would also take at least half a day. Nevertheless, the result was that everyone in the community was aware of the project, trusted the researchers and could make their own decisions about contributing. In the end, four out of five communities chose to participate fully and to receive the field guides for sale in their communities.

The communities are organized as indigenous groups, with their particular political decision-making structures. Each community is represented by the *caciques* (authorities) who have two deputies; at the same time, all communities are represented by the authorities of the Central Indígena del Bajo Paraguá (CIBAPA – the indigenous central cooperative of Bajo Paraguá).

The communities initially wanted to develop a formal agreement, and held a preliminary discussion about how to distribute the benefits that would derive from selling the guide. However, right from the beginning the communities did not expect to sell many copies; so they did not consider this aspect very seriously. In any case, they trusted that the agreement, having been made by CIBAPA, would allow the financial benefits to be channelled into a common fund to be used for school materials and medicines for the community health post; a further fund was envisaged to be invested in the production of other guides for the zone.

In the end, political processes take time; the field activities progressed, and the communities developed trust and enthusiasm through regular interaction with the researchers. Through various meetings with the villagers, field trips and a series of small workshops, they understood that the guide would be created according to their needs and preferences, and that it really was going to be useful for the communities themselves.

The formal agreement was not signed in the end; but the process and the draft document stimulated discussion, which averted possible conflicts over the dissemination of information, the distribution of the product and the possible benefits that might arise in the future.

CASE STUDY 3.8 GUIDELINES FOR TEAM-WORKING TO PREPARE FIELD GUIDES, BASED ON THE EXPERIENCE OF THE FIELD GUIDES PROJECT IN BRAZIL

Over the four years in which the Field Guides Project was carried out, we experienced various team compositions and institutional partnerships, which changed in response to the needs that came up. Through these partnerships we were able to produce the two guides (Costa et al, 2002; de Queiroz et al, forthcoming). This process brought interesting results that also provide tips about what would make the perfect team for such a project.

If you are thinking about preparing a guide, before establishing the team who will carry it out, define the authorship of the field guide or project. The following possibilities exist:

- The guide is the project of an author (physical person).
- The guide is the work of an institution.
- The guide is the collaborative work of a group of institutions, with established partnerships.
- The guide is the product (output) of a project.

As indicated in this chapter, the team can only be defined once you are clear about the:

- guide's theme and content;
- target audience;
- availability of existing information;
- time available;
- resources available.

Regardless of the format and authorship of the guide, it is very important to have a project plan that includes an:

- objective;
- methodology;
- timetable;
- budget.

Even if the planning is as realistic as you can possibly make it, you must remember that contingencies and unforeseen problems always arise; therefore, management must be flexible so that you don't compromise the end result of the project. After defining the responsibilities for authorship, the aspects of the guide and the action plan, you can define the number of people necessary to carry this out and the role/time that each will have during the project.

To help in defining a working team, we offer a few reflections based on our experience in Bahia:

- For the content of the guide, it is important to engage a specialist who is knowledgeable in the guide's theme. For example, for the guides to the legumes of the Caatinga, one author is a specialist in the botanical family Leguminosae. If you can't manage this, you will have to explain how the information is going to be acquired. Even if the information already exists and is available, the author must have the technical advice of, or must have the work reviewed by, a specialist.

- If the guide is the product of one or more institutions, it must be very clear who is going to write the guide or compile the information of the various researchers and authors. If that person is not a specialist, the participation of a specialist must be ensured either through one of the participating institutions or by contracting a consultant in order to verify that the information is correct.
- If the guide is the product of one person's work, he or she will have to ensure that various professionals can be contracted from time to time in order to carry out specific activities, with specific time and money allocated to the tasks. Depending upon his or her abilities, the author may be able to carry out some of these functions, thereby reducing costs, but must bear in mind that the time required will be greater than if a specialist is involved. In order to decide whether the author has the necessary skills, you need to define the type of product and its qualities, and give details of the format. For example, if the guide will include photographs of flowers, you must ask whether the author is capable of taking close-up high-quality photography. Furthermore, will the author have the time to do this, apart from compiling and writing the guide?
- If the guide is the product of one or more institutions, it is still necessary to have one author or person ultimately responsible, with the same need to define his or her role and responsibilities. Staff responsibility, function and hours/proportion of time allocated, as well as resources available to that person, procedures for reporting, expected results and deadlines, must all be defined within the institutional framework if this person is not to experience difficulties.
- If the field guide is the result of a particular project, there is still a need to define who will be responsible for the guide, apart from the other project activities. If the institution makes available a staff member who already has other responsibilities, it is only fair to that person and to the institution to ensure that these new responsibilities, and the proportion of time allocated, are formally recognized. Above all, the personnel assigned to the new tasks must be in agreement, otherwise they will become a member 'on paper' only. This will seriously hold up the other team members and jeopardize the whole chain of activities needed for the guide's production.
- If the guide is the result of a project carried out by a collaboration of various institutions, the same criteria apply to defining institutional and other responsibilities.
- If the guide is the result of a participatory project – in other words, based on research, together with locally knowledgeable people or with the target audience for the guide – you need to include experienced facilitators. Planning and facilitating participatory workshops and research requires experience. It will be very important and productive if this person also has knowledge of the guide's theme; but if this is not possible, the authors or specialists must be included in such workshops.
- The definition of other professional needs will greatly depend upon the specific activities and planned content and style. In particular, the illustrations, design and layout, technical editing and printing will all require expertise, time and resources.
- After defining the team involved for the preparation and technical production of the field guide, you also need to be able to rely on a support team who can take care of administrative and financial aspects. A financial assistant will manage the budget, authorize purchases and payment of expenses, and prepare financial reports for the funders. A secretary will deal with the public, disseminate information about the project, organize workshops and other project events, and send letters and invitations. It might seem that these jobs can be carried out by the same people who are responsible for producing the guide. However, these administrative tasks take time. In addition, if you have funders for your project, you will need the authority of a financial officer to report on spending.

- If the guide is the product of one or more institutions, it is helpful to appoint a coordinator or a senior figure who can manage activities and staff to ensure that the objective is reached on time. The role of this person is to manage and report on activities, use of resources, inter-institutional relations, contact with rural communities and contact with donors, as well as to plan a strategy for promoting and distributing the guide. This person must be a professional familiar with the topic of the guide, but also with experience of team management.
- If you have to contract the services of a photographer or artist, as well as other specialist services such as graphic design and editing, the coordinator must review and authorize the contract. You will need to define who will own the negatives and copyright, and how the illustrator will be credited in the guide.

In conclusion, some of these activities can be carried out by just one person whose time is dedicated to the project; but it is still necessary to outline who exactly will carry out each task, while ensuring that each person has the necessary skills to do so. Table 3.6 provides some suggestions for professionals required to produce a field guide.

Table 3.6 *Suggestions for professionals required to produce a field guide*

Team function	Staff	Comments
Team to produce the content	One person responsible for compiling the content and writing the guide	The author or person who will research, collect and compile the information, or assemble the work of the professionals
	One specialist in the guide's topic to review the technical aspects	This may be the author – but external review is always important
	One illustrator (artist or photographer)	To be contracted according to the quantity and type of illustrations, which will depend upon the preliminary consultations. The illustrator must be guided by the specialist or author of the guide.
	One graphic designer	Contracted service for specific periods
	One copyeditor	For reviewing grammar, style and inconsistencies in content
Team to test the content with the target audience	One facilitator experienced in participatory methodologies, workshop organization, evaluation methods, etc.	Must also be familiar with the guide's topic
	One professional to record the results and write the workshop reports	Must document and analyse the results; contracted for specific events
Administrative support team	One coordinator	The number of hours per week dedicated to the project must be defined since it is unlikely that this person will be working exclusively on the production of the guide
	One finance officer	Responsible for managing accounts, paying expenses, making purchases of materials, etc.
	One secretary	Works alongside the coordinator

4

Plant names and botanical publication

William Hawthorne and Stephen Harris

INTRODUCTION

This chapter concentrates on those aspects of field guides that relate to plant naming, leading into the subject of identification in Chapter 5, and the types of information required for naming and identification in Chapter 6. En route, we discuss 'botanical identity' – how a plant's name is defined – as this is central to understanding the role of any plant guide book. We concentrate on scientific names, but also discuss the use of common names. If scientific nomenclature is new to you, do not be put off: work with a botanist and the chapter will help you to understand the steps they go through.

This chapter also describes the range of publications involved primarily with botanical names. As a guide writer you should be aware of the botanical resources available in order to avoid overlooking useful information. The chapter should help you clarify the niche your field guide might fill in the botanical world, which in turn will help you to make the most efficient and appropriate choice of content and style. Should you really be aiming to produce a small Flora or checklist (see the section on 'The spectrum of botanical literature' for explanations of these terms), rather than a field guide? Should you include Latin names? What about the species' authors and synonym lists?

NAMING, IDENTIFICATION AND CLASSIFICATION

There are two aspects to 'naming': the generation of the name and the application of the name. Application of a name, better called 'identification', is a subject we take up in Chapter 5. Before anything can be identified, however, the names must be generated.

Names may be applied to specific elements, such as a person, or to vaguer, more abstract things, such as a football team (whose players change with time). Plant names are of the second, abstract type, although one name is, of course, in practice applicable to all individual plants of a particular type, unlike members of a football team.

Names might be generated in a moment of creation or evolve gradually. The origin of 'common' plant names is mostly a matter of gradual evolution in the language.

Source: Department of Plant Sciences, Oxford University

Figure 4.1 *Illustration from the* Grete Herbal *of 1526, an era when botany had not acquired a great deal of scientific rigour*

Although the scientific names accepted for particular plants change from time to time, scientific naming involves sudden name creation, deliberately divorced from the gradual evolution of the vernacular, and partly for this reason plant naming makes heavy use of the dead languages of Latin and ancient Greek. It is the job of the taxonomist to create scientific names, to link these to specimens in herbaria and to describe their features in a way that will distinguish them from all plants named previously. The field guide writer has to sort out how to apply these names to plants on a daily basis, out in the field, and how they relate to common names (see Box 4.1).

Scientists strive to give a single name to all different types of plants so that they can be referred to in a standard way. They find common plant names unreliable for general use for various reasons:

- *One name, several species*: a common name may be ambiguous, with the same one used for different plants in different places – such as 'iron-wood' or 'cherry'. Trade names particularly cover products of a range of plant species with similar properties – for example, timber trade names often address timber qualities, not the details of the living tree ('mahogany' applies to several species from around the tropics). The common name 'Madeira' is an extreme example, used now for a limited number of timber trees in parts of the Caribbean, but derived from the Spanish 'madera', or timber in general. Ambiguity also arises where colonists, finding substitutes for familiar plants from their old home, use their old names for the new species. So, we find multiple, unrelated verbenas, cherries, plums and walnuts in Anglophone tropical countries.

BOX 4.1 TYPES OF NON-SCIENTIFIC NAMES

There is wide overlap between the following; but it is useful to be as precise as possible when defining what non-scientific names to include in your field guide. It is a good idea to choose a particular non-italic font for these, to contrast with the italic convention of scientific names:

- *Common name*: any non-scientific, commonly used name, without regard to linguistics and not necessarily 'local' – for example, 'coconut' and 'gum Arabic tree'. All of the following names are types of common names; but it is better to use a more particular term from the list below, if possible.
- *Vernacular name*: name explicitly in a particular (generally non-global) language or dialect, usually with language specified – for example, *Acacia nilotica* = 'ol-erbat' (Masai) or 'chigundigundi' (Digo).
- *Folk name*: like vernacular name, but resonating with 'folklore' – that is, hint of being a name with a long tradition of use, and not necessarily a particular language, for example, *Senecio vulgaris* = 'groundsel' in the UK, from the Anglo-Saxon 'grundswelge' ('swelgan', to swallow; 'grund', ground), because it grows very quickly.
- *Local name*: any of the above, but emphasizing what people in a limited region commonly use.
- *Trade name*: transcultural names used in markets, especially international ones – for example, 'African mahogany', 'kola', 'iroko' and often applying more to a product than the tree, such as the gum of *Acacia nilotica* = gum Arabic.

- *Incompleteness*: it frequently happens that a species is not just merged with others in some generic common name, but is effectively invisible in the local culture, addressed by terms such as 'tree', 'bois-cendre' or local names that translate as 'I don't know'.
- *Many names, one species*: several different names apply to what scientists consider the same type of plant. This is usually the case for widespread species, where there are many vernacular names, and for very useful species, where the different names may strictly apply to a particular aspect of the plant. People migrate and the origin of functional names are forgotten, so even in one village you may well find disagreement on the most correct local name for a plant.
- *Impermanence*: folk names tend to disappear or evolve, often even in a few years, with the culture that invented them. They may also be supplanted wholesale, hence the Victorian move to clean up the common names of British plants, when 'pilewort' and 'pissabed' were replaced with lesser 'celandine' and 'dandelion'. There is no guarantee that a local name will continue to be used for the same plant (see Case studies 4.1 and 4.2).

What is less often emphasized, however, is that scientific names suffer from all of these same types of problem – impermanence, incompleteness, synonymy and inconsistency of application (see Case study 4.3) – albeit usually in a less chronic form. This is in spite of efforts made by scientists to place their names beyond the vagaries of normal language in the ways we summarize next.

CASE STUDY 4.1 SHIFTING LOCAL NAMES FOR THE RATTANS OF LAOS

Each of the local names given in *A Field Guide to the Rattans of Lao PDR* (Evans, 2001) was used by local people for a specimen we collected. Although these names are often used consistently in a particular village, they vary endlessly from village to village. To pick just a few examples, 'wai namleuang' (yellow spine rattan) is used for at least six species, 'wai hangnou' (rat-tail rattan) is used for at least four species and 'wai thoon', a name usually applied to the very distinctive and valuable *Calamus poilanei*, is used for at least two other large but commercially worthless species, *C. flagellum* and *Plectocomia* spp., in areas where *C. poilanei* apparently does not occur. In Vientiane Province in Laos, the name 'wai nyair' is used for both *C. viminalis* and *C. tenuis* by different people; but getting these two mixed up when you start a plantation could be a disaster – one likes dry ground, the other, flooding.

The reason for this confusing situation is simple – local names only need to distinguish the 5 to 15 species that might occur in the limited area used by a few neighbouring villages. It doesn't matter to these users if the same name is used for another species elsewhere. But it does matter to us, working across the whole country. So, be very sceptical with lists of local names, particularly when they have been compiled for a different region or ethnic group.

Source: Evans (2001)

Scientific names

Scientific names reflect the hierarchy in which species are classified (see Box 4.2). This hierarchical arrangement is also a typical, though not universal, feature of common nomenclature: combinations of names to express patterns of affinity or perceived relatedness in plants (tree, palm tree, coconut palm tree, dwarf coconut palm tree), rather like street addresses. Such a hierarchical classification in taxonomy helps the identification process by allowing identifiers to think, perhaps, first of the family, then of the genus, then the species, even if only the latter two ranks are routinely stated. A hierarchical arrangement of plant names or classes ('taxa') also helps scientists to organize their descriptive data. Descriptions of species in a particular book do not have to repeat the general details about its genus or family.

Publication of species names

Although some early botanical literature – notably Linnaeus's *Species Plantarum* (1753) – involved massive syntheses of known and new plant names, or were catalogues of useful plants, nowadays new species names are often published a few at a time in journals, or sometimes in the other types of botanical publications: Scientific plant names have to be published formally, implying copies in publicly available, printed media. Unfortunately, this does not mean that all species descriptions are easily available throughout the world, even in the age of the internet.

The most useful reference for any plant name, though, is an actual specimen of a plant (see Box 4.3). When published, a 'type specimen' is deposited in a herbarium and a short description, in Latin, has to appear in a journal referring to the type specimen and

CASE STUDY 4.2 THE LAW AND SAPOTACEAE NAMES IN GHANA

Tree species in the family Sapotaceae in Ghana are economically important; but there is confusion about their names. Several different species are routinely called akasa, adasema, kumfena and asanfena, although the Forestry Department has tried to standardize the application of these names to *Chrysophyllum abidum*, *C. subnudum*, *C. giganteum* and *Pouteria* spp., respectively. It is a constant challenge to ensure that in tree inventories, these local names are applied consistently (Latin names are too long and complicated to be recorded on inventory field forms). The timber from the trees differs in value and, consequently, royalty rates; timber concessionaires have to pay according to names assigned during stock enumerations before logging.

Some of the confusion arises because people notice no difference between the trees of these various species, with their fibrous, latex-producing bark, and discoloured crowns: this represents a simple mistake, but there is a deeper reason. Akasa is a fruit name applied originally, and in many peoples' minds, to the tasty fruit of *C. albidum*, which is often planted. However, the discoloured foliage and other aspects of the *C. albidum* tree are very similar to those of the *C. giganteum* tree (supposedly kumfena), and there is a strong tendency for people to call the latter akasa, as well, although the edible fruit is a different shape and smaller. Disagreements arise frequently because it is not strictly wrong in the vernacular sense for people to call both species akasa, or one of the species akasa and kumfena on different occasions; it is only wrong in the trade name sense, especially as *C. giganteum* is a timber tree with a higher royalty than *C. albidum*. During recent years, there have been legal proceedings in local forest offices because it appeared, apparently incorrectly, that the local timber company had deliberately misapplied local names to save many thousands of dollars in royalties. To further complicate matters, it was found after closer scrutiny of the *C. giganteum* plants during emergency training sessions that the relevant *C. giganteum* population in one forest was a local variant of the species, with several slight differences from the rest of the species, a fact not reflected in the available literature.

Notice how important the presence of the standard scientific name was to try and establish any order in the above situation. However, during the 1990s a monograph of the Sapotaceae was published that changed overnight the scientific names for African *Aningeria* into the pan-tropical *Pouteria*. At that time, perplexed timber traders were still able to say: 'What is *Pouteria*? Oh, you mean asanfena.' In other words, the local name was more widely understood and less confusing at that time than the scientific name.

So, by all means try helping to standardize local names for use in technical contexts; but expect the tide of common use to run against you. Generally, applied local names and current scientific names are appreciated by different audiences, and can function in a 'belt-and-braces' way to establish plant identity.

giving it the name (see Box 4.4). This and other rules of taxonomy are outlined in the *International Code of Botanical Nomenclature* (International Association for Plant taxonomy, 2000). Winston (1999) provides a friendly synopsis and a useful guide to the whole task of naming a species. Obtaining original descriptions and type specimens are major hurdles and expenses to taxonomy, and will normally involve you or a colleague working in a well-resourced botanic institution.

The only plant, without question, that has a particular name is the individual plant from which the type specimen was clipped. Botanists use these type specimens as reference beacons in the spectrum of plant life. Anything that looks sufficiently similar to the

CASE STUDY 4.3 SCIENTIFIC NAMES IN THE TREE FLORA OF MALAYA

Corner (1988) describes the common experience of shifting sands of taxonomy regarding the updated version of his *Wayside Trees of Malaya*:

> *Botanists have been able to visit and study critical collections in other countries for which, previously, there was neither opportunity nor funds. Not least, perhaps, there have been such improvements in postal services that the old and precious specimens – the type specimens on which names depend – can be borrowed. In tropical Asia there had grown up three traditions: the British was based on collections based in London and Edinburgh; the Dutch on collections at Leiden and Utrecht; and the French on collections in Paris. Many a plant, in consequence, had three names, and more according to the country where it had been studied … using the publications of* Flora Malesiana, *we have had to alter the names of more than 200 species of trees in this revision. Finality is not in sight because several large families await revision, and the concepts of species and genus are still fluid.*

The 200 new species names referred to had arisen for a total of 950 species, almost 20 per cent in about 40 years, or 0.5 per cent a year. None of the local names were changed between the same editions.

Source: Corner (1988)

BOX 4.2 SCIENTIFIC SPECIES, BINOMIALS, INFRA-SPECIFIC NAMES AND AUTHORS

The basic unit of scientific naming is the species – the group of all plants that look more or less the same as each other, apart from variation due to age, gender and environmentally induced differences, and that are capable of interbreeding. We will assume our readers have a basic idea of a species, but see Winston (1999) for further discussion. The scientific name for species, a binomial, always has two parts, comprising the genus, then the 'species epithet', such as *Melia azedarach*, where the species epithet is *azedarach*. In formal publications, the author (the person who formally published the original name, usually abbreviated) is indicated, as well. Usually the genus and species names are italicized, while the author is not – for example, *Melia azedarach* Linnaeus or *Melia azedarach* L. This is the scientific name that Linnaeus invented for the Persian lilac. The author might be mentioned because it has often happened, particularly with scientific names invented a long time ago, that the same name has been used for different plants – for example, the name *Psychotria albicaulis* has been used twice, by two authors (Valeton and Scott-Elliot) for different species. To distinguish these two uses, one is properly *P. albicaulis* Valeton and the other is *P. albicaulis* Scott-Elliot: only one name is allowed to be in use; but the other meaning of the name still has to be referred to by taxonomists. Furthermore, the author name gives some clues about the age and origin of the names.

Some species are subdivided and given extra names to represent local or minor variants; these so-called infra-specific names, including subspecies, varieties or forms, can then be specified after the normal species name – for example, *Antiaris toxicaria* subspp. *toxicaria*, with or without the authors. Unfortunately, many of the tools for looking up species names are incomplete for these infra-specific taxa.

BOX 4.3 THE IMPORTANCE AND METHOD OF COLLECTING HERBARIUM SPECIMENS

We have seen that plant names are originally based on specimens deposited in herbaria. Taxonomic work relies on them absolutely. However, subsequent identification of plants also relies to a great extent on specimens, and do not expect that a field guide will completely remove the need to collect specimens in the tropical rainforest if the names are to be as accurate as possible and scientifically respectable. You certainly should collect specimens as part of the work towards all but the least technical field guide. The well-stored specimen provides a permanent record of a name used – for instance, in a scientific publication or for a published photograph, which can be consulted much later, perhaps when the forest in question has been cleared and names have changed. For more information on specimen collection, visit your local herbarium or see Bridson et al (1995).

---

type specimen is then identified with that name, and, of course, the meaning of 'sufficiently similar' is the basis of much taxonomic debate. It surprises even some regular users of scientific names that they are open to interpretation and, therefore, in practice somewhat subjective. Plants vary over time and space, so their names are not as fundamental as, for example, the names of chemical elements.

Periodically, a plant is found that looks nothing like any existing type specimen, matching none of their published descriptions. A botanist will then invent a new name for this plant and define a new type specimen. Over the last few decades, about 2500 new plant names were invented per year globally (Prance, 2001) – that is, almost one per year for every 100 species that have a scientific name already. Even for the US, north of Mexico, 60 flowering plant species were described every year between 1975 and 1994, a rate that shows no sign of slowing down (Hartman and Nelson, 2003). Tropical vegetation is particularly rich in plants with no name:

- For the place of publication of names of vascular plants, whether synonyms or accepted ones, users can consult Index Kewensis or, on the internet, the International Plant Names Index (www.ipni.org/). These sources exclude infra-specific taxa and (Index Kewensis) ferns and their allies, and most frustratingly do not mention synonymy.
- Type specimens are often not very accessible; but there is an increasing number of 'virtual herbaria' with detailed images of type specimens on the internet. Search for 'type, specimens, virtual, herbarium' on the internet to find the ones relevant to you.

New species have to be named in a way that distinguishes them reliably from all other plants in the world, and for this reason taxonomists tend to focus most strongly on fertile characters (see Box 4.4). The fact that fertile characters are not always available in plants met in the field contributes to a continuing demand for field guides:

- As your field guide will probably cover a limited area, you do not need to distinguish your species from all its close relatives in the rest of the world, so small fertile characters are usually not as important as they are in a monograph or Flora. Species

---

BOX 4.4 VEGETATIVE AND FERTILE CHARACTERS, AND STERILE SPECIMENS

Flower- and fruit-related details are sometimes called fertile characters, in contrast to vegetative characters of leaf, stems, roots and general plant form. A specimen with only vegetative features is a sterile specimen. Vegetative characters usually vary more with climate and geography than fertile characters. For instance, a single species may have small leathery leaves when growing on mountain tops and larger, papery leaves when in the lowlands: fertile characters, like the hairs on stamens or petal length, usually vary less. Therefore, although some species are formally distinguished by vegetative features alone, taxonomists tend to emphasize fertile characters when species are first described. However, vegetative characteristics, such as leaf size, may be more obvious and useful differences between two species, and can be just as reliable if a field guide is very localized – for example, for one forest. The bias towards fertile details in new species descriptions tends to be carried through into the keys and descriptions of Floras and monographs, in general; but this is a bias that a field guide writer should not follow uncritically.

---

rediscovered in the field often have surprisingly distinctive, but unrecorded, features – such as long plank buttresses or a strong smell – which the author of the name was unaware of in the herbarium.

Common, scientific or both names in your field guide?

Common names have many obvious advantages over scientific names: they are mostly memorable, often short and in tune with local patterns of speech and cultural association, hence local user friendly. They frequently out-survive the appropriate scientific names, which as we have seen can change overnight. So why should we not have a strong bias towards preferring such common names in field guides? Apart from the usual problems of names cited above, which are more serious than for the scientific equivalents, there are at least three over-riding reasons for using scientific names in addition to the common ones:

- Science is global, and its nomenclature strives to be globally applicable, so its names are the keys to information available globally about the plants.
- There is a continuous coordinated effort to improve and standardize scientific nomenclature; so any ambiguity is generally very limited compared to local names.
- Scientific names do go out of use; but the old and alternative Latin names are documented rigorously, so it should be possible to translate any unused Latin name to the one (at worst, a few) name that is valid today.

Field guides should therefore include at least a cross-reference to the plants' scientific names, even if the aim of the guide is to show the plants in the context of a local community. This is for the same reason that books in libraries should have a global standard ISBN code number, as well as their title – these are universal, standard codes that allow published books to be catalogued and looked up regardless of the language.

Your guide will be of more interest and use to people from various cultures if you mention the scientific names, as well as the most appropriate common names. However, if it is to be used in a limited area it will obviously mean more to users, and will certainly be more culturally sensitive, if local names are there as well, even if they are ambiguous. If your guide in any way promotes local conservation or ethnobotanical interests, then you should mention both common and scientific names:

- As a rule of thumb, include both scientific and common names, but consult with users and other key informants as explained in Chapter 3 to define which common names to use, and which to emphasize on the page.
- Encourage your users to invent a plausible common name for species that have not been previously recognized (say where you have done so, to keep linguists happy), as the production of a field guide provides a rare chance to fix or standardize such names in the vernacular. Where one name covers several species, consider inventing qualifiers in the language of the existing common name to specify them – for example, like small asanfena and black mahogany.

Referring to scientific names in field guides

Although the Latin binomial is essential if you are referring to species names, there are some optional extras to the name.

Authors

Names in Floras and monographs always include the authors (see Box 4.2): should you include authors in your field guide? Although the cautious answer is yes, there are circumstances where they may be excluded without a problem, so explain their role to your users and see what they want. If the names can all be found in a Flora, it might make sense to save space by excluding them (as in field guides by Corner, 1988; Hawthorne, 1990; Ashton et al, 1997). On the other hand, it is a useful service to your readers to mention authors in the species index at the end of a book.

Based on feedback from a few annoyed users of an earlier field guide (Hawthorne, 1990), where author names had been excluded for simplicity, author names have been included in a more comprehensive guide book (Hawthorne and Jongkind, 2006), particularly as the number of names altered since the *Flora of West Tropical Africa* (Hepper and Keay, 1954–1972) meant that the newer book will also function as a name reference list. Although directly useful in a small minority of cases, many users demand author names from field guides only because of a convention whereby journals demand these author names whenever a species is mentioned:

- If in doubt, in a tourist guide where the names all refer to those in a standard Flora, a binomial is adequate. However, for all technical guides, include authors unless you can refer to a complete list of names in a previously published checklist or Flora.
- You should not need to list authors more than once for a species: since they make the Latin names even more daunting to non-botanists, it is best to hide them in the species index, even using a smaller font.

Infra-specific names?

Infra-specific names are cumbersome, often representing only minor variants of plants, and very commonly for field guides only one such variant will occur in the region anyway, so the infra-specific names add little information to your guide and will clutter up your pages. Infra-specific taxa are applied more inconsistently than species names, and some taxonomists ignore them altogether:

*   For simpler field guides, you may choose to ignore these names and you will still be scientifically correct.
*   On the other hand, even for simple guides you may find that there are endemic infra-specific taxa, found only in your area: this is the sort of attribute that many users find interesting and conservationists demand. If you have such cases, include the names and all other infra-specific names as well to be consistent. Ask your users whether they think the names are useful; but where there is uncertainty, include infra-specific taxa in more technical guides.
*   If including infra-specific names, where only one infra-specific taxon occurs in your area, it is helpful to put the infra-specific part in brackets – for example, *Antiaris toxicaria* (subsp. *toxicaria*), to show that for your area all infra-specific taxa belong to this subspecies. When there are two or more infra-specific names for one species in your area, leave the brackets out to emphasize that there is more than one valid option.

Be critical if you know your plants well and if the names available for the plants that you have to deal with in your guide do not do the variation justice. Scientific nomenclature is a work in progress, not engraved permanently in tablets of stone. You might even be driven to do the necessary weeks or months of work required to describe a new variety or species yourself (Winston, 1999). However, if you are not experienced, find a friendly taxonomist to help you. You will need to become familiar with the contents of a large national or regional herbarium:

*   Accept that the same name may well be applied to a plant 2000 miles away that does not look like yours, and perhaps mention this trend in your descriptive text; you do not always need names to describe variation.

Synonyms and why you need to know about them

It often becomes apparent, maybe during the preparation of your field guide, that two published names represent only one species. The newer name should then be discarded: it becomes a 'synonym' of the older (see Box 4.5).

There is a simple format for publishing a synonym, basically stating that name B is a synonym of name A, with few other details required. Many authors give little or no justification when publishing a synonym; but it is always helpful to explain nonetheless. You can publish a synonym validly in your field guide; but you should then summarize all proposed changes in one place in the introduction or index. If your guide will not be widely dispersed, it is far better to publish your synonyms before the guide is published (along with any new species) in a peer-reviewed journal. Other botanists are more likely to follow your decision on synonymy if you do so.

Experts of local flora often feel robbed when monographers dismissively sweep their local endemic plant away as a synonym, when it is said to be 'insignificantly' different from its relatives. If you feel strongly that such a mistake has been made, and you have done the required research to support your notion, you could:

BOX 4.5 SYNONYMS AND WHY SCIENTIFIC NAMES KEEP CHANGING

Independent taxonomists in different countries may be unaware of each other's publications and give different names to obviously identical plants (see Case study 4.3). Another reason for synonymy applies when, as time goes by and new names are invented for all variants of a range of plants, it becomes harder to work out to which of these species a new specimen belongs. Perhaps it has the fruit shape of species X and the petal shape of species Y. It may become increasingly obvious that all combinations of fruit and petal shape occur, like height and ear length in dogs. Maybe the flower size, so different in two type specimens, is eventually seen to increase gradually across the continent, with no single obvious place to divide the spectrum. One species name should now be used for all such plants, and the oldest name is then employed for all. All of the other names become redundant synonyms. In these cases, the species epithet will normally change; the genus part stays the same. For instance, *Napoleonaea leonensis* became a synonym of *Napoleonaea vogelii* when it was realized that intermediates existed. The placing of a name in synonymy represents a matter of opinion, and you are not obliged to stop using names once they have been published as synonyms if you are well informed and do not agree.

In other cases, two genera may be merged, or a genus may be split into parts, usually because a taxonomist has revised all of the species and decided that this describes the variation pattern most realistically. In these cases, the old genus name is retained for some species, and new ones are brought into use for the others. When a name changes in these circumstances, the genus part will differ between synonyms; yet the species part usually stays the same (maybe with slight changes to the ending to match the gender of the genus name). For instance, *Aningeria altissima* becomes a synonym of *Pouteria altissima* (see Case study 4.2) when it was decided that African Aningeria species fell within the range of variation of American *Pouteria* species.

- ignore the changes and keep using the synonym; but show that you are aware of the proposed name change and give good reasons for ignoring it, otherwise your readers may simply think you have overlooked the publication;
- formally publish the synonym name as a subspecies, variety or forma (a less divergent form than a variety or subspecies) in the new species.

However, the easiest solution might be to:

- identify your 'lost' plant with an informal or vernacular name in inverted commas in your field guide, alongside the proper species name, with a footnote explaining your reasons.

In this case, explain that taxonomists are to ignore these informal names. This will let users know both the globally accepted name and that you are referring to some minor local variant of it.

You should not, however, ignore new names just because they are unfamiliar or because your users prefer the old name. Taxonomists will usually have a better picture of the global variation pattern of the species than field guide writers, and you will not be doing your readers any favours by supplying them with names that the rest of the world will soon no longer recognize:

- On the minority of occasions when a taxonomist fortunately happens to have revised the names of one of your groups of plants, it would be churlish of you not to follow to the letter their generally careful and well-researched changes. Unless you have a very strong reason, you should follow the global expert's opinion, not your own local perception. However, if the local Flora is quite recently published, so there are only a few minor changes to its names, and you want to keep the taxonomic content of your guide simple, then it is reasonable in a technically modest field guide to follow the Flora's names for all species and to state that this is your sole source, in effect ignoring any subsequent taxonomic changes.
- Decide whether you want your field guide just to provide 'field support' to any local Flora, or if you rather want it to provide added value by bringing the taxonomy up to date. If the Flora is old (say, more than 20 years since publication), then be prepared to follow the latter route or your guide will look sadly dated from the moment it is published.
- If you have chosen to update a Flora (or checklist), include synonyms defined since its publication. Include also any other names recorded erroneously in your area in the Flora, based on specimens now allocated a different name, with a brief note to indicate the error. In addition, list in your index the synonyms that are widely used in (pre-Flora) textbooks, even if the Flora already has listed them as redundant. In all of these cases, the redundant index entry should cross-reference to the correct name. Any justification should then be included, maybe as a short footnote or endnote – for example, entries for redundant names in the index:
  - *Morus newsp* L., p20
  - *Morus oldsp* Jacq, see *Morus newsp*
- Then, a footnote entry on page 20:
  - *Morus oldsp* was recorded in our area in the Flora; but this was based on specimen Fred 23, which is, in fact, *Morus newsp* L. (see Bloggs et al, 2003).
- It is worth looking up original descriptions of disused and long-forgotten synonyms, particularly if the type specimen of that synonym was from your area. Older species names, which are the ones most likely to be in use, generally have less descriptive text and illustrations than more recently published synonyms, and there might be information in the synonym's publication that is more pertinent to your specific area than the more general description in any Flora or monograph allows.

THE SPECTRUM OF BOTANICAL LITERATURE

Taxonomic monographs and revisions: 'Spring-cleaning' in taxonomy

Periodically, taxonomists review all of the species that have been created in a genus or other group of related species, together with the new specimens collected since publication, and publish a synoptic paper. At its simplest, this is a 'revision' that may appear in botanical journals: revisions themselves often include new species names as a sort of conclusion of the work. With a larger amount of study and background information, a complete book about a particular group may be published, which is then normally referred to as a monograph.

The checklist–Flora–field guide spectrum

Botanists identifying new specimens in herbaria often follow opinions of earlier experts recorded on the original specimen label or preferably on the most recent determination slip (a 'det. slip' is a small label on which a specialist simply records their identification of a specimen), rather than relying on original descriptions; but when new species are recorded in an area, botanists must rely on the literature. Various types of publication exist to help a region develop a more consistent application of scientific names than is possible with many people independently working with type specimens and original descriptions, or copying earlier determinations for similar specimens in herbaria. Revisions and monographs summarize all plants described of a particular genus, family or other plant group. For more practical use in a particular region, synopses are made of all the available monographs and other publications for all families of plants (usually restricted to a very broad set of plant families such as 'trees', 'flowering plants' or 'mosses'). These regional syntheses include checklists, Floras and, of course, field guides:

- Frodin (2001) has summarized the content of many of these types of publication, particularly Floras.
- Checklists are, at their simplest, lists of plants in a particular region and usually the first step in producing other regional synopses (see Box 4.6). Checklists become more like Floras as more and more diagnostic information is added; but usually a checklist writer will avoid the task of identification altogether. A checklist is usually an early step towards the Flora or field guide.
- Floras are detailed descriptions of all (usually higher) plants in a region, taking care to summarize all necessary taxonomic details, and in theory allow precise identifications of plants if you have in your plant specimen(s) all the required details. They are primarily intended for use by other botanists in the herbarium, although they are often used in other situations. The Floras of the world are reviewed by Frodin (2001).

Floras tend to be the field guide writer's most useful reference books; if none is available for your area, there may be one for a nearby country that is better than nothing:

- Field guides are also primarily to help plant identification, but are designed for field use, so are generally portable and are also often designed for use by non-botanists. They have less taxonomic detail than Floras and more field-related information (see Chapter 6). It is not uncommon for a field guide to exclude some of the species from the target group, whereas this would run against the spirit of a checklist or Flora.
- Electronic identification tools represent a dramatic change of style for botanical literature, potentially confusing the boundaries, and as this change is most relevant to access methods, we defer discussion until Chapter 5.

Even a basic list of plants compiled at the start of a field guide project is a checklist. For scientifically accurate field guides, aim to make this initial checklist as taxonomically rigorous as possible, referencing literature where names were published and listing specimen numbers for your area, if you are not following a Flora with this information included already. You may be in a position to publish the checklist and then leave some

---

BOX 4.6 CHECKLISTS

Checklists are lists of plants, often from diverse families, found in a given area, often a national park or part of a country. They may be annotated, with extra information; but the most basic are composed simply of plant names. The sorts of additional information that are commonly included in annotated checklists, and highly recommended, are taxonomic details and references – for example, place of publication; specimen numbers examined; ecological and geographical range; and basic features of the plant (for instance, '5m tree'). If the list includes many descriptive details of the morphology of the plant, and especially if there are keys to help identify the species, then we have a Flora (the term 'Florula' is sometimes used for publications with Flora-like detail, but covering a small part of one country).

Many checklists were produced over the last century (for example, Hora and Greenway, 1940), which supported the subsequent development of regional Floras and field guides. Recent global or continental checklists are still extremely useful for creators of field guides – for instance, *Legumes of Africa* (Lock, 1989); *World Checklist and Bibliography of Euphorbiaceae* (Govaerts et al, 2000). The preparation of the *The Woody Plants of Western African Forests* (Hawthorne and Jongkind, 2006) was greatly facilitated by the recent completion of Lebrun and Stork's (1991–1997) checklists of African plants: even without distribution details, the literature references alone, especially for synonyms that are not otherwise available in any database, saved many months of work.

---

taxonomic 'baggage' out of your final field guide. This will help to draw constructive criticism about nomenclature from other botanists before the later stages of guide production:

- Why not aim to produce a complete checklist as an early publishable landmark of your field guide project?
- Agencies seeking to promote field guides should not shy away from subsidizing annotated checklists for large areas if such a list is not available already, however non-user friendly or non-poverty-alleviating they might appear on their own. They will have the long-term effect of facilitating field guide production.

Simple Floras, sophisticated field guides

We made a first attempt at a working definition of a field guide in Chapter 1; but there is really no clear boundary between a simpler, user-friendly Flora and a complex field guide, as Table 4.1 depicts.

On the borderline between field guides and Floras are series such as the *Tree Flora of Sabah and Sarawak* (Soepadmo and Wong, 1995–ongoing) – either a specialist Flora because it is in several volumes (unlike any self-respecting true field guide); has 'Flora' in the title; has detailed morphological descriptions of flowers; and takes many years to write. However, since it deals with only trees (and not all other members of the families); there is a separate Flora (*Malesiana*) for the area, which mentions field characteristics. This 'tree Flora' has many of the features of a field guide. Its Flora credentials outweigh its field guide ones, especially its weight and volume, averaging 150 pages per family; but we include it for the sake of discussion in 'The "pragmatic Flora" and other technical field guides' section below.

Table 4.1 *Floras and field guides: A comparison*

Floras	Field guides
Designed to be used primarily in herbaria (but also useful on field trips, though not usually in front of the living plant).	Designed to be used primarily in the field (also in herbaria and not necessarily always in front of the plant in nature).
Rarely planned with an eye on marketing strategy; usually subsidized for long-term development of national or regional natural resources (in developed countries Floras are more commercial).	Sometimes directly commercial propositions; but more technical types usually require some subsidy, as the economic value is not expected to be seen through direct book sales (except in developed countries).
Heavy and expensive, occupying much shelf space. Rarely found in non-botanist's homes.	Ideally in one portable volume. Non-botanists more often have one on their shelves at home.
Emphasize formal taxonomy, like legal documents, with lists of synonyms and often specimens of each species. Frequently with full descriptions; but some only have detailed keys.	Ideally emphasize the minimum amount of information required to identify the plant where it grows. Rely on other work (usually a Flora) to define the origin and legitimacy of the plant names.
Generally include a broad range of plants – for example, all vascular plants.	Typically restricted to a narrower subset of all species than a Flora – for example, trees.
Supposedly complete for the groups included.	May sometimes be incomplete for the botanical groups included (for example, timber trees).
Often cover complete biogeographic regions (Neotropics, the Lesser Antilles); but (colonial) politics often confuse this.	More often are aimed at one country or region within it, where the collation of field characters and local names is more manageable.
Focus on fertile characters, so are often more precise for herbarium specimens with these characters.	Focus on field characters, so are usually the only way to name plants where they are met in the field, or sterile specimens. Hence, often less precise than Floras.
Often take decades to write.	Usually take one to five years to write, sometimes even months.
Usually lack practical information on cultivation or usage.	Often include information about how to cultivate or use species.
Tend to have few (< 50 per cent) pictures, although there is a special type of illustrated Flora, intermediate in this sense to field guides.	Typically have most of the species illustrated.

Types of field guides: The spectrum continues

The spectrum from Flora to field guide continues into a rainbow of types of field guides – from intense, heavy and technical, to light, pretty and information poor; from encyclopaedias of regional field identification to tourist brochures for single parks (see Box 4.7).

BOX 4.7 HERBALS AND THE EVOLUTION OF PLANT FIELD GUIDES

Field guides and other botanical works trace their common ancestry to some of the earliest publications of any sort via medieval herbals. Herbals are practical guide books containing the names and descriptions of plants, with their properties and virtues; typically medicines. They represent the earliest field guides of Western Europe and illustrations were an important feature. The early printed herbals took advantage of earlier manuscripts, notably Dioscorides's (40–90 AD) *De Materia Medica*, the ultimate authority for over 1500 years. Similar manuscripts were also produced in China: the *Pên-ts'ao Chin*, compiled between 1 AD and 200 AD, had notes on uses, ecology ('Cannabis grows along rivers and valleys at T'ausha') and morphology, with fairly realistic pictures of the plants (Hui-hin Li, 1974).

The introduction of movable type to Europe had a dramatic impact on the availability of information about plants, albeit still to an élite defined by money or education. Its arrival saw three of the most important early herbals published in Germany: the Latin *Herbarius* (1484) (with descriptions and unrealistic woodcuts), the German *Herbarius* (1485) and the *Ortus Sanitatis* (1491). In 1530, the herbal was transformed by the publication of Hans Weiditz's naturalistic illustrations in Brunfel's *Herbarum Vivae Eicones*; but the text is of limited use. However, in Bock's *Neu Kreütter Bûch* (1539) more accurate observations were made, and in Fuch's (1501–1566) *De Historia Stirpium* (1542), the advantages of Brunfel's and Bock's works were fused into a masterpiece about 500 plants of Germany. Authors as diverse as Dodoens (*Crûÿdeboeck*, 1554), Turner (*New Herball*, 1551–1568), Lyte (*Nievve Herball*, 1578), Bauhin (*Historia Plantarum Universalis*, 1650–1651) and Schinz (*Anleitung*, 1774) made use of Fuch's woodcuts (often the actual blocks used in *De Historia Stirpium*). The 1583 *De Plantis Libri* by Andrea Cesalpino was the greatest botanical book of the 16th century and, in the opinion of some, the first general text to supersede ancient botanical writings. Many of these reference works are hardly field guides – for example, Besler's elephantine *Hortus Eystettensis* (1613) required a wheelbarrow for its transportation.

Another important technological leap was the development, during the late 1500s by Luca Ghini, of the technique of drying plants under pressure and the development of herbaria. The earliest herbaria were like herbals, bound as books and mostly used for identification of medicinal plants. Another landmark, Sloane's trip to the Caribbean, resulted in an early tropical field guide, just before the advent of modern scientific nomenclature, and linked to specimens. This 1688 guide to West Indian plants and animals – 'a voyage to the islands' – has copious, detailed (life-size) illustration; but portability was as low a priority as shortness of title (see Plate 1, centre pages). Yet the massive two volumes no doubt found a place in many naturalists' cabins on early field trips to the Caribbean.

Improvements in printing and the developments of metal engraving and lithography, for the production of illustrations, gradually reduced the price. By the late 1800s, it was fashionable for ladies to 'paint one's Bentham', a volume of illustrations to accompany Bentham's *Handbook of the British Flora*. In England, with increasing education and leisure time and ever-cheaper printing, the pre-electronic field guide was reaching maturity. For more information see Hort (1916), Thomas (1983), Allen (1984), Arber (1986), Blunt and Stearn (1994), and Lack (2001).

LANDMARKS IN THE SPECTRUM OF FIELD GUIDES TODAY

The more technical and detailed field guides tend to be more accurate than the less technical when used correctly. However, less technical guides are often usable by a wider range of people, and usually have a primary purpose other than accuracy – perhaps earning money from sales or stimulation of interest. Many of the issues in this and the next two chapters concern guides where identification needs to be accurate and are barely relevant to the other end of the field guide spectrum, where a book sometimes only needs to be pretty and marketable to achieve its goals (see the gallery of field guide types in Table 4.3).

There have been a few published reviews of field guides from various perspectives. Frodin (2001) includes some major checklists and field guides. Guides to woody plants in the tropics, including field guides, monographs, revisions and ecological papers, are reviewed by Rejmánek and Brewer (2001). Schmidt (1999) also provides literature references to some of the better-known tropical field guides, biased towards North America and including animal and mineral guides. We have compiled a bibliographic database of

---

BOX 4.8 GEOGRAPHICAL COVERAGE OF FIELD GUIDES

It is impractical to estimate the proportion of the tropical flora covered by field guides as the species overlap between guides cannot be calculated easily. However, the ratio of estimated species number to number of field guides in different regions gives some indication of the areas that are most sparsely covered. There are three regions of high biodiversity, Colombia–Brazil, Central Africa and Indonesia, which also correspond to the main areas identified by Frodin (2001) as priorities needing floristic work. They all have either no Floras or very incomplete Floras that have virtually stopped production.

Table 4.2 *Regions or countries of high biodiversity and the number of Floras for these areas*

Region/country	Number of species	Number of field guides	Ratio of species to guides
South America	98,800	122	800:1
Colombia–Brazil	70,000	44	1590:1
Central America	7380	67	110:1
Southern Africa	23,000	72	320:1
West Africa	10,340	46	225:1
Central Africa	16,320	28	580:1
Cameroon	8000	4	2000:1
D.R. Congo	11,000	7	1570:1
East Africa	7850	39	200:1
Madagascar	12,000	6	2000:1
Tropical Asia	79,500	138	580:1
Indonesia	20,000	8	2500:1
Australia	25,000	50	500:1

Source: species totals are taken from Bramwell (2002)

Table 4.3 *The spectrum of field guides*

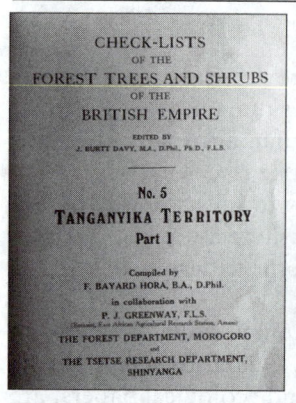 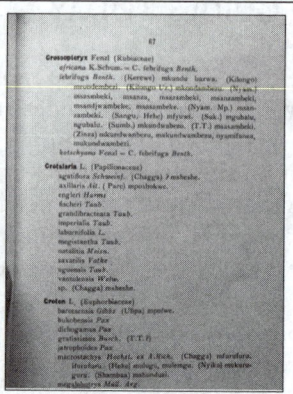

Checklist
Checklists of the Forest Trees and Shrubs of the British Empire–Tanganyika Territory (Hora and Greenway, 1940)
A starting point for subsequent field guides and Floras.

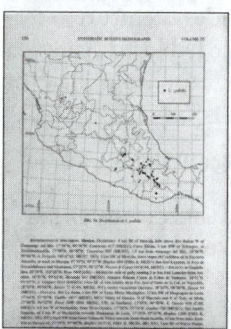 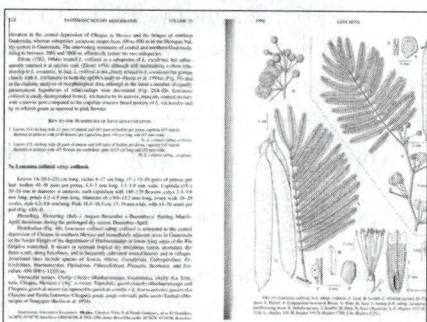

Monograph
Monograph of Leucaena (Leguminosae-Mimosoideae) (Hughes, 1998a)
Essential reference books for field guide writers; may include field guide-like sections or 'field monograph' offshoots with same data.

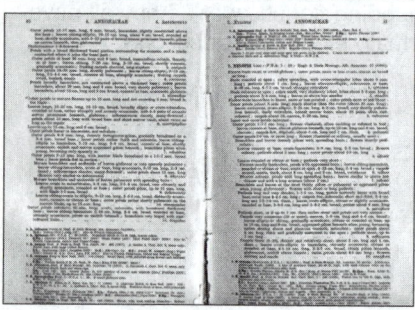

Flora
Flora of West Tropical Africa (Hepper and Keay, 1954–1972)
Totally indispensable reference for plants in a region, but rarely very user friendly, field usable or useful for sterile specimens.

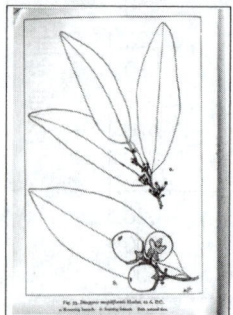 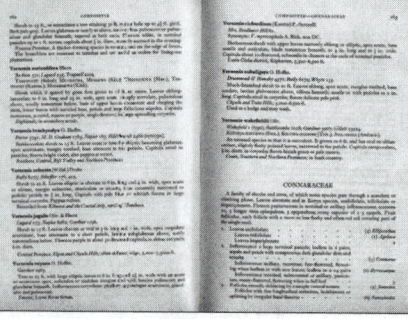

Pragmatic Flora
(technical, broad-scope, complete and not very portable field guide to trees of one country)
Kenya Trees and Shrubs (Dale and Greenway, 1961)
Bridging the gap between Floras and smaller and less technical field guides.

Pragmatic Flora (slightly technical, broad-scope, complete and not very portable field guide to all woody plants of a region. *The Woody Plants of Western African Forests* (Hawthorne and Jongkind, 2006) Very heavily illustrated, with minimal words to describe essential details of habit, morphology, ecology and geography. Designed for combination of picture browsing and analytical text. Funded by the EU to support regional development and sustainable use of natural resources. Will hopefully stimulate production of more local field guides.

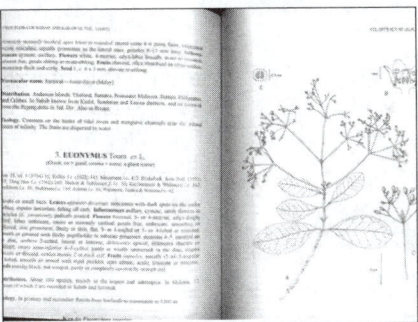

Flora/field guide borderline (Pragmatic Flora) *Tree Flora of Sabah and Sarawak* (Soepadmo and Wong, 1995–ongoing) Essentially a Flora, but could function as a field guide if necessary.

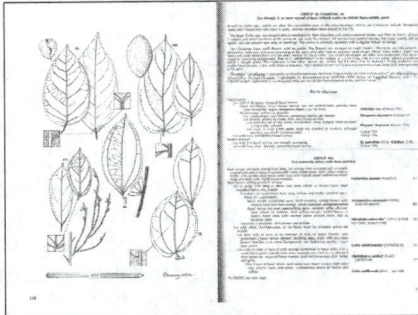

Field guide (slimmer, technical) *Field Guide to the Forest Trees of Ghana* (Hawthorne, 1990) Designed originally for technical officers in the Forestry Department for forest inventories. Concentrates on vegetative features.

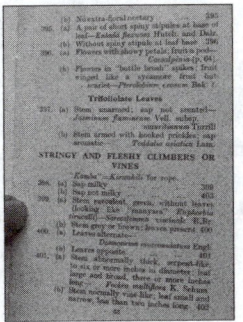

Field guide (technical, slim, not illustrated) *A Field Key to the Savanna Genera and Species of Trees, Shrubs and Climbing Plants of Tanganyika* (Burtt, 1953) A few pictures would have gone a long way to make this more user friendly, but it is admirable for its 'pocketability'

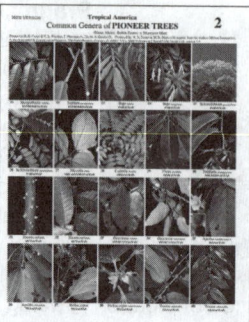

Field guide (laminated cards)
Rapid Colour Guides (Chicago Field Museum) (see Case study 4.4)
Examples here are neotropical pioneers, around letter size and laminated.
Easy to make, and can be improved or tailored with time.
Source: R. Foster, Chicago Field Museum

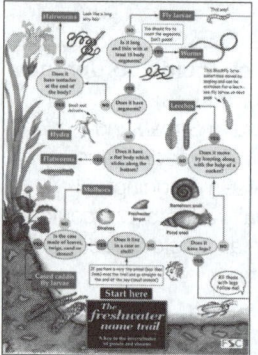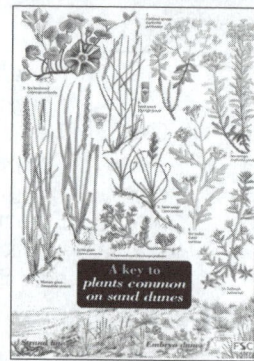

Laminated (fold-out) cards from Field Studies Council (www.field-studies-council.org/about/index.aspx)
These are ideal for school use as an easy introduction to species in a particular study area, and also make good models for guides that might be sold to eco-tourists, particularly if they double as postcards or for souvenirs/pictures on a wall.

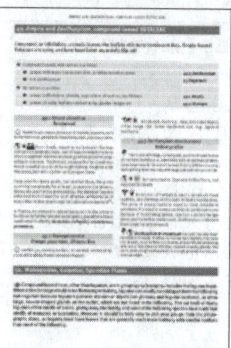

Field guide (semi-technical, heavily illustrated)
Caribbean Spice Island Plants (Hawthorne et al, 2005)
Most of the higher plants of Grenada and all the most important ones. Aimed at satisfying tourists, students, foresters and interested local naturalists, with a limited budget for production and layout. Subsidized by the UK Department for International Development (DFID) to link biodiversity benefit with poverty alleviation.

Field guide (non technical/shallow)
Trees of the Caribbean (Seddon and Lennox, 1980)
Something of interest for a casual reader or tourist, but not intended as a complete guide to trees. A larger area, but much narrower scope than *Caribbean Spice Island Plants* and therefore probably more relaxing to browse – though less likely to benefit biodiversity.

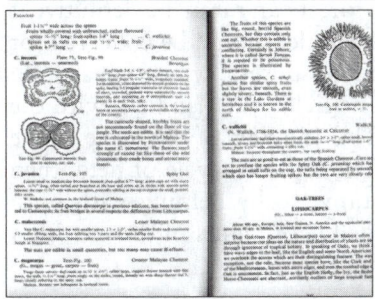

Field guide (technical, bordering on generic guide/student text)
Wayside Trees of Malaya (Corner, 1988)
An excellent and portable introductory text likely to encourage a deep interest in field botany in novices.

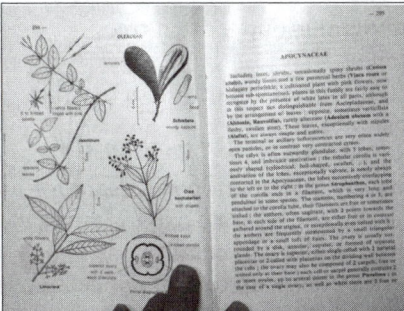

Generic guide/student text
Manual of Forest Botany
(Letouzey, 1986)
An ideal advanced student text for Africa, but not intended for species identification. Gentry (1993) has an equally admirable but different approach to the same niche in the neotropics.

tropical plant field guides with about 800 literature references, summarizing geographical and species coverage (see Box 4.8). A short summary of trends follows.

Although early field guides were biased towards medicinal plants, over the last century tropical guide development has been driven more by a need for accurate tree identification for commercial forestry, and more recently for biodiversity inventories, environmental impact assessments, long-term ecological studies and eco-tourists. The demand for comprehensive tropical field guides is stronger than ever and the proliferation of popular field guides in Europe and America has shown tropical botanists what is possible, even if publishers are not overexcited by the market for such guide books in the tropics.

The 'pragmatic Flora' and other technical field guides

More field usable than true Floras, pragmatic Floras are identification guides for use in both the field and herbarium, with emphasis on accurate identification over portability when compared with other field guides. Some will help users identify without flowers and fruits, bridging Flora-level treatments and simpler field guides if a Flora exists at all for the region, otherwise they substitute for them. The target users are often botanists or other scientists, professional or amateur, and others working in forestry, conservation and related spheres with a serious interest in plant identification. They support inventories and technical fieldwork, are useful in both national herbaria and state agricultural or forestry offices, and act as key references for resource-related non-governmental organizations (NGOs). An eco-tourist would have to be unusually enthusiastic to consider buying one.

In most of the world's biodiverse regions, one cannot expect all unknown plants to be identified immediately in the field, even with the best field guide or Flora, if the names are to be accurate. Identification of difficult plants in the forest can rarely be definitive if it is to be quick and hurried. Specimens, inevitably often sterile, should be collected for the difficult plants. In these circumstances, field guides are most useful when they help to identify individual plants as and when they are met in the field, but also help with the identity of sterile specimens in the herbarium or camp. This is a part of the niche of the extreme type of field guide we call a 'pragmatic Flora'. The repeated cycle of field, then herbarium, work is the best way to learn tropical botany; so by helping with both aspects of the work, these guides foster a deeper knowledge of plants in those with a serious interest.

Pragmatic Floras have the following features:

- complete coverage of a broad plant group – often trees
  (in 'tree Floras') or higher plants;
- coverage is often for a region of several countries, or at least
  a whole country or large subregion;
- typically include 500 to 3000 species;
- taxonomically correct, but mainly information necessary for identification;
- characters described are generally consistent across species, and fairly
  comprehensive for all basic morphological details;
- modern versions are well illustrated for up to 100 per cent of species;
- useful, like a Flora, as a general plant name dictionary;
- help production of simpler field guides by botanists or others
  (a source book of field characters for such projects);
- some botanical competence is assumed of the user – but they form an excellent
  foundation for an individual's long-term botanical education;
- take between two and ten years to produce for one or more people (albeit typically
  while doing other work); some take even longer. They are mostly made by experienced botanists with access to herbarium collections and taxonomic literature; but their production requires considerable fieldwork (see Box 4.9).

Slimmer technical field guides

Over the last 50 years, a vague trend can be seen from text-rich, less illustrated (Burtt, 1953, an unillustrated key for field use) or heavy 'tree Floras' to slimmer or friendlier guides, often with a greater range of plants and greater use of illustration. With the facility of adding colour photographs (see Chapter 8), a new wave is breaking where illustrations dominate, but where efforts have to be made to keep the book portable. The larger pragmatic Floras are inconvenient for field use, even if the library allows them out. In order to reduce the weight and the amount of work required to make technical guides, but to maintain the accuracy for those taxa that are covered, there are five main options:

1 Only deal with species of a particular (presumably problematic and important) group – the field monograph (see Box 4.10).
2 Reduce the information per species – slimmer, but all-species guides for many families (this and the next variety are summarized in Box 4.11).
3 Limit the geographic area of interest (see Box 4.11).

Box 4.9 'Pragmatic Flora' and other technical field guides

Tree (and shrub) Floras, covering countries or regions, represent a sub-type common in the tropics, including:

- *Tree Flora of Sabah and Sarawak* (Soepadmo and Wong, 1995–ongoing): far too heavy for most field trips, but otherwise field friendly compared with most Floras and useful for specimens in the herbarium or field camp. Probably cannot usefully be called a type of field guide though.
- *La Flore Forestière de la Côte d'Ivoire* (Aubréville, 1959): excellent illustrations, with fieldworker-friendly details, but not optimized for fieldwork, with large format, several volumes and a large font.
- *Nigerian Trees* (Keay, Onochie and Stanfield, 1960, 1964): fewer illustrations than previous, unusual for the time, with a multi-access key at the back supporting vegetative characters. Well used and liked by botanists in West Africa. Revised as Keay (1989); but revision sadly lost some of the unique features and rarer species.
- *Kenya Trees and Shrubs* (Dale and Greenway, 1961): unfriendly, but at one stage indispensable for fieldwork, with too few pictures and vegetative notes, though some local names to help. Identification of sterile trees in the field, even very distinctive ones, involved long hours browsing through many pages of text. Now replaced by the far more accessible field guide by Beentje (1994).

Pragmatic Floras to more than trees

- *Kenya Trees, Shrubs and Lianes* (Beentje, 1994): more compact than Dale and Greenway's (1961) guide, but easier to use, with useful distribution maps for all species and drawings for genera.
- There are many examples of pragmatic Floras for developed countries – one of our favourites being Blamey and Grey-Wilson's (1989) *The Illustrated Flora of Britain and Northern Europe*, based on paintings and text of British plants; but there are many other excellent examples, even for the UK.
- *The Woody Plants of Western African Forests* (Hawthorne and Jongkind, 2006): packed with field-appropriate photos, drawings and text, and species details are limited to the essentials (evolved from Hawthorne, 1990).

---

4 Reduce the taxonomic resolution – generic guides (for example, genus level with short notes on some species) (see Box 4.12).
5 Deal only with a subset of the species from many families – incomplete sets (see Box 4.13).

By reducing the burden of information in all of these ways at once, it is possible to make a very light field guide! These are then so lacking in information that they will rarely be accurate, and with limited coverage such guides rarely aspire to high technical standards. On the other hand, they may serve other functions, as the following examples show.

BOX 4.10 'FIELD MONOGRAPHS': DETAILED FIELD GUIDES FOR SMALL GROUPS OF PLANTS

Field monographs are field guides for single families, genera or similar groups of plants, such as rattans, and concentrate on providing the same detail as pragmatic Floras, but for a limited range of species, usually the most important and difficult to identify. To work, they should be based on a group that, as a whole, is distinctive. They could reasonably allow more information per species and still be pocketable. As the variety of plant form is likely to be limited, in most cases it is sensible for such guides to illustrate plants in a standardized format to facilitate comparison, such as Evans et al (*A Field Guide to the Rattans of Lao PDR*, 2001), Farjon et al (*A Field Guide to the Pines of Mexico and Central America*, 1997) and Timberlake et al (*Field Guide to the Acacias of Zimbabwe*, 1999). In some cases, taxonomists are producing field guides as a secondary product of monographic work (see Box 4.14). In this way a field guide can be truly portable, except that to include all species in this format would bring us back to the pragmatic Flora size:

*   It is very important that field monographs refer to similar species in groups excluded from the book wherever the subject is not in itself clearly recognizable.

Shallower guides: Non-technical, often glossy or superficial

There are many guides of this type, mostly with limited distribution. They are relatively quick to make and fall into various overlapping functional categories:

*   Introductory, tourist or enticing guides are aimed at telling short-term visitors (for example, day trippers) something of interest for a small area of vegetation; but not all species need to be named – often only the most obvious species are highlighted. Species-level accuracy is not crucial, whereas trivia, general interest and beauty are prime attributes. Often such guides include a diverse range of non-botanical information, and may include sections on animal life, history, geology or other subjects. These texts, in turn, can be subdivided by degree of seriousness expected of readers – and they will often be readers rather than serious users (compare Seddon and Lennox, 1980, Lack et al, 1998, and Hawthorne et al, 2005 – all aimed at Caribbean tourists, but with varied information content, the latter two verging on a slimmer type of technical field guide with coverage of all woody plants in the area specified).
*   Although the previous types should be eminently usable in schools, school-level texts must be cheap and generalized, but possibly usable in some cases on trips to a forest. It is helpful if examples can be made of widespread and common species in order to facilitate utility in many countries. Very often, these include technical diagrams of various plant families. These can barely be considered general field guides, except those mentioned above (see Boxes 4.12 and 4.13), but are, rather, school class notes. Some material appropriate for schools also falls under the next heading.

Box 4.11 Concise, semi-technical guides

These are field guides designed for convenience in the field, or as accurate, user-friendly introductions to an area. Any guide could be nimble if it covered few species; but here we refer to guides with perhaps 200 to 2000 species, where portability (pocket or small rucksack) is as important as accuracy, so the information per species, or species coverage is limited. The target users are those with a serious interest in learning the plants (particularly fieldworkers), who are, however, not necessarily botanists and who will be expected to check critical plants with other reference tools, such as the herbarium and a Flora.

Examples of such guides are as follows:

- *A Field Guide to Uganda Forest Trees* (Hamilton, 1981): a useful focus on leaf details of trees, with many drawings.
- *Field Guide to the Forest Trees of Ghana* (Hawthorne, 1990): all tree species (down to 5cm in diameter) and diagnostic details were illustrated, with text to support. This was written part time over three to four years (approximately three person years), including the 700 illustrations and fieldwork.
- *Flora da Reserva Ducke* (Ribeiro et al, 1999): dominated by colour photographs, arranged in a pictorial key-like manner, yet still includes much technical detail. In size, it is like a pragmatic Flora and covers all species; but to be portable and achievable in a modern project time frame, it covers only a single, albeit extremely rich, forest in Brazil (see Box 2.1 in Chapter 2). Conciseness is achieved by strongly limiting information per species and area of coverage.
- *A Field Guide to Forest Trees of Northern Thailand* (Gardner et al, 2000): rich mixture of many colour photos and line drawings.
- *Arboles de los Cafetales de El Salvador* (Monro et al, 2001): no colour and just provides annotated line drawings of leaves. Many guides still use line drawings because they can more clearly highlight diagnostic details and are cheap to print.
- *Wayside Trees of Malaya* (Corner, 1988): borders on being a student text. In spite of covering an 'incomplete set' of species (see Box 4.13), it is probably detailed enough, with enough species and accurate local names, to function as a complete guide to 'wayside trees'.

Laminated card guides

During recent years, various guides have been published with pictures, often photographs or paintings, on a single laminated sheet of card. Some are laminated by more than a standard office laminator, more like credit cards, and can then even be used underwater. Cheaper ones become yellow or frayed at the edges over years of use. Schmidt (1999) lists many such cards covering mostly North American plants, pond life, birds, fish and so on. Although all sets deal with rather narrow groups of species, often in limited areas, they can be recombined with other sets to extend the range.

There are two main design approaches:

- One approach is to arrange several species on a card according to themes, sometimes with text, or more pictures on the back. This approach is taken in the Chicago Field Museum *Rapid Colour Guide* cards: two-sided laminated sheets with 20 species per side, often many cards per theme, aimed mainly at researchers (see Table 4.3 and

---

BOX 4.12 GENERIC OVERVIEW FIELD GUIDES AND STUDENT TEXTS

There are two excellent, popular books that are well used in the field, but which are not designed to identify the majority of plants to species level. They educate and help botanists learn a new flora and put their specimens into generic order:

- Letouzey's *Manual of Forest Botany* (1986) has characteristics of both pragmatic Floras and textbooks (much technical detail and broad coverage of many families in African forests), but is light, slim, well bound and well illustrated with line drawings, with useful field information. It is apparently aimed at technical students.
- For the neotropics there is Gentry's *A Field Guide to the Families and Genera of Woody Plants of Northwest South America* (1993), which very successfully breaks the ice for a biodiverse area at a mostly generic level, without getting bogged down in all species-level details.

Although bordering on the latter type, we exclude from our definition of field guide the following types of more academic book. There are family-level treatments where one or two genera or species are given as examples, to be used in university or secondary school systematics classrooms or field trips in conjunction with specimens carefully selected by a teacher. In addition, there are keys and other guides to the families of vascular plants that cover all of the tropical regions, but which require fertile material and the dissection of flowers to succeed. Finally, there are many other student texts ranging from simple (such as Heywood, 1993) to the more academic (Geesink et al, 1981). Keller (1996) is considered in Chapter 7.

Case study 4.4). Different versions are also produced by the UK Field Studies Council; fold-out cards, each on one theme, are aimed at schoolchildren (see, for example, Edmonson, 1997).

- Another approach is to produce one card per species, such as the 67-species guide to aquatic plants, held together with a metal post, by Ramey (1995). This type of format apparently has untapped potential for biodiversity problems for reasons outlined in the discussions of modular guides in Chapter 5.

A set of laminated cards covering the same species as a typical field guide need be no different in information content. Card guides are a relatively new innovation; but since their main innovation is in the access method, we discuss these further in Chapter 5.

Electronic guides

Electronic media are fundamentally and positively affecting the manner of publication of some botanical information, both in terms of interactive internet guides, including self-assembly field guides that can be printed for field use based on the species and information you want in your guide, and applications with multi-access keys, potentially self-published on the internet. Again, because the new spirit of these guides is in the access method rather than information content, we discuss them in Chapter 5.

BOX 4.13 FIELD GUIDES TO INCOMPLETE SETS OF SPECIES

'Incomplete set' implies that not all of the plants defined by observable characteristics in the title are included. *A Field Guide to the Medicinal Shrubs of Java* would probably be an incomplete set as a field guide because 'medicinal' is not something that you can usually observe on a plant, and not all shrubs are included. Most, if not all, field guides to functional groups such as 'medicinal', 'timber trees', 'poisonous', 'edible' or 'useful' and certainly 'rare' plants are incomplete sets, as were the old herbals.

Field guides written for incomplete sets (see the section on 'Listing the species according to subjective criteria' in Chapter 3) present special problems if identification has to be conclusive in the field, although a high proportion of the potentially eligible plants in the field are ignored in the guide:

- If your guide is to an incomplete set, ensure that either identification from scratch is not important or, if it is, enough information is included to distinguish confusable species missing from the book from those illustrated and described within it. Otherwise, users will find plants in the field that are not in the book but look like ones that are, and then tend to assume the name of the similar species is correct. There is a strong tendency for this type of mistake, especially when users keen for an answer do not realize how similar related plants can be. This problem may be made worse because common names are quite often the same for similar species.
- If verification of names is important, rather than identification from scratch, then obviously the local name indexing will have to be researched and implemented fully. You will still need to be aware of the confusable species and make clear how to distinguish them.
- Try to include pictures and diagnostic text to help distinguish the included species from all the most similar ones in your area, including those that are otherwise missing from the book.

YOUR FIELD GUIDE WITHIN THE SPECTRUM OF TYPES

Your choice of guide format involves choosing an access method, format and arrangement of the information in your guide, as well as the type of information. At this stage, you may already be in a better position at least to choose the broad type of field guide you want to make, and this will determine some of its features. You might find it helpful to think about and discuss this polarity as an early step in designing your field guide, not forgetting the vast range of possibilities in the spectrum between the extremes:

- Do you need a 'shallow guide' – a short-term, attractive guide to stimulate interest, to be a souvenir to sell for profit, or to draw eco-tourists to an area? These are cheap and relatively easy to plan and make, and can often be designed as a fold-out pamphlet or card rather than a bound book. Simple ones, perhaps with 20 to 50 of the most glamorous species, can be planned and made in under three person months. However, they will probably not help serious biodiversity assessment greatly, or facilitate many other benefits from the plant community, or do much to stimulate botanical knowledge of the area. These are the fast food of the field guide world, designed for rapid consumption, on a modest budget, with less attention to the long-

CASE STUDY 4.4 CHICAGO FIELD MUSEUM RAPID COLOUR GUIDES

Robin Foster with Corine Vriesendorp, Chicago Field Museum

The Rapid Field Guides initiative is a desktop operation run by four people part time and is subsidized by grants. A few thousand people have obtained copies. The main focus is Latin American students. We sell many at neotropical congresses, at the equivalent of US$1.50 or US$2 per laminated sheet, depending upon the country. This covers the cost of materials, which at one point we calculated to be US$1.35 per sheet, but certainly doesn't cover labour and shipping. When I make trips to these countries I usually carry a suitcase full and give them to an outlet (for example, the Herbario Nacional in Ecuador), and they sell them with proceeds going to a student research fund. Since we don't make any money, there is no profit to give to the outside authors. Although I've told them they could have 100 copies free and they can sell them if they want, there has been no expression of any interest in making money from this.

So far, even though I've hawked them door to door at bookstores in Quito, and tourist outlets for the Machu Picchu guides in Cusco, there hasn't been any response, even though at the latter they said they could sell them for US$10 each and I was willing to provide them at US$3 each. I might have to have an agent in each place. I am looking into having them printed in-country; but getting the printer cartridges for these inkjets is a problem. If one had real commercial potential, maybe we could afford to do runs of a thousand or more on higher-end commercial machines. There are some 130+ guides with 700+ pages available, and I would guess maybe 8000–10,000 species pictured. If I have the pictures ready with the appropriate dimensions and size, and I know the flora pretty well or have a list given to me, I can certainly do a one-page guide in a couple of hours, a 40-page guide in maybe a week. And we can print and laminate a few hundred pages in a day. But there are all these other variables, especially with outside authors, in getting the images ready and identified: getting the images to Chicago; scanning slides, negatives, or prints, or adjusting pre-scanned or digital camera images; data-basing the images, etc. Photoshop improvements are usually less than a minute per image. Checking names can slow things down (for example, Cubans are often using many plant names that haven't been updated since the 1950s). I am getting a backlog of guides to be produced. If I dedicated my time to it, I guess I could do 100 or more different guides in a year, which averages something like two per week.

term nutrition or development of the mind. They can still benefit biodiversity through publicity and livelihood creation. There are several possible themes for such guides, and there are few universal recommendations beyond what we have said in Chapter 3. It is often only important to make your guide as attractive and stylish as possible.

- Do you need a deeper, more technical guide, such as the pragmatic or tree Floras or field monographs? You do if accuracy is really important and a proper understanding of at least part of the flora is highly desirable. Either the regional Flora is too hard to use or is impractical. Or there is no usable Flora because it is incomplete, decades out of date or non-existent. Such a guide is harder to justify on short-term economic grounds, unless subsidized by a development agency or implicitly subsidized in terms of the time for which you and your collaborators are already supported. Here are some related issues for technical guides:

- With a technical guide, think long-term education, not only short-term identification. Design your guide to stimulate learning, not only as an identification aid. This is easy to forget when testing drafts. Do not expect that users will immediately pick it up and identify all species accurately on day one; but it is important that they are at least intrigued.
- Do not underestimate the time and communication that will be involved in getting the nomenclature sorted out and in integrating your guide with the long tradition of botanical literature for your region. The more out of date or out of range the nearest Flora is, the greater this element of your team's task will be; 100 to 200 species per author year might be a reasonable estimate.

- Do you need something in between the simplest and the most technical – perhaps guides that help people to ensure that they are talking about the right species before using, eating or cultivating it, without drowning them in too much spurious information? Or do you need a sophisticated tourist guide? These may be biodiversity guides with an eye on identification or confirmation of identity; or they may be dedicated identification guides with corners cut to broaden the audience. These are neither very technical (because of the audience) nor superficial (because they need to be accurate with respect to some of the information at least). As with all compromises, the results in terms of accuracy, economics and so on may well fall between those outlined for the first two options:
  - These intermediates are the guides where the decisions on accuracy, coverage, usability and price will tend to involve compromise, and where your users' detailed advice on information content and format is so critical, perhaps much more so than in the more technical guides (where fundamental rules of science will limit choices) and in simpler guides (where the whole guide will be much simpler anyway and a book designer might have the most to say).

Better than choosing one or other of these options, why not choose more than one? Make the most of the potential synergy between different types of guides, between short- and long-term benefit.

In other words, diversify rather than compromise in your guide production plans. Here are some examples:

- Produce small, local, cheap 'shallow' colour guides based on your more technical one. Having prepared all of your illustrations, corrected all your names and so on, why not publicize the bigger project by producing shallow guides almost as advertisements? Make posters for schools; postcards, with the book title on the back; booklets for sale to tourists; mini-guides to difficult or important groups; and/or trail guides to small areas, all capitalizing on the same set of information and materials. Perhaps one commercial output could subsidize a longer-term one. Cheaper educational guides with fewer species, showing the important principles of plant identification or introducing users to the commoner plants, might encourage some students to grow into a full user of your larger technical field guide.
- In some highly seasonal vegetation, where there are many visitors all year round, you may consider a dry season guide to trees based on bark and flowers, and a wet season one based on leaves.

BOX 4.14 *LEUCAENA* GENETIC RESOURCES HANDBOOK

Colin Hughes

It is relatively easy to justify spending resources on specialist identification tools – including field guides – for groups of small numbers of species in economically important plant groups (for example, eucalypts, pines and forage legumes), particularly for difficult groups and groups with high species diversity in a small area. Specific identification tools for species of a single genus – *Leucaena* – are justified by wide cultivation, breeding programmes and environmental impacts that involve several species and artificial or spontaneous hybrids. Many cases of previous misidentification in these arenas have hindered forestry or agroforestry practice and research.

Having previously prepared a taxonomic monograph on the genus over many years, *The Genus* Leucaena: *A Genetic Resources Handbook* was made for more practical users (Hughes 1998a, 1998b). Identification is dealt with in Chapter 5 of the handbook. Identification tools include a morphological glossary, spot identification characters, composite plates illustrating character variation (leaflets, glands, pods, flowers and bark), a tabular summary and a dichotomous key. With hindsight, I can see many ways of improving the user friendliness of the chapter – for example, by including all species in all composite plates comparing flowers/glands/pods, etc., rather than just illustrative of overall diversity; standardizing species order in these plates; and better cross-referencing and navigation aids for the different options within the chapter.

Full drawings of all species to allow verification of identifications are included in the same handbook. I used a combination of photos and line drawings. Line drawings from the monograph were easy to reformat for identification. Taking more photos in the field would have been advantageous.

'Hiding' the identification chapter within the larger book has pros and cons. Many potential users, and even readers, do not realize it is there. Many people wanting to identify *Leucaena* species might not think to look there. A stand-alone identification guide would make the task easier. Limited distribution and availability of the handbook (1200 English and 350 Spanish copies have been distributed/sold and are now essentially gone) is a problem. A web version is planned that seems likely to be much more accessible, useful and permanent. I am also considering a Lucid-style e-key on the web as a better alternative.

For the taxonomic monographer, production of a variety of more user-friendly identification tools is straightforward, easy, quick and incurs minimal extra cost – one week for a group of this size. This is because the author knows the plants well and because of the availability of illustrations. However, assembling all of the other information (on uses, silviculture, ethnobotany, seed storage and pretreatments, as well as conservation) was much more time consuming and entailed approximately six months of work.

- If you have used a database to keep track of details of your species, or you have developed a digital picture library, consider using this database to make a web- or CD-based interactive guide. A website of your field guide can only increase your catchment of interested plant identifiers, provide a site for corrections, perhaps for a subsequent edition, and increase awareness of the plants or forest of your interest.
- Annotated checklists might provide an interim and publishable target output for a project. 'Modular guides', which we discuss further in Chapter 5, also offer a steady trickle of outputs rather than waiting for one end product.

5

Identification:
Keys and other access methods

William Hawthorne

INTRODUCTION

Plant identification is the process of establishing a recognized name for a particular plant or specimen. Ruling out the 'ask someone else', and potential automated methods such as DNA barcoding (see Box 5.1), there are two paths or methods to identification in terms of how we think:

1   identification through recognition apparently involves the instantaneous, ('holistic' or 'gestalt') appreciation of many parts of the plant at once;
2   identification through analysis is the rule-based method, involving a conscious sequence of considerations about individual characteristics, or 'characters'.

BOX 5.1 AUTOMATIC IDENTIFICATION

Automated methods for plant identification have been discussed seriously for a decade or more, although they have had virtually no impact yet on fieldwork and still remain a topic for research. The currently fashionable topic is that of DNA barcoding, whereby small fragments of DNA of existing species would be sampled and registered on a DNA barcode database. Identification would then involve rapid sequencing of DNA from unidentified plants, an increasingly cheap and rapid process although not yet very field friendly. This approach has apparently more chance of providing a realistic tool for automated identification in the next decade than those that attempt to analyse plant morphology, such as leaf shape (see Box 6.7, page 133). The internet has many references to these cutting edge topics, new ones appearing regularly – for example, see the BioNET archive on computer-aided taxonomy (www.bionet-intl.org/) for references on these and many relevant subjects.

> ## Box 5.2 Do you know how you recognize common objects?
>
> Consider how you identify your close relatives or friends. You probably recognize them without consciously thinking how. If you had to write a field guide with which others could identify them, you would have to think about what features characterize each of them. Experts – such as scientists, farmers or herbalists – recognize their plants apparently with just a moment's thought; but learners usually have to struggle with rules and conscious attempts to memorize facts. Confronted by a plant at the limits of their expertise, experts are like learners and have to think more analytically: 'It can't be A because it's in a swamp, so it must be B.'
>
> One might suppose that a useful way to research a field guide would be to ask local experts 'what is that plant' and then 'how do you recognize it'. Of course, it is essential to involve local experts, or other experts if you are a local expert, especially to locate and identify species in the field; but they may not know entirely how they are recognizing the plants they know. When asked, some secretly bemused experts latch onto any obvious feature, struggling to invent rules on the spot, although with practice and experience of thinking analytically, or of teaching, a few can translate experience into reliable rules better than most.
>
> Psychologists point out that recognition is largely based on '*gestalt*', or 'spirit of the whole', rather than analysis of successive questions; on computers, 'neural networks' can be trained to behave in a similar way. However, when the neural network has been trained reliably to distinguish a spanner from a hammer, it is not then possible to open up the circuit and obtain a set of rules about how to recognize hammers and spanners that could be used elsewhere. So, do not be surprised when your expert's brain struggles to speak the rules for separating two species which that expert can reliably distinguish. Unless, of course, some rules can be remembered from the field guide or expert who first taught them.

Identification tools, like field guides or herbaria, should enable us to identify plants using our powers of recognition or analysis or, most likely, a combination of both. Authors have to strike a balance between recognition and analysis that suits the intended users of their field guides.

Box 5.2 explains why you cannot create a field guide by simply publishing the information that experts have in their head. Another reason that field guides cannot emulate the mind of experts is that texture, taste, smell and three-dimensional perspectives are not well dealt with by currently practicable media, and are often very hard to characterize anyway. Recognition seems to involve a set of many fuzzy mental images or memories, covering all forms of a species; yet field guides need to be concise and intelligible when summarizing variation and must therefore stick to characters that are more reliable and with precise limits. (see Box 5.3).

One way or another, it is essential mentally to break up your plants into parts if you intend to make good use of your data on a computer, even simply to store data in a database. Furthermore, characters have to be defined if you want to promote identification by analysis. Even if you are to promote recognition-based identification and have no computer, you will find it a useful discipline to define and qualify characters – make a table or spreadsheet of species, characters and character states – in preparation for your field guide. The logical and consistent thought about the plants that this demands will

BOX 5.3 CHARACTERS

A character is any observable aspect of a plant – such as flower colour or a preference for swamps – that can be referred to with a word or phrase reliably and objectively, and itemized or quantified in terms of 'character states':

- Binary characters, such as 'thorny', have only two possible states: present and absent (or true/false, yes/no).
- Other types of character are best specified by numbers or counts, perhaps a set or range of possible values (for example, number of petals) or lengths or, in some sophisticated approaches, a probability that a character state is present.
- Categorical characters are specified in terms of multiple choice character states as words or codes – for instance, the character 'leaf arrangement' can have states 'opposite', 'whorled' or 'alternate', which would normally be codified (for example, O, W, A, or 1, 2, 3) for efficiency on a computer.

The choice of how to define a character is more about semantics, computers and convenience than botany. There is no right or wrong way of defining any particular character. Leaf arrangement could equally well be defined as a number – for example, number of leaves per node, with opposite defined by a character state of 2. Similarly, categorical character states can be thought of as, and translated to, a suite of binary characters, such as 'opposite leaves?' (true or false?). In this case, other linked binary characters, such as 'alternate leaves?', would also be needed; the binary option is the best if any species can have both opposite and alternate leaves.

Not all people in different cultures, not all languages, agree on how plants are subdivided into separate parts or characters, nor on how the various character states are to be defined (see, for instance, Berlin et al, 1973; Hunn, 1977; Atran, 1990; Davidoff et al, 1999); in fact botanists often do not agree with each other. Although, as Mendel (1822–1884) showed with his peas, some characters reflect individual genes, there is not necessarily anything so fundamental about them. The variation around the world in the boundaries between our words for colour or taste, or plant types and parts, form a whole anthropological discipline on their own. Fortunately, the degree of 'common-sense' universal agreement seems far more impressive (Witkowski and Brown, 1978; Brown, 1991; Wierzbicka, 1994), particularly for subjects that we as individuals find the easiest to distinguish and define. Colours and tastes are highly subjective, difficult to make a consistent classification of even in our own minds; so it is not surprising this is where cultural differences seem to be greatest.

force you to clarify details you might otherwise leave unresolved or unexplored, and will help you to choose the best order of species and choice of images, even for a picture guide.

Botanical identification tools, in general, tend to promote analytical identification because this is the easiest way to make a publication accurate and concise; identification rules or diagnostic characters are independently testable and easy to communicate and copy. Botanists are traditionally trained to think and write in this analytical way, and it provides a discipline that is useful for science students. The process of successive approximation, of gradually closing in on a solution, identifying the broad characteristic of the family or genus first, then gradually specifying the detail and pinpointing the

Box 5.4 General criteria for a useful set of diagnostic characters

Describing a set of diagnostic characters across many species can be a lengthy process, so prioritization of some generally useful diagnostic characters for your particular combination of users, budget, access method and species is essential. Obviously, some types of character need only be researched in subsets of species (for example, yam shape or taste among *Dioscorea*). A good character set for a particular set of species should have many of the following attributes:

- They vary much more between species than within species, or at least limits can be defined for each species that often differ between species.
- They should complement each other – that is, some should differ among species that otherwise have all other recorded characters the same. Avoid wasting time documenting characters that are more or less correlated with others that you have already recorded – for example, latex in the petiole, when latex in the bark has already been considered – even if there are some minor differences.
- They vary in a way that can be summarized and communicated reliably, with little effort. Smells and tastes, while distinctive, are often very hard to communicate on paper and across cultures. The character should be easily observable and reliably interpreted by your specific user group and by you (see Chapter 9). For instance, non-seasonal characters from low down on a large tree are better than seasonal details of the crown. The perfumed scent of leaves and bark of certain plant families (Annonaceae, Lauraceae, Zingiberaceae, etc.) are notable exceptions because, although not initially clear to many users from a textual description, they can be quickly learned and define large groups that otherwise have few completely distinctive vegetative features.
- They are straightforward to research. Characters that are often recorded in books or herbaria might have this advantage if you have easy access to these. Start by looking in existing Floras and monographs to see what characters they use. However, beware that you will still have to concentrate on field characters that we discuss in Chapter 6.
- The best characters to use in keys are often those which can most easily be reduced to simple and clear codes in a database field. If you need a sentence or even more than a few letters or digits to define a character state clearly, then it will often not be very easy or efficient to use in a key, although a short list of discrete options (for example, countries in which a species occurs) can work well.

As an example, the range in the number of pairs of lateral nerves on a leaf is a useful field character to consider, even though it varies on the leaves of one plant, because it is easily recorded, easily researched and the lower limit of many species will be higher than the upper limit of others. The texture of leaves, however, is less useful as it is harder to record, research and communicate. You will come across hundreds of such characters – 'cut wood with a slight smell'; 'older trees with rather dark crowns' – but do not ignore them altogether as they can be useful to help users confirm the correctness of an answer suggested by the other characters and the access method. You might relegate them to note fields rather than coded into neat categories in your database. As a last resort, if you do use such characters in a key, try and ensure that they are the last questions or nearly so.

species, forges a mental and information framework useful for describing and learning new species. However, not everyone needs such a mental framework; they just need to know a few names or details for plants that they come across.

Many successful field guides make good use of identification through recognition, using pictures with little diagnostic text, and there is no reason why these cannot also help users develop a useful, systematic mental framework. Field guides for birds and some other animal groups encourage more browsing than plant guides. Stevenson et al (2003) even distinguish bird field guides from 'keys', as if by definition a field guide is always less analytical – a distinction which does not apply to plant guides. Larger animals, in general, are more amenable to pictorial guides than plants as there are fewer of them, and visual signals which humans can see have often been important in their own evolution. We consider below the increasing role that browsing might have in modern plant field guides.

Your major task is to discover and document or illustrate characters that enable plants to be distinguished in the field. There may be no one in the world who consciously 'knows' all of the diagnostic rules you need in your field guide – existing botanical works will probably not contain all the answers, either – so do not expect to find them entirely by asking experts or reading books.

Decide on a good basic set of key characters as soon as possible after you have chosen your species; this will help you to focus your attention on unknown facts during fieldwork and help you take more useful photographs. Some requirements for these characters are explained below and in Chapter 6; others are more general (see Box 5.4).

TYPES OF GUIDE: TYPES OF ACCESS

Field guides provide botanical information in two main forms: the actual descriptive material, including text or pictures, and the indexing, page arrangement and keys – called here the access methods – to help readers identify or reach plants in which they are interested. Our definition of a field guide has identification as a main feature, so an access method that enables navigation to the right species based on its details is generally crucial. A suitable access method can be defined in consultation with the intended users (see Chapter 3). More essentially, it must be tested before finalizing – see Chapter 9 for methods and examples.

The descriptive element of a field guide should allow verification of the identity of species independently of the more concise or cursory information used for access. In fact, the same information ideally functions in both ways, on different occasions: if the species has been identified initially by browsing pictures, the textual description should allow confirmation; if access to the species was via analysis and reading of the text, then the pictures should help to confirm it independently:

- Promote structured browsing – that is, an effective combination of analysis and recognition. Place pictures within groups where groups are defined in a sequence, based on simple characters (for example, leaf arrangement and margin details): users can jump directly to the right groups based on rules or experience; then browse pictures to reach a matching species; then maybe check the text to identify subtle differences between similar species (we are trying to achieve this effect for image libraries of random plant images in the Virtual Field Herbarium).

BOX 5.5 TYPES OF STATIC GUIDE AND TYPICAL ASSOCIATED ACCESS METHODS

- Books and other standard printed works are the typical examples, and many access methods have evolved.
- Posters or large single information sheets for public display of information may serve as a field guide, especially if arranged as a fold-out map. Access to particular species on a poster may not be deemed crucial; but a good design may throw particularly outstanding patterns of similarity into sharp relief from a distance, with finer detail nested for closer examination.
- Laminated identification cards display all information on one sheet (for example, the Chicago Field Museum's Rapid Colour Guides featured in Case study 4.4, page 88). These do not present much of an access problem because there are few enough species to see all on one page. They are designed to facilitate browsing. If several such sheets are used together in a ring binder, the format of the guide as a whole becomes dynamic: if the sequence of cards is fixed, we have a special type of book. Likewise, collections of actual herbarium specimens or copies of them designed for field use (as with the Chicago Field Museum's Rapid Colour Guides) may have a static format.
- 'Novelty' (not very commonly employed) devices, such as identification wheels – tables arranged in a circle, with the more general character states towards the middle, and the species on the rim, but with no moving parts. These rarely represent a full guide, however, and typically lack descriptions.
- There are also certain computer versions of any of the above – for example, basic word-processed documents without hyperlinks and basic websites with no dynamic content.

Simple guides may work by browsing alone; this approach may even work for the more dogged enthusiasts with larger reference books. However, there will usually be too many species in a tropical forest guide to make browsing of all descriptions an efficient option, so a specific access method is usually needed.

We can also distinguish between static and dynamic formats of field guides:

- In static guides (normal field guides), the content, sequence and format are fixed at the time of publication. These include virtually all early field guides, notably books, and a majority of current ones (see Box 5.5).
- In dynamic formats, the order and sometimes other aspects of the content of a guide can be rearranged during use, or at least after initial publication, either on a computer or by using devices such as card indexes and ring binders. It can be assumed that dynamic format field guides will become commoner as computers become smaller, cheaper and more field usable (see Box 5.11).

Access methods in static guides: The primary sequence, keys and indexes

Primary order of species in a field guide

Static guides have the advantage that the order of the species is fixed and access and other aspects of information layout and style can therefore be optimized for this order.

For instance, the page sequence is fixed in a book, so indexing (by page numbers) to common and scientific names is trivial, as are indexes of plant appearance or keys.

In a dictionary of words, in alphabetical order, an unknown word is found by matching the first letter, then the first two letters, and so on, until by successive approximation the correct word and its definition is found out of many thousands, hopefully in a matter of seconds. If the main aim were to find a word for a given concept, a book can be arranged as a thesaurus, with words for similar concepts placed together. Similarly, the order of species in a field guide should suit the main aim of the guide. There may be various indexes to help find information by alternative criteria – for instance, the diagnostic keys, and local and scientific name indexes; but the primary page order of the guide forms a crucial part of the access design for a field guide. There are two main choices:

1   *Name order*: your typical users may think they know a name for a plant, but need to look up information about that plant in your field guide, perhaps to confirm its identity. If this were the main type of query, it would be best to arrange the information in alphabetical order of plant names, like a dictionary. The guide as a whole is then its own index. The only question, then, is should the order be common or scientific name? That will depend largely upon the relative importance you attach to these names – that is, user demand – and the reliability of local names (see Box 4.1, page 63). Keys can then provide a second access method, based on plant appearance:
    - Local or trade name order may be preferable for a guide with a limited readership, where most people are reliably using the same names for the same plants, and if most queries will be to confirm field details based on these names.
    - Scientific name order with a separate index of local names is the obvious solution for a technical or varied readership book that is sorted primarily by name. Alphabetical order of genus and species is useful if there are few species per family and people are likely often to access a species via its scientific name, perhaps having found it in a separate key or index. If there are many species per family, placing the species in family, genus and species alphabetic order, while not perfectly nature order, allows some general descriptive information to be included for each family and genus, saving space at species level.

2   *Nature order*: this is any sequence, however arbitrary, based on appearance or other plant characteristic and is used here in a more general sense than the less practicable concept of 'natural' order or affinity, supposedly reflecting the underlying evolutionary sequence or pattern, and often attempted in monographs. The primary and most demanding function of most field guides is identification, equivalent to a thesaurus rather than a dictionary; so field guides are most often in some sort of nature order with similar plants listed and illustrated together, and separate page indexes to names.

Placing species together in their taxonomic families provides a crude type of nature order, providing similar families are next to each other and species are arranged by similarity within families. However, there is no universal agreement on these sequences, so you will have to arrange families, genera and species in a sensible order yourself (see Box 5.6):

BOX 5.6 ORTHODOX AND CUSTOMIZED SPECIES SEQUENCES FOR NATURE ORDER GUIDES

Various family arrangements have been devised, and some are used to enforce a standard order on textbooks and herbarium cupboards. Although newer schemes may be more accurate and in tune with molecular data, some of the older sequences are followed in herbaria and may be appropriate in your guide for this reason. Well-known schemes are Hutchinson (1973), Dahlgren (1975), Cronquist (1988, as followed by Ribeiro et al, 1999), Mabberley (1997, an updated version of Cronquist, 1988), and the Angiosperm Phylogeny Group (APG, 1998, 2003; see www.mobot.org/MOBOT/research/APweb/).

The APG scheme is based on modern molecular analysis and is universally respected, but is not complete for all genera, and the family order is only fixed to within groups or 'clades', thus defining a tree of life showing how species, genera and families (that is, taxa) are related, but not prescribing any linear sequence of the taxa at the ends of the tree's branches. In fact, there is no reason why natural patterns of overall similarity should form a spectrum or fit smoothly along a one-dimensional sequence (try arranging your friends and relatives in a line based on overall similarity); even two-dimensional diagrams of affinity (Dahlgren, 1975) can only ever be crude approximations of the multidimensional patterns of nature. It is therefore surprising how far it is possible to do just this for practical purposes. For field use, it is relatively easy to choose a few key field characters to define a sequence, just as a picture guide to people arranged by gender, height, and skin and hair colour would be far easier to use than one arranged by their names. Decide what spectrum of characteristics you and your users want to highlight in the primary sequence; but strive to make your sequence as similar as possible to an orthodox scheme as this will help you to summarize the features of families in one place, close to where the species are listed.

For example, for three different guides to Ghana's trees:

- Hawthorne (1995) listed Ghana's tree species in genus-species order in a guide to ecological features (not a field guide) that users would be expected to reference by name.
- In a more technical woody plant identification guide, Hawthorne (1990) and Hawthorne and Jongkind (2006) used a sequence of families, reasonably compatible with the APG groupings, but with heterogeneous families split and sets of small, similar families joined, in an order optimized for a smooth sequence of leaf and other vegetative characters.
- For a tree photo field guide, (Hawthorne and Gyakari, 2006), the sequence was based purely on bark slash exudate, texture and colour.

Many less technical field guides are similarly ordered by habit, flower colour or other morphological characteristics, or preferred habitat. Beware that some such sequences have the disadvantage that one species – for example, from several habitats – may have to be mentioned in various parts of the book.

- Facilitate the ability to identify through structured browsing by adopting a sequence related to plant form (see Box 5.6). Consider ordering the species in their families as a first approximation to nature order; but you may need to break up large families and merge small ones to make all groups manageable and useful. For guides in nature order, a key can be fully integrated with the species-specific descriptions, an efficient solution for several reasons (see this chapter's 'Conclusions', page 119).

- In a field guide with a primary order other than alphabetical names, all cross-references to species names in the book – for example, from similar species or keys – should also specify the page number or equivalent (for example, 'See species X, group 22b' or 'p99'). Do not frustrate readers by requiring them separately to look up the page in an index whenever a name is mentioned (as in the otherwise well-designed guide by Arbonnier, 2004).

The benefits and limits of identification by browsing

Tropical plant guides designed to facilitate recognition – picture-rich books – have obvious potential, especially where literacy is limited or if the book has to be translated into several languages. As digital photography becomes more accessible, this potential is increasing. Picture-based books (with local name indexes) seem particularly appropriate where the guide aims to help people who know the plants in their own area to establish the scientific names. But what is the chance of making such guides promote accurate identification as a primary aim when many similar species, mostly unknown to the users, occur in the same area?

The niche for picture-based field guides to tropical plants is outstandingly unfilled. For the major patterns of variation in the plant life of typical rainforests, picture browsing alone allows at least a very useful first approximation (see Box 5.7). Some analytical guides or sections of guides, and longer-term education rather than piecemeal identification alone, are also essential if such guides are to be accurate for difficult groups. Even the most enthusiastic users need to be encouraged to study specific, often very subtle details, and there comes a point when to avoid analytical text for the sake of some users is to introduce a serious handicap in the potential for accuracy for others. If some users cannot read, and accurate identification of many difficult species is important, you and your committee of planners should question whether the combination of these users plus your field guide can solve the problem. More usually, even a low percentage of users who can read a guide in an optional analytical way will justify adding some technical, analytical text to support the images for difficult species.

Keys and other ways of diagnosing species by their characters

The classic method for botanical identification by analysis is the diagnostic key, which has not changed radically since the 18th century (see Pankhurst, 1975, 1991, 1993; Tilling, 1984; and Edwards and Morse, 1995). A key is basically a 'decision tree', a figurative treasure hunt, where the answer to each question leads to another question until the right name is reached (the key might be formatted or phrased as a pair of optional statements; but each step can still be considered a question). Each key question filters out some of the remaining species until only one species is left. Keys can be displayed or formatted in various ways (see Table 5.1 and Plate 2, centre pages).

There might be one character considered per question, with character states representing the possible answers; or two or more characters might be combined into one key question – for example, if a combination of two makes the dichotomy workable in different seasons, or the individual characters define a set of species less reliably than their combination. The character states define the possible statements in a key; so, in order to make a truly dichotomous key, all multi-state characters can be translated to binary ones. It is often better for categorical and some numeric types of character to have the three or more optional answers all listed together ('polychotomous') at a partic-

---

BOX 5.7 CAN PICTURE-BASED GUIDES BE ACCURATE IN SPECIES-RICH PLACES?

Can browsing of picture-rich guides be accurate? This issue is one of those investigated by the UK Department for International Development's (DFID) Forestry Research Programme (FRP) Field Guide Project R7367 (see Case study 8.1, page 184). The three main sets of trials in this project are all directly relevant to the question.

A trial photo guide to large trees in the Ghanaian rainforest was made showing bark slash and other tree details, containing 128 picture cards, one or more species per card. With about 30 minutes of training, users from villages and towns with little prior knowledge of local trees could use this through structured browsing of pictures to identify more trees (about 80 per cent accuracy averaged across all trials) than professional tree spotters knew without the guide. The tree-spotters themselves were able significantly to improve their own performance with the same guide. The poor-performing minority of photographs could easily have been anticipated: they had slash patterns that looked very similar to other species and the minor differences visible were not consistent ones.

We also ran picture recognition tests in a wide range of Grenadian vegetation, from montane forest with many similar species, to drier lowlands where the differences between many species (stilt-rooted mangroves to fruiting mangoes) were easy to recognize. Obviously, the levels of accuracy in the easy patches were much higher, reaching more than 80 per cent even with vanloads of schoolchildren. In the difficult vegetation, more than half of the 20 sample plants were still correctly matched. Intriguingly, people preferred photographs to drawings or paintings, but were not significantly more accurate with them overall. There was a slight trend for standard botanical drawings, which we presume induce a more analytical approach, to perform better with difficult species.

Various illustrative devices and even minimal basic text can be added to improve the results slightly: practice, user need and experience would also improve accuracy in the longer term. However, tests on *Cola* species on Mount Cameroon revealed the limitations. Only about half of all *Cola* treelets from 19 species were matched correctly to their pictures, and it made little difference whether the pictures were photographs of live or herbarium specimens, or line drawings, or with or without small marks to highlight important details.

In summary, browsing helps almost any user distinguish plants within a heterogeneous set (that is, most crucial differences are easily seen), encouraging novices to realize that plant identification can be easy. A general average of 50 to 80 per cent species accuracy covering the studious, the gifted, the bored and the occasional half-drunk should be possible in a species-rich rainforest by browsing pictures whose primary order has been optimized for this task, and which are broken into smaller groups of 20 or less species.

For difficult groups of plants, one should not expect a browsing/recognition approach to yield accurate results.

---

ular point in the key. In any case, users consider one question at a time before moving onto another question in a predefined order.

In a 'multi-access key', also known as a polyclave, the user does not have to follow a predefined sequence of questions. They are based on complete lists of taxa and their characters, and therefore require more data to construct than simple keys which need only focus on the details in specific questions. The user selects the characters to be defined and the order in which they are considered. Missing characters on incomplete specimens can be avoided. Although these are mostly implemented as dynamic keys, static versions can be made where one character perhaps defines columns and the other rows in a table, the answer being in the cell where the chosen row crosses the chosen column. Users still think about one character, or question, at once; but by placing the options in a table, the species that show various combinations of characters are clearly exposed. More than two characters can be considered in this way, for instance in a triangular table. A multi-access table may also subdivide into successive and more specific options, with rows and columns splitting (see Box 5.8); but such polyclaves can soon become too complicated and inefficient to use.

Table 5.1 *Various formats of dichotomous or similar keys*

a. Numbered	596	Leaves opposite	597
		Leaves alternate	599
	597	Flowers red	Species A
		Flowers blue	598
	598	Leaves serrated	Species B
		Leaves entire	Species C
	599	Leaves serrated	Species D
		Leaves entire	Species E

b. Indented	Leaves opposite		
	Flowers red		Species A
	Flowers blue		
		Leaves serrated	Species B
		Leaves entire	Species C
	Leaves alternate		
	Leaves serrated		Species D
	Leaves entire		Species E

c. Indented and numbered	596a Leaves opposite		
	597a Flowers red		Species A
	597b Flowers blue		
		598a Leaves serrated	Species B
		598b Leaves entire	Species C
	596b Leaves alternate		
	599a Leaves serrated		Species D
	599b Leaves entire		
		600a Leaves truly alternate	Species E
		600b Leaves sub-opposite	Go to 596

d. Numbered, with return number	596	Leaves opposite	597
		Leaves alternate	599
	597	Flowers red	Species A
		Flowers blue	598
	598	Leaves serrated	Species B
		Leaves entire	Species C
	599	(596) Leaves serrated	Species D
		Leaves entire	Species E

Note: Return number only necessary when the 'parent' question is not immediately above: helps retracing steps.

e. Flow diagram, with boxes and text

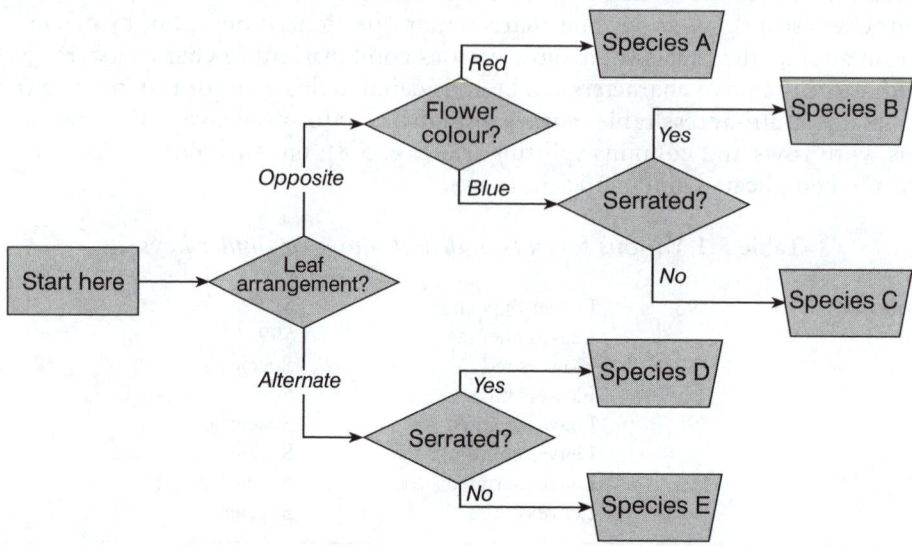

Note: Although they can be very clear, flow charts occupy a surprising amount of space compared to a normal key with the same information content.

f. Flow diagram with pictures

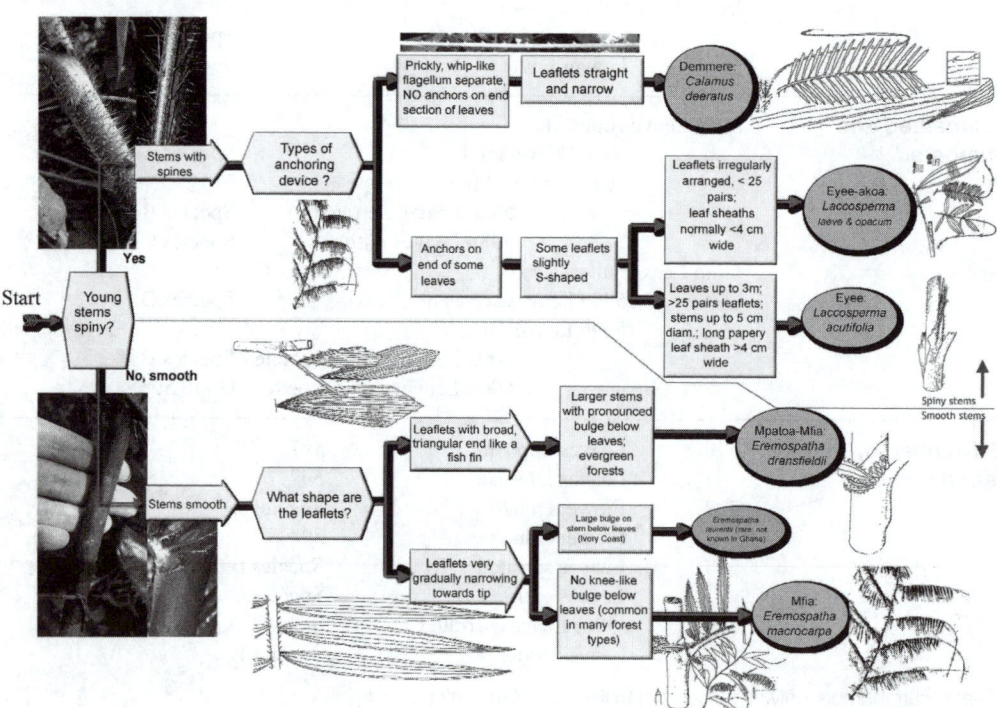

g. Numbered, as with (a), with icons to designate character states

596	Leaves opposite		597
	Leaves alternate		599
597	Flowers red		Species A
	Flowers blue		598
598	Leaves serrated		Species B
	Leaves entire		Species C
599	Leaves serrated		Species D
	Leaves entire		Species E

Note: As with (e), suitable for showing a limited amount of information in a simple, clear but spatially inefficient way.

---

h. Table with successive division of columns only

Leaves opposite			Leaves alternate	
Flowers red	Flowers blue		Leaves serrated	Leaves entire
	Leaves serrated	Leaves entire		
Species A	Species B	Species C	Species D	Species E

Note: Obviously, this type of tabular key can have added images as well.

i. Circular version of hierarchical divided table shown in (g)

Note: The illustrated hummingbird guide is basically a circular list with words associated with each picture. In more complex versions, an inner circle represents the first choices of a key; each of these semi-circles may then be split into smaller sectors of the circle, leading to a species name in the outer rim.
Source: Texas Parks and Wildlife Publications

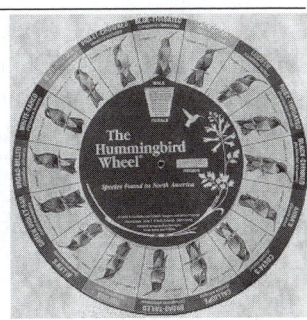

BOX 5.8 DAWKINS'S *GRAPHICAL FIELD KEYS OF UGANDA TREES*
TWO-DIMENSIONAL MULTILEVEL TABLE

Dawkins's (1951) multi-access key to Uganda trees based on bark and leaf details has inspired many writers of tropical tree guides. The primary table was divided in the following manner. The numbers refer to groups; further details were given for each species on a separate page. Names were put in these boxes as well. Box 6 of Table 5.1 is filled out as an example.

Table 5.2 *Dawkins's primary table*

			Leaves alternate		Leaves opposite	
			Slash white, yellow, brown	Slash red	Slash red	Slash white, yellow, brown
Leaves simple	No latex, etc.	Not trinerved	1	2	21	22
		Trinerved	3	4	23	24
	Coloured resin		5	6 *Pycnanthus Staudtia Spondianthus*	25	26
	Latex		7	8	27	28
Leaves with 2–3 leaflets			9	10		
Leaves pinnate	No exudate		11	12	31	
	Red		14			
	Latex		16			
Leaves bipinnate			17	18		
Leaves digitate			19	20	39	40

Source: adapted from Dawkins (1951)

Hawthorne (1990) used a similar approach, but added drawings and indented keys to vegetative features to separate the almost 700 species in Ghana. Pictorial multi-access keys (see Figure 5.1) were added as a graphical alternative for those who preferred it.

However, most users in Ghana preferred the simpler indented keys to these multi-access keys and the latter also take up more space and more time to make. They should be seen as often something of a gimmick, more of aesthetic satisfaction to the key creator than of benefit to practical users.

Multi-access keys are very appropriate for flower, fruit and other seasonal and other optional data, which may be missing when the plant is observed in the field.

An extra dimension for diagnostic information can be added to books (or bound sets of cards) by colour coding or by using simple marks or icons on the edges of pages in a book. In Ribeiro et al (1999) the pages have such marginal marks and the individual pages hold simple multi-access keys, with the leading questions also colour-coded in the centre of the page spread and photographs inserted around the page centre. This

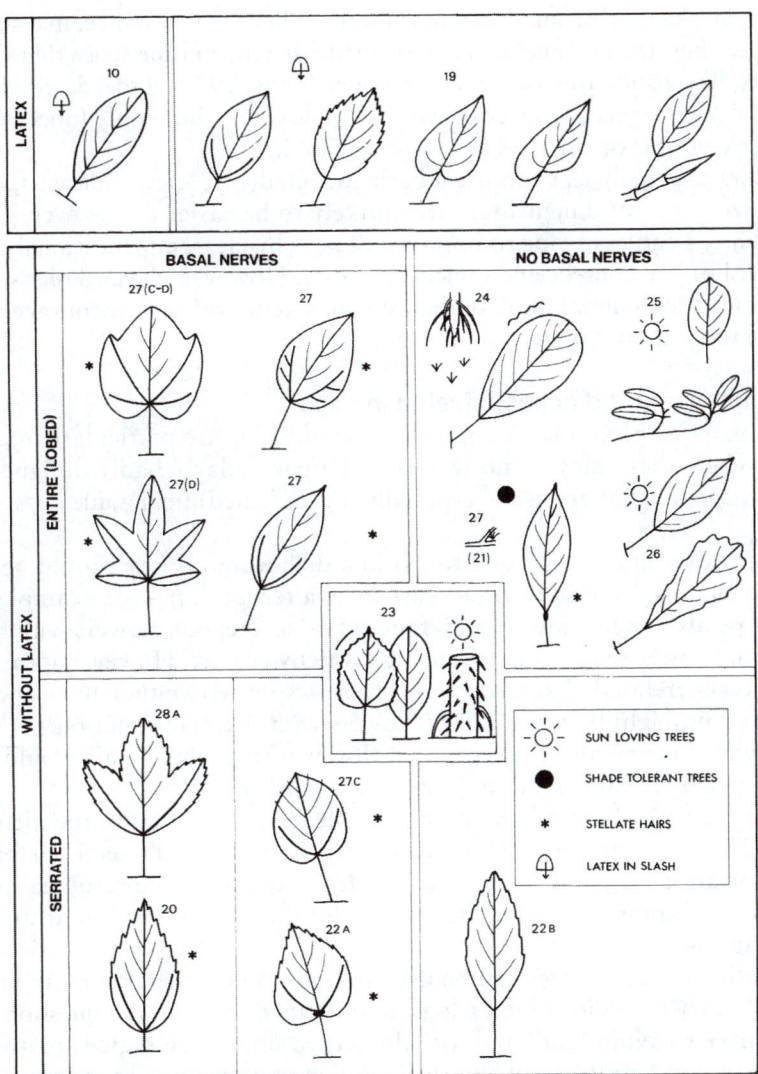

Source: Hawthorne (1990)

Figure 5.1 *Simple multi-access key to groups based on latex (top row) and leaf form*

arrangement of colour-coded information can take a significant time for the novice user to digest, and although more stylish than simpler keys, such use of colours is not necessarily easier to use than straightforward black-and-white indented or tabular keys, especially in the dim light of a rainforest understorey. Full-colour books are also much more expensive than guides with many non-colour pages.

Apart from the simplest types of table and few-species guides (for instance, Westfall et al, 1986), multi-access keys are perhaps most suitable where they are in a dynamic format – that is, where they can be mechanically manipulated or are electronic. The simplest dynamic keys are a small step beyond static keys. For instance, in a static, circular multi-access key, the arrangement can be made dynamic in the sense that the key has moving parts, like a slide rule (see circular key in Johns, 1978). Indeed, simple 'identification wheels' may have a sliding cover with a window in, whose only function is to hide information except for one species at a time (see Table 5.1i).

Most users can easily learn to use a basic indented key; 'clever' designs, and multi-access keys with several dimensions, are unlikely to be easier to use even if they save space; but there is endless scope to improve all keys by clearer, professional design and careful control of key content and logical structure. However, clever designs that avoid the old-fashioned schoolbook look of dichotomous keys probably encourage more non-botanists to take an initial interest in a field guide.

Some principles of good access design in keys

Although most principles of key design are general, some are particularly important in static keys, where there may be no way round a particularly badly designed section. Here are some points that are useful especially for (indented) field guide keys:

- Each pair of statements (or questions) in a dichotomous key should be mutually exclusive (that is, opposites, or at least strict alternatives) – for example, 'flowers with five petals' versus 'flowers with four petals' is fine; but 'flowers with five petals' versus 'blue flowers' is not fine, even if it is strictly correct. However, it can be useful to mention correlated characters to help users spot where they have gone wrong. The latter pair might be rephrased as 'flowers with five petals, not blue' versus 'blue flowers with four petals'. A user with a flower of five blue petals would therefore know they had probably made a wrong choice earlier.
- Use simple, easily observed and more reliable characters first in the identification process. There may be a conflict between easily observed and reliable characters; but it is important to try and reach a workable compromise. For tropical plant field guides, a good compromise for the 'first cut of the cake' is the leaf arrangement as outlined in Chapter 6.
- Combinations of characters can be used to make a key question more precise and reliable; but try to avoid complex logic in questions. In your key questions or statements, strive to avoid 'and' and 'or' altogether, unless the logic is really basic, in which case you should limit yourself to a maximum of one 'and' or 'or'. For example, 'flowers red or pink' is alright; but 'flowers red and white, or blue and pink' may already stretch the overheated field botanist's patience. Avoid constructs such as 'statement 1, or if not statement 1 then statement 2'.
- Never include more than two optional answers if you are using characters combined with 'and' or 'or'. When checking for errors of logic, note that if you combine two characters in one question, one option will probably include 'and' and the other should then include 'or'. Make the 'and' and 'or' stand out – for example, with bold or italics.

Although you may think your logic is easily comprehensible at your desk, even very simple questions can appear as an impenetrable fog at the end of a long hot day in the rainforest, when users are being pestered by mosquitoes and failing light. In other words, this need for logical simplicity is more of a constraint on field guide design than on herbarium keys, where generally well-ventilated users will have more time to work through such statements. It will usually be possible to restructure your key to simplify.

Bad, over-compact key
- ❶Leaves hairy, or if glabrous then not serrated — *Examplus tomentosus*
- ❶Leaves without hairs and serrated — *E. serratus*

Longer but clearer key
- ❶Leaves without hairs
  - ❷Leaves serrated — *Examplus serratus*
  - ❷Leaves entire — *E. tomentosus* (below)
- ❶Leaves hairy — *E. tomentosus*

Limit the number of choices of answer for any one question to two (the classic 'dichotomous design') unless there is a good reason for more. Users may not notice the third or subsequent options, and even if they do, choosing one of three is often far more taxing than choosing one of two. There are cases where this point does not apply, as follows.

One situation that justifies more than two options is where more than two options are exactly 'compatible', referring to a categorical character with a few distinct states (such as leaf arrangement):

Slightly awkward design
- ❶Flowers not red
  - ❷Flowers blue — *Exampla coerulea*
  - ❷Flowers white — *E. albida*
- ❶Flowers red — *E. rubra*

Box 5.9 Efficient key characters for a given point in a key

The most efficient key (MEK) characters for a given point in the key are those that split the remaining species into groups of equal number, ultimately enabling identification with the fewest steps. This is best illustrated for dichotomous keys, where MEK characters split the remaining taxa into two halves. So, if a dichotomous key is made of successive MEK characters, one character is needed to differentiate two taxa, two characters for four species, three characters for eight species, and so on. Define ten characters correctly, and you find your plant among 1024. In this context, the worst key characters overall are those that are only found in a single taxon – we call these 'fingerprint characters' if they uniquely define species and occur in all of a large set of them: 1023 fingerprint characters might have to be examined (or answered 'yes/no') to differentiate 1024 species in the worst case. Infrequently, unless very common species are listed first, users might hit the right species after considering just one or two fingerprint characters, but the 10 MEK character route is much faster, on average. Fingerprint characters (for example, bark slash pattern) can, however, be ideal as the focus for structured browsing if they can be arranged in a reasonable sequence (for example, more to less fibrous). In this sense, browsable characters could be thought of as the 1024 possibilities for a single key question of a polychotomous key. Compromises between two, or more, choices, browsing pictures and reading about characters, analysis or recognition have to be considered together.

Better design
  ❶Flowers red   *E. rubra*
  ❶Flowers blue   *E. coerulea*
  ❶Flowers white   *E. albida*

Arrange for key steps to divide into subgroups of similar size (see Box 5.9); but learn when picking off one species at a time is the best solution.

Here are the three occasions when halving the species with each choice is far from ideal – that is, when you should consider ignoring the two rules of dividing into equal groups and of keeping the key dichotomous:

1   To make the subsequent subdivisions clearer, you may want to get species that are particularly distinctive, yet variable, 'out of the way' so that they do not have to appear in both branches of subsequent questions. In this example, losing a species with very variable petiole lengths makes the subsequent divisions easier:

      ❶Plant with red leaves
         ❷(petiole 1–10cm long)   *Species c*
      ❶Plant with green leaves
         ❷Petiole < 2cm long
            ❸   *Species d*
            ❸   *Species e*
         ❷Petiole > 5cm long
            ❸   *Species f*
            ❸   *Species g*

2   In 'difficult' groups, species may differ by subtle differences in several characters combined. In these cases, it may be safer and easier, however tedious, to 'pick off' species one by one: in effect, the user reads a list until they reach an answer. Similarly, you may choose to list 'fingerprint characters' where every species is unique in some distinctive character, especially if associated pictures that are opposite the key can be browsed in tandem (for example, 'Choose shape from the list and from the accompanying illustrations of shapes A–Z', rather than 'shape A: not shape A, shape B: not shape B, etc.').

3   Try and pick off commoner species first: users may then rarely have to answer the subsequent questions. If one species is much commoner than all the rest, it is worth using the otherwise awkward construct of the type in the key below.

      ❶Large canopy tree with steep buttresses;   *Triplochiton scleroxylon*
         leaf lobes divided to halfway … more
         details … very common …
      ❶Not *Triplochiton*: description otherwise
         ❷(Key to less common species starts)
            ❸   *Species a*
            ❸   *Species b*
         ❷   *Species c*

Most beginners will correctly identify their (common) tree with the first question, and most experienced users will know *Triplochiton*, and will therefore ignore the first question.

Make retracing steps (to previous questions) easy in a key; facilitate trial and error, and support the 'what if' approach to identification that most users use when confronted with difficult questions in keys.

In the case of electronic designs, a web browser or document with hyperlinks, this simply requires a 'back' button: a major advantage of electronic media over their printed equivalent, one would assume, although they are not always used well. For static keys, a strictly hierarchical arrangement of questions – where a question can only be arrived at from one previous question, rather than a web-like arrangement, with questions being arrived at from more than one possible previous question – will greatly help users to retrace their steps if they need to. Indented keys are better in this sense than numbered ones because it is easy to find the previous, less indented option. Although you can put the 'return to' numbers in numbered keys, they are awkward and often confusing (see Table 5.1d).

Make the structure of the keys and guide logical and memorable so that users can learn to recognize and jump straight to particular groups or sub-groups. If the groups correspond to plant families or genera, then there will be educational benefit to be gained through regular use of static formats.

In some types of guide book the keys are fully integrated with the species descriptions (see, for example, Hawthorne, 1990; Ribeiro et al, 1999; Hawthorne and Jongkind, 2006), rather than the keys in one place and the descriptions and pictures in another. This saves space by reducing cross-references and the need to repeat the key features in the descriptions; above all, it facilitates the ideal mixture of browsing (recognition) and key use (analysis). The keys lead directly into the descriptions of species at the end of the keys, and the species order (nature order) follows the structure of the key. The pictures that relate to the species follow the same sequence, ensuring structured browsing and, indeed, reducing the need to illustrate key questions separately. This design aspect can be planned in consultation with users (see Chapter 3).

Note that the sequence of species even in an indented key can be manipulated within reason by swivelling the sequence (usually a pair) of options at each level.

A common complaint of indented keys is that the number of levels is limited by how far you can indent the text, and that the heavily indented text is a waste of space. However, this is only a problem if you try and arrange keys to tens or hundreds of species in one block. Keys with more than one page of questions can be broken up into hierarchical groups, so the entire structure for each sub-key can be seen on one page. Hawthorne (1990) breaks indented keys to 674 trees in Ghana into groups of about 5 to 12 species, each group on one page, all illustrated on the facing page. The indentation is never more than five steps deep.

Dynamic guides and associated access methods

In dynamic guides, the order of species and other aspects of the content of a guide can be rearranged during use, or at least after initial publication, to suit different users, seasons or places (see Boxes 5.10 and 5.11).

If only the order or species content is dynamic, as in a basic ring-bound file, users can remove species that do not occur in the current patch of forest, or life forms they are not interested in, perhaps leaving a small enough number to browse (as with Hawthorne

BOX 5.10 CARDS WITH PUNCHED HOLES AND/OR OTHER INFORMATION

There are two main types of access methods based around sets of cards (which can be reshuffled) with holes punched in them. Both have novelty or educational value for a field key, although they are largely superseded by computerized multi-access keys today.

In the 'species-per-card' type, each card represents a species (or other taxon), and holes around the margin represent different characteristics, perhaps 'fleshy fruit'. If the species represented by the card does not make a fleshy fruit, the relevant hole is clipped to make it into a notch. When a pin is passed in this position through a pile of cards and lifted, only the cards that represent species with fleshy fruits are left dangling on the pin.

In the other 'character-per-card' type a single master card has all the species written out at their specific point in a matrix and each punched card represents a character state, say fleshy fruit. Holes are made in the middle of each card, at positions corresponding (on the master card) to all those species with fleshy fruits. By collecting together several cards for different character states applying to the specimen being identified, it is possible to see through the holes on the combined cards only those species that have that character combination.

Punched hole cards have been used in the past for certain types of plant identification guide (see, for example, Hansen and Rahn, 1969; Simpson and Jones, 1974; Hyland, 1982), with the species-per-card type more appealing for many field guides because species can be added as time goes by, and other notes or photographs about species can be added to the card. Keay et al (1960) appended to their tree field guide a 'numerical key', which, although usable in the static form in the book, was in a format designed to be used in a reader's home-made card index.

Although these can be satisfying to use, like a game, especially with large sets of species, one problem is that each hole can only represent a binary character. This is efficient for some characters, but less useful for multi-state characters, such as flower colour, or smell for which separate holes are needed – for example, flower blue (yes/no); flower white (yes/no). At least it is possible for a single species to have more than one possible flower colour; but there is usually only a limited amount of space for characters around the card.

Hence, species-per-card packs are best when the number of index characters is limited, and then some other method – possibly just browsing of the pictures of the species – is used for further refining the search within the selected set.

Alternatively, you could leave out the punched holes altogether. The suits (hearts, etc.) of classic playing cards can be seen as index icons, and you could design similar icons to represent leaf arrangement, for instance, with other details to separate species on each card. Such playing cards have been used to stimulate interest in plant identification rather than for field guides *per se*. For field use, we would recommend some binding to prevent the pack from becoming dispersed (see Box 5.7 and Case study 8.1, page 184).

and Gyakari's *Photoguide to the Larger Trees of Ghana's Forests* (2006) in Box 5.6). In other dynamic guides, access involves the guide responding to user input. In the most dynamic guides on computer, access and other aspects of the 'behaviour' of the guide can be indistinguishable and such programmes, customizable in many ways, will no doubt become more common.

BOX 5.11 MAIN TYPES OF DYNAMIC FORMAT GUIDES

The main types of dynamic (field) identification guides are as follows:

- *Sets of cards* – for example, with access information represented by punched holes, and/or with various types of illustration; see Box 5.10.
- *Pages in ring-bound files.* Ring binders hold together pages, while allowing for additions to or removal from the species dealt with in a field guide – for instance, to include only species for one forest, or to add newly discovered species. For the pages to be independent, a single page with two faces has to cover one species – hence, probably pictures on one side, text on the reverse – so the pictures cannot face the text without having half the guide as redundant white space. Where this is not the case (as with Thikakul, 1985), it is hard to see any advantage of a ring binding.
- *Various mechanical arrangements*, as with a slide rule, where bits of card can be slid against each other or two circular cards are rolled over each other (as in wheel guides; see Table 5.1i). Usually these will be small – in effect, a stand-alone index or access method – and therefore designed for use in conjunction with books.
- *Computer databases used as multi-access keys* – for example, a Lucid database. A few of these for particular groups of plants are available on CD-ROMs, such as Euclid for identifying 690 *Eucalyptus* spp., produced by Brooker et al (at www.anbg.gov.au/cpbr/cd-keys/Euclid/) (see Figure 5.2).

Web pages or otherwise linked HTML files or documents are designed to react to user input in a similar way to multi-access keys. Guide pages may appear different to different users – for example, with alternative languages, fonts, with more or less jargon, perhaps always including drawings rather than photographs, and so on.

Interactive computer identification and e-keys

Interactive identification on computers includes both interactive documents (including web pages) and specialized software tools built around databases and polyclaves. At the time of writing, computers are rarely ideal as methods for field use, particularly for the rural poor in the tropics; but this may become less so as the internet permeates ever-smaller tropical settlements, as wire-free links are developed, and as devices for using this information become smaller, cheaper and more capable. Meanwhile, there is some relevance to the current manual because:

- field guides do have some role in the office or laboratory;
- some field visitor centres have computers;
- static guides, especially modular ones, can be generated and printed from dynamic computer guides as well (see Box 5.13).

Get to know the intricacies of your word processor – use the hyperlinks and so on to facilitate cross-referencing of keys to groups (see Box 5.14).

Hyperlinked documents on a computer do not necessarily lead to greater accuracy or speed. However, cross-references are very useful for linking keys and other indexes to descriptions, and cross-linking species that are similar to each other, even in documents destined to be printed (see Box 5.15).

Box 5.12 Modular guides: An efficient solution to the biodiversity identification bottleneck?

A one-species-per-card identification pack that can be assembled by users to suit their interests can be called a 'modular guide'. Modular guides are dynamic field guides because the contents of the guide can be rearranged by the user. A project focused on producing modular cards would have a number of obvious benefits to the project workers, the funders and the ultimate users. The following conclusions were drawn from Forestry Research Programme (FRP) trials on the subject (see Case study 8.1, page 184):

- Usable outputs would be available from very early on in the project, and progress could be followed and used monthly as successive cards were produced. A target of about 15 to 20 species per month, averaged over a year or so, is reasonable for a researcher with assistant. It should be possible to complete a 200 species guide in a year. This incremental approach is encouraging to the guide producers, and they can get feedback on efficacy before they produce too many species in a poor format.
- Tests on the guides can easily be designed to pick out poorly performing cards – that is, those that turn out to be associated with poor identification accuracy, or which users do not like for other reasons. Cards can be added to or improved as time goes by (for example, to correct textual inaccuracies) without republishing a whole book.
- The cards have to be designed as picture based since browsing rather than analysis is to be promoted in this approach. This reduces language problems and the need to produce detailed diagnostic keys. However, for larger sets of cards (more than 20) it is useful to reduce the burden on the browsers by defining broad categories (for example, slash exudate and texture) that will always break up the set of species into groups of manageable size, no matter which species are included.
- If the infrastructure for browsing the cards is well planned, it is possible for different sorts of users to select very different sets of species, yet use the same framework – for example, a ring binder. Timber cutters might only choose cards for large trees; forest managers might select these and trees of conservation interest; forest guards might include only the species in their local forest.
- The pictures should be designed to highlight crucial details in the same position on each card. Textual keys to particularly difficult groups can be slotted into the ring binder where necessary.

Such guides are not as easily published as printed sheets, especially if incomplete sets are to be sold. For this reason, the *Photoguide to the Larger Trees of Ghana's Forest* has been published bound as a book (Hawthorne and Gyakari, 2006).

The internet *per se* may not currently be an appropriate medium for interactive tropical rainforest guides; but it is useful for distributing printable, free field guides. Such a service would, anyway, be very useful for helping tropical plant identifiers in tropical herbaria, where even static format guides are in short supply.

There are various classes of computer-based identification systems (such as expert systems, statistical classifiers and neural networks; see Webb, 1999; Ripley, 1996); but for botanists, electronic multi-access key types (e-keys) have predominated and are a natural progression from paper-based multi-access keys and especially punched hole

---

BOX 5.13 DYNAMIC FIELD GUIDES FROM DATABASES

Many readers will be familiar with 'Mail merge' features of word processors, where a template document is arranged to have some static and some variable data. The variable data area is then filled in from a separate data table when the mail merge option is run.

For instance, a form may be:

<Address>
Dear **<Name>**, I hope you are well. You owe me £ **<Debt >**,
Bank Manager

The data table might be as follows:

Address	Name	Debt
Department of Plant Sciences	William Hawthorne	500.20
Environmental Change Institute	Anna Lawrence	264.30

Personalized letters are then sent to both parties. Another report template might summarize records from the database on one sheet. In this way, the data in the letter could then be said to be 'repurposed'. This is a basic feature of all database packages (for example, Microsoft Access or Foxpro), where reports can be generated from data in various formats. Botanists may be familiar with the use of one set of data to generate herbarium labels, then checklists and so on. Today, images can also be added to the reports so that a field guide of user-definable format and content can be generated from a field guide database. This is obviously useful if you want to make field guides customized for particular areas or forests because it is a trivial matter in any database to filter out some of the records. On the other hand, compared to static formats, there is less scope for the personal touch, to optimize paper space or to allow more room for difficult species.

If the database interface is the internet, field guides can, in principle, be customized for many types of user. This approach, embryonic but developing at the time of writing, is bound to evolve over the coming years, with data exchange potentially facilitated by the formal separation of style from information using XML (World Wide Web Consortium, 2002). Ideas vary from simple production of sheets with pictures and text to full use of the internet, with cross-linked databases and shared resources.

Further information can be found from the Openkey (www.isrl.uiuc.edu/ ~telenature/about/index.html#openkey), Hopscotch (www.hopscotch.ca/guides-on-demand/about.html), Enature (www.enature.com) and Bibe (www.biobrowser.org) Initiatives; and also on the Virtual Field Herbarium (http://herbaria.plants.ox.ac.uk/VFH).

---

cards (see Case study 5.1). There are at least 15 published e-key packages; but some, such as Pankey, have been superseded. Others are only available as published keys with data or, like CABIKEY and Linnaeus II, linked to publishers and may not be suitable for small research projects; so the practical choice for most field guide creators is more limited. At the moment, Lucid (see Figure 5.2) is probably the leading e-key package designed for both authors and users. See Pankhurst (1991, 1993), Bridge et al (1998) and Dallwitz et al (1998), Dallwitz (2000).

Box 5.14 Word processor files, Acrobat PDF files and indexes

Word processors are all you need to make an interactive key: web pages have many of the same features. A word processed field guide, possibly saved as Adobe Acrobat (PDF) or HTML files, can be published directly on the internet. Here are some aspects of electronic documents that can help you to make your key more interactive and information rich:

- Use tables (with invisible grid lines) to help format keys, with species names or groups aligned in a right-hand column.
- Use outline-numbered styles for the group headings. Insert cross-references (hyperlinks) where relevant from the end point in one key to the start of the next key so that users can navigate back and forth, as in web browsing.
- Create indented key levels as styles (special fonts, etc.), using a number or other symbol as the bullet to designate each level. Create styles for descriptive text and species names. Also use different colours or fonts for the different levels of indent in a key. Use of consistent styles for different types of information is helpful in itself for maintaining consistency, but should also facilitate transfer to an XML format for data exchange.
- Use the outline level functions for keys to groups (level 1), sub-groups (2) and even indentation levels within keys. Users can then collapse or expand outline levels, or navigate using the document outline.
- Create a glossary and designate the technical words in it as bookmarks or headings. You can hyperlink these words in the main text to the book mark to facilitate glossary use by people reading the document on the computer.
- For guides with many species (hundreds), create documents for large groups as separate files. You can index and interlink these documents in Word and Acrobat, so the files can be used independently or as a whole guide.
- Include references to useful websites.
- Experiment with the index functions in your word processor: it is possible to make indexes to glossary entries, and to species names, synonyms and local names without all of these alternative names necessarily being visible on the relevant page. Indexes to glossary entries can be developed as a quick, basic multi-access key.

In Acrobat PDF files, experiment with photographs that are of higher resolution than needed for printing. Users can zoom into photographs to investigate details of the plant.

Available e-keys work in a similar way, based on a matrix of characters (sometimes called 'features') or character states ('attributes') by taxa, in a database that can be sorted or queried in any order. A standard called DELTA (Description Language for Taxonomy) exists for communicating between character databases. Some programmes allow users or authors to score the characters for reliability, ease of use or interpretation, rarity, etc. The easiest characters can be considered before the more difficult. Other uncoded textual information and pictures may also be shown, and picture browsing is also more or less supported.

At the time of writing, the image browsing, zooming and related functions are much more limited than in dedicated image database software; this aspect shows the greatest

Box 5.15 Experiments on the value of interactivity in keys

In interactive documents, hyperlinks can be used extensively in a bid to facilitate identification. Surprisingly, Wright et al (1995) and Edwards and Morse (1995) found that users were slower and less accurate with a hypertext version of a key, and were more inclined to become 'trigger happy' and less likely to retrace their steps than with a paper key. Morse and Tardivel (1996) tested on zoology undergraduates a dichotomous key (with or without the hypertext links discussed below) and a multi-access key to woodlice. Multi-access keys were generally slightly slower to use than paper dichotomous keys and did not produce the right answers significantly more or less often (the overall accuracy was 74 per cent). Paper keys were associated more often with confident, but wrong, answers than electronic ones with hyperlinks.

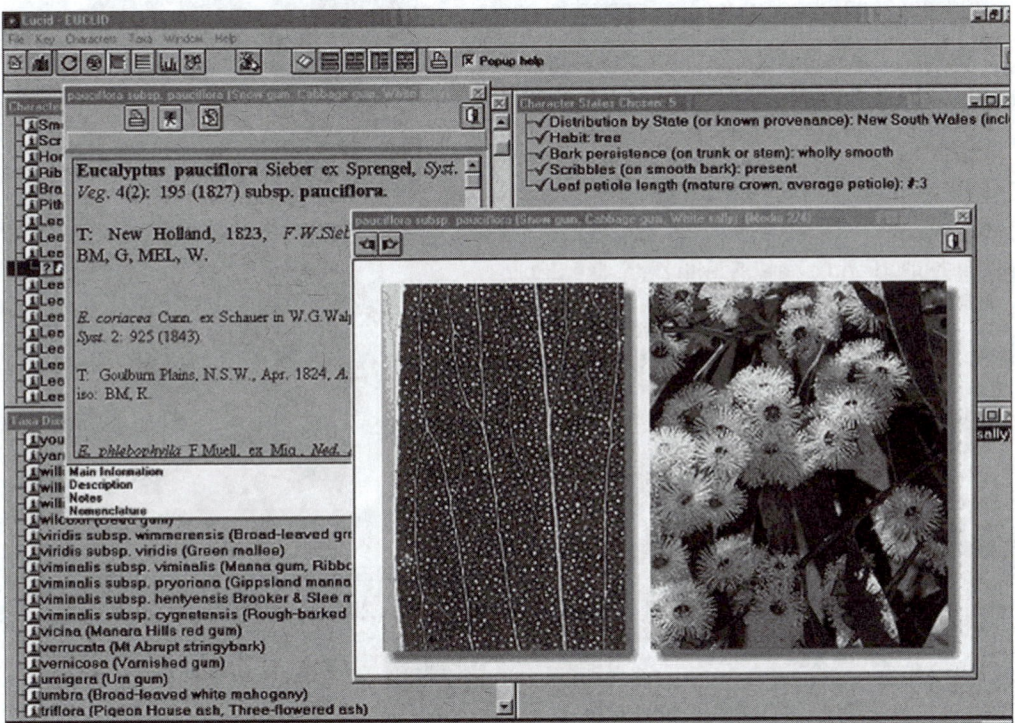

Source: from Euclid – an implementation of Lucid software with *Eucalyptus* database – see www.anbg.gov.au/cpbr/euclid/euclid.html

Figure 5.2 *Screenshot of an e-key in action*

potential for future improvement. Until then, it is an open question how far computer guides will be able to facilitate recognition-based identification, even if the computers can be taken where they are needed on a budget that is realistic for rural, tropical communities.

CASE STUDY 5.1 AUSTRALIAN RAINFOREST KEY

One of the best working examples of an interactive key for rainforest plants is Hyland and Whiffin's rainforest key, which also shows an interesting evolution from card-based polyclave to a computer-based key. In 1971, this covered 584 taxa on 80-column computer cards, with 48 bark features and 45 leaf features. This grew until 1982, when it covered 799 taxa, the limits of the cards – with the same features, but extra information added for families and geography. This was converted to a computer format in 1983 covering 1058 taxa, and this was coupled with a leaf atlas and extra computer data for flowers, fruits and seedlings. In 2000 the system had expanded to all 1733 Australian tree species in a Windows interface. By now, four people were involved. The most recent 2003 version covers shrubs and vines. Unfortunately, the system is not designed for other authors to use, unlike the Lucid system where similar packages – ready filled and available with data, like Euclid – are increasingly common.

Characters in similar software are normally defined per species; but the rainforest key is more painstakingly based on an underlying core database of specimen-level records, facilitating the update of the dataset when taxonomic opinions of the specimens shift.

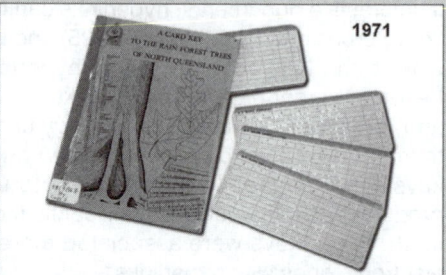

Figure 5.3 *The evolution of the Australian rainforest key*

Sources: Images reproduced by kind permission of Trevor Whiffin; text based on www.anbg.gov.au/cpbr/cd-keys/rfk/history.html

CHOOSING ACCESS METHODS AND THE MEDIUM FOR YOUR FIELD GUIDE

There are many factors to weigh when selecting the format appropriate to your needs. Here is a summary of some of the pertinent points:

- Since all user groups are different, use the consulation methods described in Chapter 3, and consider performing accuracy, confidence and other tests on your own field guide users to optimize your proposed access method (see Chapter 9) – you may well be surprised by the results.
- Critics who decry paper keys are often confusing the access method, which could hardly be simpler, with the (technical, jargon-rich, picture-less) content of traditional biological keys: 'For non-experts traditional keys are often difficult to use because a scientific language is used and illustrations are often lacking or placed elsewhere' (CABI, www.pest.cabweb.org/Identification/BIOSYS.HTM). Until computer identification systems are as cheap, robust and future proof as field guide books, traditional dichotomous keys should be the first default type of key you try out with your users.

Computer-based dynamic guides and field use

- In e-keys, users can avoid or delay questions that they cannot answer. This is particularly valuable for fieldwork, where only fragments of plants may be available. The flexibility of data display in an e-key is undoubtedly a huge boon.
- Some e-keys do allow commoner species or more important characters to be prioritized; this option is usually taken for granted in static keys; but potentially, at least, an e-key could adjust this option depending upon where you are and the species remaining. Sensitivity to user skill is another key asset in principle, although this is hard to implement. An e-key could prioritize characters based on user skill, species remaining, location, and feedback from past instances of the use of this character. This would be harder to set up, but probably worth it for e-keys with large markets. We look forward to further developments in this direction.
- Modern students are generally comfortable with the 'point-and-click' browsing approach to information, and interactive software may draw some to tropical botany if the interface seems modern, regardless of the content or actual usability. An interactive CD version of your book need only involve hyperlinks to be a useful accessory.
- If a decision is bothering you as author, or there is a conflict among potential users (Which species should I include? Should I emphasize local or Latin names?), maybe you could supply both formats, or species lists, with software 'switches' to change between them.
- Evolution of e-keys is slow compared to other software, but they do increasingly allow reasonable illustration of taxa, with multiple images, maps and textual information, to be viewed when necessary to confirm an identification by selecting the appropriate link. In book format, all of this information would soon add up to a key heavier than a portable computer.
- Dynamic computer formats will probably revolutionize field guides by making the access of information more user friendly and more flexible, even if the guide is

ultimately to be printed for field use. Sites on the internet or databases on a CD-ROM will increasingly produce guides customizable for species and geographical coverage. You can prepare for this now by collecting digital imagery and defining character databases as a prelude even for a book project, and maintaining your data and documents in as logical a format as possible.

The potential for non-computer, yet dynamic, field guides

- A printed (or printable) modular guide project (see Box 5.12) could provide a platform whereby sponsors pay per species and see them used variously in different environments; independent workers collaborate to contribute to a wide field guide effort; and users from many backgrounds can take their results and adapt them to their own need. Identification would be based largely on browsing, facilitated by a structure put into place by the consortium, and this would be useful for facilitating the international aspects of such projects.
- Modular guides and other dynamic formats can be updated without a major revision.
- Dynamic, unusual formats (like punched hole cards) often attract more interest among students whose botanical interest has yet to be turned on than, say, a static format book because they are interactive and different. As novelties, they may be more sellable than standard books. For an eco-tourist venue, think up educational games that could be built around them.

Static formats: Classic field guides are still the best option for field users

- Do not underestimate the value of a basic indented dichotomous key and crisp black text on white paper as a good access method. While they are not the most fashionable, such keys represent the clearest and an efficient way of displaying textual information for a decision tree. Multi-access keys are useful, but often over-rated: certain characters will have to be observed, anyway, if a plant is to be identified, so there is no harm in steering all users through the easiest and most reliable of these questions first, and little advantage to allowing users to avoid answering them early on in their decision-making process, as is advocated for multi-access keys.
- Books or laminated cards are mostly more practical for fieldwork in tropical forests than dynamic formats. When computers are involved with dynamic formats, the hardware may end up being less convenient, portable or affordable than a basic book. Personal digital assistants (PDAs) are not yet powerful enough (in 2006) to substitute.
- Books do not need technical support and are 'future proof'. Computers consume bench space and require air conditioning and a reliable and protected power supply. They are likely to be hijacked for other uses.
- Book users need less training than computer users, especially if they are not comfortable with computers. The layout of a book is globally well understood.
- The more familiar printed medium suits the purpose of many authors adequately, earns more academic credit and works during power cuts. Dynamic formats are currently harder to publish for scientific citation. If you are a scientist or are working with one, their future employment may well depend upon the production

of easily peer-reviewed publications in a static format. This will presumably change as more information is published electronically.

- In educational terms, the lack of a rigid structure engendered by dynamic formats might make learning of the plant groups harder. Some e-keys allow characters to be prioritized for ease of use, or reliability, even though users can choose to ignore the recommended next best question. If one encourages complete flexibility of identification path, the benefits associated with learning a taxonomic structure, or at least memorizing where certain types of species are to be found in a field guide, will be reduced.

- More information is needed for a complete data matrix for an interactive key than for a static dichotomous key, as all possible routes to an answer have to be planned for; yet, not all character states are even worth codifying for all species, and missing field data is normal for rare species, but can usually be steered round in a static key. Dynamic keys often therefore involve more unnecessary work and non-botanical skills to produce than static guides.

- E-keys often (allow authors to) rank the best characters to use, including those with multiple states. Because the author will not, in general, know the context that the character will appear in, nor the other species that will be possibilities when the question is to be addressed, this can be harder to optimize than with a static key.

- There is a danger that machine-customized field guides look somewhat uninspiring, like automated catalogues. Designers of static guides can tweak the format to suit the species and users.

CONCLUSIONS

Interactive guides or keys have several major advantages over conventional guides; but they are not replacements: at the moment they cannot easily be taken into the field and more people potentially have access to books than computers. However, with the software available it is possible to produce an interactive guide as a secondary output with little overhead when the primary output is a published guide in book form. Why not create both a static and dynamic field guide (for example, a CD-ROM or website accompanying a book)? A realistic target for a computer guide that helps field botany is to support the use of field and sterile characters for identifying specimens. But beware – there is a danger that the computer component of the work will consume disproportionate resources.

Modular guides and structured browsing can work well, and have other advantages for managers of field guide projects, and especially sponsors seeking efficient solutions for plant identification in the tropics.

Facilitate browsing for and within groups of distinctive species; but if parts of your guide deal with difficult species, list characters and make a key for them. Keys are difficult to plan for in modular guides; so it might be best if one key to all species is made for all species of a difficult genus in the modular guide, and the local implementers of the modules are helped to create keys to the fewer local species.

For difficult groups, dichotomous keys work well – and well-planned indented keys are clearer than numbered ones. Ask your users what they think, after some practice. You may be able to devise simple multi-access tables if the defining characters are simple; but they are not necessarily any easier to use or more efficient than dichotomous ones, however succinct and satisfying they are to the guide authors. Test your key with a sample of the users (Chapter 9), before finalizing it, to be sure.

Do not expect to necessarily be able to model your guide on expert skills; but by all means see what range of characteristics various experts look at, smell or taste in their own identification. Go hunting for characters both in the field and in the herbarium that no one before you has found, to make your access methods as foolproof as possible. It is these characters that are covered in Chapter 6.

6

Plant characters suitable for field guides

William Hawthorne

INTRODUCTION

Plant characters were introduced in Chapter 5 as the foundation of botanical identification. In this chapter we focus on field characters that tend to be most useful in tropical forest field guides. But due to limited space, the chapter can only be an aperitif: many more topics, specific examples and details are explained on our linked website (see Box 1.1). Just a few common sample cases are included, biased strongly towards woody plants that dominate rainforests; but the principles and tips for field guide writers that these illustrate are generally applicable (see Box 6.1)

Field characters are generally less well understood, with less standardized terminology, than the classical fertile or anatomical characters that form the backbone of most other botanical publications; but there is no shortage of relevant jargon. Out of the jungle of myriad structures and terms, you have to find a set that are understandable and observable by your prospective users, and that are, at the same time, useful from a diagnostic point of view. In some cases, you will have few decisions to make, especially when dealing with distinctive groups – grasses, palms, bamboos, mistletoes, orchids and so on – for which monographs highlight the useful and often rather unusual or specialized field characters you need to know. For instance, for cacti, you will probably refer to size and shape of the plant, spines and stem ridges, no matter what form your guide takes. In other cases, including most woody rainforest plants, you have more choice of characters to focus on.

Classical characters can certainly not be ignored when considering the preparation of a field guide; but there is no need to cover them all here. Just read the glossary of your local Flora or botanical website. Stearn (1966), Harris and Harris (1994) and others in the References section have provided well-illustrated glossaries for classic characters (see Box 6.2).

Beyond the essential words for your own field guide, it is important to understand jargon in order to make good use of botanical literature, and to understand where published information is compromised due to lack of clear standards about its meaning.

BOX 6.1 FIELD CHARACTERS AND CLASSICAL CHARACTERS

A field character is one that is useful for identifying a plant living in nature without special equipment (hand lens, bush knife, binoculars, catapults and other field equipment excepted), in all seasons and potentially for plants of any age. Some field characters are also useful for identifying sterile herbarium specimens.

The classical school botany lexicon – from *Abaxial* to *Zygomorphic* – represents the basics of the scientific tradition of botany, but is far from ideal as your only source of characters for field guides. It is the language that describes the characters used by taxonomists, anatomists, morphologists and other indoor botanists: characters we call 'classical' here to contrast with the field characters on which field guide writers have to concentrate.

As we pointed out in Chapter 4, most plant names are defined with respect to classical characters of pressed, dried herbarium specimens – usually seasonal details of flowers and fruit – and this bias diffuses into Floras and other botanical literature; but field guide writers should not follow the trend uncritically.

There is considerable overlap between field and classical characters and no possibility of dividing them into two exclusive sets. Some characters – for example, leaf type and arrangement – are useful in all circumstances. However, the emphasis with respect to how these ever-useful characters are described depends upon where they are to be used. For instance, it is reasonable to provide greater detail on leaf venation in a field guide than in a Flora because for fieldwork it is more likely that a sterile plant will have to be identified. Flower details in a field guide might focus more on the superficial characters, such as colour and size of the whole flower, whereas the Flora might concentrate on numbers of stamens or ovules and other 'deep', but more obscure, characters with a more fundamental and global significance.

BOX 6.2 AN UNFORTUNATE DIVERSITY OF JARGON FOR CLASSICAL CHARACTERS

Even 40 years ago, you could have filled a small library with literature whose sole purpose was to define words for biologists. The Systematics Association (1960) made a list of about 350 'authoritative' publications of this type. The choice is bewildering; but the situation is particularly difficult for field characters of tropical plants, which tend to have been dealt with less meticulously than classical characters. A major problem is that glossaries of botanical terms frequently contradict each other or exclude some vital, modern standards of botanical description, even where the standards do exist. For example, there has been an attempt to make words used by botanists for outline shapes (such as leaf or petal shape) more precise by defining ratios of length/breadth for each term (Systematics Association, 1962); but these are missing from widely used glossaries by Harris and Harris (2000), Bell (1991) and several others published or re-edited since the standards were set, and many writers use the terms with their older, imprecise meanings (see also Jackson, 1928).

Be circumspect and critical of others' choices of terminology, and define with your users the jargon to use in your field guide without confusing the standard terms that are well accepted (see Box 6.2, and see Chapter 3 for methods).

> ## BOX 6.3 OTHER REVIEWS OF FIELD CHARACTERS FOR TROPICAL FORESTS
>
> There are a few previous overviews of a wide range of useful field characters for tropical plants. Rosayro (1953) discussed field characters for tropical tree identification, for instance, and Wyatt-Smith (1954) also tried to standardize terms for Malayan trees. Letouzey (1986) has reviewed more classical characters, albeit in a user-friendly way: these and similar treatments border on generic or family field guides, discussed in Chapter 4. In fact, for many purposes, the best general reviews are in the introductions or glossaries of actual field guides.
>
> Keller's (1996) book on vegetative characters is one of the very few general overviews that even attempts fully to review tropical forest field characters, alongside many characters that are of little use in the field but which enable plants to be identified without flowers and fruits. Perhaps rather ambitiously, Keller's book is, in part, a key to tropical plant families or other large groups. It makes few concessions to amateurs, using a full gamut of jargon, albeit mostly well illustrated, and requiring microscopic or careful analysis of detail. But this is still an interesting and original vegetative guide to plant family identification. For certain field characters, particularly tree architectural models, it provides a useful illustrated reference, and writers of technical field guides will benefit by trying to work through the keys with proposed guide users, if only to show which types of character are practical. The 1996 edition is very far from complete with respect to tropical plant families; but hopefully it represents a work in progress.
>
> Similarly highly detailed, almost encyclopaedic, but not always practical or complete sources for field characters are Metcalfe and Chalk's botanical classic (1979, and other editions and volumes, especially volume 1), Metcalfe (1988) and Keating et al (2003, likewise in several volumes).

Because many standard botanical works, and certainly original species descriptions, underplay field characters, field guide writers should discover and publicize, rather than simply précis, published information.

The following section and the associated web page (http://herbaria.plants.ox.ac.uk/VFH) will help you to decide which jargon to use and to make definitions in a working glossary for your own purposes. Find out if your prospective users understand these terms after an acceptable learning period. Your glossary should be one of the first products of your field guide project (after the species checklist) and distributed to co-authors as a list of allowed jargon. Make your definitions precise enough, with copious illustrations so that you and your co-writers and readers can follow it strictly. You may, however, need to refine it as your research progresses.

Jargon: When 'pyriform' goes 'pear-shaped'

It is tempting for the radical field guide writer to avoid all jargon as it can be off-putting to casual users and students:

- Translate jargon: field guide writers are the interface between the public and academia. They are therefore more obliged than other botanists to translate jargon to normal language wherever appropriate; but also to educate readers where necessary.

- Some jargon can be substituted with illustrations (for example, of shapes), a good reason to make profuse use of illustrations. The conciseness afforded by specialist words is of no benefit if those words also put users off using the field guide.
- Some jargon terms are hardly necessary in any type of botanical literature, let alone a user-friendly field guide.

However, while not all botanical terms will be appropriate in your field guide, many unfamiliar words that are not often heard on the high street will have a useful role. Like scientific nomenclature (see Chapter 4), one of the advantages of jargon over common language is that jargon words can be given very specific fixed meanings by scientists and others who depend upon precision – for instance, apiculate is more precise than pointed, and tomentose or puberulous are more specific terms for hairy. Learn to judge when hairy suffices, or perhaps when tomentose increases the fitness of your guide for its purpose. However much you like plain words, surely you wouldn't think of removing 'tree buttressed' in favour of 'tree non-cylindrical at base, with triangular outgrowths supporting the tree' throughout your guide? Some jargon is almost indispensable for keeping your field guide short and light – and the weight of a field guide book is likely to be a major design constraint.

- 'Good' jargon is concise and highlights the crucial features in a description, forming a simpler mental picture and therefore making the point stand out, much as a diagram does in the pictorial world.
- Even if you are illustrating profusely, you may have to explain certain points with words. For instance, in an 'incomplete set' guide (see Chapter 4), you may want to explain in a footnote, without a picture, how a rare plant differs from the common one illustrated. Rarely encountered species may justify usage of unfamiliar terminology.
- One of the fieldworker's advantages over the herbarium botanist which you should exploit is that there is greater scope to explore in the field the limits of variable characters, comparing leaves on shade shoots, old branches and so on that rarely find their way into the herbarium.
- When discarding jargon, do not 'throw out the baby with the bathwater'. Egg-shaped is not the same as the more precise ovate (in the proper usage of ovate), and ovate is a shorter word, so is potentially better for use in a field guide for both reasons. An illustration may show one example of an ovate leaf, but the word allows for a range of shapes. You can define such words in a short glossary inside your front cover; this will make the whole guide more concise and accurate for almost all users, even if the text appears slightly less friendly to some.
- Do not exclude jargon, fine details or other technicalities just because a focus group says that they do not like or understand it the first time they see it. People are initially 'shy' of new concepts and small details – the sort only visible with a good hand lens; but field botanists rely on them. Most amateurs soon discover a universe of interest in the fine print of plant life, and it is this factor above all – attention to small detail – that separates good from unreliable field botanists. However, do exclude small details and disliked words when you are sure that they are not needed for reliable identification.

CASE STUDY 6.1 JARGON LEVELS IN THREE FIELD GUIDES

Consider three field guides produced recently showing how one author and colleagues have attempted to resolve the need for conciseness with user ability:

1   *Photoguide to the Larger Trees of Ghana's Forest* (Hawthorne and Gyakari, 2005): an identification guide targeted at farmers and others from rural backgrounds, possibly seeking employment as tree-spotters or eco-tourist guides. The book was designed around photographs of bark and other whole tree features. The basic key to bark groups includes words such as 'latex' and 'gritty'; but it was envisaged that those unable to read the English could, in any case, be taught by non-governmental organizations (NGOs) or forestry staff to recognize the groups and browse the pictures. Twenty minutes of explanation on our trials proved sufficient for many to reach 80 per cent accuracy.

2   *Caribbean Spice Island Plants* (Hawthorne et al, 2006): a guide to Grenadian plants, designed for secondary or higher education, eco-tourists (as a commodity to be sold by tour guides and also for identification), and English-literate but non-botanical Grenadian tour guides, foresters, conservationists, etc. The book is heavily picture based, so it can be used to some degree regardless of jargon. Most of the text is dominated by usage, folklore and historical information with little botanical jargon, but with some chemical or medical terms. Brief descriptions for the keener readers (in a small font) use words such as inflorescence and corolla, but leaf stalk and flower stalk instead of petiole and pedicel. Venation patterns are described by photographs. Slash details are not covered, and descriptions are limited to latex because this can be found in cut twigs. Keys use more jargon, explained in a glossary, but should be limited enough to intrigue the curious, while not putting off the casual browser.

3   *The Woody Plants of Western African Forests: A Guide to the Forest Trees, Shrubs and Lianes from Senegal to Ghana* (Hawthorne and Jongkind, 2005): for technical users to identify any of 2140 species of tree, shrub and climber in West African forests, and others needing a reference of African plant names or pictures. Many technical users might have limited prior knowledge of botany, but should be able to use the book as the basis for learning, in herbaria or on field trips, but probably not often while walking in the forest. More than 5000 illustrations (drawings and photographs) are provided to help interpretation of jargon; but keys use many technical words for conciseness. For leaf arrangement and form, words such as petiole, petiolule, rachis, mucronate and scalariform were indispensable. Bark and bole characters are explained in detail, and include gritty, latex, resin and concave/convex buttresses. For distinguishing closely related species or in family descriptions, words such as disc, corona, cystolith and androgynophore are explained and used within certain groups. Words such as megaphanerophyte and campylodromous are avoided completely.

The level of jargon should therefore be tailored to the skills of your proposed users, possibly making the content slightly more jargon rich than they feel comfortable with at first sight (see Case study 6.1).

An interactive and more comprehensive glossary on the Virtual Field Herbarium (see Box 1.1, page 6) uses the definitions provided in Table 6.1.

Table 6.1 *Jargon level: How unnecessary is that word or phrase?*

Undesirability, in terms of cost/benefit	Examples	The desirability of using these words in your field guide
0 Generally desirable	Ovate; acute; bark; buttress; leaf blade; leaf stalk; petal; corolla; fruit; buttress; lateral nerve; kidney-shaped; sand-papery	There is almost no scope to ignore these words in any field guide unless you are explaining everything with pictures, or you want to substitute these merely unusual, but concise, words for mealy-mouthed imprecise sentences.
1 Often reasonable in a user-friendly guide	Petiole; petiolule; lenticel; bole; 3° venation; rhizome; scabrid; saprophyte; small serrations; mucronate	Any field guide user with some technical or school background can make good use of these words with little ambiguity; but you may still be able to do without them in some field guides.
2 Technical, concise	Reniform; secund; serrulate; Corner's model; mucronulate	Unless your field guide is for boffins – for example, a 'pragmatic' Flora used only by other scientists – or needs to be short on illustrations for weight or expense reasons, you should rephrase these words, and there is generally a good substitute.
3 Undesirably technical	Suberous (use corky); fistulose (hollow or pipe-like); complanate (flattened); trichome (be specific)	Avoid these words: although they are sometimes used by botanists, they are ambiguous and/or synonymous with a simpler word or short phrase. There is a better way of saying or showing the same thing in your field guide.

Source: William Hawthorne

CHARACTERS OF YOUNGER STEMS AND LEAVES

The young plant shoots – that is, young stems (sometimes called branchlets or twigs) – and the fresh leaves, stipules and bud scales that they support are most important for identifying virtually any type of plant: large or small, young or old, woody or not. Such details almost always deserve a prominent place in your field guide, even if only as descriptive text; many examples are on http://herbaria.plants.ox.ac.uk/VFH, but some important examples follow.

Describing hairiness on leaves or other (generally young) parts

There are very many terms for hairs, both for individual hairs and the covering ('indumentum') they constitute (Payne, 1978; Theobald et al, 1979), and their general importance for distinguishing related species, even when flowers are available, can hardly be overemphasized.

Trichome is a general term including hairs, scales, colleters, superficial prickles and other hair-like outgrowths of the epidermis, without vascular tissue (Hewson, 1988). Trichome and colleter can usually be avoided in non-technical field guides (use hair(s) or

Table 6.2 *Definition by various authors of some hair-related terms*

	Hirsute	Hispid	Villous	Pubescent
Payne (1978)	Long, rather stiff	Long, very stiff	Long, soft, curly, not matted	With trichomes; or hairy, with soft hairs
Hewson (1988)	Coarse, long hairs	Long, erect, rigid hairs or bristles, harsh to touch	Long, soft, weak hairs, the covering somewhat dense	Somewhat dense cover of short, weak, soft hairs
McCusker (1999)	Coarse, rough relatively long	Stiff bristly	Shaggy, long, weak	Short, soft, erect
Harris and Harris (1994)	Coarse, stiff	Rough, firm, stiff	Long, shaggy but unmatted	Covered with short soft hairs; or any hairs
General	Both terms imply rough hairy, with longer hairs than 'scabrid', but hirsute–hispid distinction varies		Not matted; some say straight, some curly, some allow appressed hairs	Some use it for any sort of hairiness

scales, etc., as appropriate). Even the word 'hairy' can be ambiguous, as some people use it to mean a surface with even a single hair on it, or a fine coating of microscopic hairs; but others use it only for surfaces that are obviously hairy all over, to touch. The terms villous, pubescent and tomentose among many others have also been used ambiguously, so such terms must always be defined in a glossary in your field guide if you want them to be useful. It seems that most botanists have fairly precise definitions of such terms in their own minds; but these do not necessarily align very closely with the concepts of other botanists.

Two of the most used reference works, Harris and Harris (1994), a simpler one, and Hewson (1988) differ in some of the details. Hewson's short handbook is more thorough, but also complex, and goes into much detail – for example, about how the individual cells are arranged – that is of little use in a field guide.

Hairs can be produced on all living surfaces, and the indumentum on different parts of one plant is often similar and diagnostic. However, they generally disappear, becoming bald (glabrous) with age; so try to specify the indumentum for recently formed parts. Your users may be expected to have access to fresh, young foliage, whereas taxonomists may consider the indumentum on leaves excessively variable because in the herbarium there is less chance of specifying age or relative position of leaves. In many cases, where a taxonomist might refer to the indumentum of the calyx or pedicel in a Flora, you may be able to substitute the indumentum of youngest shoots, apical bud or petioles in your field guide.

In a technical field guide to many species it is useful to be as precise as possible about the form, length, density, colour and pattern of location of hairs or scales, even more so than in the Floras and monographs. Indumentum tends to change with altitude and habitat, so monographers will often see no merit in describing details very precisely for wide-ranging and variable species. But you may be in a position to be more specific.

Glands and similar details

The word gland covers a multitude of details in a plant, secreting water, nectar, oils and other substances. These are among the most useful of fine details to examine in certain families, and almost no value in others. A full review for West African plants is given by Hawthorne and Jongkind (2006).

There is a natural tendency when collecting specimens, taking photographs or making field notes of fresh shoots to sweep away and disregard ants and their associated debris, as well as other insects. Think again – maybe your plant always has these features and you could count them among its field characteristics? In any case, they may well indicate the presence of glands (extra-floral nectaries).

Strong scent in the Annonaceae, Myrtaceae, Rutaceae and other families is generally indicated visually by the presence of oil-producing 'glandular hairs' or dot-like oil pockets in the leaf tissue.

Glands and other small structures on leaves and young shoots represent an area where, by exploration with a good lens, even in a herbarium, you are likely to discover previously undocumented field characters.

Leaf types and arrangement:
The primary questions in most field guides

The most useful characters when first trying to identify a higher plant in the field are, as a rule, the leaf type and arrangement. These divide plants into useful groups of families and are usually available. There are, of course, exceptions – opposite-leaved species in alternate-leaved families; or simple leaves in plants from predominantly compound-leaved families, such as the mango amongst the golden apples and other Anacardiaceae; even old leaves or leaf scars may be hard to find in leafless deciduous trees or high in the canopy. Nevertheless, leaf type and arrangement are the most common choice for the first subdivision of the species list in keys in field guides (see Chapter 5) to tropical plants, wherever many families of plants are involved. But the difference between simple and compound leaves involves more than one line of definition. It is therefore a crucial judgement to make when planning the access method or arrangement in your guide if it is to be used by complete amateurs (see Box 6.4).

You are not fully informing your readers if they do not end up understanding fundamental differences between types of plants, such as whether they have simple or compound leaves. If your field guide is appealing enough otherwise, a small learning period should be acceptable to most users.

Non-technical guides might avoid the problem of defining different types of leaf by showing pictures of each category, and not describing technical differences in words.

Compound leaves present other dilemmas in a field guide because the jargon can be confusing, and fieldworkers may only be able to retrieve a single leaflet from the canopy:

- The numbers of leaflets, or leaflet pairs or pinnae, on a compound leaf is useful in a field guide; but herbarium specimens of fertile branches will rarely show the shade or sapling leaves of a tree, which almost always have a different number of leaflets than sun leaves (see Box 6.5). In Meliaceae, Rutaceae and Sapindaceae, pinnate-leaved species often produce simple or trifoliolate seedlings, rising to a maximum leaflet number in shaded 'adolescent' saplings, then declining again on exposed adults.

BOX 6.4 ISSUES WITH SIMPLE AND COMPOUND LEAVES

For simple, non-technical guides, one may question whether it is worth labouring the casual reader with the detailed differences between compound and simple leaves. If you have decided to base your guide on a few species of flowers, for instance, then you may not need to discuss finer details of leaf arrangement – just illustrate them. However, whenever a large number of plant families are to be included in your guide, leaves are likely to be obtainable or visible for many of them: you need an exceptional reason not to emphasize the leaf arrangement.

In field tests in Grenada (see Case study 8.1, page 184) we found that non-botanists could usually match pictures of whole compound or simple leaves to real plants, without any textual assistance at all. At the other extreme, even experienced botanists make mistakes with exceptional cases – the apparently compound leaves of some *Phyllanthus* and *Panda*, for example, and the confusion caused by a compound leaf having an apical growing tip (suggesting a stem with simple leaves) as in *Guarea* and *Dysoxylum* species – these are the difficult exceptions, not the easily graspable rule. Take precautions to catch such easily made errors. Read through any keys you have made; but put yourself in the shoes of a beginner and imagine you have erred. Then place notes in the appropriate part of the wrong side of the key. Work out where the user would end up in the key if the *Phyllanthus* branch was perceived as a compound leaf and place a note there.

Also, beware of the common confusion between similar terms. The axis of a compound leaf is divided into two parts: the rachis is the part beyond the first leaflet; the petiole is the part below it. There is usually no other visible distinction or cut-off line between the petiole and rachis, and the separate terms therefore often cause confusion, particularly as many users are also prone to confuse the word petiole with petiolule, the stalk of each individual leaflet. It may be useful to clarify this in keys wherever the question is critical – for example, 'Petiole (stalk of the whole compound leaf) < 2cm long.'

BOX 6.5 SEEDLING GUIDES

Seedlings, short unbranched stems with only cotyledons and no adult leaves, present particular challenges (Duke, 1969). Their presence in a particular area of forest is often ephemeral. To make a good seedling guide, it is normally necessary to collect seeds from adults that are identified and vouchered in the normal way, and to germinate these in a nursery. Hence, purely seedling guides are seldom available and often not called for, except for problem weeds of agricultural land, where early recognition is vital. In many guides, seedling characters are included alongside adult details (for example, Taylor, 1960; Hyland et al, 2002). Seedlings can be photographed as a whole, or scanned or pressed, dried and laminated on card easily (see Chapter 8). Published seedling guides for agricultural weeds (many can be found on the internet; search with key words 'weed seedling identification') are mostly based on single, detailed photographs for each species, with perhaps some notes on key points to look for.

Even if you do not include all seedlings in your field guide, it is useful to illustrate seedlings for species (usually shade-bearing ones) that characteristically have profuse regeneration in their vicinity. The seedlings in these cases are like field characters of the adjacent adult plant, and will help to confirm or refute initial diagnoses.

- If your users expect your guide to work for saplings, do not underestimate how much fieldwork it takes to record the sapling details for compound leaves accurately and to modify any herbarium-based description. You will have to identify the saplings by finding and linking all stages between sapling and adult. Try not to base keys on leaflet numbers when saplings have to be identified as well. Other features such as glands, venation and hairs are usually more constant.
- In bipinnate leaves with many small leaflets (for example, *Acacia*, *Piptadeniastrum* and *Parkia*), the individual leaflets or even pinnae often vary little as the plant grows up (the leaflets are often only slightly larger in the shade); but the total number of pinnae and size of leaf typically varies more.
- Check carefully whether the leaflets on a pinnate leaf are precisely paired and opposite or sometimes slightly unpaired. The closely paired arrangement with no terminal leaflet (absolutely paripinnate) occurs more commonly in legumes than the type of 'paripinnate' leaf where the leaflets are not quite opposite (that is, sub-opposite).
- Be careful to indicate what type of 'imparipinnate' leaf you mean when specifying pinnate leaves with some unpaired leaflets – are the leaflets precisely paired with one unpaired leaflet on the end (paired + 1), almost paired +1, or alternate? Species with sub-opposite leaflets common on herbarium specimens are frequently found in nature to possess juvenile or shade leaves where the leaflets are unpaired to the point of being alternate (or with only one leaflet).
- The terminology associated with bipinnate or tripinnate leaves where lobing occurs on some leaflets and not others is complicated; but these characteristics are easy to demonstrate with silhouette-type diagrams, easily made with a scanner and easily converted to small monochrome diagrams (see Figure 8.1).
- In other cases, it is useful to illustrate large compound leaves with a full view of the whole leaf at one scale and a single leaflet with more detail shown closer to the camera or artist.

Leaf shape and margin

Characters such as leaf shape and margin are amply catered for by virtually all botany textbooks, dictionaries, Floras and so on (see Figure 6.1). Rather few words are routinely used to describe the shape of a leaf, and although it is generally much more desirable to include a picture of leaf shape than words, a few shape terms are useful in even a non-technical field guide – for example, in a guide to an incomplete set of species – to describe a rarer unillustrated relative that differs in leaf shape. However, even these terms are used inconsistently (see Box 6.6). Software developers have not yet achieved an ideal way of indexing shape, although this is likely to happen soon – and this will revolutionize pictorial e-keys (see Box 6.7).

Marginal details such as teeth and lobes are very important in most field guides. For a useful manual primarily for workers on fossil leaves see the Leaf Architecture Working Group (LAWG, 1999), where it is pointed out that the most reliable characters of a leaf are entire versus serrated margins, lobing, and primary and secondary venation. For non-technical field guides, it is enough to distinguish lobed, serrated (toothed) and crenate from entire margins; but one can specify much finer detail, preferably with illustrations, to distinguish subtly different types of tooth for species that are hard to distinguish.

Box 6.6 What exactly is egg-shaped?

Consider the words ovate (egg-shaped) and lanceolate (lance or spear-head shaped). Both of these have been defined for botanists (Systematics Association, 1962; followed by Stearn, 1966, and many others) as shapes broadest below the middle, the ovate with a length/breadth ratio of between 2:1 and 3:2 – in other words, shapes between twice as long as wide and one and half times as long as wide. Alternatives such as (very) widely ovate can approach 1:1 – that is, almost round but still broadest before the middle. Lanceolate leaves are much more slender, at 6:1 to 3:1. This still leaves open to question what to call a shape between 6:3 (= 2:1) and 6:2 (= 3:1). More serious is the fact that many people still use the ambiguous 'egg-shaped' definition, while accepting some very dubious shapes of eggs. Compare the *Flora of Australia* glossary distinction between ovate and lanceolate (see www.anbg.gov.au/glossary/webpubl/splitgls.htm): this is significantly different from Harris and Harris (2000), whose illustration at least looks egg-shaped. Furthermore, some botanists seem to ignore obovate and oblanceolate, where the broadest point of the leaf is near the apex, choosing instead to use the words ovate or lanceolate no matter which way round the leaf is. We strongly recommend using the 'ob-' forms for leaf shapes in field guides, and to follow the standards for the numeric limits (see Figure 6.1).

There are many aspects of leaves that reflect a plant's ecology, guild or functional group: for instance, leaf size, inclination from horizontal, serrated margins, cordate bases, drip tips and many more traits are loosely associated with ecology (for a summary, see Givnish, 1987, and Press, 1999). By choosing to emphasize some of these characters in a key, it is often possible to distinguish meaningful ecological groups – for example, where single pages have similar leaves from similar habitats to ease comparison (Gillison, 2002)

Leaf stalks

Leaf stalk is a non-scientific term for petiole, but more familiar to the public and therefore often appropriate in simpler guides:

- Beware of the very common confusion between the terms petiole, petiolule and rachis (see Box 6.4).

Petioles provide many useful field characters in themselves – for example, if swollen at one or both ends ('pulvinate'), channelled, winged, many-grooved, twisted, articulated, hairy or twining. But they are also useful at providing an easily locatable, standard part of a leaf for characters that tend to vary from one part of the leaf to another, such as hairs and glands:

- The hairs that occur on petioles are often little different from the range found elsewhere; but it is often worth specifying the indumentum specifically on petioles (defined positions on the midrib or along the apical bud are also useful) where there is variation across a plant.

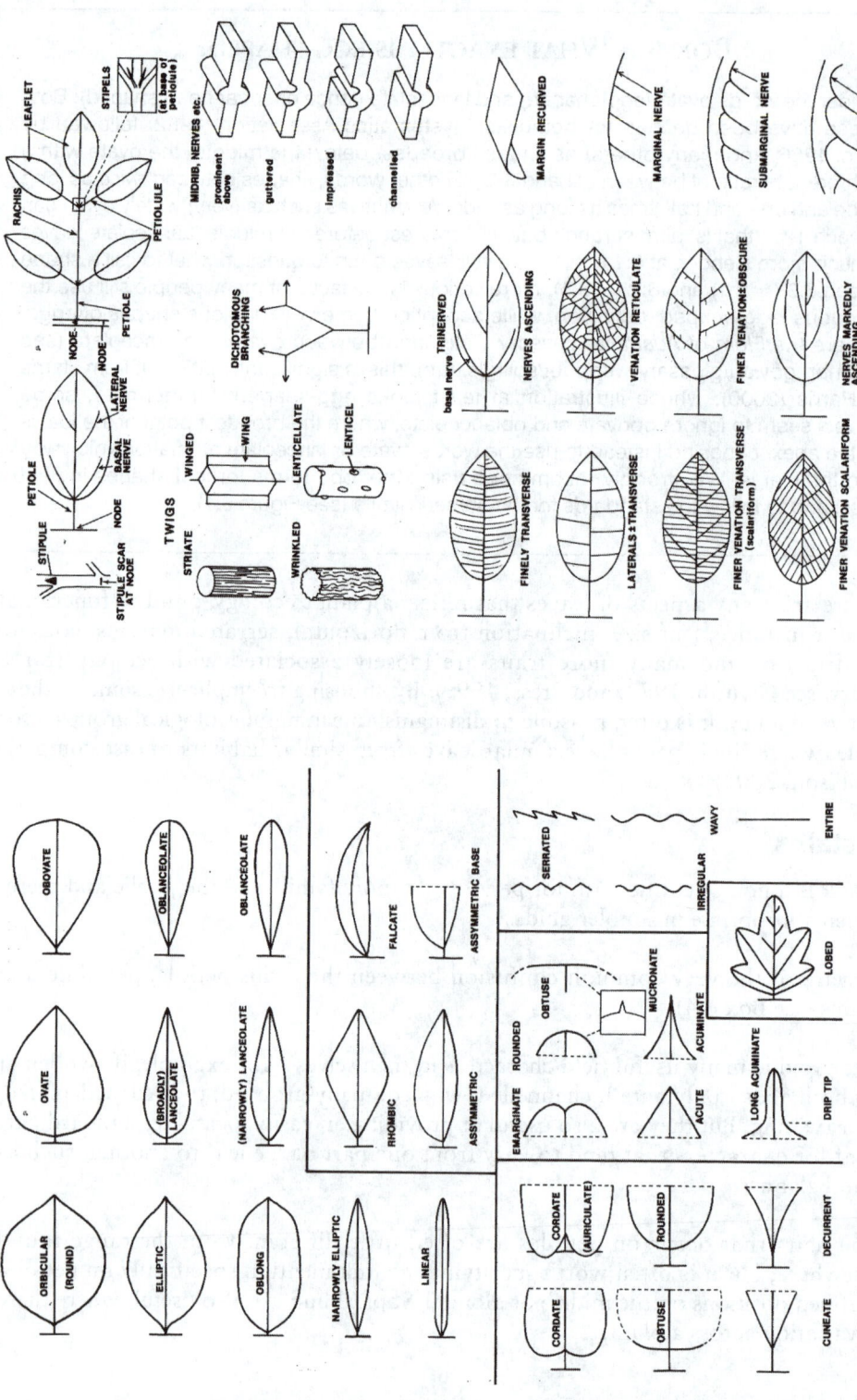

Figure 6.1 *Moderate levels of jargon in a field guide glossary*

Source: Hawthorne (1990); Hawthorne et al (2005)

BOX 6.7 DEFINING AND ANALYSING LEAF SHAPES IN DATABASES

How might shapes be represented in a database so that they can be matched, perhaps automatically, to a specimen to be identified? There are no off-the-shelf solutions today, so should field guide writers give this a moment's thought? If you want to be at the cutting edge of the subject, maybe you can organize your data to make the most of such developments when they arrive. The problem of subtle shape-detection software is a mathematical one with biological constraints (see, for example, Ledig et al, 1969; Dale et al, 1971), and various approaches have been proposed and compared (see Freeman, 1961; Dickinson et al, 1987; Jensen, 1990; Loncaric, 1998). Some programmes and algorithms are still under development, or recently reported but far from commercially available or reliable (Abbasi et al, 1997; Liu and Sclarof, 2000; Gandhi, 2003). It is not difficult to match exact shapes, but generally inconvenient to codify a leaf to be identified, especially in the field, and to deal with acceptable variation and cases where, for instance, a spectrum of possibilities exists for one species from, say, three to five lobed to unlobed leaves:

- A useful set of recommendations for basic leaf measurements to include in your database is given by the Leaf Architecture Working Group (LAWG, 1999), starting with midrib length multiplied by lamina width (for lobed leaves, draw an ellipse joining the lobe tips and treat this as a leaf), and distance along midrib of greatest width. Such a simple shape index can be measured and typed in manually (LAWG, 1999) and used to shortlist species in a database, but has much lower discriminatory power than is theoretically possible (for example, based on matching by eye).
- Database searches for words such as 'ovate' or for the length/breath ratios that define them may be of some use for narrowing options, but are far from subtle unless the shape is very unusual. However, the rarest shapes have no precise word to describe them, the ratios are likely to miss their essential oddness, and these species are the easiest to identify from pictures anyway.
- Do not spend long typing in complicated shape data; soon software will, one assumes, be available to scan images in databases and to extract indexable details. Rather, start now to build up your digital picture library of clean, isolated leaves on a plain, unpatterned (black or white) background. Such images are also ideal for orthodox use in a field guide. By contrast, most images of herbarium specimens or living plants show too much overlap of leaves, ripped or ragged margins, perspective distortion or three dimensional 'artefacts', such as shadows on the mounting paper, and are unlikely to be easily searchable or indexable for a number of years (see also O'Callaghan, 1970, and Ray, 1992).

- Many petioles have clear 'abscission lines', or lines of weakness marking where the leaf will break off when their time is up – this is a more reliable and useful character than referring to a plant as 'deciduous', although it is not necessarily the case that the correlation is absolute.
- The maximum petiole length is a useful character to record for all species; emphasize to your users that it is important to look across many stems of a plant to find this.
- When describing the size of leaves, be sure to explain where the leaf length is measured from and to. Many authors do not, and in these cases the length is presumably of the petiole and lamina (leaf blade) combined. It is usually more useful to divide total leaf length into ranges for the length of the petiole and length and width of the fully developed leaf blade or lamina.

- Sometimes it is not actually the absolute length of the petiole that is significant – for instance, for reducing leaf overlap – but the length relative to the lamina. Petiole/lamina length ratios can sometimes, therefore, be useful in a key.

Some of the characteristics of petioles apply to petiolules (leaflet stalks in compound leaves); for instance, abscission joints, with an abrupt change of texture or colour between petiolule and rachis, are common at the base of petiolules of legumes and various vegetatively similar families. In many legumes, the petiolule is often short, fat and wrinkled like an earthworm, or else a so-called 'cushion' where a leaflet blade with an asymmetric base is hinged directly onto the rachis. These can be useful features for distinguishing them from other pinnate-leaved groups. The petiolules of the leaflets of compound leaves are usually short (< 1cm long) and not pulvinate; but in *Dacryodes* and other Burseraceae they may become longer or swollen at the top.

Finer details of the leaf blade (lamina)

Leaf texture

There are various ways of describing the obvious variation in thickness of the lamina of fresh leaves, especially leathery (= coriaceous), papery (= papyraceous) and even thinner than paper, such as many of the more delicate fern leaves (= membranaceous). This is very far from an exact science, and although the (bracketed) terms are important in descriptions, they can often be ignored in favour of other characters in keys. For instance, in leathery leaves, margins are often recurved, and midrib or vein prominence may be quite different from close relatives with different leaf blade thicknesses. Between leathery and papery, some leaves have the texture of a thin sheet of brittle plastic, cracking when folded. The term 'plastic textured' can be used for these, the ancient Romans not having invented plastic.

There is scope to develop a mechanical leaf texture index to use with a field guide as the character is potentially more useful than the jargon allows for. Perhaps you could bind flaps of different types of material in your book or actual dried leaves for a herbarium guide?

Leaf colour

Some leaves, particularly of ornamentals, are variegated or strikingly coloured, making them very distinctive in pictorial guides. For non-cultivated plants, a distinction between otherwise similar species could be made in the field on the basis of shades of green, associated with whether the plant is evergreen or the leaf is leathery. However, it is difficult to record this accurately, even on camera, and to print it out successfully; often, one has to be satisfied with mentioning extremes only. However, for difficult groups, leaf surface colour and related details visible only with a good lens might be useful in technical guides (see, for example, Stace, 1965).

For a tree or liane guide, the best source of leaves is the forest floor, and the fallen leaves of many species turn a distinctive colour – for instance, fallen *Calophyllum calaba* leaves are usually mottled red and green, and are usually to be found below an adult. In the African swamp species *Spondianthus preussii*, lacy leaf skeletons are always found below the tree. The distinctive colours of dried specimens may also be useful for identifying them in the herbarium (for example, the reddish, black or greyish shades in various

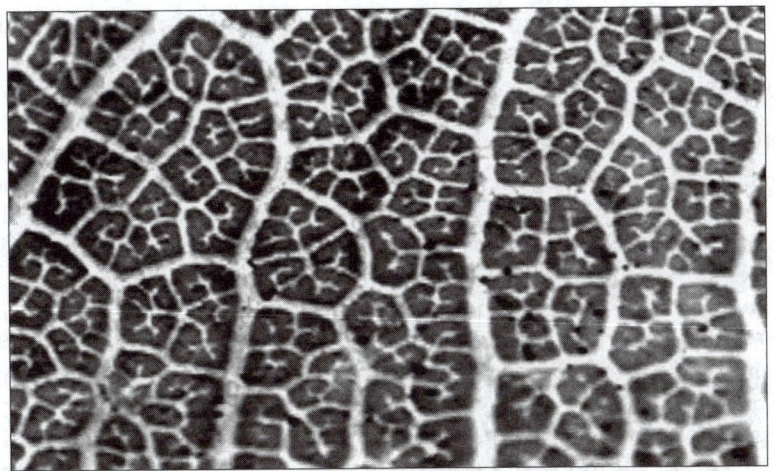

Note: Leaf venation, often so distinctive, is best illustrated. An easy method is to photograph fresh leaves against the light, converting if necessary to black and white.
Source: William Hawthorne

Figure 6.2 *Leaf venation*

Psychotria species); but be careful because different methods of drying can result in different colours.

Glaucous leaf surfaces, often pale blue or white due to a wavy layer, are very distinctive, often diagnostic and survive drying well.

Leaf venation

The basic patterns of venation are best expressed by illustration, especially photographic (see Figure 6.2), although there are some terms that are easily understood without illustrations and others that are useful for emphasizing features that may otherwise not be noticed (Hickey, 1973; Hickey and Wolfe, 1975, although their jargon is not very user friendly). For many descriptions, it is important to refer to the venation order (1°, primary, for the largest order of veins; 2° for laterals; and so on). Although the casual definition of vein order seems simple enough, problems arise when trying to be absolutely precise – for example, when comparing closely related species with subtly different venation, or when specifying venation patterns accurately in databases (see Hill, 1980; Spicer, 1986):

- The minimum and maximum number of pairs of lateral nerves (2° venation) is a very useful character to record for all species.
- Illustrate venation by photographing a leaf with a macro lens, held up to a bright light. This can be manipulated to form a monochrome diagram-like image (see Figure 6.2 and Chapter 8).
- It is usually possible to pick on some arbitrary aspect of the venation when only two species are compared – for instance, if the finest venation looks more lax in one species than another, try comparing the number of areoles (finest, closed vein fields) crossed on a line between two adjacent laterals in the middle of the leaf, halfway to

the margin. These sorts of indexes can be surprisingly constant. The angle of lateral nerves to the midrib is sometimes useful; but few field botanists carry a protractor, so try to use this character for difficult groups or extreme differences only.

Midrib and vein prominence

There is much variation in the conspicuousness of veins, partly due to their width, partly due to their prominence (above or below the lamina surface), and partly due to how opaque the surface of the leaf is, possibly hiding finer veins. 2° and finer veins may be 'obscure', meaning not clearly visible. It is important to specify whether this applies to the upper or lower leaf surface, and what minimum order of venation it applies to (for example, 3° venation partly obscure; 4° and finer venation completely so). Is the appearance something that is only apparent at arm's length, or are all finer veins invisible on close inspection, as well?

The degree of prominence of the midrib on the upper surface of the leaf is a significant character in some groups and largely survives drying well, so the information can be gleaned from herbarium specimens very quickly. It is possible to go beyond the three main character states of prominent, channelled and flat (see Figure 6.1) and to distinguish 'impressed' from 'channelled' and 'guttered' from 'prominent'. For the midrib, it is usually best to specify a part of the leaf where this character is to be checked; the midrib, for instance, may be channelled where it runs into the petiole and prominent halfway along the leaf.

For finer venation (3° and higher order), the degree of prominence on either surface can vary with drying; in particular, finer venation that is prominent on the upper surface of dried leaves is usually less so in the field (although fallen leaves may be dried in this respect). The degree of prominence on the lower surface is more constant, and veins that are impressed, flat or guttered on either surface in fresh leaves tend to remain so when dried.

Smells, taste and bark: The gourmet field botanist

Smell and taste, whether of tree barks or fresh leaves, are often useful clues to a plant's identity (see Box 6.8). Obviously, fleshy fruits are frequently sweet or sharp and pleasant tasting and smelling, and nuts and leaves are sometimes edible and tasty. More intriguing and less seasonal, though, is the range of other testable or scented plant parts. Tasty leaves are more common among savanna herbs and shrubs than they are among rainforest woody plants; but a few forest species have distinctive tastes. Some *Dialium* species (oxalic acid taste, like rhubarb) and *Tamarind* leaves have a pleasant, sharply acidic and fruity taste, useful for distinguishing them from otherwise similar legume saplings. The leaves of some *Begonia* species are tasty (sour) and palatable enough to be collected as a salad vegetable.

Certain plant families are characteristically more scented than others. Of course, the range of scents is much greater when flowers or fruits are included; but some families are notable for being scented in stems and leaves, such as the Annonaceae (custard apples), Lauraceae (laurels and cinnamon), Myristicaceae (nutmegs) and Piperaceae (black pepper family). Among the monocots, the Zingiberaceae (gingers) are particularly notable for their scented leaves and stems. Although most grasses are unscented, a few are widely cultivated for their scent, such as lemon grass relatives and patchouli. In

BOX 6.8 SMELLS AND TASTES

Smell and taste are related senses. Some elements of taste are detected primarily in the mouth; but most of the subtleties of taste – for instance, in food – are derived from the aroma or smell (thus, the sense of taste declines if the nose is blocked). There are also certain other mouth-related sensations, such as the cooling effect of peppermint oil and the heat of chilli pepper, which are not strictly taste, but are usually discussed with it.

Some plants are poisonous, so the tasting of unknown plants is not to be recommended wholeheartedly. On the other hand, poisons generally taste very bad – if not immediately, then as an aftertaste. When tasting bark or leaves, first nibble the tiniest amount possible with your front teeth and always spit fragments out after a few seconds. Never swallow after tasting plant parts, and have a bottle of water to wash your mouth out if you are left with a bad aftertaste. The author, who has tasted most Ghanaian forest barks and leaves, nevertheless disclaims any liability should you die after eating any plant parts! There are some poisonous or allergy-causing groups that should certainly be kept well away from your skin and mouth, including the Anacardiaceae, Euphorbiaceae (especially those with hairs or latex) and Urticaceae. For leaves, it is advised that you only consider a small taste once you have ascertained that there are no other field characters which can distinguish it, and there is no bad reaction from handling the crushed leaves.

Our noses can distinguish more than 10,000 different smells, and it is thought that there are hundreds of different olfactory receptors, each recognizing different odours. For example, the distinctive smell of bananas is due to isoamyl acetate, and the primary smell of an orange comes from octyl acetate. These chemicals account for the basic ingredients of a smell; but plants blend such molecules to different degrees, creating endless possibilities. Some people are 'blind' to particular chemicals. Although you should not primarily rely on smells in a field guide for this and other reasons, smells are a highly useful source of information to support plant identification (see Worms, 1942; Moskowitz, 1975; Classen et al, 1994; Civille and Lyon, 1996; de Garine, 1997; Bubondt, 1998; Casagrande, 2000).

addition to these, scents are common in some of the families with translucent dots, or oil sacs, in their leaves, such as the Rutaceae (citrusy in all parts) and Myrtaceae (including, and often scented like, cloves; the bark usually does not smell strongly, though). There are a few plants with scents so unusual that they deserve special mention in your field guide, such as the foliage and bark of *Afrostyrax lepidophyllus* (Huaceae) and *Cordia alliodora* (Boraginaceae), and the bark of *Cedrela odorata* (Meliaceae), all of which emit a fetid smell like onions or garlic; or *Chione* and *Chiococca* (Rubiaceae) and most Montiniaceae, with peculiar ammonia or floor polish-type scents:

- Always smell the bark slash. Try to develop your powers of description, like a wine expert. Always ask others from your user group what they think a smell is like.
- Smells are useful for identifying many fungi – for instance, agarics produce a wide range of subtle fragrances, from aniseed to almonds. Your challenge will be to describe them to your audience using words for smells that they can relate to.
- As any universal smell vocabulary is not very subtle, the potential to make the use of scent clues is almost lost. A standard reference set of chemicals in small bottles, with common bark, essential oil and other smells ('vic', 'cedar', 'onions', 'eau de cologne', 'lily of the valley', 'mushrooms', 'citrus', etc.) would be a good start for helping

technical guide writers and users to express their experiences, and would probably not challenge the skills of modern odour chemists or a budget unduly. Such smell sets might even enhance the saleability of field guides and interest in eco-tourism.

CHARACTERS OF WHOLE PLANTS OR PLANT POPULATIONS

Habit or life form

Habit is the word used to describe the general appearance of a plant – for example, whether it is a tree, herb, shrub or climber. Although this is obviously a very significant field character, it is difficult to apply the terms precisely. There is no agreement about their definitions; gardeners may refer to a shrub as a low (say < 5m) and many-stemmed plant; but this is the definition others prefer to reserve for bush. The American Society of Foresters (http://soilslab.cfr.washington.edu/S-7/EcolGlos.html) defines a shrub as:

> ... *a woody perennial plant differing from a perennial herb in its persistent and woody stem, and less definitely from a tree in its lower stature and the general absence of a well-defined main stem.*

However, the society does not then define tree. Although the first decision in Keller's (1996) key to tropical families is 'tree or shrub', as against 'liana or weakly prostrate plant', these terms are not defined in that book, and there is a considerable grey area from shrub to 'rambling shrub' to liane. Habit categories are very vague, and we advise users to define their use of terms carefully, perhaps choosing an arbitrary cut-off, possibly in height or diameter, between shrub and tree (see Box 6.9).

Raunkiaer (1934) defined life forms according to how and where the growing points of plants are protected. However, these are not very suitable categories for rainforest, nor do the words roll smoothly off the tongue – for instance, trees > 30m tall are 'megaphanerophytes'. The plain English is shorter and clearer:

- Look for links between functional or morphological groups and habitat preference. Any links you find might help you to choose appropriate divisions in your keys – for example, 'Leaves < 1cm wide; plant always along rivers.'
- Apart from the extreme differences (such as bromeliad-, grass-, palm- or cactus-like plants), do not expect an easy and clean division of rainforest plants by habit unless you have a limited number of species and they cover diverse habits. However, stem texture (woody, herbaceous and succulent) is a useful trait to concentrate on.
- Maximum recorded size, or minimum size of fertile plants, can be expressed as height or DBH (diameter at breast height, taken as 1.3m above the ground or above buttresses) recorded for fertile herbarium specimens of larger trees and lianes. Include other descriptive adjectives – for example, 'liane to 15cm DBH, capable of looping between ground and 30m canopy several times over'; or 'small spreading tree to 20cm DBH, often with straggling, half-climbing branches'.
- For a field guide to trees, define at the outset a minimum diameter for trees to be included – perhaps 5cm or 30cm DBH – which can be easily checked as fieldwork progresses. Then perhaps also include (with a note to this effect) species that have only been found just below this diameter, say 4cm or 28cm DBH, as one may expect

---

BOX 6.9 HABIT CATEGORIES IN *THE WOODY PLANTS OF WESTERN AFRICAN FORESTS*

The following quote from the Introduction to Hawthorne and Jongkind's (2006) field guide to Western African woody plants summarizes the problems faced by the authors, where the 2130 species include a similar proportion of trees, climbers, shrubs and herbs:

We use the terms liane to mean large woody climber (as distinct from barely woody or herbaceous small twiners, such as the garden bean). We do not distinguish very precisely the terms tree, treelet, shrub and shrublet, but use the terms descriptively as follows.

A tree is an erect woody plant with a well-defined main bole or trunk. A treelet is a small type of tree that is always in the lower layers of the forest; if pressed, we could suggest an upper limit of 5cm trunk diameter for treelets; but we have not been able to apply this definition rigorously. Shrub is used variously for other, smaller woody plants that are not well described by the previous terms for various reasons: either they show little tendency to have a single straight main stem; or some of their branches sprawl around in a half-climbing way, but other branches behave as a small tree; or because they are too small even to be a treelet, perhaps never exceeding 2m in height [other habit terms are discussed similarly]... We initially struggled with the proper application of these terms; but there is so much scope for error, lack of accurate records, and so many species change their habit depending on growing conditions that we have ended up using the terms in an explicitly vague way. Note that in all cases the terms refer to the typical plant when mature, so immature trees are referred to as saplings rather than shrubs or treelets.

Source: Hawthorne and Jongkind (2006)

---

the larger sizes to be discovered eventually. Users will be more likely frustrated if you miss out species that should be included than if you include a few too many. It is useful to check forestry organizations for inventory data, at least to see how many common species are known in various size classes.

Architecture and crown form

The overall form of a whole plant depends, to some extent, on their architectural 'rules' or branching pattern, but also on other factors. Hallé (1971, 1995), Hallé et al (1978) and Keller (1994, 1996) have approached the issue of tree architecture formally. However, although the extreme types of architecture, such as 'Corner's model' can be distinguished easily, these characters are, in general, hard to assess, more of academic than practical interest, and often involve analysis of where flowers develop. For the easily observed architectural patterns, it is less confusing to use in a field guide terms such as '*Terminalia*-type branching', or 'un-branched, papaya-like habit' rather than Aubréville's model or Corner's model, respectively. Similarly, related characters of the buds and leaf arrangement can usually be specified and used more easily (Cullen, 1978; Keller, 1994).

Figure 6.3 *Distinctive forms of two species of Bombacaceae in West Africa
(left:* Rhodognaphalon brevicuspe; *right:* Ceiba pentandra*)*

It is often possible to see in a distant crown, either across fields or in the canopy above, distinctive shape, pattern and textural effects; but these are hard to put into words. One solution is to photograph tree silhouettes and convert them to high-contrast black-and-white photographs (see Figure 6.3; Figure 6.4 shows some of the variety that can be captured in silhouettes). But, apart from a few species with unusual crowns, most species are not distinctive enough to allow identification by this method in a practical guide (see http://herbaria.plants.ox.ac.uk/VFH).

The architecture of lianes (Putz and Mooney, 1991) tends to go unnoticed, intermingled as they often are among tree crowns. Hawthorne and Jongkind (2006) review liane architectural terms useful for West Africa field use, and these apply elsewhere in the tropics. Little-branched or small trees or shrubs may be distinctive looking; but their distinctiveness is generally easily describable with common language, perhaps helped with a few key architectural adjectives.

Older woody stems and wood anatomy

Rosayro (1953) and Empire Forestry Association (1953, 1957) summarized some of the characters of tree stems; but there are many more to be found in numerous specific field guides to tropical trees. Wood anatomy is rarely of any use in a tree field guide, unless perhaps the guide is aimed at loggers where there is a close working relationship

Figure 6.4 *A minority of species have crowns that can be illustrated with silhouettes*

between fieldworkers and the sawmill. However, consideration of liane wood anatomy can be useful, firstly, because some of the patterns are extremely distinctive, even without a lens, often with repercussions visible from the profile of uncut stems, and also because cut lianes are more likely to be available than cut tree stems. Some foresters spend a lot of time cutting down lianes.

Although lianes frequently have very distinctive wood, there is not much published other than the works of Caballé (1993) and Carlquist (1991), and some publications for specific plant groups (Villiers, 1973; Vliet, 1979). For Celastraceae, a globally important liane family and one of the most interesting for unusual wood, Hallé (1962) and Mennega (1988) have remarked on the great taxonomic and diversity value of wood structure. Hall and Lock (1976) discuss *Salacia* stems in this family in Ghana, recognizing four main types (normal, annular, lacunose and sulcate). More recently, Hawthorne and Jongkind (2006) have summarized what is known for all liane families in West Africa. See Plate 4 for a sample of the spectrum. Some sample terms and definitions for liane wood are summarized in the same book.

Many of the extremes of liane wood pattern are manifested in unusual stem shapes (such as the ribbon-shaped stems of various *Bauhinia*, *Millettia* and *Dalbergia*); so even if you do not consider wood anatomy useful, it is worth considering its external manifestation forms as a 'stem shape' character.

Bole and liane stem shape and tree bases

It is generally easy to distinguish irregularities on the surface of the tree due to a combination of patterns in the underlying wood and more superficial patterns within the bark. The tree trunk or bole may be cylindrical or variously distorted by fluting, sinews, knee-like bumps or knobs and various more bizarre conditions. In some cases, the spines or prickles of the younger stems are carried on the main bole, as well. See Plate 3 for the main types of bole and base, and Plate 4 for some of the range of stem forms found in West African tree boles and bases:

- Sometimes the utter lack of irregularities or special characters is as striking as their presence, and this applies when the main trunk of large trees is completely cylindrical to the ground. In Africa, these strikingly cylindrical-when-huge boles occur in genera from many families (for example, *Daniellia*, *Gilbertiodendron*, *Petersianthus* and *Hannoa*).
- Small buttresses or other outgrowths around the base of trees are age dependent, so buttressing can be unreliable for identification unless the guide is meant to work reliably only for very large trees. However, they can be very distinctive, and should be recorded in plant descriptions and photographs even if not in keys.
- In a general field guide, consider making one key for all species and another, perhaps, for very large trees (see, for example, Hawthorne, 1990). In the latter case, detailed descriptions of buttresses are almost indispensable; but in the former they are useless if the guide has to work for small trees.
- For buttress details, note whether the top edge of the buttress is straight or curved, concave or convex. Buttress height and width obviously increase with age; but their ratio (extent from tree at ground level/height reaching up bole) is more constant, distinguishing tall and narrow from low and spreading forms. It is particularly useful to estimate the thickness of a buttress, halfway between the bole and the

buttress edge: 'plank buttresses' are thin, not much thicker than floor boards; but there is no common term for thick buttresses. You may be able to define a very clean-cut division between species with plank, or normal and thick, or no buttresses in your area.

- The more subtle bole irregularities can be very hard to photograph – the best way of describing them – as it is important to illuminate the bole from the side in order to create shadows. This can be achieved by selecting a time of day when the sun is appropriately positioned relative to the camera, or more conveniently by obtaining a 'remote flash' or a very long flash cable, positioning it with the help of an assistant to shine across the tree and downwards. Some degree of trial and error is generally needed, so a digital camera with a preview function is very useful.
- Be alert for trees on the forest edge where the buttresses are clearly visible and not obscured by others, and for lone trees on recently cleared hill tops where crown form is obvious. Take their photographs at any opportunity.

Roots

Roots are rarely of much interest in a field guide, except where they are found above ground level, as in swamps and on epiphytes, where stilt, strangling, breathing and other unusual aerial roots are typical (see Figure 6.5):

- Look around your trees for any surface or breathing roots that are partly exposed in the soil. These are diagnostic for some species.
- In a few species with medicinal bark or wood, the roots are collected since the tastes, smell and presumably chemical content are often stronger there. If your plant is supposed to be scented or medicinal tasting, but is not convincingly so in the main stem, dig a root from the foot of the tree and encourage your guide's users to do so.

Bark

Bark is the protective outer coating of old stems and roots characteristic of shrubs, trees, and lianes ('woody dicots'); it is for these that bark is a most useful field character (Foxworthy, 1927, 1932; Wood, 1952; Chattaway, 1953; van Wyk, 1985). Bark should be described from two points of view: by external appearance and by slash (= blaze), which is the appearance of the oblique section of the bark soon after being cut. Whitmore (1962a, 1962b, 1962c, 1963) classified bark primarily by external appearances, or manifestations, subdivided by the internal anatomical structure that gives rise to that pattern, defining seven major bark types for 29 manifestations of dipterocarp bark. A particular manifestation of bark – such as roughness – is associated with a limited number of anatomical or slash patterns. However, this approach involves a heavy burden of jargon and microscopic detail inappropriate for most field guides, even technical ones. For instance, the first issue in Whitmore's (1962c) key to bark types includes the option as follows: 'Expansion tissue uniform, continuous at surface in wedges and/or fingers confluent externally into a pseudocortex'. A few subsequent authors have tried to develop this approach to more than Malaysian dipterocarps (for example, Yunus and Yunus, 1990; Trockenbrodt, 1990). However, because of the complexity, most actual field guide writers concentrate instead on simply describing or illustrating the more obvious visible slash patterns (for example, Hawthorne and Jongkind, 2006).

BOLE AND BASE TYPES

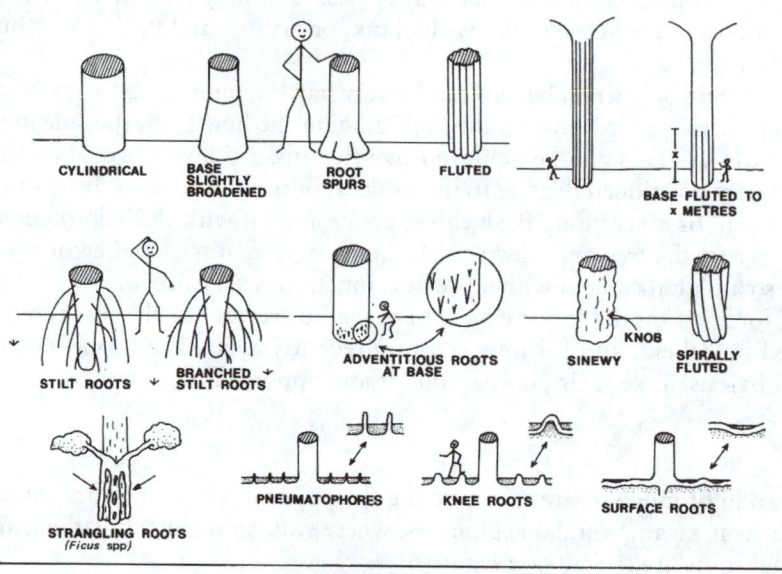

BUTTRESS TYPES

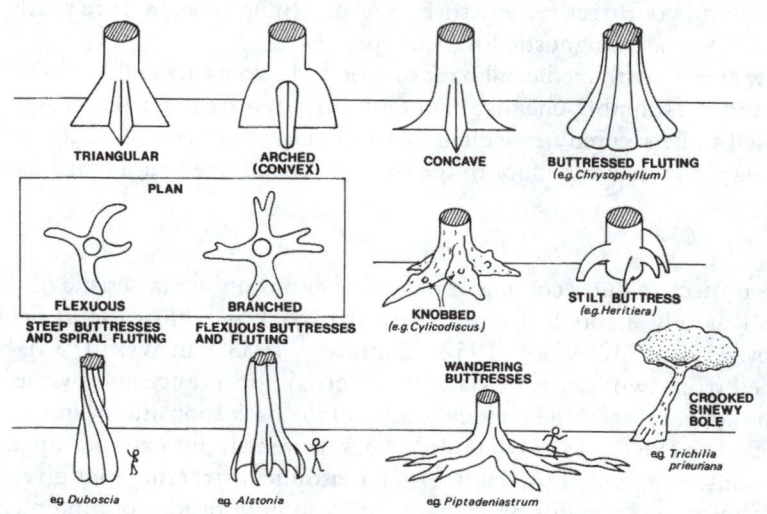

Figure 6.5 *Standardizing use of terms for a tree field guide*

One of the commonest side effects of the dead outer bark not growing with the tree below is for it to break up into vertical fissures or cracks, especially where the bark is very fibrous – that is, largely composed of vertical fibres. There is no agreement about how such rough barks should be categorized; but Junikka (1994), adopting earlier recommendations by Wyatt-Smith (1954) and others, recommends various descriptive phrases. This is not all suitable from a field guide writer's perspective either, and you will

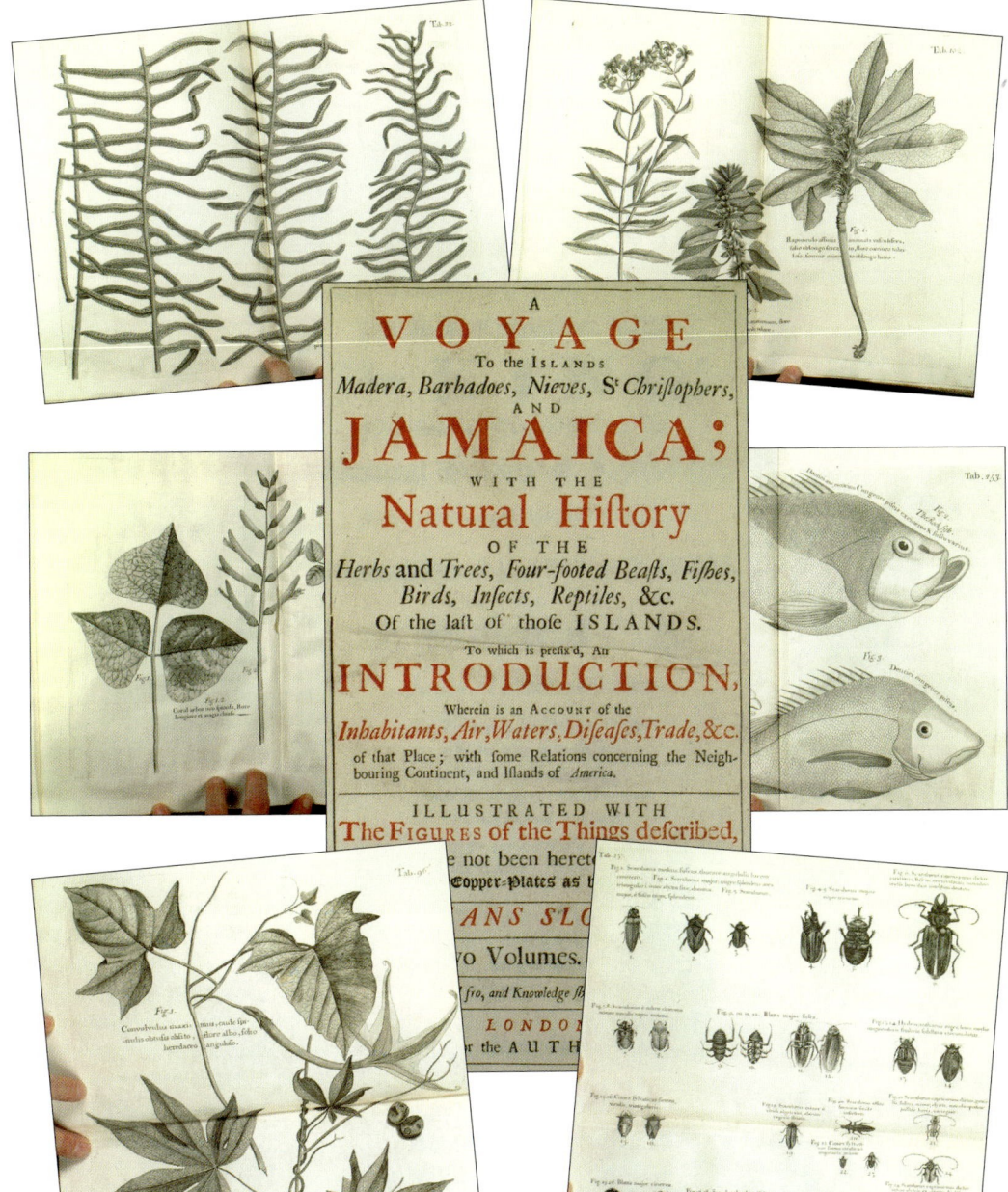

Plate 1 *Copperplate engravings from Hans Sloane's early guide to Caribbean plants and animals*

Source: Sloane (1707); scanned by William Hawthorne with permission of the Department of Plant Sciences, University of Oxford

Bignoniaceae

All species have opposite compound leaves. Sometimes the leaflets are serrated, usually not, but this can vary on the same tree.

Choose the best description of the venation and lower surface of the leaflets

Scalariform
with dense hairs or scales below

Strong ladder-like 3°venation, but finer venation all forming similar-sized islands

Undersurface with many hairs or with a dense covering of scales

Reticulate
with 3 or 4 levels of veins between the laterals; few hairs but with minute scattered dots at the end of the veins

3° venation not strongly ladder-like; broken up into lesser islands by 4° and then finer veins. Lower leaf surface hairless or with very few hairs.

Small scattered dots can usually be seen within the smallest vein islands with a hand lens

Scalariform type. How are hairs arranged on lower surface of leaflets?

Reticulate type. What are the bases of the leaflets like when viewed from below?

No tuft domatia: Hairs all over the young leaves, but these disappear with age

'Tuft Domatia' i.e. small tufts of hairs in the axils of some of the main lateral nerves. Few other hairs on leaflets, but yellowish scales

Basal glands?

Scaly twigs?

No clear leaflet stalk, with glands by midrib near base; sometimes with **tuft domatia**

Slender leaflet stalk (petiolule) present, with base of leaflets folded over into petiolule channel; no domatia

Leathery leaflets; base of leaflet folded over around glands; often planted in villages, or in secondary forest	**Papery leaflets;** margin not curled round at base; pointed buds at leaf base Savanna or disturbed dry forest	leaves often slightly shiny or yellowish below due to scales, but not hairy; leafy '**pseudostipules**' (like St.ac.) between the leaves Dry forest trees;	Almost always with sharp teeth and often long leaflet tip; Drier forests, often boundary as a living fence	Teeth few, except saplings; basal glands; leafy pseudostipules; leaflets dry red-brown; dry forest; 1m thin pods <1cm wide	Variable, but without long leaflet tips; mostly dries greyish to yellowish green; small tree often by streams 40 x 15 cm sausage shaped fruit
Spathodea campanulata	*Markhamia tomentosa*	*Markhamia lutea*	*Newbouldia laevis*	*Sterospermum acuminatissimum*	*Kigelia africana*

Plate 2 *Example of a diagrammatic, dichotamous key based on images*

Note: the images were scanned from herbarium specimens.
Source: William Hawthorne

Plate 3 *A sample of the wide range of tree bole and base forms found in West Africa*

Plate 4 *A sample of the wide range of liane wood found in West Africa*

Source: Hawthorne and Jongkind (2006)

Plate 5 *Part of the spectrum of bark slashes found in West Africa*

Note: Colour photographs are the best way to document these.
Source: Hawthorne and Jongkind (2006)

Plate 6 *Colour photographic* Cola *leaf guidelets tested in Cameroon*

Source: S. Cable, W. D. Hawthorne, R. Lysinge and E. Ndive

Plate 7 *Samples of modular photoguides tested in Ghana*

Note: printed as laminated cards; sizes of A5 and A6 were compared.
Source: Hawthorne and Gyakari (2006)

Plate 8 *Samples of the photo-cards, paintings and drawings used in format trials in Grenada*

Source: William Hawthorne (photographs) and Rosemary Wise (paintings and drawings)

BOX 6.10 BARK FLAKES OR SCALES?

As another example of where there is no agreement on a widely used term, both scale and flake have been used to describe (thin) patches of outer bark that become detached. Rosayro (1953) used flakes for large rectangular pieces and scales for smaller ones; but he did not specify, and there is no general agreement about the cut-off point. Corner (1988) and Letouzey (1986) use them interchangeably, a definition that Junikka (1994) recommends; but we suggest that a distinction is made in your own glossary – for example, specify that flakes are flexible or papery, often curved at the edges, and scales are barely flexible and especially used for large plate-sized ones. Flakes that are thin and flexible like paper can be called papery flakes, or the bark as a whole may be 'flaking off in papery sheets', or exfoliating. This can be called 'paper-scrolled bark' when the scrolls are more than 1 cm in diameter. Papery scrolls are typical of several *Bursera* species and various Myrtaceae, for instance, and familiar to residents of temperate climates in the papery scrolled species of birch (*Betula*) and cherry (*Prunus*).

---

still need to choose your own definitions, probably starting with Junikka's (1994) summary (see Box 6.10).

Slash characteristics

Bark is made up of various layers and patches of different texture and colour visible in the slash. Every tropical forester knows that the tree slash is one of the best diagnostic tools for identifying large trees, but converting what can be learned from a 'recognition' point of view to a diagnostic key of some sort is hard (Beard, 1944; Symington, 1943; Rollet, 1980–1982; Tailfer 1989). It is often possible to distinguish various layers in a slash, above the generally harder sapwood. Some authors, for example Wyatt-Smith (1954) and Wood (1952), show how to describe the slash in terms of various layers; but few field guides have made good use of such jargon. We recommend describing the patterns as below, without using special terms.

Living tissues in the inner bark (mostly secondary phloem) can contain resin ducts or laticifers that exude liquids when cut (Serier, 1986). Similar exudates can also be produced from the sapwood of some trees:

- The first consideration to make for a slashed bark is whether there is any 'significant' exudate, like latex or other coloured thick liquids. Many barks exude colourless sap or other watery substances when cut; this is widespread, fickle and not counted here as significant. It is useful to note the colours of any latex and other slash parts in the first 10 to 20 seconds of exposure. This is the about the time taken to cut the bark a few times to make a neat slash, put down the bush knife, take out your hand lens, open your notebook and look closely. In many cases, the colour will change, usually to a darker colour over a period of minutes or days, a fact that should also be recorded where possible.
- The slash pattern and colour is usually hard to describe in the field without technical language and great patience, and is best done with photographs. However, it is also useful to refer to the texture of its components with words such as gritty, granular and fibrous. The overall texture might also be brittle, fibrous or corky, in their

common English sense. In a bid to specify the bark colours accurately, Hawthorne (1990) tried calibrating slash colours with Royal Horticultural Society (RHS) Standard Colour swatches. Apart from colours that darkened rapidly, this did support the notion that at least a distinction between reddish ('greyed red') and orange-yellow barks (RHS definitions) were reasonably constant for a species, as proposed by Dawkins (see Box 5.8, page 104). Even with these terms and tools, a user-friendly key for tree barks is made difficult by the mixtures of subtle textures and gradients and changes of colour.

- A detailed photograph is by far the best approach to bark description in a field guide, paying attention to record the true colours, particularly the 'difficult' shades between yellow and white. For this reason digital photography is highly recommended (see Plate 5, centre pages).

Smells and tastes are very important for characterizing barks as they are for some other field characters (see the earlier section on 'Smells, taste and bark: The gourmet field botanist').

Ecology and distribution

Your field guide will have been planned in the context of a specific region; but not all plants are found throughout. Although it is usually appropriate to mention species range and global rarity – for example, for conservation planning – this is only likely to be relevant as a field character if your guide covers thousands of square kilometres. If your guide does have a broad geographical range, and if you have very good herbarium or other survey data, you may well be able to make use of the distributional information to identify plants.

Local endemics are species found only in a particular, limited place, such as an island, mountain range or river valley. Use this fact in your field guide if you are reasonably confident it is a true pattern and not due to under-collection. Conveniently, 'sister species' that are otherwise generally the hardest to distinguish purely on how the plants look often have distinct ranges.

When distribution is determined by obvious environmental factors – rainfall pattern is one of the most important, so check rainfall maps – the constraint is 'ecological'. Try to understand which part of the landscape (swamp, riverbank, hill top, etc.) each species prefers. Beware that the ecology of a species in one part of its range is often different from that seen elsewhere, perhaps under a different climate. Many species that are only found along rivers in savanna are frequently found away from them – for instance, on rocky slopes under wetter climates. Other species are truly swamp specific, or are restricted to particular altitudes or limestone soils or very exposed, disturbed areas. All such ecological characteristics can help your users to identify their plants and can be used like physical field characters.

Herbarium specimen databases can be very useful for helping you to determine whether species are always, often or are merely randomly found along rivers. In many areas, such as Amazonia and the Congo Basin, historical collections have led to most specimens over large areas being recorded from riverbanks on herbarium notes or when the collection locations are mapped, but only because most of the collectors moved around on boats, so you have to see beyond this sampling bias. See http://herbaria.plants.ox.ac.uk/bol/home for free herbarium database software and what can be done with it.

It may be useful to calculate from your database the proportion of specimens for each species that have been collected along rivers (or in a swamp, etc.) and divide this by the proportion for all species combined. This habitat preference index will give you some idea of the true preference of various species – a score of, say, 5 would be a species five times more common along rivers than the sampling bias would produce by chance. You will need to exclude specimens of collectors who make poor ecological and location notes, a common trait of specimens more than 100 years old.

Some species are characteristically found in stands with few other species – that is, they are gregarious and locally dominant or at least locally very common, such as *Gilbertiodendron* trees and *Rinorea* shrubs, contrasting with the majority of species that are less so. Furthermore, adults of these and other tree species may characteristically have abundant seedlings around them. In extreme cases, the local dominance should be mentioned as a confirmatory character, but is rarely useful as a key character because other species may, on occasion, become gregarious. In species that form dominant patches due to due to local vegetative spread (such as bamboos and creeping herbs), the local abundance of stems is really a feature of the habit or life form, and is more likely to be worth emphasizing.

CONCLUSIONS

We have barely scratched the surface of the ranges of characters useful in field guides; but it is clear from even this sample that there is a vast range of relevant literature, though it has to be used very critically. Out of all the above types of field characters for flowering plants, distinction between all species in any one area ('local resolution') can, in general, be obtained by leaf and shoot details alone. For larger trees and lianes, slash characters of the bark can provide almost as much accuracy; but you will need to use colour photographs and pay attention to detail when taking your photographs. For shrubs, and especially herbs, which may be in flower or fruit for more of the time, you may be in a position to use some classical characters, possibly in simple terms ('petals 5mm long, white').

Whether or not you are planning a detailed type of publication, your research will benefit if you scan, first, through all species in the herbarium for field notes and details from the specimens. Of course, for many of the most important characters, there is no substitute for seeing the plant in the field where the guide is to be used. Even for these cases, though, you will benefit by first noting what others have learned before you, and by making yourself aware of ways of checking the identity of your plant and of issues that need resolving through fieldwork.

Some whole-plant field characters are not seen in the herbarium, and others do not survive the drying process, limiting the potential of the herbarium reference collection. On the other hand some useful characters for distinguishing sterile specimens – for example, colour and wrinkling on drying – are seen only on dried specimens (see Table 6.3).

Table 6.3 *Where to look for and use various classes of character*

Type of field character	Usability	Herbarium/field
Microscopic details (i.e. sub-hand lens) and chemistry	Only generally feasible with lab/herbarium equipment.	H
Leaf type/outline/shape	Identical for herbarium and fieldwork.	HF
Leaf margin/midrib prominence	Midrib prominence or channelling usually stays the same, but a smooth (channelled, flat or prominent) midrib of fleshier leaves will often become more wrinkled and grooved on drying.	HF
Leaf venation and surface	The venation pattern does not change with drying, but prominence of minor veins will often increase with drying as the softer leaf tissues collapse. Patterns visible with transmitted light on fresh leaves are often more obvious in the herbarium.	HF
Leaf indumentum, glands, translucent spots, domatia (see Hamilton, 1897; Schnell et al, 1963; Jacobs, 1966; Belin-Depoux, 1989)	These are generally well conserved on dried specimens, and you will usually need to allocate yourself a lot of time with a bench and a good lens and light to discover them. In the field, study the behaviour of ants (Uphof, 1942) on your plants: are they showing an inordinate interest in one part? If so, expect to see some form of glands or shelter there. In the field, you may also find it useful to inspect the leaf by holding it up to the light.	HF
Stipules, lenticels, buds	Generally identical in herbarium and field, although dried stipules are sometimes slightly more inclined to fall off than fresh ones.	HF
Leaf, twig and hair colours	These vary greatly and are often diagnostic, especially for herbarium use on dried leaves. Dried leaves on the forest floor correspond in relatively few cases to the herbarium version, usually because the leaf will have died and turned brownish before falling. Hair colours do often stay the same (white or silvery ones on dried leaves will usually be the same on fresh plants), but some do not (e.g. some hairs only become really red-brown after drying).	H or F, but often not both with the same information
Leaf scent (and taste)	Stronger scents are retained for years in a herbarium, but decades-old material almost never smells anything like living plants. Recently dried Annonaceae, etc. leaves are frequently very similar to the fresh plant. *Dialium* leaves retain their acid taste when crushed; but do not even think about tasting herbarium specimens since they are often sprayed with poison, and curators do not appreciate visitors eating their specimens.	F

Table 6.3 *continued*

Type of field character	Usability	Herbarium/field
Exudates	Although some exudates can be noted from dried specimens (e.g. black stains on cut Anacardiaceae petioles; gum on *Gardenia* and *Coffea* buds), most exudates should be checked for in the field: look in the slash and on cut petioles and twigs.	F
Bark/periderm of young twigs	Lenticels and other bark patterns, such as small scales and even colours, are usually well conserved in herbarium specimens when they relate to the rhytidome (dead parts – e.g. corky patches). However, green young stems will often become black or other colours when dried, although in certain families such as Olacaceae they are more stable.	F(H)
Bark details for larger stems	Almost impossible to do anything useful except in the field. Photography is a good solution for comparing these sorts of characters, as field notes rarely capture all subtleties. An anatomist can make some use of dried bark specimens, however, and anyone can use them to distinguish – for example, lenticels and extremes of texture.	F
Bole, base, crown	Likewise, field only; but start building your herbarium photo library now.	F

7

Information: Finding it and presenting it

Anna Lawrence

INTRODUCTION

The access systems and botanical information outlined in Chapters 4 to 6 form the basis of any field guide, together with illustrations, described in Chapter 8. However, a field guide usually contains a considerable amount of additional information other than simply botanical description. In Chapter 3, we described ways in which to decide how much information is appropriate to the purpose and user group of the guide. This might include background information about the area and the plants to be included, in an introduction; details about the uses or ecology of each species; and sources of further information, such as conservation organizations that the user might like to contact. But where does this information come from, how do we know that it is accurate, and what is the best way of organizing and presenting it? This chapter provides guidance on methods for collecting, checking and organizing information. It considers various sources of information and methods for gathering material from these sources; questions of accuracy, validity and comprehensibility; and sorting your results in a manageable way and preparing them for inclusion in the guide. As well as checking the accuracy of the information, we emphasize the need to check that typical users can understand and access the information once it has been written up and formatted on the page.

KINDS OF INFORMATION

Begin by listing the different types of information that you need. This comprises the information needed for each species, which should be systematic and consistent. It is confusing and appears careless to provide detailed information on, for example, the medicinal uses of one plant and nothing on the uses of another. Therefore, in order to ensure that you collect the information in a systematic way, and do not have to repeat your research or publish an incomplete guide, plan your information needs at the beginning. It can help to set up your database or spreadsheet at this stage, as well (see the following section), because the field names or section headings of your template will be the same as the categories of information you need to collect.

The list will include:

- All of the categories of information that you need for the individual species descriptions (see Chapter 3 for suggestions). By this stage you should have a clear idea of what the users are looking for. The list may cover soil type, growth characteristics, how to manage or cultivate a species, where to find it, some interesting historical information, and the uses and cultural meaning of a species. The choice of these kinds of information will depend, of course, upon the purpose and use of the manual, as explained in Chapter 2.
- Any information that you need for the introductory sections. Again, Chapter 2 provides a list of the kinds of information that you might include in an introduction, such as an overview of the ecology of the area or group of plants; a history of their management, conservation or use; an explanation of the key characteristics that users must familiarize themselves with in order to identify plants in that category; or perhaps a description of how to reach the area.
- Any information that you need for the glossary, index and 'Further information' chapter at the end of the book. Usually information in the index will already be included in the species descriptions; but you may need to consider researching sources of further information, from books, organizations or people, to be included in a final chapter.

With this list you will be able to make a plan to collect the information in a consistent and reliable way.

MANAGING INFORMATION IN A DATABASE

While you are gathering information, you will be filling notebooks, probably in chronological order. It can be difficult to find the pieces of information you need afterwards unless you organize it. The main part of the information in a field guide is centred around the individual species, so the key element here is to organize the data that you collect in the same way. You may choose to:

- fill in standardized forms for each species, with subheadings for each category of information about that species, such as description, uses, ecology and distribution;
- complete standardized forms in a word-processing package;
- make a table with a separate line for each species; in this case, you can include column headings relating to each category of information, such as description, uses, ecology and distribution; or
- use a computer database or spreadsheet.

In fact, all of these are versions of a database, and the table is the underlying structure of a database, which broadly defined is a large amount of data stored in a systematic way so that you can find and use it easily. Computers are particularly useful for storing and organizing information, and it is likely that most authors of field guides will have access to a computer. The value of databases, especially on computers, is that you can sort the information in different ways. On file cards, each card usually refers to one species or specimen; it becomes difficult to find out which species have yellow flowers or are used for fodder or occur on riverbanks without laboriously reading through all of the cards and making a note of the species. In a computerized table, spreadsheet or database, you can sort all of the records according to any of the subcategories of information, so this task becomes easy. Table 7.1 summarizes some of the advantages and disadvantages of these means of storing and accessing data.

Such sorting is important when it comes to deciding how to organize the species within the field guide. For example, will species be presented in alphabetical order, or grouped according to flower colour, habit or habitat? This is also useful when preparing indexes for the guide, which may help the user to find species by common name, scientific name, habitat or use.

A manual in the People and Plants Initiative series provides much more detail on botanical databases (Berjak and Grimsdell, 1999) and is available on the internet at www.peopleandplants.org/whatweproduce/Books/botanical/Databases.html. Its key recommendations are summarized in Box 7.1. Essentially, it is important to:

- Define the information categories required for each species.
- Set up a format for each species – even if it is not the final format, at least each piece of information will be clearly retrievable.
- Ensure that all of the information concerning each species is linked to a unique, internationally recognized name (see Chapter 4) so that information from different sources can be combined under that species.
- Update your information as necessary – for example, when specimens are identified, add the scientific name immediately.
- Record the sources of your information (see Box 7.1).

Tip: Backing up your computer files

Many people working in tropical countries, especially in rural locations, will know how often power failures can occur. When a power cut happens, all of the data you have entered on the computer is lost unless you have saved it. Even saved data can be lost if the computer becomes corrupted, whether because of a virus or because of damage to the hard drive. To avoid the catastrophic situation of losing months' of hard work, make sure that you take regular copies of your files and store them safely. Even if you do not lose data, you may change your mind about how files are structured, and it can be very useful to be able to go back to an earlier version that may turn out to be closer to your final intentions.

NOMENCLATURE

Recording local names for species is a task that falls to the authors of the field guide, and it can be a complex one (see Chapter 4). It is very rare, indeed, that all local informants agree on the same name for a given species, and even more variation is found between

Table 7.1 *Comparing methods for storing data*

Method	Advantages	Disadvantages
Paper and pencil	• Reliable: remains functional during power cuts. • More personal: spending more time processing records means more familiarity with your informants and data • Affordable: may be all that you can support	• Time consuming • Inaccurate: susceptible to human error • Isolating: as more work is done on computers, there is increasing pressure to work in the same media as colleagues and sponsoring agencies
Spreadsheets	• Time saving: data is entered once and can be selectively linked to other data to use for many purposes (timesheets, reporting hours, etc.) • User friendly: once a programme is set up, it does not require extensive expertise to use • Cross-functional: data doesn't need to be translated from another programme	• Unwieldy: as more data is added, the document expands across the screen • Limited sorting: all data entered is displayed at once; if you want to see the uses of a particular species, you have to sort through every other bit of information to find the one piece, or pull the selected information into another sheet • Not text friendly: text can be entered (and lists even sorted alphabetically), but no lengthy text such as long accounts of local uses can be included
Pre-packaged databases	• Fast learning curve: not necessary to be a programmer to use the database • Offers all of the best features of a database: time saving; displays only relevant data; multipurpose; doesn't become unwieldy • Buy and use: aside from data entry, no set-up required • Built to fit: some databases are built specifically for biodiversity data; usually effective at anticipating the needs of users • Help is at hand: technical support available if problems occur or new needs come up	• Inflexible: unlike a customized database, it is difficult or impossible to add new features • Limited: may not offer all the functions you want • Text oriented: not as good as spreadsheets at managing numerical information, although this is unlikely to be a problem in field guide production
Customized databases (such as that used for the Flora Reserva Ducke)	• Flexible: customized databases can grow and change • Time saving: once the initial time is put in, customized databases are generally the most time saving of the four options • Avoids the irrelevant: because 'reports' display only the desired information, you don't have to	• Time-consuming set-up: extensive programming is required to develop the database • Requires expertise to maintain: if no one in the organization is familiar with the programming (because either the person who set it up has left or an outside consultant was used), the programme cannot be further refined

Table 7.1 *continued*

Method	Advantages	Disadvantages
	weed through extraneous data to find what you're looking for • Multipurpose: can easily generate the same information in different formats (checklists, draft field guides, etc.) • Streamline: can grow extensively without becoming unwieldy	• Text oriented: not as adroit as spreadsheets at managing numerical information

Source: adapted from Berjak and Grimsdell (1999)

communities and ethnic groups. On the other hand, the same name is often used for quite distinct species, or by different groups of people for distinct species or to refer to all of the species of a given genus. Variation in names tends to be higher for plants that are less well known or that are known only in the wild. There is usually more consensus over names of cultivated and traded species because people discuss those species more in everyday conversation (Berlin, 1992).

When working with indigenous people whose languages have not traditionally been written down, there are further pitfalls. Great care must be taken in transcribing the names – in other words, deciding how to spell the name. If anthropologists or linguists have produced guidelines on this, it is important to follow them so that your field guide is standardized and others can compare it with their findings. Even slight differences in the sound of the name must be recorded as these may later be found to vary geographically, or between communities or ethnic groups, in a systematic way.

BOX 7.1 PRINCIPLES OF DATABASE DESIGN

1 *Atomize your data*: divide your data into their basic parts (their atoms). This makes it easy to obtain very specific results from the database, if required.
2 *Keep your data in raw form.* In other words, keep your original observations or measurements just as they were noted or recorded.
3 *Each record must have a unique designator in at least one field.* Clearly, without such a designator, some records might be the same and could not be separated from one another.
4 *Standardize as far as possible.* This means using standards in common use. For instance, there may be list of standard plant names for the country or region where you work; these, in turn, may follow an internationally agreed standard.
5 *Be consistent.* This means adhering strictly to the ways in which you decide to record data entries and the titles of databases and fields (that is, spelling, style, and the use of upper and lower case letters and any other characters on the keyboard).
6 *The source of information should be recorded.* This principle really applies to larger databases where data comes from various places, people and organizations. If the source of the information is noted, then one can check this material in order to judge how reliable the data is.

Source: adapted from Berjak and Grimsdell (1999)

Most important of all is to make sure that the names you are given refer to the species you are thinking of. The only way to be certain of this is to take a voucher specimen for verification in the herbarium later.

The names that people supply when asked are affected by a range of factors – some of them intrinsic to their lives, some of them dependent upon the circumstances of the interview. People's knowledge of plant names depends upon their daily activities and experience of the forest, fields, gardens, etc., in which they work, upon their own personalities and level of interest, and upon their position and relationship to the rest of the community. It is important to separate differences in names given by 'knowledgeable' and 'less knowledgeable' people from those given by people with varying kinds of specialist knowledge. Different names supplied by people who are equally knowledgeable are equally valid.

However, there is a further range of pitfalls to be overcome, related to the conditions under which you ask about names. In his classic work on ethnobiology, Brent Berlin (1992) noted that names depend upon people receiving correct stimulus – in other words, the diagnostic characters that they use in identification; upon the perceived knowledge of the researcher; and upon the perceived usefulness of the exercise. One study found that men in an Amazonian tribe were able to identify birds much more accurately than women; but the study was based on dead bird specimens. The women were used to hearing the birds, rather than seeing them, so specimens were not helpful to them in identifying the bird. In another study, he reports that women provided much more detail about the names of manioc varieties to female researchers than to male researchers simply because they did not perceive that men could possibly be interested in such knowledge or find it useful.

SELECTING, SAMPLING AND RECORDING YOUR SOURCES OF INFORMATION

If your sources are real people, how do you decide whom to interview? As was the case in Chapter 3, where we explained how to interview potential users of the guide, your sources of information do not need to be a statistically representative sample of any particular group of people. Random sampling is not appropriate here. You are not treating your respondents as the object of study, but as collaborators in the production of a useful consensus document. Your sources should be people who are recognized as knowledgeable about the topic in question (such as the local uses and ecology of the plants in the guide), and there should be agreement that the resulting information is correct. That means that information gathered from key sources should be presented and cross-checked with other members of the same stakeholder group, and should come from those who are considered by their peers to be the most knowledgeable. Nevertheless, as pointed out in the section on 'Nomenclature', there are different kinds of experts, and a sample should be inclusive of differences in gender, ethnic group and occupation.

Each type of 'expert', whether scientist, rural community member or outreach worker, has many demands on his or her time; so polite requests for interviews with explanations of the purpose, as well as flexibility are needed.

Box 7.2 BRAHMS AND ALICE: EXAMPLES OF SOFTWARE TO CREATE YOUR OWN BOTANICAL DATABASES

One software tool to help with producing field guides is the BRAHMS (Botanical Research and Herbarium Management System) database (see http://herbaria.plants.ox.ac.uk/bol/home). Species names, collection data, bibliographies and images can be assembled and formatted to create an almost limitless range of checklist styles. The concept of 'checklist' is treated broadly, but always has a list of species names as the central theme. This includes inventory-type lists of taxa from a specified geographic area (a forest reserve, a park, a country, continent or any other geographical area). It also includes taxonomic lists and synopses, not necessarily geographically restricted. Lists may constitute little more than a sorted record of names, perhaps with authors. Alternatively, a list may be richly annotated with nomenclature, descriptive text, references and other facts and features about the species, including images. Checklists may vary greatly in size and content. Some examples include:

- aquatic species found in a garden pond;
- *Shorea* in the central Philippines;
- a world checklist of conifers;
- a checklist of vascular plants of Mount Cameroon;
- the lianas of East Africa;
- commercial trees of Brazil.

Alice is another database management system for the creation, management and publication of information about organisms, designed for use by small or large collaborative projects working at different locations (see www.alicesoftware.com). Databases can be constructed about species, genera, varieties or cultivars, and Alice is flexible, so those producing the database decide what information to include. The basic data types are scientific names, vernacular names, uses, geographical distribution, habitats, text and user defined descriptors, and the Alice system can be configured on request to support any taxonomic hierarchy.

Data can be imported into Alice databases from other sources in a standard set of formats, including Description Language for Taxonomy (DELTA), using a merging tool kit. This means that Alice can be used with other tools for managing biological data. Tools, which do not require sophisticated technology, are also available for web publication of entire or subsets of databases. Alice webs are highly indexed, so finding taxa of interest and locating taxa with specific attributes is easy.

Examples of the use of Alice include the creation of species checklists and descriptive databases of:

- the world's legumes;
- cultivated plants such as potato, wheat and peas;
- endangered species of ethnobotany;
- plant usage of medical and poisonous plants, and other plant properties.

Always make a note of your sources for each single piece of information. For example, if you have a note of a local name, it is essential to know who gave you that name. This is important for three reasons:

1 When you are looking through lists of local names later, if you find discrepancies, you know who to check with.
2 If you find patterns (for example, women always use one name, men another; or different ethnic groups use different names), you can note this in your guide.
3 In case information is questioned after publication, you can refer back to the source.

In some guides, the authors explain in the introduction where they found the information about the species. This can help the user to decide how authoritative the guide is, and to understand why there are variations or gaps in the information. It can also stimulate guide users to note their own observations and provide feedback to the authors, which can help in producing later revised editions or even contribute significantly to scientific knowledge (see Box 2.1, page 17).

PRIMARY DATA: INFORMATION DIRECT FROM PEOPLE

There are many different methods available for gathering information using interviews and participatory techniques, and it is important to understand the suitability of each for the kind of information you need, and the person or other source you intend to get it from. Table 7.2 gives guidance on this. Both semi-structured interviews and questionnaires have a role to play in information-gathering for field guides; but in addition, a number of participatory tools are useful when seeking more local knowledge about the plants, their significance and uses. Finally, various documented sources of information can be searched to support your findings. All of these methods are described below.

Semi-structured interviews

As explained in Chapter 3, a semi-structured interview is one in which a relaxed but focused conversation discusses relevant issues but allows the informant to provide depth and indicate other issues of relevance. It is based on the preparation of a checklist of topics that covers all of the aspects the interviewer needs to know; but instead of reading out questions that cover the topics, the interviewer aims to have a naturalistic, flowing conversation with the informant by skilfully steering the discussion to cover all of the topics.

In order to do this, it is very important to avoid suggesting an answer to the informant; instead, the semi-structured interview relies strongly on open questions – questions to which it is not possible for the informant to guess a 'correct' answer, but instead will feel encouraged to reply from his or her own experience. The opposite of open questions, closed questions are often phrased in such as way that the answer can be 'yes' or 'no'. Open questions, which use phrases such as 'What do you think about X?' or 'Why do people do Z?' are much more productive.

Other techniques that are important in semi-structured interviewing are designed to ensure that you have really understood what your informant knows about the topic. Probing refers to exploring a topic more deeply, using techniques such as:

• waiting for further information;
• repeating a question;

Table 7.2 *Linking the method and source to the kind of information needed*

Kind of information	Source	Method
Distribution management uses Characteristics of related species Ways to avoid confusion with other similar species	Botanical specialists	Semi-structured interviews
Uses Cultural meanings/folklore Distribution and habitat preferences Management and cultivation	Rural experts	Semi-structured interviews Ethnobotanical surveys and questionnaires Observation Participatory workshops: • ranking • sorting • seasonal calendars • timelines • maps
	Other key informants	Semi-structured interviews
Distribution Ecology Uses	Herbarium specimen labels	Herbarium specimen search
Uses in other locations Cultural meanings	Internet	Internet searches with cross-checking of reliability
Generalized guidance on management for plants in that genus or family	Published work	Literature searches

Source: Anna Lawrence

- asking for an example or an explanation;
- asking for further information by asking 'what other things ...' – for example, 'what other species have this name?';
- repeating what the respondent has just said.

Don't forget to record the results in a way that is acceptable to the informant. Tape-recording the interview often seems like the best way to retain all of the detail; but there are two disadvantages – it may make respondents feel uncomfortable, and transcribing the results afterwards can take four or five times the total length of the interview. Nevertheless, if the respondent agrees and you have the time to transcribe it, this is the most accurate way of recording interviews. Otherwise, take care to write all the information you need in a notebook, together with the date, place and name of your informant. Box 7.3 provides more advice on how to make sure the interview goes well.

BOX 7.3 GUIDANCE ON CONDUCTING INTERVIEWS

This applies to any kind of interview, whether an in-depth unstructured discussion, a semi-structured interview with checklist of topics or a structured questionnaire.
   A good interviewer:

- is well prepared and understands the topic thoroughly;
- listens attentively to the respondent and does not impose his or her views;
- is courteous and friendly, and easily establishes rapport in the given cultural context;
- inspires confidence and trust by making sure that the respondent understands why he or she is conducting the interview;
- records the interview in a way that is both accurate and acceptable to the respondent.

A good interview:

- is held in an environment where the respondent feels at ease, and at a time which suits the respondent;
- begins with introductions and an explanation of the reasons for the interview;
- makes the respondent feel comfortable by assuring them of confidentiality and avoiding expressing an opinion of their responses;
- allows the respondent to talk as much as he or she wants to;
- keeps an eye on the time so that all of the questions can be addressed in the time available, without wasting the respondent's own time;
- ends by thanking the participant for making his or her time available.

Questionnaires

A structured questionnaire is highly appropriate for collecting information about each species in the guide since each description will contain the same categories. The questionnaire can simply be prepared as a form with the same categories of information that appear in your database. Questionnaires help to gain information from a large number of people, or about a large number of species, in a way that is easily analysed because the same specific questions are asked about each species. Although the terms 'questionnaire' and 'survey' are often used interchangeably, a questionnaire is a written form containing questions that people fill in, while a survey is a more general term that might include this, as well as face-to-face or telephone interviews. Both are good ways of gathering information systematically, but often reveal less about people's perceptions and concerns than more flexible methods such as semi-structured interviewing (see the previous section). Box 7.4 explains how to write and use a questionnaire.

   It is very important to field-test questionnaires before using them to gather your data. It is possible to waste much time talking to people before realizing that they have misunderstood some of your questions or you are missing an essential question, in which case you have to revisit all of your respondents. Field-testing means taking your draft questionnaire to a few friendly respondents who are happy to answer your questions on the understanding that you are testing and, therefore, that you welcome feedback on how easily they understand the questions and whether you have covered all of the possibilities.

Box 7.4 How to collect information using a questionnaire

- *Method*: producing, using and analysing a questionnaire.
- *Objective*: collect information from different stakeholders in a structured manner.
- *Output*: information regarding what different stakeholder groups want from the guide, and what they would like to be included in the guide.
- *Staff*: two researchers (do not need to be so experienced as those conducting semi-structured interviews).
- *Participants*: key informants or representatives from each stakeholder group.
- *Time*:
  - *preparation*: half a day;
  - *testing and amending*: one day;
  - *completing*: although questionnaires should be short (half an hour to one hour), it is rarely possible for an interviewer to complete more than four questionnaires in a day;
  - *analysis*: very dependent upon the number of questionnaires; allow one day per eight questionnaires for data entry and word processing, and a further two weeks full time for reviewing and editing the information, and planning follow-up.
- *Equipment*: if possible, computer with word-processing software to set up questionnaire, and spreadsheet software to analyse results.
- *Materials*: photocopied questionnaires; pens.

Planning

When planning a questionnaire, it is worth considering the following questions:

- What information do you need and from whom?
- Are these respondents going to be able to fill in a questionnaire?
- If not, do you have the resources to take the questionnaire to them and ask the questions in person?

In order to address these questions:

- Make a list of specific items of information that you need. Work backwards from the outline of your field guide to make sure that you haven't missed anything.
- Are you going to ask people face to face, by telephone, by email, or distribute printed copies of the questionnaire? If you will be present or on the phone line, you can help to explain the questions and fill in the answers yourself; but if you are sending out the questionnaire, you need to make sure the format and design is very clear so that people can fill it in for themselves.
- How precise does your information need to be? This will affect your choice of open-ended questions or multiple-choice questions.

Different types of questions

Closed questions are those that can have only a limited range of responses. They can be numerical responses. For example:

- How often do you visit this national park every year?

Or you may offer the respondent a list of possible answers and ask them to tick those that apply. For example:

- Which of the following help you to identify this species:
  (a) flower colour;
  (b) leaf shape;
  (c) bark;
  (d) smell;
  (e) other _____. (Please describe)

The last example, 'other', is, in fact, an open question. Open questions can involve any response. They are useful when you have fewer preconceptions about the answers you may receive and are still looking for new ideas. For example:

- What are the features of this tree that tell you it is species X?

Such questions can give you a rich variety of responses; but it is more difficult to analyse them in a structured way.

Writing the questionnaire

- Write an introduction to explain to respondents what the survey is about and how their response will help. If you are going to interview respondents in person, you can use this as a reminder to yourself of what you need to say.
- Explain why the questions are being asked.
- Start with interesting and easy questions.
- Avoid intrusive or sensitive questions. For a field guide, there should be little need for such questions in any case; but you might need to explore issues about ownership of information, or perceptions of why other guides have not worked. Many people do not like to be critical and will certainly avoid being so early on in the interview. They will be more likely to give their frank opinions once they are in their stride.
- The specific content depends upon the stage at which you are doing your planning. If you simply want to produce a popular guide that will encourage tourists to visit the area and take an interest in the plants, you will take a relatively open approach to finding out what sort of guide appeals to them most. If, however, you have already decided that you want to produce a guide to the mosses of a small nature reserve, you will not want to waste time on questions about people's favourite species, but instead move directly to questions about how familiar they are with plant identification procedures, how useful the scientific names are to them, etc.
- Conclude in a friendly way, thanking them for their time and informing them what feedback you will be able to provide, if any.
- Include a space to record the respondent's name and the place and date of the survey.
- Check your questionnaire carefully – and cut it down as much as possible. The world is full of questionnaires that are much too long and whose results have never been fully analysed.

Testing your questionnaire

- There must be no doubt about the meaning of your questions.
- The questionnaire design is the most important part of your research: if you get it right, the responses and analysis will follow smoothly.

- Pre-test everything – the questions, the questionnaire as a whole – with everybody who will give you the time of day.
- Does it really need to be that long?

Analysing the responses

- Enter data into a spreadsheet as you go along – this saves time and makes comparisons and analyses quicker and easier.
- Open responses can be categorized and grouped once all the responses have been received. This is useful to see general trends; but detail can be lost and bias introduced by the person categorizing the responses.
- Remember to give feedback from the questionnaire to respondents if this is appropriate.
- Since every question should have been asked for a reason, all responses will be useful in your project.

For example, it is common when asking a multiple-choice question to give respondents the option of answering 'other'. You might, for example, ask:

- Would you describe this leaf as:
  (a) oval;
  (b) round;
  (c) pointed;
  (d) other _____? (Please describe)

If, in your field test, you find that most of your respondents are answering 'other' and giving the description 'heart-shaped', it is more useful to revise the questionnaire and include that option in your list, rather than have everyone answer 'other'.

Case study 7.1 gives an example of a questionnaire used to provide all of the information needed for the descriptions in the guide to forage legumes of the Caatinga (Costa et al, 2002). However, it was by no means the first version of the questionnaire. It took several revisions to make the questions as clear as possible, to include all of the information categories needed and to avoid repetition between questions.

Ethnobotanical studies

Ethnobotany is the study of local knowledge about plants, usually referring specifically to knowledge held by indigenous people. It is not a separate methodology, but rather an interdisciplinary field that combines methods from biology, anthropology and more quantitative social sciences. It follows the principles of interviewing and questionnaire construction given above. However, some extra guidance may be needed when interviewing indigenous groups about their knowledge and use of plants, both because their worldview may be quite distinct from that of the field guide authors, making it difficult to understand each other's perceptions of the plants and habitats, and because plants, animals and natural habitats may be so important to the indigenous people that they feature significantly in the culture and in a way that respondents may be reluctant to divulge. It is important to respect this and avoid pushing for more information than

CASE STUDY 7.1 QUESTIONNAIRE TO COLLECT INFORMATION ABOUT THE FORAGE LEGUMES TO BE INCLUDED IN A BRAZILIAN GUIDE FOR COMMUNITY USE

Note to the interviewer: this questionnaire is for use with key informants from the communities and with agricultural development workers. It is important that the respondent feels comfortable and willing to give the information. It is a long questionnaire. You should make sure that the person does not feel obliged to answer all of the questions. If this is not the case, the person could give an incorrect answer.

Place of interview: _____

Person interviewed: _____

Date: _____

_____

1   Scientific name:
2   The most used popular name:
3   Other popular names known in the region:

I Morphological characteristics

4   What is the habit of this plant? ( ) herb; ( ) bush; ( ) shrub; ( ) tree

Height:
5   Shape of the crown:
According to the farmer:
According to the interviewer: ( ) rounded; ( ) elongated; ( ) spreading; ( ) other
6   Does the plant have thorns? ( ) yes; ( ) no
7   Do the thorns fall off the plant easily? ( ) yes; ( ) no
8   Where do you find the thorns? ( ) on the trunk; ( ) on the branches; ( ) on the leaves; ( ) other:
9   What is the shape of the thorns? ( ) straight; ( ) curved
10 Behaviour of the trunk: ( ) peeling bark; ( ) non-peeling bark

Question for the interviewer:
check whether there is any difference between the outer and inner bark.
11 Texture of the trunk: ( ) smooth; ( ) rough
12 Colour of the trunk: ( ) light; ( ) dark
13 Are the hairs visible on the leaves? ( ) yes; ( ) no
14 Texture of the leaves: ( ) brittle; ( ) not brittle
15 What is the colour of the flowers?
16 Shape of the fruit:
17 Shape of the seeds:

II Phenology

18 When does it begin to flower? ( ) dry season; ( ) during the first rains; ( ) other:
19 During which months?

20 In which season is the plant covered in leaves?
21 When is the plant flowering (period when it is in full flower)?
22 When is the fruiting season (period during which it is in full fruit)?
23 When is the plant completely without leaves?
24 When is the plant completely with leaves?
25 Any other observations:

III Uses

26 Eaten by which type of animal? ( ) goat; ( ) sheep; ( ) cow; ( ) donkey; ( ) horse;
     ( ) birds; observations:
27 Which part of the plant is eaten? ( ) leaf; ( ) branches; ( ) pods; ( ) flowers; ( ) bark;
     ( ) trunk; ( ) seeds; ( ) wood
28 How do the animals eat this fodder? ( ) stall fed (in which case, do you dry it?);
     ( ) directly from the plant; ( ) on the ground
29 Which fodder does the plant produce in the dry season? ( ) leaf; ( ) pods; ( ) flower;
     ( ) seed; ( ) bark; ( ) branches
30 Which other uses does the plant have? ( ) medicinal; ( ) firewood; ( ) soap; ( ) hay;
     ( ) honey; ( ) human food; ( ) charcoal; ( ) timber/fence/furniture/benches; ( ) others:

IV Management

31 Do you know what coppicing is?
32 Does the plant coppice? ( ) yes; ( ) no
33 Under what conditions: ( ) following fire; ( ) after being cut
34 Do you know people who plant these trees? ( ) yes; ( ) no
35 How do they do it? ( ) stakes; ( ) seed
36 Which plants do people worry about conserving around here?
37 Why?
38 Do you collect the seeds of pods of these plants? ( ) yes; ( ) no
39 During which season?
40 How do you ensure the conservation of these seeds/beans?
41 How do you make the seed germinate, and does it germinate easily? ( ) plant directly
     in the field; ( ) make a seed bed; ( ) other:
42 What is the procedure utilized for forage? ( ) cut, dry, store and give; ( ) cut and give;
     ( ) cut, dry, make hay, store and give; ( ) cut, grind, make silage and give;
     ( ) others:

V Problems or restrictions in use

43 Problems or difficulties when the animal tries to eat the plant: ( ) the seed punctures
     the stomach; ( ) the plant is very high; ( ) poisonous; ( ) others:
44 Is this plant toxic to the animal? ( ) yes; ( ) no
45 When is it toxic? ( ) when it is green; ( ) when it is withered; ( ) when it is cut;
     ( ) others:

VI Other information

Source: research for Costa et al (2002)

informants are willing to provide, at the same time avoiding jumping too quickly to conclusions about the meaning of the information provided.

Several detailed books on ethnobotany and its methods are available, including two in this series (Martin, 1995; Cunningham, 2001) and two other highly recommendable volumes (Alexiades, 1996; Cotton, 1996). Producing a field guide may seem like only the tip of the ethnobotanical iceberg, and yet many ethnobotanical studies either start, or end, with the decision to produce a guide, often with the aim of 'conserving traditional knowledge'. We cannot go into all the issues around this here, but note that issues of self-determination (the right of indigenous peoples to decide what is documented and how) and intellectual property (see below) are paramount.

The choice of respondents needs particular attention in an ethnobotanical study. An ethnobiological description, or field guide based on such a study, may consist of only that knowledge unanimously agreed on by all informants or the combined knowledge of all. But some knowledge is more important in that is it more salient and widely shared, while other knowledge is unique to individuals (Berlin, 1992).

A major task of ethnobiological description is to find relationships between folk and scientific classifications. While a field guide is not usually a work of ethnotaxonomy (indigenous systems of classification) in itself, it is often the result of such studies and may well be organized in such a way as to reflect local classifications. It is useful, therefore, to understand how ethnobotanists go about understanding such systems. There are two well-established systematic ways of gathering basic data from which the patterns of variation in informants' classifications may emerge:

1   use of prepared specimens, which multiple informants are requested to view and name independently of one another;
2   use of several different informants who identify multiple plant or animal species in their natural state at the time of collection, but none of whom see the full set of collections.

Such studies are also important for finding out the local names used for the plants in the field guide. However, naming is not the same as classification. If an informant tells you that a plant is 'a kind of fern', that means that he perceives it to belong in the group of plants that he knows as ferns. It does not mean that the name of the plant is 'fern'.

More important in the context of field guide preparation is to find out how different people identify different species, and what are the characters that they rely on. This can help to develop user-friendly identification keys as described in Chapters 5 and 6. One approach that has been used to elicit the characters employed by different local forest users is described in Case study 7.2.

Participatory visual methods

The tools developed under the umbrella of participatory rural appraisal (PRA) often rely strongly on using visual methods to stimulate discussion and to record information. This is for several reasons: visual information, such as maps and diagrams, is more easily shared by a group, thereby avoiding the sensitive situation of a researcher writing down data on a form that she then takes away without locals sharing in the results. Visual information is also more easily shared with people who do not read and write – or who

Case study 7.2 Methods developed on Mount Cameroon to elicit characters used in indigenous plant identification

Penny Fraser

If we want to talk or write about plant identification, or to teach others how to identify plants, then we need to work out which characters are being used in the identification process. The characters used by formally trained botanists are well documented. But do people from other cultural and knowledge domains use the same characters? Researchers working on Mount Cameroon were aware that people from different backgrounds not only speak different languages, but can think, see, perceive and interpret in different ways. They therefore designed a series of exercises to elicit information on the characters and processes of plant identification used by local plant experts with contrasting backgrounds and relationships with plants. Mount Cameroon was an appropriate site for this work because it hosts great diversity of species, habitats and ethnic groups: 2435 plant species; 28 rare animal species; a rise from sea level and 34°C to 4094m and 20°C in less than 14km. Rainfall also rainfall varies greatly, from 800–11,000mm within 40km.

The teacher–student role-playing exercise

The objective of this exercise is to elicit which characters and processes plant experts use when they are identifying plants. The output of the exercise is a ranked list of the identification characters for each participating user group. Analysis enables calculation of the total number and relative importance of different characters and character types, within and between sample groups. A suitable sample for the exercise is 3 to 15 plant identification experts, working with a staff of two facilitators. Essential equipment comprises pre-prepared recording sheets and an audio tape-recorder, and, most importantly, a location containing habitats and plants familiar to participants.

Method

The rationale behind the exercise is first explained to participants:

- Identification is something we do every day, without giving it much thought.
- In order to teach plant identification, it is necessary to know what it is that we do unconsciously each time we identify, and which criteria are used.

In order to make people think about how they identify plants, they will pretend that they are teachers who have to teach their students how to identify specific plants. The researchers will be the students; participants have to choose a plant that they know and teach the researcher how to identify it. Participants have to try and teach well, and students to learn well. The information that passes between them will be recorded.

The procedure is then explained before commencing.

Procedure

The group will go on a walk during which each participant, in turn, will act as a teacher, selecting a plant that they know and teaching the facilitator (who acts as the 'student') how to identify that plant. Participants need to imagine that they want to send the 'student', unaccompanied, to collect the selected plant; so the student must know exactly how to distinguish it from other plants. Teachers can choose any plant in the bush, farm, forest or garden that they know well. Live in situ plants will be used as teaching material. The group must choose a route for the walk that includes a range of habitat types and plants, enabling all members to find plants that they would like to use for their teaching.

'Teaching' should take place in front of a small group, one facilitator recording the identification characters provided by the teacher, the other acting as student. The student asks questions, probing the 'teacher' for information, until satisfied that sufficient information has been provided to fully identify the plant. Using a banana plant as an example:

- Teacher: 'You know this plant because it has long fruits in a bunch and long huge leaves. It also has a smooth and green stem, not as hard as a tree stem.'
- Student: 'But a plantain is also like that; how can I know that this is banana and not plantain?'

The teacher then continues with further characters – 'banana fruits are smaller than plantain fruits … and there is a white powder, etc.'. Enthusiasm for the exercise can develop as the floor is thrown open – when student and teacher flag, other participants can assist them, pointing out gaps in the character list. Some participants will need encouragement to adopt the teaching role and may prefer to role play on a one-to-one level, or with a sub-group. Facilitators must mediate and ensure that all personality types participate.

If you have different livelihood groups among your participants, you can test for different character use between them by asking everyone to gather together after the walk and produce a matrix of the most important characters for each sub-group. Define 'important' as the first characters that they would teach a plant identification novice. Participants may agree among themselves on the choice of characters and their ranking, or the exercise may require facilitation, first eliciting a list of the ten most important characters, and then discussing and reaching consensus on the ranking. Statistical tests can be applied to the matrix to test for significant difference between groups.

Results

The knowledge elicitation exercises were tested on a sample of plant experts who live and work in the forests of Mount Cameroon. Five user groups were sampled: hunters, farmers, timber exploiters, spice collectors and herbalists. The results indicated that context is important. People from different user groups identified plants in different ways, using different characters perceived in different ways, as well as a different total number of characters. There was greater similarity within user groups than within communities. The process of identification was linked to a person's relationship with the plants that they deal with. Timber exploiters, for example, use the shape of the tree – the stem and branches (important in terms of timber value). Hunters also work with many tree species, but were more tuned in to features of fruits and ecology (when trees fruit; whether and which animals eat the fruit, or sleep in the trees), traits important to their trade. Timber exploiters used many characters that require action before they can be perceived (30 per cent of first characters used): they cut wood and look at the colour and texture inside. Hunters used 'active' characters first only 5 per cent of the time. Different groups used different parts of the plants to different extents. Herbalists and spice collectors emphasize leaves: flowers were used by only two user groups. Herbalists used a suite of characters most similar to that of taxonomists; characters they gave importance to included leaf traits and hair cover. A person's background determines which part of the available information they use. From the full suite of characters, 42 per cent were used in a single community; only 21 per cent were used in all four. In contrast, the number of characters used in different farmer, hunter and timber exploiter communities was consistent. Timber exploiters, on average, used the most identification characters and herbalists the least, with greater variation among spice collector communities.

do it so rarely that they feel uncomfortable and nervous when expected to. Finally, visual methods are more fun and attract more participants to join in the discussion around them. They are particularly suitable for use in workshops or small groups.

Two of these methods, ranking and sorting, are described in Chapter 3. These are helpful at the early stages of planning a field guide when a method is needed to prioritize the species to be included. They can also be used at this later stage of gathering more information about each species because they often stimulate much discussion about why people have decided to put them in the chosen categories, or to rank them in the order they have given. One particularly useful method for elaborating upon these reasons for ranking, which thereby provides considerable additional information about the species being ranked, is the matrix scoring diagram (see Box 7.5). This has the advantage that the categories of information about the species are defined by the local people most knowledgeable about those species, and that all categories are covered for all species – hence, providing the kind of systematic information that we have seen is so important.

Three other participatory visual tools that can help in acquiring information suitable for the field guide, depending upon its users and purpose, are seasonal calendars, timelines and maps (see Box 7.5). Participatory mapping, in particular, can help a community group to discuss the kinds of habitats that different species are found in, and to indicate where particular individuals might be found for sampling purposes. Seasonal calendars demonstrate the annual cycle of growth, management and use of a given species. Timelines are used to explore the longer-term history of (in this case) a community's resource use, and can highlight changes in availability, abundance or use of a given species.

As with all methods for collecting information, whether questionnaires or more participatory methods, it is important to keep your eyes open and observe the species and vegetation around you, and constantly cross-check that reported information and reality match up (see the section 'Accuracy and reliability' later in this chapter).

SECONDARY SOURCES: INFORMATION FROM EXISTING DOCUMENTED SOURCES

In most cases, your field guide will not be the first to publish information about the chosen species. Valuable additional information on medicinal uses, chemical content, management or conservation status can often be gleaned from scientific journals, books, botanical databases and the internet. Even field guides in relatively neglected areas of the world can benefit from a literature search. When the authors of the guide to trees and shrubs for agroforestry systems in the inter-Andean valleys of Santa Cruz (Vargas et al, 2000) conducted a literature search, they found useful published information about 32 of their 60 chosen species, adding greatly to the advice on management and use of those trees.

There are now so many scientific journals that might contain useful information, it has become impossible to physically search each one. If possible, try to gain access to bibliographic databases. This is more likely in a university or research institute, and in a relatively wealthy country, so colleagues can be useful in this regard. Such bibliographic databases allow keyword searches on numerous scientific databases. The internet provides many more opportunities to search for published information. Search engines

Box 7.5 Visual participatory methods

Matrix scoring diagram

- *Objective*: participants assess different items (in this case, species), using criteria that they themselves identify.
- *Outputs*:
  - a set of criteria for differentiating or describing species, and the reasons for including them in the guide;
  - species-specific information for each of those criteria;
  - where relevant, differences between different stakeholder groups in terms of their perceptions of the criteria.
- *Staff*: one experienced facilitator with, if possible, an experienced observer to record process and results.
- *Participants*: representatives from each stakeholder group.
- *Time*: half a day.
- *Materials*: this depends upon what the informants feel comfortable with. A large sheet of paper, with pens to draw the outline of the table, is ideal for the purpose of taking the information back to the office to copy into the field guide. However, it is also common to draw the matrix on the ground.

While some participants will want to write the information in the table boxes, others will feel more comfortable allocating the appropriate number of beans or stones to each species.

- *Methods*: a common matrix scoring diagram takes the form of a table, with species along the horizontal axis and the elicited criteria along the vertical axis. The job of the facilitator is to encourage the participants to:
  - Name all of the species they would like to include in the matrix (this may already be decided if the species list for the guide has already been agreed).
  - Discuss what the important criteria are to describe each species. This is often a confusing terminology, and it is easiest to explain what you are looking for by asking the group to compare two species and write down the factors that they give; compare another two, and write down any additional factors; and finally ask them to look at the list of factors that differ among all of the species and complete the list.
  - Prepare a table with the names of the species along the top row, and the factors differentiating them down the left-hand column.
  - Ask the group to assign a value or a description to each species for each factor. If assigning values, it is useful to indicate a range – for example, you could suggest that a score of 10 indicates a 'very good' or 'very strong' characteristic, while a score of 0 indicates a non-existent characteristic. For instance, if one of the criteria is 'useful for fuelwood', then a herbaceous species might score 0, while trees might score 5 (some use) to 10 (best use).

Note that scoring is not the same as ranking; the species are not being placed in order; instead, each factor is being weighed up for each species.

Seasonal calendars

- *Objective*: document seasonal trends of species phenology (seasons of leafing, flowering and fruiting) and use.
- *Outputs*: a description for each species of seasonality of appearance and use.
- *Staff*: one experienced facilitator.

- *Participants*: a group of local knowledgeable respondents; the aim is to achieve consensus rather than to explore differences of perception as the field guide should indicate a pattern that is helpful to the user in identifying the species.
- *Time*: two hours.
- *Materials*: a large sheet of paper and pens of various colours. It is also possible to make a seasonal calendar by improvising with locally available materials, such as sticks, leaves and stones. However, the facilitator will still need pen and paper in order to note the results and incorporate them later within the guide.
- *Methods*: seasonal calendars begin by drawing a long line to indicate the course of the year. Events can then be marked along the line, or stones and beans may be used to show varying availability or abundance during the year. Simple line graphs can be drawn to show seasonal increases or decreases.

Timelines or historical profiles

- *Objective*: document historical trends of vegetation and species condition and use.
- *Outputs*: a description of changes over time (usually over the course of living memory) of the state of the vegetation and (where possible) particular species. This provides valuable context for the introduction to the guide.
- *Staff*: one experienced facilitator.
- *Participants*: a group of local knowledgeable respondents; the aim is to achieve as much detail as possible, as well as consensus. Older people who have lived all of their lives in the area are especially valuable in this activity.
- *Time*: two hours.
- *Materials*: a large sheet of paper and pens of various colours. Alternatively, a line can be indicated on the ground, and group members write events on cards which they place at the appropriate time point on the line. This allows people to move cards around if they decide later that they need to accommodate more events or realize that events happened in a different order. The facilitator will need pen and paper in order to note the results and incorporate them later within the guide.
- *Method*: people share accounts of the past, condition of the forest or other wild habitats, ecological histories, changes in land-use and species-use patterns, changes in customs and practice, and relevant changes and trends in human behaviour.

Participatory mapping or resource mapping

- *Objective*: indicate vegetation, land-use patterns and specific locations of species of interest for the guide; understand people's perceptions of why the vegetation is that way and why species occur in those habitats. This provides useful information as context for the introduction and specific to each species.
- *Outputs*: a map that indicates habitats and species, preferably with landmarks and indicators that help participants to locate those habitats and species later on for further discussion and/or botanical sampling.
- *Staff*: one experienced facilitator.
- *Participants*: a group of local knowledgeable respondents; the aim is to achieve as much detail as possible, as well as consensus. A range of local stakeholders who know the area in different ways through their different daily activities will work well in this activity.
- *Time*: two to three hours.
- *Materials*: a large sheet of paper and pens of various colours. Alternatively, the map can be drawn on the ground using locally available materials. The facilitator will need pen and paper in order to note the results for use in later field visits and interviews; often the participants will themselves want to keep the original or a copy of the map for themselves.

BOX 7.6 HOW TO ASSESS INFORMATION THAT YOU FIND ON THE INTERNET

Great care needs to be taken with information found on the internet. Anyone can create a website and publicize their personal opinions. But it is often difficult to tell who the author is, what his or her sources were, when it was written or revised, whether it is quoting, copying or stealing (accurately or inaccurately) from someone else, and whether it has been edited, refereed or otherwise approved by a third party.

Don't include information from internet sources in your field guide unless you feel confident that you know about:

*   The website itself: if it is just someone's homepage, ask yourself why they have not published the information somewhere more reliable. A moderated discussion, where others have the chance to respond and critique information, is more reliable, as are websites of known institutions, such as universities and natural history museums.
*   The author and his or her occupation and qualifications: what does a search for their background and other work indicate about them?
*   The sources of their information (what do they tell you about them?): if the information conflicts with everything else written about this species, for example, distrust the website.
*   The reasons for putting the information on the website: does the host or the author have a bias?

Of course, many knowledgeable people put valuable information on the internet because it is such a convenient way to communicate quickly. Take a careful approach to checking your sources and make the most of this amazing resource.

---

such as Google, Yahoo, MSN and Excite allow you to type in the species name and search for any information that has been put on a website. A word of warning, however: while the increase in information access over the web is exciting, there are no checks on accuracy. Anyone can put information on a website, and much of it is anecdotal and consists of one-off observations. Although such observations may be perfectly valid and correct, without the external reviewing system that applies to scientific journals, it is sometimes hard to know what you can trust from the internet. Of course, if the information is on a website of a respected institution, that helps. Box 7.6 provides some tips on the reliability of internet sources.

Another valuable source, if you can obtain access to them, is the range of botanical databases that have been established around the world. These are often for a specific botanical group, and data is related to the scientific name of the species. The most useful, for the purposes of writing a field guide, are those which store data on the geographical distribution of plants or plant characteristics (for example, medicinal properties). Some international databases are listed in Box 7.7, and botanists at your local herbarium or university will know of any relevant ones for your area.

Finally, herbarium labels can be a rich source of secondary information about plants. Many botanists record habitat, behaviour, details of interactions with animals or information given about the uses of the plant at the time of collection.

> ## BOX 7.7 EXISTING BOTANICAL DATABASES THAT CAN HELP WITH NAME CHECKING AND KNOWN USES, DISTRIBUTION AND CONSERVATION STATUS
>
> Existing botanical databases include the following:
>
> - TROPICOS (Missouri Botanical Garden's database): www.mobot.org/W3T/Search/vast.html;
> - Threatened Plant Database of the World Conservation Monitoring Centre (lists conservation status of threatened species, together with a range of other valuable databases, such as medicinal plants and tropical trees): www.unep-wcmc.org/index.htmlwww.unep-wcmc.org/cis/~main;
> - International Legume Database and Information Service (ILDIS): www.ildis.org/;
> - Survey of Economic Plants for Arid and Semi-Arid Lands (SEPASAL) (a database and enquiry service about useful 'wild' and semi-domesticated plants of tropical and subtropical drylands, developed and maintained at the Royal Botanic Gardens, Kew): www.rbgkew.org.uk/ceb/sepasal/.

OWNERSHIP, INTELLECTUAL PROPERTY RIGHTS AND COPYRIGHT

Whenever you are working in a situation where information is passed from one person to another, for publication or possible commercial use, issues arise over ownership of the information. This may be a matter of simply taking care of professional sensitivities; but in some cases it can be a legal matter.

Ownership of an idea is covered by intellectual property rights, which are addressed by a rapidly developing body of law, both international and national. Much of this originated from commercial interests, and the recent concern about biodiversity and intellectual property rights has arisen mainly because of the commercial use to which biodiversity information can be put. This has raised issues of social justice, particularly where indigenous people have useful knowledge about medicinal or agricultural plant uses, which has been made use of by unscrupulous corporations without due reward to the original holders of that knowledge. The situation starts from a very un-level playing field, and it is now a major concern of non-governmental organizations (NGOs) and indigenous organizations to win a share of the benefits from their custodianship and knowledge of biodiversity. The situation is described in detail by Dutfield (2000). The key points for writers of field guides are to make sure that informants are aware of the use you want to make of their knowledge and agree to it (through what is known as 'prior informed consent'); and to understand the law in the country of publication relating to distribution of benefits resulting from use of that knowledge. Specialists advise that it is often better from the indigenous people's point of view to publish their knowledge so that it is clearly identified as their property, with due reward applied if commercial use is made of it. However, there are numerous complexities involved in identifying the legitimate original holders of knowledge (for example, is it the medicinal specialists in the community, the men, the women, a particular family, an individual or the whole ethnic group?), and clear agreements should be obtained with any communities involved in the guide production (Laird, 2002).

Copyright is a different and less complex matter. Copyright does not protect ideas. It protects the way in which the idea is expressed in a piece of work; but it does not protect the idea itself. So the actual form of words in the field guide, or the illustrations, are copyright, and others do not have the right to copy them for personal gain or commercial use. However, because field guides are sometimes produced with the intention of reaching as many people as possible, the authors may explicitly waive copyright with a statement at the beginning of the guide to the effect that 'users are welcome to photocopy this guide' or 'users may quote the text or use the illustrations as long as this source is acknowledged'.

Of course, the copyright works the other way round as well. If you use other authors' published words or illustrations, make sure that you obtain permission first. Chapter 8 provides specific advice on copyright of illustrations.

ACCURACY AND RELIABILITY

Authors of any non-fiction book are concerned that the content is as accurate and reliable as possible; but with a field guide, there are a number of extra pitfalls relating to certainty over the identification of the species and the linking of information to those species. It would be quite disastrous to find out some fascinating medicinal uses of a plant and publish those under an incorrect scientific name next to the wrong illustration simply because of a muddle over local names. Therefore, particular attention needs to be paid to:

- the steps to ascertain the scientific name;
- the guidance on local nomenclature given above;
- linking ancillary information on uses, ecology and cultivation to a specific plant which the authors have seen with their own eyes, and have positively identified with its scientific name, or from which they have collected voucher specimens for later identification in the herbarium (see Box 4.3, page 67, for information on how to collect voucher specimens).

There are several aspects to accuracy, and the most relevant ones relate to the concepts of validity, reliability and objectivity:

- Valid results are ones that we believe represent the 'truth' of the findings, and that are also applicable in other contexts or with other groups of people than the ones who provided the information. For example, if you describe a plant as useful for curing stomach ache, you want to be sure that it really does cure stomach ache, whoever uses it. If you are unable to verify the information, you can, instead, report that 'people in such-and-such a region use the plant to cure stomach ache'.
- Reliable results are ones that would be the same if you repeated the research again in a similar situation. For example, if you ask only a few people about the plants or you conduct your survey in a hurry, you might miss out the most knowledgeable people or annoy the informants so that they give incomplete information. Under

different circumstances, you might, by chance, interview other representatives of the community, more in sympathy with your objectives, who might give you different information. The only way to avoid this is to take great care over your research procedures and follow the sampling and interviewing guidelines given above.

- Objective results have not been affected by the biases, motivations and perspectives of the researchers or facilitators. For example, a facilitator who assumed that only men know the plants because they are the ones who go to the forest might forget to interview the women of the village and, hence, overlook medicinal or nutritional information about the species.

These criteria are often used in social research; but where participatory approaches are used, and particularly where culturally specific information about plants is to be included in the guide, authors may need to recognize that different informants or stake-holders perceive different 'realities'. They see the natural world and the plants in different ways. Instead of finding one 'true' perspective on knowledge and use of the plants, a good balanced description of the different uses by different people, or in different places, is more reasonable.

Because participatory approaches use terms such as 'informal' and 'qualitative', they are sometimes assumed to be less rigorous and accurate than more conventional social research methods. But careful attention to the process means that results can be just as reliable and valid as a more structured research approach. Jules Pretty and his colleagues (1995) have developed a list of criteria for 'trustworthiness' which serve as a checklist to make sure that you can trust the results of your data-gathering (see Box 7.8). The most important of these are triangulation (use of multiple sources, methods and investigators) and asking participants to check your interpretation of the results. You can also cross-check with the published literature. They point out, however, that it will never be possible to be certain about the trustworthiness criteria – all we can say is that X is trust-worthy because certain things happened during and after the process of joint investigation and analysis.

In the end, you may have to make a judgement about who is right. If respondents cannot agree (which is unusual), you can do several things:

- You may feel the range of opinions is interesting in itself, particularly if there is a pattern, such as women mentioning one use and men mentioning another; in this case, you can include the various uses in the guide, with information about who provided the information.
- If there is an alternative way to verify the information, such as direct observation, do it. For example, if local informants give varying opinions about the habitat of a particular palm, it may well be that they have in mind two different palm species with similar names. Such confusion can be easily cleared up by asking the infor-mants to accompany you to specimens of the tree growing in its natural habitat.
- Try to work out whether there might be a reason why people are giving you inaccu-rate information – is there confusion over the species name? Do villagers suspect that you are going to steal their traditional knowledge? Try to address these concerns.

Box 7.8 Criteria for trustworthiness

Criteria for trustworthiness, adapted from Pretty et al (1995), that are relevant in producing a field guide are as follows:

- Know the informants well through prolonged and/or intense engagement with them in order to build trust and rapport.
- Persistent and parallel observation: keep your eyes open and check that what people tell you matches what you see.
- Triangulation by multiple sources, methods and investigators: broadly speaking, this means using at least three sources or three methods or three different interviewers to cross-check information, increasing the range of different people's realities.
- Peer or colleague checking: this involves periodical review meetings with peers not directly involved in the enquiry process.
- Participant checking: this entails testing the data, interpretations and conclusions with people with whom the original information was constructed and analysed.
- Parallel investigations and team communications: if sub-groups of the same team proceed with investigations, in parallel, using the same approach, and come up with the same or similar findings, then these findings are more trustworthy.
- Enquiry audit: the enquiry team should be able to provide sufficient information for an external person to examine the processes and product in such a way as to confirm that the findings are not a figment of their imaginations.

Whatever steps you take to ensure that your information is correct and valid, it is helpful to document the processes and explain them in the introduction to your field guide so that the reader can understand the basis for trusting the content of the guide.

WRITING

Collecting the information is only half of the process; it must also be assembled into clear, easily understood text. Start to write as early in the process as possible, even before you have all the information you need for each species. It can easily take several hours to write a description for a species, and sometimes much longer for guides at the botanical end of the spectrum (see Case study 7.3). Authors often underestimate the difficulties of writing clearly for other types of readers, and it is advisable to start with a species that you know well to help you find out what the challenges might be. The process of putting together species descriptions can also help to finally decide which species are to be included, and whether aspects of the guide need to be redefined.

It is the written parts of the text that require most checking and testing because it is through written language that humans experience most differences of style and meaning. Authors therefore need time to check the accuracy of the content and to test comprehension of the text.

Several aspects of language need to be taken into account – not only the dialect and local or national language to be used, but also the choice of technical or non-technical terms. Guides that are produced with and for indigenous peoples may be written in languages which have only recently been documented, or for which the phonetic rules (the relationship between the spoken sound and the written spelling) have recently been changed. In such cases, it is important to consult an expert in that language and to take particular care when testing that the users have really understood your meaning. In other cases, you might think about the message that your choice of language will send to the reader. The eco-tourist guide for Rio de Contas described in Box 2.1 was written in Portuguese and English, attracting a range of visitors to the area; the *Flora da Reserva Ducke* is written solely in Portuguese, making it accessible to botanists from countries across Latin America and motivating students to identify species for themselves.

In addition to the main language of the guide, it is common to include the vernacular or local language names of each species, often in a range of local languages and dialects (see Chapter 4 for more nomenclature).

Writing well

Some principles of clear writing apply widely, regardless of the education or interests of the reader. Obviously, technical words have their uses; but they are not necessary as often as is thought. Using short and familiar words is a skill that many technical and academic writers could refine. The advice of the Plain English Campaign applies to all languages (see Box 7.9). In the end, the best way to proceed is to find an example that works for your target audience (through the consultations at planning stage – see Chapter 3), analyse it and try to write in the same style, and finally test it before publishing the guide (see Chapter 9).

Formatting and layout of text

Experiment with different models for setting out the information on the page. Take into consideration:

- font;
- size;
- spacing;
- number of columns of text;
- heading and subheadings – number, format (bold, italics or underlined), as well as spacing around them. (Headings help to break up the page and affect the understanding of the material. Consider which word is the most prominent on the page – this forms part of the access system – see Chapter 5 – as it is the word that people will see when leafing through the guide. In many guides this will be the species name in its version that is most relevant to the user group.); and
- mixing of text and illustrations (using pictures and diagrams to break up the text helps to make it more accessible to people who are not used to reading).

The authors should have a good idea of the users' preferences from the consultations at the planning stage (see Chapter 3). However, it is always necessary to test again at this stage by comparing different formats for comprehensibility.

BOX 7.9 ADVICE ON WRITING WELL

Advice on writing clearly and simply is provided by the Plain English Campaign (see www.plainenglish.co.uk/). Wherever possible:

- Use short words.
- Use everyday English; avoid jargon and explain
  any technical terms that you have to use.
- Make sure that sentences have no more than 20 words.
- Do not include several ideas in one sentence.
- Use active verbs rather than passive verbs (for example,
  'the local people use this plant to cure stomach pains' is preferable
  to 'this plant is used by the local people to cure stomach pains').
- While writing, imagine how you would talk to the reader;
  use a sincere, straightforward style.

Writing a species description

The species description is the botanical part of the guide, and you will need to be familiar with Chapters 4 and 6 before you can embark on this. However, while botanists are trained to write complete and detailed botanical descriptions that are perfectly comprehensible to other botanists, this art form is not so accessible to users from other backgrounds, and it is in writing and testing the botanical description that most care will be needed not to resort to technical language. As Jorge Costa points out in Case study 7.3, describing the key characteristics of a species in layman's language can often take more space than using the carefully defined specialist terms of botanical language, and it may be more feasible to use some technical terms in the text which are clearly defined in a glossary.

If you take this route, though, it is especially important to check that your intended user group can understand how to use the glossary to look up the meaning of a technical term and, furthermore, that they can actually understand the definitions given there. The Brazilian team producing the guide described in Case study 7.3 also produced the much simpler guide to 21 leguminous species based on the questionnaire in Case Study 7.1, to be used by communities and outreach workers in the Caatinga. They were surprised by the difficulties of writing a glossary. However, because they applied a careful and rigorous testing procedure, they discovered in good time that the users could not understand the definitions, and they rewrote it twice before they could be sure that it was acceptable.

Structuring the species descriptions should be relatively easy because the template has already been defined by the initial consultations with users and by the plan for information-gathering. However, because the data-gathering process can be iterative, and can help you to redefine the content of each species description, species descriptions may turn out to be structured a little differently from, for example, your questionnaire.

Writing other sections of the guide

Apart from the species descriptions themselves, there are, of course, other essential parts of the guide to be written. The introduction to the guide might be the most important

CASE STUDY 7.3 EXPERIENCE OF WRITING SPECIES DESCRIPTIONS FOR NATURALISTS' GUIDE TO LEGUMES OF THE CAATINGA (DE QUEIROZ ET AL, FORTHCOMING)

In the text below, Jorge Costa describes the steps involved in the lengthy process of producing 250 species descriptions in a field guide intended for naturalists – in other words, for users with some education in biology, but no familiarity with the details of botanical jargon or classification. This example illustrates the need to plan carefully and to be quite systematic in gathering and presenting the information. It also shows how a number of different people may be needed to carry out the work. The student who was preparing the descriptions had some botanical training, but was not a specialist in the Leguminosae family and therefore had to consult with a botanical expert. Even though the guide was intended for non-specialists, the information that it was based on had to first come from an expert source, and then be 'translated' into more easily understood language:

1   *The first step was to limit the species content of the guide. The species of the Leguminosae family found in the Brazilian Caatinga were chosen because we could rely on an expert in this group who could subject the data collected and used in the descriptions to closer analysis, thus increasing its reliability.*

   Even so, having limited the content of the guide, we were faced with the need to survey and collect data on about 250 species of plants, which would inevitably prove time consuming. We decided to employ a student with some specialist knowledge in this area to undertake this task. The work consisted of surveying all of the features of each species using detailed descriptions. These descriptions were made in accordance with a diagnostic form specially designed for the project, which made it possible to transfer the information into a database and to standardize the data on the species. The difficulties involved in producing the descriptions were corroborated by the student, as some specialist knowledge of the family was required for the process to go ahead smoothly. The time taken on this task is an important consideration: all of the later stages of a project to produce a guide depend upon the surveying of this data.

   Because of time constraints, another person was employed to produce the descriptions. It is essential that this stage is carefully planned, taking account of the time available and the degree of experience of the individual(s) who are to complete the descriptions of the species for the database.

2   *Once all of the species had been described and the information fed into the database, the next step was to extract the data surveyed to build up a standardized description of all species. The information contained in the database had to be prepared to meet the needs of a description, in paragraph form. It is important to allow plenty of time for this and to choose the person responsible with care, as the job demands a certain degree of knowledge of the subject.*

3   *The third step is to make sure that all of the species descriptions are fully standardized and complete – that is, they contain all elements necessary to describe their salient features. The descriptions should be diagnostic*

in nature (in other words, focus on the characteristics that help to identify them, not on a full description of every feature of each species) and emphasize those features which characterize each species, without introducing too many elements outside the standardized model.

4   *The fourth step involves testing the descriptions on target users. This test showed us that the language adopted must be carefully graded in order to make it easily comprehensible for the user. Different language will be needed for each target readership.*

5   *The fifth step is to refine the language used in the descriptions in order to make it appropriate for the target user group, removing technical terms as far as possible that might cause difficulties for users without specialist knowledge. These adjustments to the language used bring with it another problem, that of space. If botanical terms have to be explained instead of used, the author will need to employ more words and, thus, more space. One way around this problem is to include a glossary for technical terms; but the language used in the glossary must also be suitable for the target users. To complement the glossary, an illustration can also be designed to show the morphology of the plants, with technical terms marked.*

To sum up, the descriptions must be succinct, clear and diagnostic in nature so that the target users can understand and use them. It is sometimes necessary to supply extra information to aid comprehension, although this information can be left out if a glossary and/or appropriate illustrations are included.

Source: based on an interview with Jorge Costa

chapter in terms of encouraging your target audience to buy the guide or use it, or to put into practice the information contained in it. Chapters that might come towards the end of the guide include a glossary, indexes and names of further contacts. The exact position of these in the guide will depend upon consultations with users and key informants that you conducted at the planning stage, and much of the content will come from the interviews and participatory research tools described above. Here is a checklist of the kinds of information that you might consider including:

- *Preface*: often a very brief section written by a senior person who recommends the guide to the users, perhaps indicating how it was funded and why it was produced.
- *Acknowledgements*: here the authors recognize and thank the efforts of all of those who contributed to the production of the guide; this may be a rather long chapter if the production process has been participatory. It is important to think carefully about this chapter as professional colleagues, as well as rural informants, are often delighted to see their name mentioned or are offended if it is omitted. This is an opportunity to show appreciation for their time and knowledge.
- *Contents page.*
- *A section or chapter on 'Who and what this guide is for' near the beginning*: this should be kept short and direct, and will help prospective users to decide whether to buy or use the guide. It also helps to personalize the guide by introducing the user from the beginning.

- *Geographic or botanical area covered*: indicate to the user how you selected the species that are in the guide. It is very important to indicate here whether you are offering a selective (subjective) range of species (such as 'useful species' or 'attractive flowering plants') or have included every possible species that occurs in that area or that botanical group (see Chapter 3 on species selection). This will help users to understand whether they can be sure that the species is in the book, or whether they can propose new species to be included.
- A *map of the area*, indicating key geographical features and ecological zones within the area, as well as human settlements or conservation designations (such as 'national park') where relevant.
- A *chapter or section on 'How to use this guide'*: again, keep it short and prominently near the beginning of the book. Tell users what to expect, and point to the tools that you have included to help them find their way around. Explain what order the species are in and why, and give step-by-step guidance on how to identify an unknown species. It will help your users to understand if you provide them with a couple of examples of these tools.
- A *chapter or section on 'How to identify plants in the field'*: this covers what to look for and particular features that might be confusing. Also include a section on 'What to take with you to the field'. This section will depend upon the existing knowledge of the target audience.
- *The key characteristics of the plant group covered by the guide, as well as main diagnostic characters*: for example, the team producing the guide to legumes of the Caatinga in Bahia, Brazil (de Queiroz et al, forthcoming) debated, at length, the value of including a section on 'How to identify a legume'. In the end, the team chose to include a section on 'Easily confused species'.
- *An introduction designed to inform the reader, whet their appetite and encourage them to use the guide*: this chapter will depend greatly upon your users and their level of interest and formal education, their occupations and their reasons for using the guide. As indicated in Chapter 2, for example, eco-tourists are likely to take the most interest in the general features of the area or plant group included in the book, and to enjoy reading about the history of ecological change, conservation and use of the plants. Others will be interested to know the relevance of local knowledge and plant use for conservation, or to read about the organizations involved in producing the guide.

Testing

All of the descriptions, introductory/explanatory text and layout of the text will be based on specifications prepared at the design stage, using the guidelines in Chapter 3. However, it is still necessary to check that the results are correct, understandable and useful. Every stage must be tested: analysed and formatted information must be cross-checked with the original sources of the information; and the language, style and layout must be checked with the potential users. Ultimately, it is important to be clear about roles – who owns the guide and who makes the final decision about what is correct or acceptable. In Bolivia, for example, the scientific authors of the guide to the useful plants of Bajo Paraguá (Vargas and Jordán, 2003) saw themselves as the technical team who oriented, supported and collected information, and analysed and presented results back to the communities. The ultimate decisions about content and format were made by the indigenous community members.

Chapter 9 provides guidance on testing the content, layout and usability of your guide.

8

Illustration

William Hawthorne and Rosemary Wise

INTRODUCTION

In earlier chapters, we saw how illustrations reduce the need for jargon, and work where literacy is limited or the audience speaks various languages. They facilitate a browsing approach to identification, which can be at least a useful starting point for identifying plants, and can show where details fit in the context of the plant as a whole in ways that words alone cannot. Even where the users think they know the plants, images are useful to confirm identification and for drawing attention to differences that might not otherwise be noticed. All users strongly prefer field guides that are illustrated and might not even try to use guides without them. They usually make the guide more attractive, more useful and likely to be used.

Illustration of one form or another is therefore likely to be essential in your field guide; yet the preparation of illustrations may well be your major task. In this chapter we summarize the pros and cons of various types of illustration, making frequent reference to trials on the subject in Cameroon, Ghana and Grenada (see Case study 8.1). We assume that anyone who is preparing a million-dollar field guide will have the services and advice of a professional photographer or illustrator; so on the basis of this, we are targeting our advice at projects with a more modest budget.

As with all aspects of the guide, the decision about what kinds of illustrations to use will be based on informed knowledge of, or consultation with, the user (see Chapter 3) and tested (see Chapter 9) before final publication.

THE CONTENT OF A PICTURE: SOME GENERAL PRINCIPLES

The choice of the characteristics of a plant to illustrate should be obvious from our earlier discussion of characters (see Chapter 6) and your own calculations and consultations on what it will take to make the guide work (see Chapter 3). Clearly, some important characters, such as smells, cannot easily be illustrated ('scratch 'n' sniff' type patches being too unrealistic, unsubtle and short-lived); but the need for other characters

CASE STUDY 8.1 DFID–FRP (PROJECT R7367) TRIALS OF ILLUSTRATIVE MATERIAL IN FIELD GUIDES

William Hawthorne, S. Cable (Plant Sciences, Oxford), R. Lysinge, E. Njenje (Limbe Botanic Gardens, Cameroon), M. Abu Juam, N. Gyakari (Forestry Department, Ghana), D. Jules (Forestry Department, Grenada)

In the UK Department for International Development (DFID)–Forestry Research Programme (FRP) Field Guide Project, we evaluated graphical aspects of field guide formats, based directly on empirical trials in Cameroon, Ghana, Grenada and Oxford. The full details and results will be published elsewhere (see Box 5.7, page 100, and http://herbaria. plants.ox.ac.uk/VFH for an update on this publication). Briefly, workshops were held to discuss the needs, formats and styles of field guides, and a set of species and image formats were chosen for trial. In each country, 20 to 150 species were selected and a series of comparable 'guidelets' made for them. A **guidelet** is a set of pages or cards with features of a field guide to be investigated by practical field trials (in reality, we would expect many field guides to have more species; but a subset of 20 to 100 species for browsing should be easily filtered by major divisions in a guide). More than one format of guidelet was made for each species to allow the effect of format to be evaluated in a standardized way. We tested guidelets for **accuracy** (percentage correct in a trial, usually of 20 plants in the field); and we recorded the respondents' subjectively assessed **confidence** of answers, **usability**, **beauty** and **monetary value**. Around 1500 respondents and about 30,000 plant person-guidelet events were evaluated. We also compared these attributes in two types of trial. Most were '**name that plant**' trials, where users were asked to match a numbered tree to a species in a guidelet. We also conducted **species recognition** trials, to test whether a picture reliably brings the correct species to mind or could be used to communicate to respondents which type of tree they were to find in a patch of forest.

In Cameroon, at Limbe and around Mount Cameroon, we tested eight formats of guidelet for 19 species of *Cola* (small trees, many rare or economically important) (see Figure 8.1 and Plate 6, centre pages). Respondents only knew of the species earlier in less than 10 per cent of cases. The formats, from photocopies, dried specimens, drawings and photographs of various types, made little difference to the accuracy – which was generally poor (40–60 per cent) for this difficult genus.

In Ghana we tested one modular format of the guidelet to 125 large tree species in two sizes (see Figure 8.2), mostly with villagers around forests. Prior knowledge was minimal; but after using the guide, accuracy increased to an average of about 80 per cent.

In Grenada, we tested card guidelets in shuffled packs of around 20, containing equal numbers of paintings, drawings and photographs (see Figure 8.3). Each species was in the respondent's hand only once, in one of the formats. Again, prior knowledge of plants was low. Here we found significant differences in overall accuracy between habitats (averages from 60 per cent for montane forest to 80 per cent in other vegetation types). The slight differences in format were insignificant.

In all test sites, photographs were overall the most successful, with some gain in subjective scores or accuracy for different formats in different subsamples.

The full results are published elsewhere (see Hawthorne et al, 2005, and http://herbaria.plants.ox.ac.uk/VFH for publication details).

Illustration 185

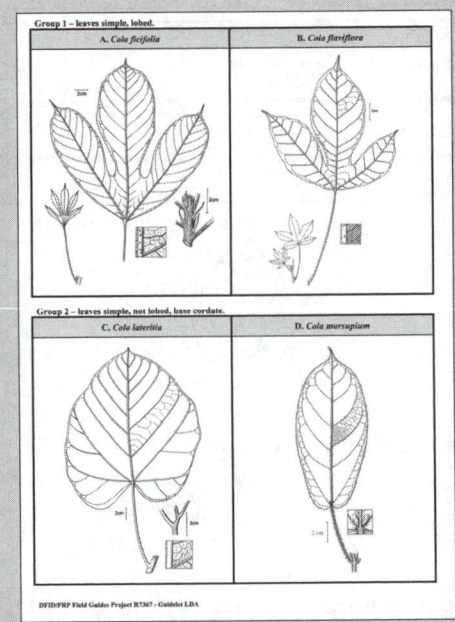

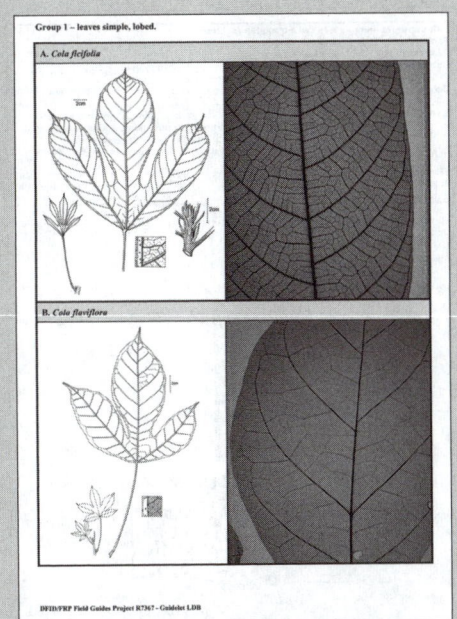

Source: S. Cable, R. Wise & W. D. Hawthorne

Figure 8.1 *Sample guidelet pages from the formats tested in the DFID–FRP Field Guide Project for Cameroonian* Cola

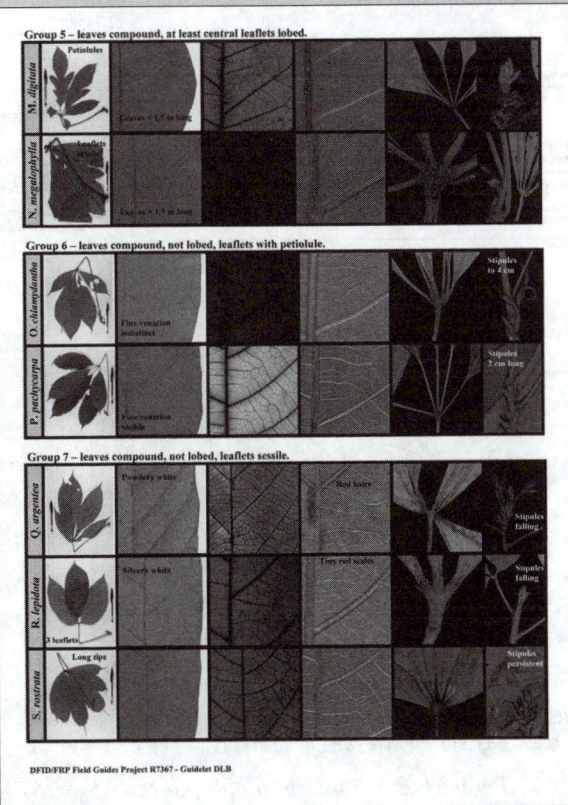

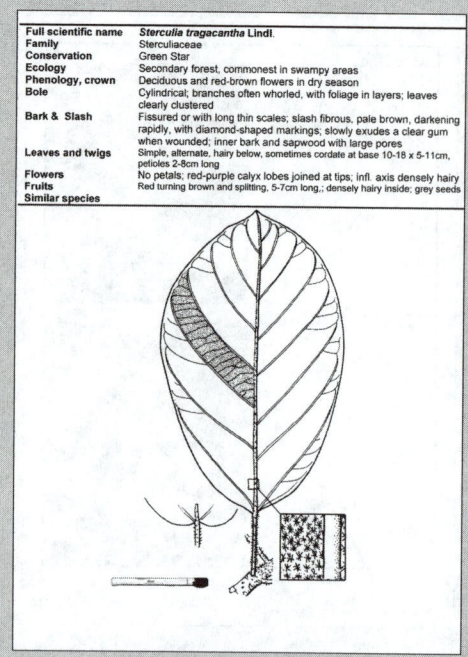

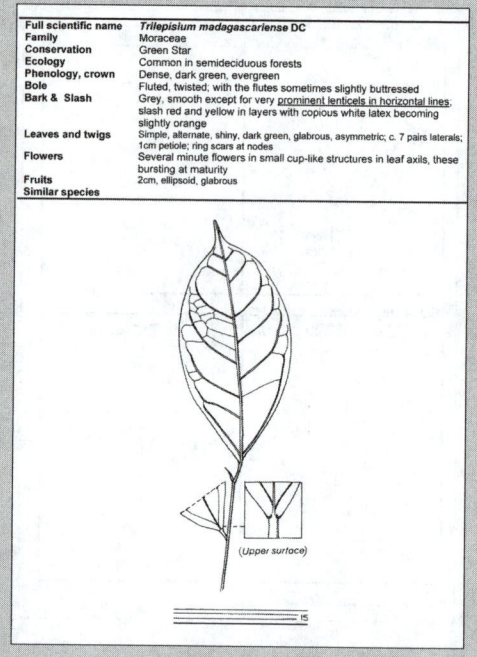

Full scientific name	*Sterculia tragacantha* Lindl.
Family	Sterculiaceae
Conservation	Green Star
Ecology	Secondary forest, commonest in swampy areas
Phenology, crown	Deciduous and red-brown flowers in dry season
Bole	Cylindrical; branches often whorled, with foliage in layers; leaves clearly clustered
Bark & Slash	Fissured or with long thin scales; slash fibrous, pale brown, darkening rapidly, with diamond-shaped markings; slowly exudes a clear gum when wounded; inner bark and sapwood with large pores
Leaves and twigs	Simple, alternate, hairy below, sometimes cordate at base 10-18 x 5-11cm, petioles 2-8cm long
Flowers	No petals; red-purple calyx lobes joined at tips; infl. axis densely hairy
Fruits	Red turning brown and splitting, 5-7cm long.; densely hairy inside; grey seeds
Similar species	

Full scientific name	*Trilepisium madagascariense* DC
Family	Moraceae
Conservation	Green Star
Ecology	Common in semideciduous forests
Phenology, crown	Dense, dark green, evergreen
Bole	Fluted, twisted; with the flutes sometimes slightly buttressed
Bark & Slash	Grey, smooth except for very prominent lenticels in horizontal lines; slash red and yellow in layers with copious white latex becoming slightly orange
Leaves and twigs	Simple, alternate, shiny, dark green, glabrous, asymmetric; c. 7 pairs laterals; 1cm petiole; ring scars at nodes
Flowers	Several minute flowers in small cup-like structures in leaf axils, these bursting at maturity
Fruits	2cm, ellipsoid, glabrous
Similar species	

(Upper surface)

Full scientific name	*Triplochiton scleroxylon* K.Schum.
Family	Sterculiaceae (Malvaceae)
Conservation	Red Star
Ecology	Very common tree in semidecidous forests, including secondary patches
Phenology, crown	Deciduous; fruits mainly once every 7 or so years; crown massive, with star-like leaves visible from a distance
Bole	Rough and scaly, often yellowish orange
Bark & Slash	Soft fibrous, yellowish, with coarser darker fibres, darkening
Leaves and twigs	Leaves 5-7 lobed glabrous, lamnina c. 10-15cm but larger on saplings;
Flowers	1cm petals very hairy, white, red to purple at base; 30-50 stamens fused at base; In axillary panicles
Fruits	With single winged, 6cm, 1 seeded
Similar species	*Cola millenii* is a smaller tree with similar, larger, mostly 3 lobed leaves

Full scientific name	*Symphonia globulifera* L.
Family	Guttiferae
Conservation	Green Star
Ecology	A slender tree of swamp forest
Phenology, crown	Narrow, with short horizontal branches like spokes of a wheel around bole
Bole:	Slender, often but not always with stilt roots but unbuttressed
Bark & Slash	Thin, pale grey to yellowish, brittle with yellow latex
Leaves and twigs	Simple, opposite, c.10cm long, hairless, with many vague lateral nerves
Flowers	On old twigs with 5 green sepals and 5 red petals, with 15 stamens in 5 groups
Fruits	Spherical, c. 4cm diam; 5 compartments, with 5 stigmas remaining on top
Similar species	See *Pentadesma*; *Symphonia* has smaller thinner leaves without obvious resin channels

Note: see Plate 7 for the colour component of each card.
Source: W. D. Hawthorne & R. Wise

Figure 8.2 *Sample guidelet pages (A5 or A6) tested in the DFID–FRP Field Guide Project for Ghanaian large trees*

Illustration   187

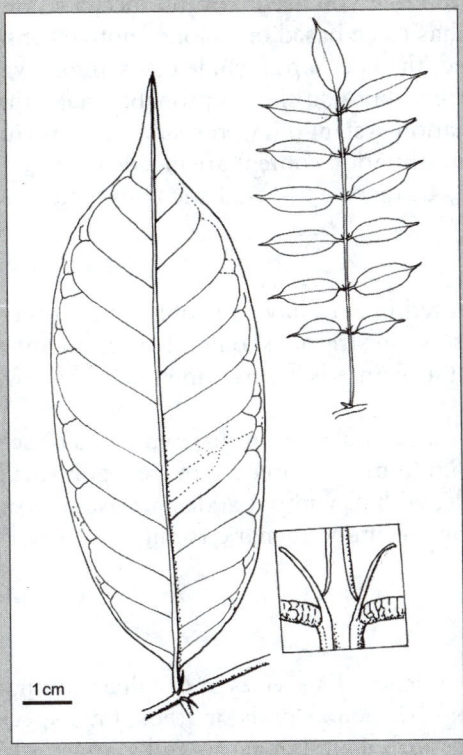
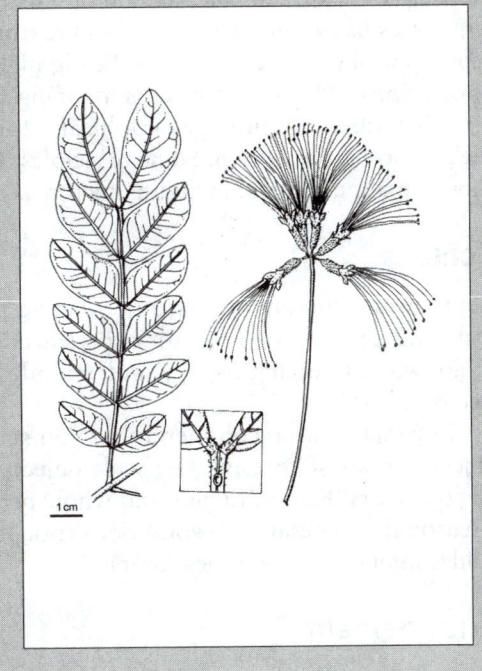
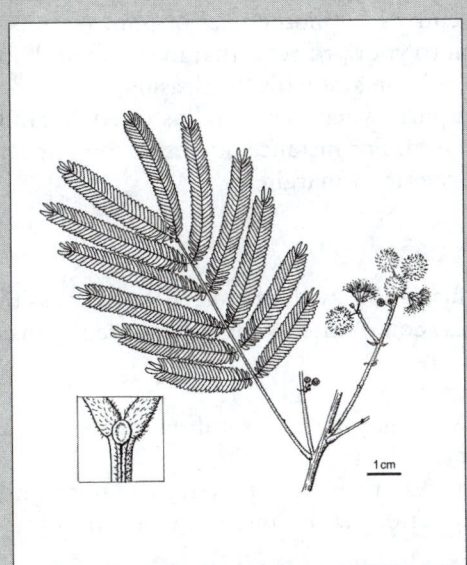
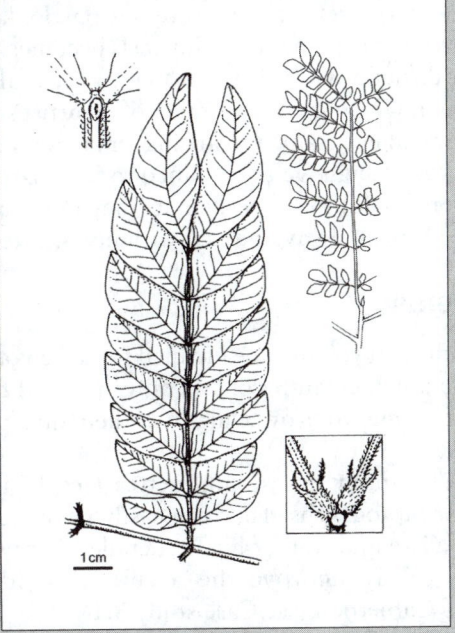

Note: see Plate 8 for optional colour cards these were compared with.
Source: R. Wise & W. D. Hawthorne

Figure 8.3 *Sample guidelets (A6 cards) with drawings of Grenadian plants, tested in the DFID–FRP project*

will help to determine the medium of illustration that you need. For instance, a guide to large trees based on slash colour and texture has to be based on colour photographs. If geographical distributions are to be highlighted, then perhaps include maps among your illustrations. We will not discuss mapping further; but you should probably make them directly with a computer geographical information system (GIS), the subject of a whole shelf of books on its own. Some principles of information content are independent of the subject matter, though, including picture scale, arrangement, detail and copyright.

Scale

Many users who are not used to viewing printed images have a problem interpreting scale and perspective. Even for experienced users, illustrators should plan for an appropriate way of helping the eye understand that a picture is a close-up view or far away (see Box 8.1).

In general, we recommend that you select a standard set of different sizes of scale objects for all of your images; scale objects should be of simple shape, recognizable by all your users. Hands, fingers and whole people, with or without added precise sizes, are a reasonable general scale solution, although pure centimetre markers might be better in guides intended for technical users.

Arrangement

You may sometimes want to include all characteristics of a species in one illustration, or you may prefer to separate out particular details, such as pods or seeds, on a special plate for comparison. This task becomes easier with digital imagery, and inappropriate or difficult if you have chosen to use real specimens or photocopies or photographs of them. One of the advantages of an artist's input to your project is that they will probably have an eye trained to arrange images on a page in an aesthetically pleasing way.

Although we are inclined to idealize plant parts when they are illustrated, it can be more useful to show them as they are usually seen. For instance, leaves of some species are almost always riddled with holes, eaten at the tip or margin.

Detail

Although you may be inclined to make your illustrations with as much detail as possible, too much detail becomes confusing, and the less complicated your images are the easier it becomes to browse many of them quickly:

- In many cases, silhouettes (see Figure 8.4) may be as useful as more detailed photographs. They can easily be made in many ways.
- The addition of highly detailed X-ray pictures of venation patterns did not significantly improve the accuracy of identification with line drawings in Limbe, Cameroon (see Case study 8.1).
- Details are usually best added to drawings in 'detail boxes' (or in circles, representing the view through a hand lens). These are easily implemented for digital photographs and enable you to use a low-resolution version of a photograph, with an inset of, for example, part of the venation, with higher resolution. This can be emulated easily on photographs; but it may be clearer to include a second

Illustration 189

BOX 8.1 DEPICTING SCALE

There are six main options for representing scale:

1 Show all at life size. This is appropriate for less experienced users where appreciation of scale depicted by any means fails, and where you have decided it is possible to make the guide work on items such as leaves or parts of leaves. This will seriously limit your choice of subject matter and prevent depiction of detail, but is inevitable if you are using real plant specimens in lieu of illustrations and a reasonable solution if you are using photocopies of specimens. It should be emphasized that people who have never seen photographs can have a very difficult time coming to terms with scale even with very strong visual clues such as elephants and *Acacia* trees.

2 Show images at various scales and rely on background clues in each to make scale obvious. If you use a black cloth as a background, the weave of the cloth can provide some scale clues for close-up photographs. We can intuitively tell that a photograph of a whole tree on the edge of a forest is not life sized because we have never met trees and forest-like objects that are only a few centimetres tall, and there may be clouds in the sky anyway. The flattening out of shadows or lighting associated with photographs of leaf surface details also seem obviously not to relate to, say, a football pitch-sized area. A mass of yellow flowers on a street tree might be so distinctive that the precise length is not important anyway. In these ways, it may be possible for some images to work without adding explicit scale information. This option seems to apply especially to photographs; similar visual clues are generally missing from drawings.

3 Magnification factor: some technical images have a 'x 10' or 'life size' caption, to inform the users of the scale. We advise against these (unless all pictures are life size) because they become complicated if images are reproduced at different scales – for example, with a photocopier – and because they can be hard to understand anyway.

4 Include a scale bar. A small 1cm line is the standard practice on many technical drawings. These are generally better than the previous type as they are still correct when images are reproduced at different sizes. However, many non-technical users may not be familiar with centimetres or inches.

5 Include a scale object in your pictures. You can substitute for clues that might be naturally present by adding your own. This is standard practice in some photographs, where coins, for instance, are often used. We advise against lens caps (which vary in size and are unfamiliar to many); but matchboxes, biros (especially Bic biros), pencils, disposable cigarette lighters and paperclips are well known to many. Parts of the body such as hands, feet and whole people are useful since they are generally available to the photographer, although this is not much use where a precise scale is needed. For close-up photographs, however, the hand or clutching fingers are useful inclusions as you probably need to hold the specimen still anyway. These can also work well for drawings. Rosemary Wise's drawings in the field guide to Ghanaian trees and African *Acacia* (Hawthorne, 1990) use cartoon people to help scale large trees, and pencils in diagrams of leaves.

6 The world's pencils or people are of very roughly the same magnitude, yet variable in precise size; their usage as a scale object therefore sends the message that the true size of the plant part depicted is approximate due to natural variation. But the pencil or other scale object can still have a precise length or width written where this is important – that is, scale objects can be left as imprecise sizes if the subject of the image is variable in size anyway, or have added dimensions written where the precise length is critical.

Note: Some compound leaves are complicated and the jargon is mostly unspecific regarding how lobing merges gradually into separate leaflets (2–3 pinnate, with deeply toothed lobes), so it is often better to avoid the jargon and use pictures or icons. These images were made in 45 minutes by scanning a fresh leaf, cleaning up the background, increasing the contrast to make the image more diagram like and reducing the resolution (with edge smoothing).
Source: William Hawthorne

Figure 8.4 *Leaf silhouettes created using a scanner*

photograph (zoomed in) showing the details, with the location of the details indicated on the first, especially if the photographs are printed in small sizes (< 4cm across).

Copyright: What can you 'borrow' from other artists?

Of course, one of the easiest ways to illustrate your book might be to copy images from Floras, monographs, or the internet. However, under the Berne Convention (see Box 8.2), you can only copy images 50 years after the artist has died, although most countries have extended this term to 70 years. This does mean that you can, in principle, scan and use without permission 19th-century and earlier drawings, although you will probably need to obtain permission from the library where you have found this material, in case there may be more specific restrictions.

It is always advisable to obtain permission to use material found on websites, even if the image seems to be public domain; often, the web artist will be happy for you to do so in exchange for some acknowledgement, particularly if your rendition is a lower resolution version of an original anyway. Ask the publishers and editors of Floras in your area for their opinion on this (liability for getting copyright clearance lies with the author, not the publisher or the person who gave permission to use the work).

Illustration   191

BOX 8.2 COPYRIGHT ISSUES

The Berne Convention is an international copyright treaty signed by 160 countries. The regulations of the Berne Convention are more far-reaching than, for example, US copyright law. The convention requires member states to recognize the moral rights of integrity and attribution. Authors or artists have exclusive rights to translate, reproduce, perform or adapt protected work. As soon as a creation appears in some tangible form (that is, not just an idea expressed in a conversation), it is protected. No notice (for example, the © symbol) is necessary, although it helps legal cases. The correct form for the notice is 'Copyright [dates] by [author/owner]'.

Therefore, under the convention everything is copyrighted unless the creator explicitly puts it in the public domain – for example, 'I grant the public freedom to use these images as they please.' Granting something to the public domain is a complete abandonment of all rights. You cannot grant it 'for non-commercial use'. Indeed, other people can modify one spot on a public domain picture and claim copyright for it themselves.

You cannot copy work without permission for the life of the author plus 50 years. The Berne Convention now represents a minimum requirement for copyright protection, however, and most countries have now voluntarily established copyright protection for 70 years after the author's death.

However, although your national laws may be different, artists can sell or license the rights to others. When artists are paid to produce pictures for someone else, they *may* have, in effect, sold their right to copyright in advance: it will probably depend upon the precise wording of their contracts, and the legal subtleties seem frequently to become very complex.

'Derivative works' – that is, copies, modified slightly – are in most countries also protected by copyright laws and are considered owned by the creator of the original.

THE OPTIONS FOR ILLUSTRATIVE MATERIAL

We will be stretching somewhat the definition of 'illustration' in this section: illustrative material seems more appropriate, especially for our first category. We discuss the three main categories of illustrative material that have often been used to depict plants: real plants, machine-made imagery and artist's images. A synopsis of their pros and cons is included in Table 8.1.

Real plants

Fresh plants

Imagine that you want to produce a guide to medicinal plants to enable people to perform an inventory in the forest around their village. They recognize most of the plants anyway; but the guide will be used to increase accuracy and standardize the names used in the inventory. The inventories in question are localized and will be repeated only once every few years.

In this case, it might well be most appropriate and efficient for you to forget about printing, words and pictures. Perhaps you should just use your budget to arrange for someone to turn up for a day or two at the start of each inventory, collect fresh examples of the plants in question and attach names to these, allowing people to have parts of the

Table 8.1 *The three main categories of illustrative material with their advantages or disadvantages*

Type	Realism	Expense	Other good points	Other bad points
1 Real plants, in general (see next two entries for specifics)	Maximum (for parts that can properly be used in this way). No scale problems.	Cheap, except time to collect.	Smell, texture and hairiness, etc., can be compared. Details can be examined with a lens wherever the user wants.	Cannot include all aspects – for example, buttresses and large leaves. Limited scope to draw attention to important features. Hard to publish (impossible via the internet). For eco-tourists, there may be a legal problem taking specimens home. Can be fragile, short-lived and bulky.
1(a) Fresh plants	Almost complete.		Smell, taste (hence, good for medicinals).	Short-lived solution
1(b) Dried plants	Good for showing form, but often poor for colour.	Bags, card, etc., and probably a box.	Can have novelty value; doubles as a 'field herbarium'. Can be long-lived.	As above, although less ephemeral Specimens are fragile and may gradually decline in quality.
2 Machine imagery	Varied.	Generally cheap after capital costs.	Some of the fastest and most accurate. solutions where there is no artist. More compact than dried plants.	Can absorb a lot of time and expense. Aesthetically pleasing layout not guaranteed.
2(a) Photocopies and scanned leaves	Good for shape and, for example, main nerves only.	Cheap if you have the hardware and a herbarium.	More durable, flexible and lighter than specimens, and easily made from them. Many copies can be made at once.	Often bad for the photocopier or herbarium specimens. Only appropriate for small, flat leaves Difficult to include areas of detail such as might be seen with a hand lens. Hard to depict textural effects due to no angle of lighting. Cannot be used in the field.

2(b) X-rays	Good for shape and detailed vein patterns. No scale problem (life size).	Cheap if you have access to hardware, else expensive.	Ideal where leaf venation is very important – for example, for archaeologists. Often aesthetically attractive.	Need access to X-ray equipment, which is potentially dangerous. The veins in the image may not be visible in fresh material. May still need to be scanned and tidied up digitally. You may as well take and enhance a digital photo in the first place. Cannot be used in the field, and probably not even in your herbarium.
2(c) Film photography	Good; but scale has to be dealt with.	Slide film is very expensive.	Field usable. Colours and image 'vibrancy' still marginally better than digital prints. Good to have slides for larger images – for example, posters and slide shows.	Film and optical equipment can be ruined by fungus in the forest. No immediate feedback on exposure, etc. Will still need to scan slides for electronic layout, then lose most of the image quality advantages over digital photography. It is not realistic to make back-up copies of slides, and slides deteriorate with time.
2(d) Digital photography	As for film.	Hardware is expensive. Optical equipment as for film; many more images affordable on the same budget.	Image preview in forest to ensure that difficult exposures at least approximately work out. Scope to record audio notes on pictures. Easily processed to enhance details and to integrate with text. You probably have some of the hardware anyway. Field usable.	Electronics and optical equipment can easily break down. Need for computer, electricity or many expensive memory chips and batteries on field trips.

Illustration 193

Table 8.1 *continued*

Type	Realism	Expense	Other good points	Other bad points
3 Artist's imagery		Depends upon artist, but probably a significant part of your budget and more expensive than photos.	Artist design should help with attractive and functional guide layout. Can be easily idealized, leaving out some details or parts. Details clearer than equivalent photos. Details easily emphasized; sometimes less information means more realism. Very compact: more species or details can be fitted on a page than with photos.	Specialist artist required. Not as accurate as the above. Generally poor for field characters such as bark slash and crown shape.
3(a) Drawings	Generally low, by design. Key points are abstracted from the rest.		Good for leaves, flower and flower dissections. Cheaper to reproduce than colour. Can be prepared entirely in a herbarium.	No colour. Off-putting and 'unrealistic' to many amateurs.
3(b) Paintings	Nearer photos than drawings.	High; slower production rate than drawings.	Colour and surface texture information. Might attract the more sophisticated and rich end of the field guide market for best artists.	More critical to have a good artist than for drawings. Expensive to reproduce. Structural detail less clear than in drawings.

Source: William Hawthorne

Illustration 195

real plant to touch, smell and examine. Cultural differences in perception of abstract images will surely rarely or never apply to the use of living specimens.

We do not intend to worry about whether fresh plants really can constitute a field guide; but they do indisputably mark one end of a spectrum of illustrative material. There are many advantages of real plant material over printed images. The material might be free to produce, it could hardly be more realistic and people can focus on any aspect for identification. For species that show regional or ecological variation, it is easy to add 'local' representative specimens. Smells, taste, texture and touch can be judged clearly only if illustrated by actual leaves.

This proposed solution will be inefficient under these circumstances:

- if there are too many plant samples to learn before the plants wilt or rot;
- if the village has a changing population and the inventory is to be annual; the travelling demonstrator may then soon represent an expensive solution;
- when the sample plants are so many and so dispersed that the work involved in collecting all of them in one place, especially if a regular event, is long;
- where the parts of the plant useful for identification do not survive picking well or are uncollectible; tree boles and bark fall into this category.

One possible solution to some of these problems is the establishment of small botanic gardens in the villages, with the plants permanently labelled – a sort of living field guide like the forester's arboretum (this access to material for teaching and identification was one of the justifications for the establishment of early European botanic gardens). While this may substitute for the need for illustrations, and they may, in some circumstances, perform well when used in conjunction with printed guides, we can hardly pretend that the trees of an arboretum come under the heading of 'illustrative material found in field guides'.

Dried leaf specimens: A portable field herbarium

Even if you are sceptical that we should be including living plants under a section on illustrations, dried plant specimens continue the grey area between illustration and living plants and are often used as illustrative material. Specimens are pressed flat between newspaper and dried in the manner of all field botanical collections (see Box 4.3, page 67). Why not take the herbarium reference material itself into the field? In fact, some or the earliest proto-field guides from the 16th century were books of specimens (see Box 4.7, page 76). It is not an uncommon practice for tropical field ecologists – for instance, those involved in enumerating many plants in sample plots – to do just this, and thereby to do away with any need for a printed field guide (see Box 8.3).

Deciding when to use dried plants

Dried plants solve some of the problems of fresh ones, but some attributes are lost in the process. The texture, smells and tastes, and many of the colours, will probably have deteriorated during drying, for instance. Dried specimens are cheap to make; but storage and organization are not negligible (hundreds of white cards and sealable polythene bags) (see Box 8.4).

BOX 8.3 RECIPE FOR PREPARING A DRIED LEAF SPECIMEN GUIDE

- Make dried, flat leaf specimens as in Chapter 4 (see Box 4.3) (make enough for all reference copies that you will need).
- Cut sections of (white) card 5mm smaller than the dimensions of plastic re-sealable ('Zip-Loc') bags. You may need two or three sizes of bag; but do not use more than three sizes, as different sizes will have to be stored in different sets to facilitate sorting and indexing. A4 size or slightly larger is generally the most convenient.
- Put the dried specimens from your press in the polythene bags, backed by the piece of card.
- Write names and notes on labels slipped in the (back of the) card.
- Store these cards in a box, for easy browsing.
- If necessary, introduce dividers or other index methods (see Chapter 5).

For species that show regional or ecological variation, it is easy to add 'local' representative specimens. The same material can be put to very good use for identifying other dried specimens collected when the plant is not easily identified in the field.

A photograph of a living plant will usually provide more accurate colours than a dried specimen. Large leaves have to be fragmented (or stored in an impractically large folder) and can therefore be hard to recognize, and some aspects of a living plant cannot be shown using portable plant parts at all. It may be inadvisable or impossible to provide material for rare plants; yet these may well be precisely the plants for which the guide is needed. Mass production may be impractical and many potential users may be put off by the crudeness and weight of this reference material.

Novelty tourist guides or related illustrative material can be based on dried specimens – for instance, actual leaves (such as those of *Ficus religiosa*) are sold on greeting cards in India. However, export of dried plant material from or to certain countries might present problems for eco-tourist guides based on them.

BOX 8.4 GRENADA FIELD HERBARIUM

Proper herbaria are expensive to make and maintain, so Grenada had none in 2000. Herbarium curators will naturally not usually allow the specimens to be used by schools or on field trips. This presented problems for the Grenada Forestry Department, not least when trying to produce field guides: the nearest reference material was in Trinidad and a major use was likely to be educational. We therefore produced a minimalist herbarium, made of specimens in resealable ('Zip-Loc') bags; these, in turn, were filed in box files (see Box 8.3). As the specimens are sealed, sets could be taken out into the field, and damaged specimens can be replaced. Furthermore, notes and photographs can be inserted into the back of the polythene bags. 1500 named and labelled herbarium specimens were already available as an output of a field guide project. Requiring only about UK£5000 for stiff white card, 'Zip-Loc' bags, box files and shipping costs, and the assistance of three occasional volunteers, the field herbarium was completed for the 1500 species (allowing room for expansion to double this) in about three weeks, with the bulk of the work finished in one week.

Illustration   197

Results of field trials of real (dried) leaves

Dried leaf specimens were compared in the field trials in Cameroon (see Case study 8.1). They did not perform significantly better than other material for accuracy in the name-that-plant trials, although dried specimens were marginally the best in the species recognition trials. Even in the context of these short-term trials of many formats, we decided that the supply of fresh plant specimens would be impractical; but we suspect that these would have been the most accurately matched format.

Machine-made illustrations

These include the only sensible choices for field guides today, where there is an adequate budget, a need for many published copies, and when no artist is available or affordable.

General guidelines

- Prepare the material carefully to clarify shapes and details – for example, trim to prevent overlap of layers of leaves. Often, 'less is more'.
- Choose a neutral, un-textured background for your subject if necessary. Edit the images electronically to remove distracting or incomplete parts.

Photocopies and scanned specimens

The next approach along our spectrum from reality to abstraction is where the dried leaves of the previous section are replaced by photocopies or scanned images made directly from fresh or dried leaves on a digital scanner. Although most photocopiers are black and white, colour photocopiers are very similar to scanners, the main difference being that a file can be saved from a scanner for future printing or scanning. Since cheap scanners are now widely available, the only potential asset of a photocopier is if it is black and white, producing cheap and simple copies, and can be used for rapid and instant output. Colour scans can be almost as realistic as photographs of leaves, although lack of choice of shadow orientation may prevent you from creating a reasonable impression of texture or other surface effects. Scanned colour images are considered together with digital photography. Here we consider black-and-white photocopies made on a standard office photocopier, and black-and-white scans can be deemed, for most purposes, equivalent to photocopies.

The Chicago Field Museum used to make and sell bound 'micro-herbaria', or sets of photocopies of herbarium specimens reduced to 66 per cent (see http://fm2.field museum.org/plantguides/microherbaria.asp) as field reference material. More recently, they have started to use scanners to produce colour versions of the same. Either way, this clearly represents a cheap and convenient way to make a basic field guide; they even sell their micro-herbaria on the internet in volumes at ten specimens per US$1.

See Table 8.1 for a summary of the pros and cons of photocopies or scans. One of the most frustrating problems is that the leaves to be scanned have to be flat and are limited in size to the glass plate of the copier or scanner, although they can be reduced or enlarged from this size.

Limbe field trials of photocopied plants

Photocopies of herbarium specimens were compared in the Limbe field trials (see Case study 8.1) and performed similarly to most other formats in the accuracy trials, although respondents did not rate them very highly for other attributes. The addition of the simple textual key made a slight but significant improvement to their accuracy, possibly because although some details are visible from a photocopy, others (which may be implicit in a key) are not.

Photocopies can provide a cheap, relatively light replacement for real leaves. There is little need to laminate the pages since photocopies (unlike cheaper inkjet inks) are fairly water resistant and new copies can be made easily anyway. However, it is not much harder to photograph leaves, and the potential benefits of ease of arrangement of digitized images in a document may well outweigh the speed of photocopying. Photocopies suffer many of the same limitations as real plants – for instance, only small to medium-sized leaves are suitable; other plant parts are not.

In many cases, people reproduce guides by photocopying; so if you want to encourage this, it is worth checking how well your illustrations of another type come out when photocopied.

X-rays

X-ray photography, or radiography, of leaves produces high-quality black-and-white images of venation patterns that surpass line drawings and conventional photography for accuracy and detail. They are cheap and quick to produce, but require specialist equipment that may only be available in hospitals or industrial laboratories. There are few published examples, notably Christophel and Hyland (1993) and Hyland et al (1998). The example in Figure 8.1 shows a portion of a leaf of *Cola*. It was taken with an X-ray machine used to test seed viability. The radiograph was scanned using a desktop scanner equipped with a transparency hood.

Results of field trials of X-rays

X-rays of leaf specimens, as an additional detail with line drawings, were compared for usability, accuracy and saleability on the field trials in Cameroon (see Case study 8.1). In a way, this became a test of the usability of leaf venation as a character for identification, and the X-rays did not improve the accuracy of identification of line drawings in the trials, nor were they particularly liked by the respondents. While veins are, in some cases, like fingerprints of the plant and provide subtle identification hints, they are hard to match correctly; as highlighted by our respondents, other characters such as hairs and colour are not only often equally or more important, but also more easily recognized in the field and not visible on X-ray images.

If you have the equipment, X-ray images represent an easy way of providing accurate images of venation pattern and leaf shape. However, the venation that is visible in the field can be made more simply with a digital camera. There are very few circumstances when it is worth considering X-ray pictures in tropical plant field guides. In the unlikely event that your only access to illustrative tools is a friend in a local seed-testing centre, then experimentation may be worthwhile. If your users have technical jobs that requires them to identify fragments of leaves – for instance, those used in nesting material – or poisons eaten by livestock, then a library of X-ray images of candidate species can be recommended. Finally, X-ray pictures can be very beautiful abstractions of leaves, and for this reason they might find a place in a more artistic or aesthetic type of field guide.

Illustration 199

Film photography and photographs, in general

Increasing numbers of colour photographic guides are attractive, affordable and useful, and can be produced on modest budgets (see, for example, Gardner et al, 2000; Hawthorne et al, 2005). There are many books and courses, and much experience in photography, so we will not cover general aspects here. Many of the principles of basic camera technique that are especially applicable to plant photography apply whether you are using film or a digital camera (see Box 8.5).

Until recently, in order to obtain good-quality photographs, the only viable solution was to use slide film (transparencies), which is expensive and deteriorates after some time in the tropics. While it may still be the best way to take the highest-quality photographs – for instance, for posters and art exhibitions – the days of the superiority of slide film for small photographs in reasonably priced books is over. Nowadays, it is often impossible to see the differences between the best digital photographs from those made in traditional ways. There are some remarkable photographic field guides where the photographer used slide film (see Box 2.1, page 17). However, these often required massive and generally unrealistic financial subsidies. Today, digital photography stands to increase the viability of similar initiatives (see Box 8.6).

Slides can be used as the basis for public talks with less expensive equipment than required to project computer images. Many (although a rapidly declining number) institutions may have slide projectors, but no equipment for projecting digital images. The main reasons for using slides will soon be inertia to change and a heritage of old slide libraries. Slides might be returned from the developers with disappointing results, by which time the field trip or opportunity for taking pictures is long past: at best, one can never be sure how accurate subtle colours have been rendered, and these subtleties are important for bark slash, for instance. Digital cameras of adequate quality are declining rapidly in price and the recurrent costs (mainly batteries, hopefully rechargeable ones) are lower than film. In most cases, scanned images of your slides are not likely to be as high quality (colour accuracy and resolution) as the originals, especially if they have not been treated with absolute care. We therefore strongly advise field guide makers to use a digital camera.

Many readers may have access to an archive of historical images. The best advice we can give for these is that you scan them into digital format early on in your field guide project. Early digitization of slide libraries will considerably facilitate the demonstration and discussion of plans for field guides and, in conjunction with a good image database (see Box 8.8), will help to highlight priorities for new imagery.

The main problem for printing photographs – whether for final publication or, more acutely, for draft versions (see Chapter 9) – is the expense of high-quality colour printing, relative to black and white. At least now it is cheaper and more practical than it was, with an A4 photo sheet costing around US$1 (see Box 8.7).

Photo guide trials

Photographic guide materials of various types were evaluated in Ghana, Grenada and Cameroon (see Case study 8.1). In all cases, photographs were at least as accurate as any other format, and users rated the format very highly, whether photographs of fresh leaves in Cameroon, photographs of whole tree characters in Ghana or for general photographs of plants in Grenada. They are also one of the fastest formats to create and can be made without employing an artist. However, the medium is up to four times as

---

BOX 8.5 SOME BRIEF NOTES ON HOW TO CONTROL YOUR CAMERA

Even if you are inclined to set your camera to 'Auto exposure, auto focus', there will be times when you will only get good results by manual control. The following key points should be known to all photographers to get the best out of your camera:

- Read a guide to photography to help you understand exposure, depth of focus and so on.
- Make sure that the blur due to motion in the subject or vibration of the machine is minimized by keeping a high shutter speed or using a tripod. Shutter speeds below 1/125 may well lead to blurring, except with a tripod or flash.
- You will benefit from a tripod if you are taking many pictures of tree bases in the forest.
- Use depth of focus (DOF) to control whether details at a broad range of distances from the lens are in focus (high DOF), or whether a sharper picture is taken of a specific point or plane (low DOF). High DOF is obtained by a narrow aperture (small gap to let light in), which obliges the shutter speed to be slower.
- On a digital camera, at least, slight underexposure is preferable to slight overexposure. It is usually possible to enhance the former to reveal details in the shadows, whereas 'burnt-out pictures' will often have nothing retrievable from the highlights.
- In the tropics, use an ultraviolet (UV) filter if you taking pictures in the open. Ultraviolet light causes slight fogging or overexposure and loss of contrast. You can also compensate for this by setting your camera's automatic exposure over-ride to reduce exposure by one 'F. Stop'. This may be indicated by '–1'.
- Use flash sparingly, but try and find natural light patches in the forest. If you do use a flash, beware that the camera-based flash will make bark textures, mild fluting, etc., look more flat and featureless due to loss of shadows.
- You can compensate even on some digital cameras for low light by increasing the 'film speed (ASA or 'DIN setting'). This will inevitably lead to a grainier or (on digital) more speckled or 'noisier' picture; but that may be preferable to using the flash.
- Try to ensure a neutral background – for example, black is often best. Take a non-shiny black cloth to the forest with you and, where the ground is rarely flat, a small black-board as well.
- Make sure that you buy a camera with a close macro lens. Of the cheaper models, the Nikon Coolpix 4500 and similar models have generally been the best for this. Furthermore, invest in a small LED ring light (not a ring flash): capturing rainforest details without one can be very tiresome, and the internal flash does not work well up close.
- Beware of subtle yellow and other pale shades in bark and flowers. They frequently become overexposed to glaring white if you set your exposure to automatic, especially if the flash is deployed.
- Study other field guides to work out what subjects, views and composition rules work best.

expensive to print as monochrome images. Respondents were unwilling to pay four times as much for published photographic field guides, even though they preferred them, and line drawings were often just as accurate for appropriate subjects.

Illustration 201

BOX 8.6 PHOTOGRAPHY AND THE FORESTRY RESEARCH PROGRAMME PHOTO GUIDES

During the early part of the Forestry Research Programme (FRP) Field Guide Project (see Case study 8.1), we started using existing photographic equipment to develop photo libraries for guides in these countries. These images were scanned onto Kodak Photo-CDs, and have subsequently been included into our digital photo library. Soon after, the Nikon Coolpix 990/5 digital camera came on the market, so after some experimentation, and considering the inconvenience of slide film, we decided to use this as the main means of photography. It made the capture of tropical plant imagery several times easier, and some types of image that were infamously difficult to take with slide film (for example, yellow bark slashes with a flash) were reasonably easy through trial and error, changing the flash intensity or shutter controls.

Special or enhanced imagery

One of the options opened up by digital handling of imagery is that it is possible to enhance the images – for example, to make a more usable contrast or more healthy green colour – or to modify your photographs more substantially to more diagram-like images. In Figure 8.5 we show two of many possible ways in which venation, outlines and other key features of your leaf can be prepared for monochrome printing with a little practice in a cheap digital editing package. Remember when manipulating images like this to take and maintain copies of the original photographs in colour.

BOX 8.7 EQUIPMENT FOR A DIGITAL PHOTO GUIDE

The resources needed to produce a guide are modest, compared to standard film photography:

- a good digital camera with several 256 megabyte (MB) or larger memory chips and at least 5 megapixel capability;
- rechargeable batteries for as many days as your field trips require, or camps or bases with electricity;
- a laptop computer (or stand-alone hard drive) with appropriate software (see Box 8.8) and a memory chip reader;
- a robust external hard disk (at least for back-up) capable of holding about 1 to 2MB times the number of photographs to be captured (before perhaps downloading to a desktop computer) – 40 gigabyte (GB) portable hard drives recommended;
- a black matt cloth, large enough to back the largest compound leaf you will need to show;
- an external flash for the camera is often useful, as is a tripod, for taking tree bole pictures in the forest;
- specimen collection and normal field work equipment.

BRAHMS (http://herbaria.plants.ox.ac.uk/bol/home/) and Thumbs Plus (www.cerious.com) software can be used to help you organize and rename your photos and link them to relevant specimen information.

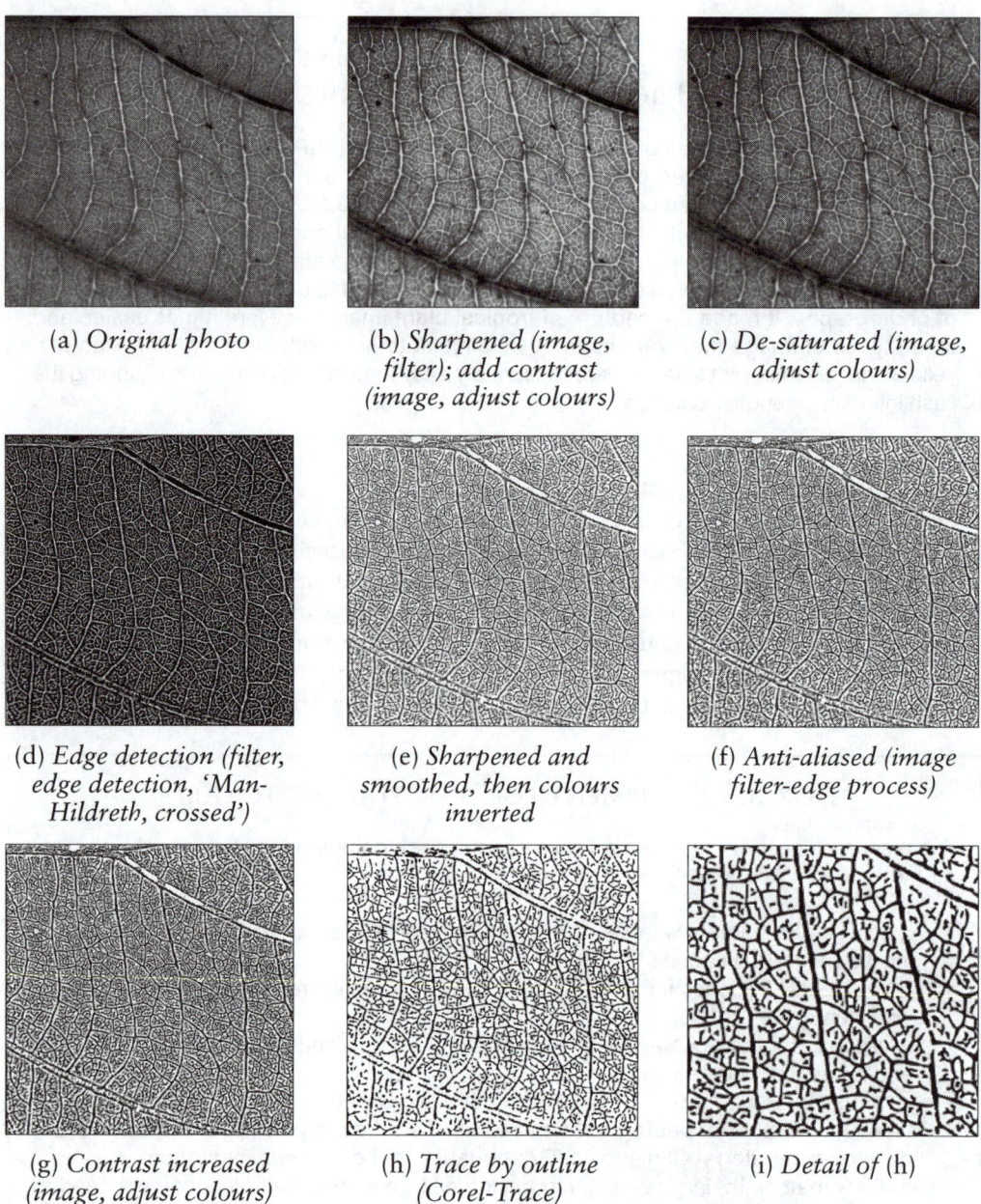

(a) *Original photo*

(b) *Sharpened (image, filter); add contrast (image, adjust colours)*

(c) *De-saturated (image, adjust colours)*

(d) *Edge detection (filter, edge detection, 'Man-Hildreth, crossed')*

(e) *Sharpened and smoothed, then colours inverted*

(f) *Anti-aliased (image filter-edge process)*

(g) *Contrast increased (image, adjust colours)*

(h) *Trace by outline (Corel-Trace)*

(i) *Detail of* (h)

Note: A *Diospyros mannii* leaf photo was obtained by holding the specimen up to the light and photographing it with a Nikon Coolpix macro lens, showing scalariform venation. Various digital manipulations using basic view/edit options in Thumbs Plus are shown. Figures 8.5 (a)–(g) above refer to Thumbs Plus menu options (www.cerious.com). Similar functions are available in all image-editing packages. Figure 8.5 (h) is performed in the Corel-Trace package, allowing the image to be enlarged indefinitely without introducing 'aliasing' (stepped diagonals). See also Figure 6.2, page 135.
Source: William Hawthorne

Figure 8.5 *Making an image that can substitute for a line drawing from a digital photograph*

Illustration 203

Botanical illustration

Drawings

Drawings have traditionally been the most important medium for botanical illustration, and for this reason many botanists are familiar and comfortable with the use of them in field guides. Most botanical works include some of them. There are still circumstances when drawings are to be recommended in field guides even if they are being reduced in importance by advances in printing and photography.

One of the main problems is the availability and cost of a specialist artist. One of us (Rosemary Wise) has much experience of training complete amateurs to create drawings, and perfectly usable drawings can be produced by more than half of the global population with a few weeks of practice and a few days' training, so why not think about trying yourself? Some basic pointers to creating your own botanical artwork are included on our website (http://herbaria.plants.ox.ac.uk/VFH).

Costs and practicality

When considering the costs of drawings, think about the convenience of drawing from herbarium specimens. Most of your plants will likely be found together, hopefully largely correctly named, in a dried and pressed state in a herbarium. This also applies if you want to take photographs or photocopy the same specimens.

In contrast, to make most use of your camera for a field guide, you should be out in the field photographing fresh plants and many more parts than seen in the herbarium. Travel costs vary – perhaps you are lucky and they are insignificant because your forest is next door. But in some cases, for large-ranging field guides covering many rare plants, illustrations based on herbarium specimens may be your only option for financial reasons. For a large print run of a cheaper monochrome guide, it will also be worth investing in line drawings.

Results of trials with drawings

We compared drawings with other media in our FRP tests in Grenada and Cameroon (see Case study 8.1). We also have experience of the pros and cons of drawings related to Ghanaian trees, as we have witnessed many years' use of *Field Guide to the Forest Trees of Ghana*, with all circa 700 species drawn (Hawthorne, 1990), and the more recent *The Woody Plants of Western African Forests: A Guide to the Forest Trees, Shrubs and Lianes from Senegal to Ghana*, with 2600 drawings (Hawthorne and Jongkind, 2006; see Case study 8.2). In general, non-technical audiences do not rate drawings very highly for beauty or usability; indeed, in some circumstances, they produce slightly less accurate answers with them. In most cases, though, the distaste is not matched by a significant loss of accuracy. These issues do not, in general, apply to technical users, however, who are more likely to appreciate the simplicity, efficiency or parsimony inherent in a good drawing, and understand and use the artistic conventions that have evolved over centuries of botanical illustration.

Botanical painting

We include some details on the Virtual Field Herbarium website (http://herbaria.plants.ox.ac.uk/VFH) to help general watercolour artists produce botanical paintings. Paintings are less commonly encountered in modern field guides than drawings as they are the most expensive format to create, and are no more accurate to use or cheaper to print than colour photographs. They do, however, have some potential to combine the advantages of photographs and drawings. The results at their best are aesthetically pleasing, selling a field guide on their own merit, and doubling as publicity material or the originals as gifts for sponsors. A good painting can capture the 'soul' of the plant; a good photograph, unless you are a very lucky or inspired and patient photographer, can usually only manage to capture its body. When the Ministry of Lands in Grenada chose a design for T-shirts for publicizing World Food Day from our collection of 300 images of Grenadian plants, they chose paintings, rather than photographs or drawings. Furthermore, we are perhaps saturated with photo and video imagery, and paintings of plants make the statement: 'we are attaching importance to this species: it is special'.

To create paintings, you need the services of a good botanical artist, otherwise you should forget the idea; so check the price before thinking further. Fine details – for example, in inset boxes – are not as commonly included in paintings if they are to double as aesthetic objects; but a good design can incorporate all the necessary detail. Many beautiful, highly practical and popular field guides have been illustrated mainly with paintings (for example, Blamey and Grey-Wilson, 1989; Wise, 1998). These might, on the whole, come under the heading of labour of love, rather than a practical model for aspiring field guide creators in the tropics; but they do show the massive potential of painted field guides.

Even when your local artist is too expensive or busy for you to consider for the job of illustrating your entire field guide, it is well worth thinking of commissioning a few inspirational plates – for example, for the front cover, publicity posters or occasional insets – as it may well increase sales or stir a deep interest in your publication and in any plants you want to publicize.

Field tests of painted images in Grenada

Amateurs in our trials in Grenada (see Case study 8.1) marginally preferred photographs to paintings as they were perceived as more realistic. They were of about the same accuracy as photographs in name-that-plant trials, and slightly more accurate than drawings. The medium is not ideal for difficult colour subjects such as bark slashes and tree trunks, even if you can persuade your artist to work inside the shade and discomfort of the rainforest and in an environment that is not ideal for watercolours.

USE OF COMPUTERS FOR HANDLING ILLUSTRATIONS

In some cases, illustrations for field guides of any format may be destined for use on a computer as well as, or even instead of, on paper. In other cases, a printed field guide may be illustrated with images from a digital camera or scanner. In both of these cases, use of a computer for manipulating your illustrations is inevitable. However, even where computer use is not essential, field guide creators who have access to a computer have much to gain by digitizing illustrations and managing them on a computer. Software for facilitating various aspects of imagery on a computer is discussed in Box 8.8.

Illustration 205

BOX 8.8 LAYOUT AND OTHER SOFTWARE TOOLS

When preparing simple illustrated documents of a few pages, normal word processors such as Microsoft Word provide tools for the layouts of images and text. For more professional layouts, particularly where all or many pages follow a predefined template, a desktop publishing programme, such as Adobe Indesign or Quark, is more appropriate. We laid out the pages for all our test guidelets for the Forestry Research Programme (FRP) trials using Microsoft Word. This allowed good colour printing of subtle bark shades, large file sizes, reasonably accurate alignment, and so on. Tables, into the cells of which you drop photographs or text, are useful alignment tools. If all pages are to have the same layout, make a document template – for example, containing tables, text boxes and dummy text in various defined styles to ensure consistency. Although top copies were created on an ordinary Epson inkjet printer directly, to produce six laminated copies of the 120-page colour guide, we decided to use a printing agency. For this purpose, and because we wanted the printer to produce all guidelets in various sizes for single files, we created Adobe Acrobat files of the guidelets (see Box 8.9).

Digital image databases

There are a number of software packages that facilitate the handling of images on computers. Two leading contenders are Thumbs Plus (www.cerious.com), which is currently slightly more advanced and slightly more expensive (at US$60), and ACDsee (www.acdsystems.com), which is slightly cheaper and had fewer database functions. However, this software is evolving very quickly, so by the time you read this there will probably be other contenders. We have used Thumbs Plus extensively on the FRP guides project (see Case study 8.1) and consider it very easy to learn and hard to find fault with.

Key points to look out for in such image-handling software are:

*   ability to automatically analyse and show thumbnails for all files on your computer and on removable disks;
*   ability to perform basic image handling (for example, contrast enhancement, cropping and rotation) from within the software;
*   batch renaming, editing (for example, file size reduction) and conversion of formats;
*   database functions, such as user-defined fields (like linked specimen numbers) – it is useful if the database file can be accessed by external database software;
*   gallery functions, where the same picture can appear in multiple virtual folders without the image file being duplicated (for instance, if you have your images arranged by plant family, you could have one gallery for bark types, one for rare plants, one for medicinal plants, and an image occurring only once on your disk would appear to be present in four separate folders);
*   when printing slide sheets, or multiple images per page of your image collection, make sure the software does not simply print the thumbnail, but recomposes each image from the original in order to make the best quality possible of the allocated space on the printout;
*   ability to make distributable CD-ROMs or web pages directly from selected folders or galleries;
*   linked view mode, where you can open two similar files, and when you zoom into or pan across one, the equivalent portion of the other files are shown side by side;
*   annotations and user fields for image descriptions should be printable adjacent to the images.

It is important to understand and use appropriate file formats for your digital imagery – without care you might lose important information or use up unnecessary disk space (see Box 8.9).

Advantages of handling your illustrations on computer

- It is easy to lay out, scale and modify text and drawings on a computer.
- It is therefore easy to 'repurpose' your information – for instance, to make a poster or computer key with the same images as used in a printed guide, or to publish your images to a web page.
- Digital imagery can be backed up and archived.
- Digital imagery can be exchanged through email, and this circulation can be useful for verifying the utility, accuracy and name of the plant in question.
- For limited print runs of guide material of limited circulation, it may be economical to print all of your field guides directly from the computer, and do without a printing agency altogether.

Disadvantages

- Computers with a high enough specification may not be available, even if adequate for handling the text of a field guide.
- It costs time and money to digitize images from drawings and paintings.
- New skills may have to be learned to operate the software.

BOX 8.9 GRAPHICS FILE FORMATS

When you save a file on a computer from most image-editing software, you have an option to choose one of the many, often more than 20, file formats supported by that software. A file format is like a language for storing and communicating information. Image formats are very far from being equivalent; so an important early decision when developing a set of images for your field guide project is what format or formats to use. Most programmes, for instance Adobe Photoshop, Corel Draw and Paint Shop Pro, have their own native format. If you are creating an image, you may as well use their own format while working on the image; but these are not the best formats to use when you want your image to be employed more widely – for instance, in your field guide document or web page – even if some of these proprietary formats are widely 'understood' by other graphics applications. Translation from one format to another is usually as simple as opening the file and saving it in a different format; but there is a high chance that some of the information content will be lost in the process.

The internet has many pages devoted to discussing the various strengths and weaknesses of the different formats. We can simplify the various pros and cons to a choice between the following.

Vector (and metafile) formats for maps and diagrams

There is, in principle, a distinction to be made between vector type images, which store image information as abstract shapes, fill patterns and so on, and raster imagery, with information on the pixels, or points, of which pictures are made, much like the dots on a traditional film or printed article. This distinction is blurred by certain formats being able to

Illustration 207

represent images in both formats – for instance, EPS (postscript format) and Windows metafile (WMF) or enhanced metafile (EMF), and the newest SVG (scalable vector graphics) format designed for use on web pages. Maps and CAD (computer assisted design) images (for example, architect plans or technical drawings of engines, or in principal floral diagrams) are generally best produced as vector images. Anywhere that the illustrator is likely to want to adjust and edit the path of lines, the shape of outlines or the relative position of objects rather than the subtle shifts of colour or fill density is best represented in a vector format – only in this format is the line itself retained in the file format. One of the main assets of vector imagery is that you can reproduce these images at different sizes, and straight lines never display jagged edges as you 'zoom in'.

Maps themselves represent a special, largely vector-based, type of image often useful in field guides. Map-making for field guides is a specialized pursuit that we cannot cover in any detail here; but many levels of geographical information system (GIS) software such as Arc View, MapInfo, Atlas GIS, IDRISI and so on are available for this purpose. GIS applications usually support their own specialized suites of various file formats. If you convert an Arc View or MapInfo map to DXF (drawing exchange file) format, or export to a bitmapped format like JPEG (Joint Photographic Experts Group), you may retain an image resembling your map, but you are likely to lose much of the underlying and linked geographic data.

Bitmap images

This is the ubiquitous format used by most modern computers for displaying images on your screen. The display area is broken up into a metric of dots of pixels, whose colour is defined. The number of colour types possible for each pixel (colour depth) and the number of pixels in the picture determine the quality of the image. There is little problem converting vector files into a bitmapped format; but the converse is not so easily achieved.

Resolution

Printers will generally work with up to 2400 dots per inch; but 300 dots per inch will still produce realistic images. When considering what resolution you need for your imagery, consider the maximum possible physical size you may need the image to appear at in your publication. If the guide is intended to be a document, then you can establish the minimum number of pixels required by multiplying the final printed size (say, 2 inches) by 600 dots per inch (speak to your publisher or printing shop early on in the project). This would suggest an image size of 1200 x 1200 pixels; so whether you are scanning a picture or choosing a setting on your digital camera, this picture resolution is what you should have in mind.

There are other factors, though, and a picture with 300 dots across it can be perfectly usable in a field guide. Many say that for colour images you only need to assume a 300 dots per inch resolution when scanning – and that any more is superfluous, more dependent upon the colour quality of the image and the printing device. However, for line drawings, where sharpness is vital and images might be examined very closely, we would recommend a higher resolution. The authors prefer to work on the safe side and scan all original artwork at 1200 dots per inch. This has the advantage of always providing a safe margin in case of changed decisions or better printers:

- Remember that it is easy to reduce the resolution of your image later, but impossible to increase it usefully. Taking pictures or scanning images is always time consuming, and one should not need to repeat it later.

Table 8.2 *File space required (kilobytes) for different formats and types of image*

Image type:	Line drawing	Line drawing	Painting	Photograph
	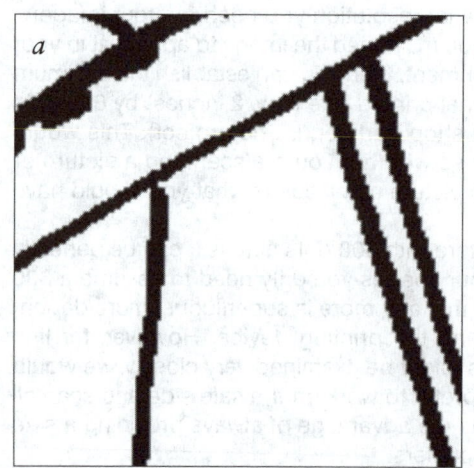			
Number of pixels	1802 x 1928	1000 x 1000	1000 x 1000	1000 x 1000
BMP or TIF without compression	3300	978	2900	2900
TIF (with LZW compression)	93	109	1100	1800
PNG	99	87	853	1500
JPEG 95%	353	189	172	467
JPEG 75%	353	115	120	167
JPEG 50%	288	86	77	97

Note: JPEG percentage figures are for quality (high quality, no compression = 100%)
Source: William Hawthorne

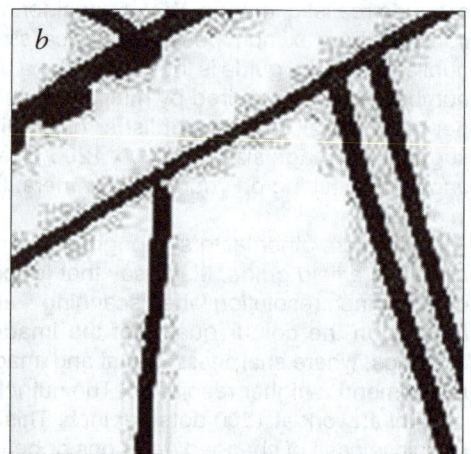

Source: William Hawthorne

Figure 8.6 *The problem with saving the same compressed JPEG file too often: (a) detail from original scan; (b) detail from 50% JPEG quality (saved five times)*

Illustration 209

- There is no point scanning above the optical resolution of your scanner. You can interpolate extra points later using basic image-editing software.
- Scan line drawings at a standard resolution, at least 600 dots per inch (dpi), preferably 1200 dpi, even if they have already been drawn larger than the size required. By scanning all images at the same resolution, it will be easier later to arrange for all images on the same page to be at the same scale.

Colour depth

24 bit or 48 bit colour images are needed for colour photographs. 8 bit colour images are useful only for diagrams. A line drawing is best scanned with 1 dot per pixel and high resolution, although in some cases they have to be converted to grey-scale images (with 8 bits to represent shades of grey for each pixel) before they can be edited.

Table 8.2 shows the savings of file space (and therefore faster transmission across the internet) possible for colour pictures with increasing JPEG compression (the bottom three rows) – the more colours and the blurrier the original, the better the compression. Figure 8.6 shows the minor artefacts that arise in a JPEG picture, After opening and saving the same file five times in a row with the JPEG quality set to 50%. Although relatively minor, they can become worse with every resave. Better-quality settings lead to similar, but smaller, blemishes. The problems are not likely to be noticed even on printed field guides.

Which image format is best for use with botanical field guides?

- Use tagged image file (TIF) format, with the compression options set to 'on' (for example, LZW) for line drawings.
- If you want to use a standard format for all your images, line drawings and colour, a good all-rounder is the newer Portable Network Graphics (PNG) format (with appropriate settings – for example, full 24 or 48 bit colour.
- Where space or transmission speed on your computer is an issue, use Joint Photographic Expert Group (JPEG) file interchange format with around 75–95 per cent (fairly high) quality setting. This will reduce time for downloading files and storage space by a factor of six to ten times over the next best option for compression, which is PNG format.
- Digital cameras often produce images with JPEG format anyway, so there is nothing to be gained by then converting them to PNG format (since the minor damage is already done) unless you intend to repeatedly edit your photographs.
- Keep an archive copy of all digital photographs before they are edited.
- If you ever need to edit and repeatedly save a JPEG file, convert it to TIF or PNG format, and only convert it back to JPEG after you have finished the last ever edit. The quality deteriorates every time you save a JPEG.
- There is no obvious reason ever to use JPEG format for line drawings.
- The only reason you might want to use BMP files or uncompressed TIF files is if you have some old software that cannot read other formats. In this case, it may be better to upgrade your software.
- Some cameras have a native RAW format that professionals use to avoid making JPEGs – the file sizes are very large for JPEGs at the same resolution and they can be awkward to process (to set the white balance manually, etc.). If you are confident handling these files, then you probably do not need to read this. Anyone else should stick to the higher-quality JPEG options from the camera.

See Table 8.3 for a summary of file formats.

Table 8.3 *Summary of image file formats*

Format	Type	Pros	Cons	Conclusion
JPEG (JPG)	Joint Photographic Expert Group file interchange format. Bitmaps with variable 'lossy' compression, or 24 bit or 48 bit full colour images, or greyscale.	Small files for good images; allows users to set compromise between file size and data loss; 1MB file size can support a >10MB image with no serious loss of picture quality. 'JPEG 2000' gives even better compression; commonest format for photographs on internet, and common output from digital cameras.	Repeated editing and saving of files introduces increasing, albeit initially subtle, artefacts.	Use instead of TIF where size of colour photographic images needs to be minimized – e.g. for large image libraries or transmission by email. Not ideal where images are likely to be repeatedly edited.
TIFF or TIF	Tagged image file format. Bitmap with lossless ('LZW', or no) compression; 1–48 bit images.	Widely accepted, used and very flexible format. No information is lost every time the file is saved. Detailed line drawings can be compressed to moderate file sizes with the compression option.	Large file size of colour images even with compression activated. Optional compression settings when saving can confuse software reading it.	Good for line drawings, and for archived colour photo libraries where storage space and transmission space not a problem.
BMP	Windows bitmap; 1–32 bit.	Very standard and basic image format for Microsoft bitmapped images.	Compression options usually not implemented, so file size tends to be unnecessarily large.	A common format, but not ideal as a photographic standard image format, as the format is rarely adopted with its compressed options and not favoured outside Windows.
GIF	Graphic interchange format bitmap. Palette based, maximum 256 colours, with lossless compression.	The main traditional format of the internet and other screen imagery and diagrams where full colour is not used anyway; single image can be an animation.	No good for full-colour (>256 colour) photographs. Some developers do not approve because of a copyright issue.	Not really relevant to field guide imagery except where image is to be only computer based.
PNG	Portable Network Graphics. Bitmap with lossless compression in 8 bit (256 colour), 24 or 48 'true' colour, or 16 bit grey scale.	A new format designed for the internet, similar to GIF but without copyright restrictions for software developers; the 24 bit is more suitable for photos than 8 bit or GIF. Some technical improvements over GIFs include slightly better compression, variable transparency (e.g. to display non-rectangular images), two-dimensional interlacing and gamma correction (useful for standardizing brightness on different computers).	24 bit image files typically four to five times larger than effectively identical JPEG.	Probably a good future-proof solution for image databases designed for web use or otherwise on your computer, although at the time of writing many users still have older web browsers and other software that cannot read it.

Illustration 211

Table 8.3 *continued*

Format	Type	Pros	Cons	Conclusion
PDF	Portable document format. Adobe Acrobat document format. All image types contained within, with text.	Good for transferring images and text over the internet; users on different machines and of the printed output will see very compatible colours and layout.	Special software needed to create the images. Few programmes write this format directly.	Good for distributing completed, formatted guides across the internet or different types of computer, and for taking your images to a printer.
EPS	Encapsulated postscript. A page description language. Vector, raster and text.	Related to and similar to PDF format; can be used for exchanging images alone. Widely readable.	Not appropriate for fully functional document format; different software tends to treat the files slightly differently. Some software can print, but not display images imported in this format.	A standard medium for vector-based imagery; not recommended as a general standard for exchanging your field guide images.
WMF, EMF	Windows metafile format. Enhanced metafile format. Windows metafiles (24–48 bit colour).	Convenient way of transferring vector and simple colour images between Microsoft Windows applications.	Not good for colour photographs; not optimized for bitmap images.	You may well find it convenient to use these formats while developing your guide, especially for graphs, diagrams and other vector imagery.
DXF	AutoDesk Drawing eXchange format.	Widely adopted standard for CAD drawings.	Very large files; vector files only.	If you are stuck trying to manipulate a vector image, this may be the format to allow other packages to read your file.
PICT	24 bit Macintosh picture format.	Standard within Macintosh computers for metafiles (raster or vector).	Not much used on non-Macintosh computers.	Not widely usable.
PCD	Kodak Photo CD.	Standard for storing scanned images on CDs.	Software mostly cannot write to this bulky format.	If you scan slides to CD, you may receive this format; but it is not a convenient format for image manipulation.

Source: William Hawthorne

CONCLUSIONS: CHOOSING AND USING IMAGERY

Real plant specimens can be used as a type of, or in the place of, field guide illustration, as *aides mémoires* or for reference to repeatedly visited forests – for example, to permanent sample plots. They are ideal for temporary familiarization and standardization of names for small sets of species and small groups of people. For a more permanent solution, a dried leaf specimen guide could be considered; but this is not much use where you have to include either many plants with large leaves (for example, palms), or where identification is to be primarily on aspects other than leaves (for instance, bark and bole guides), or if many people over a large time period might need the guide. Forest or education institutions might consider mass-producing such field guides for training purposes. The niche for real plant field guides, though, is otherwise limited. Dried plants are hardly practical for use in field guides for which many copies are needed or where more than a few hundred species are to be included. It is probably impossible to include them in a proper publication, for libraries and easy citation. A more standard 'publishable' guide, or at least a guide that can be copied, is then needed.

There are not many circumstances in which it is best to use photocopied imagery, standing as it does between the options of using real dried leaves or photographed (or scanned) images. However, if the only tool at your disposal is a photocopier, you may as well try and solve your illustration problems with it, particularly for rare plants of which you have limited real dried leaf material. If you are in charge of a student course or need to perform a local inventory, at short notice, of plants that are recognized largely by their leaves, and you have limited access to equipment, a photocopier as a potential illustrative tool should not disregarded totally – the results are about as accurate as other formats. Colour scanners are marginally better, and enable you to modify and manipulate images. For certain plant groups, where outline shape is the main characteristic to show (for example, many ferns), a scanner can enable a guide to be illustrated very quickly and cheaply.

In general, unless you have a very low budget, or limited requirements for numbers of users and time scale, we recommend concentrating on line drawings and digital photography for a published field guide. If you are a good painter or know one, then by all means use paintings to liven up the book, or the front cover, or for use on publicity material, such as postcards, pamphlets or T-shirts; but the practical work of making accurate plant identification guides is generally served more efficiently by photographs and drawings. Both have their advantages; but consider using a combination of the benefits of drawing (artistic licence to simplify where necessary; cheaper printing) and photography (colour and the illusion of texture).

Digital photography is in the process of revolutionizing tropical field guide production. Black-and-white photographs and images such as line drawings can be created from digital images without much extra effort; so it is possible for a non-artist to create usable diagrams and drawing-like images from pictures of plants, and these will allow printing costs to be reduced considerably – compared to colour photographs, black-and-white line imagery will be about one quarter the cost to print.

Digital photography could be said to have a higher capital cost; manual artwork requires less equipment but requires the services of a competent artist, and the per-species costs are therefore much more expensive. If the relative values of drawings and photographs were similar, the break-even point, where it would be cheaper for non-artists to buy their own digital camera and equipment, would be somewhere in the range of 10 to 100 species. However, the equation is not so simple, and the main criterion will almost always be: do you want or need photographs, drawings or something cheaper altogether? For a technical audience and cheap compact guides, drawings still have an important niche (see Case study 8.2).

We have based our recommendations in this chapter on the rigorous trials described in Case study 8.1. Illustrations for a field guide should always be tested with groups of potential users, and methods for doing this are described in Case study 8.1 and Chapter 9.

Illustration 213

CASE STUDY 8.2 ILLUSTRATION AND *THE WOODY PLANTS OF WESTERN AFRICAN FORESTS*

The Woody Plants of Western African Forests: A Guide to the Forest Trees, Shrubs and Lianes from Senegal to Ghana (Hawthorne and Jongkind, 2006) covers about 2140 species (a few are mentioned in footnotes or the introduction only), 2600 drawings, 2600 photographs, slightly above 1000 pages and 358,000 words. There are more than 4000 species names in the book, including synonyms. Only one species is illustrated with a photograph of a herbarium specimen because it could not be obtained on loan for drawing, and the size of the leaves alone distinguished it from relatives.

This field guide is an output of the European Union (EU)-funded Ecosyn/Ecodes project, with some input from the UK Department for International Development (DFID)–Forestry Research Programme (FRP) Field Guides Project, in terms of the use of many images. It covers trees, shrubs and lianes, as well as many types of non-woody climbers and larger herbs – for example, Marantaceae – that occur in the forest zone of Upper Guinea (West Africa, from Togo to Senegal). This represents more than 75 per cent of the whole Upper Guinean flora, the main groups excluded (15 per cent of the flora) being ferns and orchids, which are distinctive as a group but could justify their own regional field guide, especially as most are epiphytes with wide geographical ranges and are very incompletely inventoried. From inception to publication, the guide took ten years. Although all of the contributors have been working on the guide for only a small part (less than 20 per cent) of this time, it has nevertheless taken the four main contributors (excluding project administration) more than 2000 person days of work in total, including two artists to complete the drawings. One of the authors (Carel Jongkind, primarily a taxonomist) concentrated on nomenclatural issues and the taxonomy of some notoriously difficult climber groups, notably the lianes of the Combretaceae, Celastraceae and Annonaceae, while the other (William Hawthorne, primarily a field botanist and ecologist) dealt with the other families, the main structure, linking text, keys and the field characterization. A few genera, notably *Pandanus*, remain unresolved because someone else is in the process of monographing them, or at least because fertile specimens are far too sparse for us to do so without waiting another five years (by which time many of the other names would have changed again).

The main target users are not taxonomists from developed countries, although we hope such readers will find it useful; rather, they are users with some technical or scientific background in (West) Africa, including foresters of all ranks, wildlife officers, university students, medicinal plant researchers, non-governmental organizations (NGOs) interested in conservation, and hopefully the many plant enthusiasts scattered throughout rural West Africa who are literate, yet have no access to relevant literature. It is hoped that this guide will be a long-term learning tool, as well as a quick reference guide, for these people.

One main task has been to sort out the correct names for all woody plants in the forests of the region, and defining the scope has been a problem in itself. We have adopted a broad span, including thicket and many coastal swamp species in the forest zone, as well as all strictly forest species. Another challenge, especially since Sierra Leone and Liberia have frequently been too dangerous for fieldwork, has been to highlight field characters. We have been beaten in this aim by a few groups, where reproductive details are therefore used (notably various Annonaceae lianes); but for most of the flora we hope we have substantially facilitated identification for a wide range of users, compared to what could be achieved with existing literature, not least through our copious illustrations. Photographs are used particularly for flowers, fruits and bark or wood details, where colour is generally important or fine details and textures would be hard to draw. The drawings are mainly of leaves, stems and associated structures, with a significant proportion showing inflorescences without much detail. Where space and images were available, or for recently published species, we have included a few detailed images – for example, of flower cross-sections. Because mistakes and missing information are inevitable for a book of this size, it is supported by extra images and corrections on the Virtual Field Herbarium (see Box 1.1, page 6, and http://herbaria.plants.ox.ac.uk/VFH).

9

Testing the field guide

Anna Lawrence, Patricia Norrish, Maria Theresa Stradmann, Israel Vargas, Edwin Magariños, Jorge Costa, Claudia Jordán and Teonildes Nunes

INTRODUCTION

Throughout the process of writing a field guide, decisions on, for example, content, the type of illustrations and keys will have been taken with representatives of the end users and balanced against the resources available. Such activities reduce the possibility that a guide will be unacceptable and incomprehensible. However, the ultimate test of the guide is not only that it contains useful information, presented in a format that people like and understand, but that it is usable for the kinds of tasks which people want to perform. Chapters 5 to 8 have all pointed out the need to both pre-select formats in consultation with users, and to test the chosen formats at an early stage to ensure that they are understood by the users.

Both the format and content of each component, as well as a full mock-up of the guide, must be tested in realistic conditions by the kinds of people who will use the guide. The mock-up should also be as realistic as possible without going to the expense of final printing. This stage of testing is often called usability or performance testing.

Because the basic process of testing is the same for components and for the whole guide, we describe a model (outline) of the process first, and then give specific examples of how to elaborate upon this for the different aspects of the guide that need to be tested. This chapter discusses the need for usability testing; the ways in which a reasonable mock-up can be prepared; what needs to be tested; ways of carrying out the testing; and how to analyse and use the results to make adjustments to the guide.

Reasons for testing components

As explained in Chapters 3 and 7, users of the guide do not necessarily have the same knowledge, perceptions, worldview and communication style as the people who produce the guides. It is often surprising to authors to find out not only that their language is impenetrably technical, but also that people from different cultures or educational backgrounds may be put off by certain fonts, letter size or density of uninterrupted text, or, perhaps even more surprising, that different people interpret pictures in different ways. In tests conducted in northeast Brazil, highly accurate ink drawings of medicinal plants had been prepared carefully, with parts enlarged inside circles, as if under a microscope, to show key identification characters such as hairs or glands. The agricultural technicians testing the guide did not recognize the enlarged parts within circles as magnifications, but instead perceived the illustrated plants as diseased, having extraordinary distortions of certain parts.

In another example from Bahia, Brazil, a workshop with farmers was used to test the usefulness of photographs for plant identification. A selection of photographs was chosen for each species, and among these was a photo of the flower on its own, enlarged if the flowers were small. For the botanist, it was clear that this picture was important, and that it would often help them to identify the plant. The farmers, however, who are not used to seeing the flower in isolation, sometimes did not recognize it in this type of photograph. The photos that helped them to identify the plants were those which depicted the branch in flower or fruiting, illustrating the plant in its natural environment. Without this test, resources would perhaps have been wasted on producing images that would not be useful for the target users, and the guide would have failed in its objective. Even more importantly, the farmers felt deeply involved in the production process and enthusiastic about the product.

Reasons for testing usability

As explained in Chapter 2, 'usability' refers to the properties of the guide that enable users to achieve their objectives successfully – in other words, to identify plants, find information about those plants or to recognize that the plant in question is not in that particular guide.

Usability testing of a mock-up of the guide is about seeing how people find their way around the guide, and whether there are any serious obstacles to using it that need to be addressed before final printing. It can pick up issues that may not have been noticed earlier during pre-testing of individual components of the guide, such as portability, durability, binding defects and, most importantly, identifying the right species among the whole mass of species in the guide.

This final evaluation of the field guide is obviously useful for authors to help improve the accuracy and usability of the guide; but it is also an important stage for users who have participated in the production to reinforce their feeling of involvement. One user made the following comment: 'Seeing our names in the book alongside the others has given us an incentive to keep helping with the production of the book.'

OVERVIEW OF THE TESTING PROCESS

It is difficult to test several components of a field guide all at once. For example, if the aim is to test whether or not the diagnostic characters of the species described in the text are important and helpful for the user to identify the plants, the materials used in the test must consist only of the text with the information you want to check, as well as samples of the plants that are the object of identification. It is important that neither photographs nor drawings should be used since these will make it impossible to ascertain whether it is the clarity of the text or the characters described that enable identification.

The first step, therefore, is to define exactly what it is that you are testing. If illustrations, are you testing which illustrations people *prefer*, or which ones help them to reach an accurate identification? What are the possible options? They may include preferences already stated by users at the consultation stage, as well as innovative ideas for illustration that the authors have seen elsewhere. How can you gather or prepare material to test these options? And how many species would you want to include? For example, if you want to compare the usefulness of ink drawings with photographs for identifying trees, you might prepare illustrations of both kinds for a sample range of species that covered all the difficult aspects of identification – such as leaves, bark thorns or fruits.

Table 9.1 sets out some possibilities for testing procedures. Each test must have an underlying question, such as 'Which format leads to the most accurate identification?', and materials and method can be chosen accordingly to match the question. But, of course, there are many more detailed questions to be asked, such as 'What is it that you like/dislike/understand/don't understand about this picture/description/key, etc.?'

There are also decisions to be made about how the testers will get on with their task. Sometimes the testers (who represent potential users of the guide) are left to examine the material or to carry out a task, and then the facilitators can interview them to ask these questions. At other times, especially if the testers are not used to following written instructions or may become nervous about doing so, the facilitator can guide the tester through the steps. However, with usability testing the testers must be left to find their way through the guide without assistance since this is the point of the test.

In all of this, the role of observer is extremely important. Often, the testers will find it hard to explain how they used the guide, or will not notice factors such as their speed in identifying something, puzzled expressions on their faces or repeated looks at one particular illustration. All of these are clues to the facilitators about how easy or difficult it is to use the guide.

After these activities, it is important to round off with a discussion to summarize the testers' experiences and probe into their reasons for liking or not understanding something. If possible, this should take the form of a group discussion so that opinions can be shared and consolidated.

In summary, then, the whole process involves the following:

- *Plan*: what will you test, and what needs to be recorded and observed?
- *Invite*: who will test this? Invite them, explaining why you want them to test the field guide and what the arrangements are.
- *Gather or prepare materials*: specimens must be freshly gathered and display the characters of interest; plants in the wild must be easily found and clearly marked; illustrations, descriptions or the mock-up must obviously be ready in time for the testing workshop.
- *Prepare instructions for the test itself*: these should be read by the testers or be used by the facilitators.
- *Prepare forms for the results to be recorded*: these are filled in by the testers and facilitators (who must record their observations).
- *Organize logistics*: plan travel, food, space and workshop materials.

- *Run the tests*, usually in the form of a workshop.
- *Record results, observe behaviour, discuss and explain experience.*
- *Reflect on outcomes* after the workshop.

These steps are described in more detail in the following sections.

Timing of testing

As indicated in Figure 2.1 (page 16), testing occurs at various stages of field guide preparation. Some components of the guide need to be tested as early as possible in the production process in order to avoid wasting time and money (for example, in producing illustrations that are not of the required type) or in order to guide the information-gathering process (for example, by finding out which diagnostic characters your guide users find more practicable to use in the field). Other components cannot be tested until you have enough information to prepare the content. This applies particularly to a thorough reading of the descriptions of all species to check for any incorrect or contentious information and, of course, to the final testing of the full mock-up, which must contain as many of the final descriptions and illustrations as possible, in the right order, and with keys and indexes where required to help the user find the correct species.

METHODOLOGY

An important issue to consider when planning and choosing a suitable methodology is selecting an approach that is appropriate for the readership. This necessitates a clear definition of the target users of the field guide as the participants in the tests must represent a sample of this group. When testing material for farmers, for instance, given that the material to be tested (content of the guide) contains a specific type of language, the methodological approach used must also be in a language understood by this group and in accordance with their education. For example, if the users include people who cannot read or write, there is no point in creating a questionnaire for them to read and answer. It will be necessary to think up ways for them to analyse the material, perhaps involving helpers to aid them with the tasks, although it is, of course, important that the participants should not feel embarrassed. Equally, if the target users are eco-tourists, there is no point in preparing long tests or questionnaires with a large number of questions as these users, on holiday, are focused on enjoying themselves and are not going to spend a long time answering a boring questionnaire.

Each test explores the ability of the guide to answer a particular question (for example, 'What species am I looking at?'). The basic aim is to define a method that challenges that particular question, to carry out this defined task using the materials available, to record the process followed by the testers and the conclusions that they reach, and to analyse the reasons for them following that process and reaching those conclusions. In short: present task; ask testers to do task; record and observe; analyse through interview and reflection. Table 9.1 shows how this basic core method is used in a range of tests for illustrations, text, keys and the whole guide.

Thought must be given to how you will make the testers feel comfortable and how to explain the purpose and procedure. In order for the tests to have validity, there needs to be uniformity on this, and what is going to be said should be set out in some way, either as a statement to be read or as a set of guidelines on what must be covered. It may be important to relax and reassure people that it is the guide (not themselves) that is being tested, and that inability to use the guide is nothing to be ashamed of, but rather a very useful result. Many people can lose their concentration if they think they are being observed or feel under pressure. For this reason, it is sometimes better to conduct evaluations where people are left alone to get on with the guide use at their own pace. If necessary, usability can be assessed by asking users questions at the end once they have been shown which species they identified correctly and which they did not, discussing at this later stage where the guide was misleading.

The skills needed by the facilitators are:

- structuring a task based on the guide:
  - carrying out structured observation of how people address the task to find out if and where the process breaks down;
  - recording of the structured observation;
- preparing a semi-structured interview:
  - carrying out a semi-structured interview with the potential user (before, during and after the task as necessary) to determine existing levels of skill in using a guide and the specific problems/successes with the guide being tested.

Semi-structured interviewing is described in Chapters 3 and 7, and the section on 'Questionnaires' in Chapter 7 will also be helpful. Thought needs to be given to the questions you will ask at the start in order to determine whether people have experience of working with guides or not (their experience will affect the speed and ease with which they carry out the task), and questions that need to be asked at the end of the task to determine why people did what they did.

Setting a task that tests the aspect of the guide you are interested in is a logical process. Make sure that all aspects of the component are tested. For example, if you are asking testers to name the species illustrated, ensure that a range of different kinds of species are included, and that different parts are illustrated or different types of illustration are used. Sort these randomly so that one illustration does not help the tester to recognize the next. Some examples of tasks are given in Table 9.1.

In addition, the facilitators need to be particularly skilled at detached observation, and at recording the behaviour and discussion that occurs during the test. Observation and interpretation of a situation, informed by an understanding of the situation from the point of view of the participants rather than the observer, is a particular challenge if you have been closely involved in the development of the guide and have strong opinions about how it 'should' be. But the tests will not be objective if you let your concerns get in the way of understanding the blocks and responses that the testers have to the guide. These observation skills are particularly useful in the usability test, which is a procedure specially designed for testing the use of the full mock-up.

The usability test

The aim of the usability test is to see the guide being used to solve a set task, in as realistic a situation as possible. This will preferably be in the field. If it is difficult to conduct the usability test in the field, a simulation can be organized by bringing the specimens to the

Table 9.1 *Some approaches to testing*

What are you testing?	Example of a task	Examples of questions to ask	Materials needed	Method
Illustrations that help to confirm identification.	Recognize the species illustrated in a range of illustrations.	What species is this? What do you like/dislike about the illustration?	Range of illustrations for each species. These may be different *types* of illustration (drawing, photograph) or illustrations of different *parts* (flower, fruit, whole tree, branch, bark) depending upon what you are testing.	Testers work individually or in groups to identify randomly sorted pictures. Depending upon the testers, facilitators can ask them to report verbally what species they think it is and why, or to write their answers on a form. Facilitators observe testers for signs of confidence or worry. Interview testers afterwards to understand their reasons for successful or unsuccessful identification.
Comprehensible text	Read and comment on species descriptions or other written components of the guide.	What do you not understand? Which do you read fastest and why? Which do you prefer and why?	The same species description formatted in different ways, or the same species, described using different words.	Individual testers read texts. Facilitators observe testers for signs of confidence or worry. Testers and facilitators discuss texts in groups to reach consensus and also to seek alternative words for those which are not understood.
Diagnostic characters that are observable, understandable and help to reach an accurate identification	Comparison of pairs of species that differ in few but significant ways, asking testers to note differences between the species. Examination of single specimens to describe character state represented.	What is the difference between species X and species Y? How do you know they are those species? On this specimen, would you say character X was a, b or c (for example, would you say the leaves are simple, pinnate or bipinnate)?	Specimens for comparison or marked species in the field. If you are asking the testers how they recognize the species, the specimens must be in the field so that all possible characters are available, and must be species known to the testers. Species used to test diagnostic characters must be carefully chosen to represent a range of states of those characters (e.g. pairs of species that have different types of hairs, different thorn shape, etc.).	Testers work individually or in groups to examine specimens or pairs of specimens. Depending upon the testers, facilitators can ask them to report verbally what characters they observe or differences they find between the species, or to write their answers on a form. Facilitators observe testers for signs of confidence, worry or confusion. Interview testers afterwards to understand their reasons for successful or unsuccessful completion of the task.

Usable keys	Use two or more key formats to identify a range of species chosen for testing a range of diagnostic characters.	What is this species? Which key format enables you to reach a correct identification and to feel confident of your identification?	Specimens for comparison or marked species in the field. Keys prepared using different structures and formats. To ensure that the testers are using the keys and not their own knowledge, the selected species must be previously unknown to the testers.	Depending upon the testers, facilitators can ask them to report verbally their conclusions and points of difficulty in the keys, or to write their answers on a form. Facilitators observe testers for signs of confidence, worry or confusion. Interview testers afterwards to understand their reasons for successful or unsuccessful completion of the task.
Usability	Identify a range of species using the guide, or correctly conclude that the species is not in the guide. Find information contained in the guide, such as a range of species appropriate to a chosen purpose.	What is this species? How did you decide that? What did you like/dislike about the process of identification and why? In this guide, which species might be suitable for annual fodder? This can be presented as a quiz, including questions suchas 'why should species X not be used for medicine in winter', which requires testers to use indexes, possibly linking local to scientific names, locate the species description and find the correct information.	A mock-up of the whole guide. Specimens for identification or marked species in the field. A mock-up of the whole guide (as close as possible to the final product). Photocopies of the mock-up for observers to record comments.	Testers work individually or in groups to identify species or answer questions. In this case, it is best if facilitators do not interact with testers while they are performing the tasks as it is important to see if the task can be completed using the tools available in the guide. Facilitators observe testers for signs of confidence, worry or confusion. Observation is particularly important in the usability test as it is the most complex of the tasks that can be set and involves using the whole guide, so careful attention must be paid to the parts of the guide used. Interview testers afterwards to understand their reasons for successful or unsuccessful completion of the task.

Source: Anna Lawrence

testers rather than the other way round. The basic process is much the same as for the usability test carried out in the field. However, particular attention needs to be paid to the quality of the specimens in this case (see the section on 'Preparing materials for testing').

Steps in a usability test

The first step is to consider the purpose for which the guide is intended and to decide on a task that exemplifies this purpose. If the purpose of the guide is to enable people to identify particular trees, then the task for the usability test will be identification. If the purpose is to help users confirm identity in order to then find information about a species, then the task could be to find some specific information about a plant or about its use (for example, 'use the guide to find out how to prepare chamomile in a tea', or 'use the guide to find which species are suitable for animal fodder in the dry season'). Setting the task involves thinking through the various ways in which people might use the different components of the guide to successfully complete the task. It may be helpful at this stage to think back to your initial consultation and to remind yourself what kind of questions the guide is designed to answer (see Chapter 3).

Having made a decision about the task, the next step is to select the species to be identified using the guide. This should be done in relation to each potential user who will be involved in the usability testing. It is important that the range of species to be identified covers various possibilities. For example, of six species selected to be identified, two might be well known to the testers, two less well known and closely related (so that they have to be examined particularly carefully to be separated), another rare and currently flowering, with another presented in a vegetative state so that other characters have to be tested.

Once the species have been selected, then the user and the specimen need to be brought together. There are various options for this:

- *Take the user to the plants (a field test)*: plan a route through the forest/field that takes the respondent to various pre-selected plants. These may be labelled – for example, each with a number – so that the tester has no hints as to the names, but the facilitators can cross-check on a list of correct identifications against each number. This could be tested by numbering ten random plants in a forest and seeing whether the ones that *are* in the guide are accurately picked out by users, and those that are *not* in the guide are all noted as being not in the book. Another approach involves asking users to find plants in real life situations using the guide. For instance, a field guide promoting local medicines may aim to allow people to locate the plants (perhaps prior to using them) and allow no confusion with non-medicinal plants (that are not in the book). This involves choosing an area where some of the target species are present, perhaps along a path to make the test easier, and asking users to locate any of, for example, five species from the guide that they find. In this case, plants are numbered.
- *Take the plants to the respondent (a simulated test)*: bring plant specimens to the place where the interview will be held. This requires care because the identification of plants in the field often depends upon characteristics, such as the bark, latex or habit of the plant, that cannot be observed in small specimens (for example, branches); but it is the next best thing if a field trip is impossible.

Decisions now need to be made on what has to be observed and noted down during the usability test. It is important to remember that each potential user participating in the test will need to have one observer watching them throughout the task. What you are looking for is confidence that leads to a successful search and the points at which the search breaks down or becomes difficult. You should look for signs of hesitation, annoyance, revisiting the same part of the book more than once, starting over, etc. These must be noted down as they will form the basis for discussion after the task has been completed.

The next decision to be made is how the observation will be recorded. This can be as a set of notes or on pre-prepared forms (see Table 9.2) in which tables can be used that list all of the components of the guide, with columns for entering what people did and for your own comments and queries that you want to take up with users at the end of the test. Preparing the tables, which are essentially a description of the guide and its constituent parts, can take some time. An example is included in Table 9.2, and can be adapted to specific situations.

You may find it much faster and safer (in terms of recording all that the user does and says) to note sequentially what is being done, said and observed by the user. Nevertheless, if the tables are not completed, you run the risk of losing (or not recording) other information. For example, it is important to know which components of the guide are being used and which are not. If a table is not made for the usability tests, then the interviewer may forget to ask important questions about the components that are not being employed. We therefore strongly recommend that the tables are used during, or immediately after, each test has been completed as a means of recording the data. This will be invaluable when it comes to analysing the results.

You need to pilot the usability test, preferably with a member of the potential users – but if that is too difficult, certainly among yourselves. Then revise the test in order to overcome any confusion. For example, in Ghana, a theoretical test protocol was devised for comparing various formats with the same species content. However, early tests using two or three invigilators showed that the tests took too long, and so were simplified. In the early tests, we asked participants whether they had enjoyed themselves and how the tests might be improved. Many people found the tests interesting, but said that if the test was shorter they would have got just as much interest out if it and would not have become so tired at the end. Based on this, the tests were shortened and lasted about 1–1.5 hours of actual testing (excluding transport to the site) per participant, rather than twice as long in the original design. Other minor changes to the wording of questions and to the size of the forms were made in this early phase.

ORGANIZING WORKSHOPS FOR TESTING

Planning the methodology will help you to decide:

- whether the team conducting the test needs training;
- how to allocate the resources;
- how to choose suitable target users to invite for testing;
- the most appropriate dynamics for creating the best possible group interaction for the tests.

Table 9.2 *Completed usability form in the case of a specific guide to medicinal plants in Paraíba, Brazil*

Component	Used?	Comments
Preface		
Contents		
Acknowledgements		
Summary		
Introduction		
Study area		
Methodology		
Format		
Species descriptions		
Common name	3	Checked the name.
Scientific name		
Synonyms		
Family		
Description	4	Read the description to make sure; remained a bit uncertain of the identification because common name was different from the one he knows.
Comments		
Ethno-medicine		
Chemical constituents		
Biological activities		
Representative sample		
Illustration	2	Leafed through, looking for the species. Stopped at p37; recognized the photo.
Glossary		
Bibliography		
Index of common and scientific names	1	Started here, looking for the common name of the plant he wanted to identify; didn't find the name.
Index of chemical constituents		
Index of uses and activities		

Note: The 'Used?' column indicates the order in which the tester used components.
Source: Ana Paula Ferreira and Anna Lawrence, results of testing usability of Agra (1996)

All activities must be planned, however simple they might seem. Who is to lead the activity, what material will be needed and, especially, what the aim is and why that particular technique is being used – all of this must be decided beforehand. One technique is suitable to help a group relax and another to wake them up after a long presentation.

When there are activities to do in the field in order to test material, it is better to do these in the morning and leave the afternoon session for theoretical discussions, seminars, debates, presentations, reading, etc. If there are long presentations, it is also advisable to hold them in the morning session as people are more awake and alert then, and keep the afternoon for more dynamic activities, such as group work or debates.

Planning meetings should be held in advance to allow enough time for materials to be produced, for a suitable methodological approach to be designed, and to issue invitations to those individuals who are to take part in the testing workshop as a sample of the user group in order to ensure their presence and participation. It is advisable that the first meeting should be held at least two months before the testing, and a second one between a month and a fortnight before.

It is also necessary to hold a meeting with the entire test team the day before the workshop. It is vital that all those involved know the aim of the test, and the materials to be used and tested. It is also important to check all of the materials, the set-up and the facilities available, and to be able to resolve unforeseen hitches and make methodological changes should team members or members of the target user group, for instance, be missing.

The time dedicated to each activity should be calculated carefully since there may be a variety of different tests to be performed. It is worth remembering that the individuals taking part in the testing are not necessarily used to identifying plants or animals, or to the discipline of recording each step involved in the process, or to being critical of another person's work. A workshop like this will usually take a whole day.

Remember that the testers have made themselves available voluntarily, whether out of self-interest or not, and that they are giving up their time to take part. The organizers must do everything possible to encourage them to take part, making the logistics as easy as possible for them.

Location, facilities and materials

The venue where the workshop is to take place should be easy to get to, and if this is not the case, transport should be provided for the benefit of the participants and the team. If the workshop is held in an area where the participants do not live, all board and lodging should be covered by the test organizers.

As far as possible, the facilities at the venue should offer a reasonable standard of comfort and be well enough equipped for the activities that are to take place at the workshop. All of the material to be tested and associated methodological material must be ready for use so that participants are not kept waiting unnecessarily.

Conduct of the tests

We recommend that the team, or at least one team member, arrives at the venue half an hour early to welcome the participants. A punctual start to proceedings is important.

The workshop should begin by welcoming all participants and outlining the aim of the activities that are to take place. All of those present should be introduced to each

Box 9.1 How to run a usability test

- *Aim*: to test the efficiency and accuracy of the guide in helping users to identify species or find out information about the species contained in the guide. Essentially, there are two tasks: find the species in the guide and confirm that this identification is correct using the information contained in the description of the species, based on the important features of the species.
- *Location*: an open area containing all or some of the species included in the guide, with some in flower or fruiting, or a communal area to which specimens have been brought.
- *Material for the participants*: mock-up of complete guide; numbered plants or specimens to be identified, or list of questions to be answered by using the guide.
- *Material for the team*: photocopied mock-up of complete guide; list of answers to each question or species to be identified; evaluation forms for the observer (see 'Documentation: Instructions and forms for the test').
- *Logistical guidelines for the activities*: it is helpful to have two facilitators for each group of testers. If you have more than five testers, consider dividing them into more groups, each with two facilitators. One will present the activity and provide guidance, and the other will observe and record responses, analyses, comments, other observations, problems, etc.

Each tester group should have a complete printed guide and should identify two or three designated species. Each group should be allotted different species, which will facilitate testing of many of the species in the guide. Encourage different group members to identify each species in turn, with assistance from the rest of the group.

- *Method*:
  1. Start by making people feel comfortable and by explaining what you are going to do and why. They should *not* feel that they are being tested, although this is hard to avoid at some level. Say something quite simple covering:
     - what the research is about and why it is being done (why you are here);
     - their role in the research (how they can help);
     - thank them for their time;
     - make sure they know that it is the manuals and their designers who are on trial, not them;
     - the fact that you want to make notes on what they say/do (do they mind this?);
     - how you will go about the interview (you will start by asking them some general questions and then go on to detailed questions about the guide).
  2. Find out what kind of experience people have with using guides; the feedback from those who are less experienced may be more important than that from practised users. Ask the following questions:
     - Do you use guides?
     - What do you use them for?
     - What do you think makes a good guide (you could ask them to name a guide that they find practical to use and probe as to why this is).
  3. Explain the task and hand him/her the guide. Give him/her time to look at this and ask questions about it and about the task. Reassure them once again that they are not on trial – the manual is. Emphasize that they can ask for help at any stage of the test.

4   Observe the task and record your observations, including all 'finding/searching' activities on a form such as that in Table 9.2. What do they do first – for example:
- Look at the book to see how it works?
- Look in the index?
- Look in the contents pages?
- Look at any preliminary information?
- Flick through the book randomly?
- Make a closer observation of the specimen; if so, what are they looking at?

Where do they go next? Watch carefully to see what people do from first action to the end of the task.

Note any hesitation or annoyance, as well as the following actions: repeatedly going back to the same place; trying to use more than one part of the book at the same time; keeping their fingers on more than one page to keep them all open.

Note any questions asked and your answers.

5   Use semi-structured interview methods after this activity in order to probe about the use of the guide by asking the users why they used the components in that way, and reminding them to give their opinions. At the end, ask the following questions:
- Are you sure of the identification/information that you have found?
- Why/why not?

If the respondent did not use some of the access tools, ask why not. For example:
- Why didn't you use the key?
- Did the index of common names help?
- Do you think it is necessary to include the distribution maps?

6   Record the results – for example, on the photocopy of the mock-up. Note:
- How long did it take the respondent to identify the plant when using the guide?
- Was the identification correct or not? (If the interviewer does not know the plants well enough to be absolutely sure of the identity, the only way to conduct this test properly is to collect a voucher specimen of the plant used in the test and to send it to a botanist who can give you the correct scientific name.)

See 'Documentation: Instructions and forms for the test' for some suggested ways of documenting the results and observations.

other, and it should be made clear that they are valued representatives of the target user group.

It is vital to ensure that the team conducting the tests understands the importance of adopting a respectful attitude towards the participants. The team is there to guide, provide information and help the testing process run smoothly, and in no event to assume the role of an interrogator or presume greater knowledge than the participant, even if this is, in fact, the case. An attitude of this kind may make the participant, or even the whole group, feel inhibited or under attack, and this could greatly reduce the value of the entire testing process, as well as perhaps never being able to work with those individuals in the future.

At both the beginning and the end of the workshop, thank the participants for giving up their time, and re-emphasize the importance of their taking part in the tests to find out more about the target users.

Dynamics of the workshop

Dynamics are not only important when it comes to putting participants at their ease or introducing an element of fun into the workshop, but also when planning the methodology used in the activities and exercises themselves. The dynamics exert an important influence on the success of these, both in terms of achieving the objectives of the tests and maintaining the cohesion of the group so that the workshop goes as well as possible.

As far as the introduction of team members and participants is concerned, it is important that all individuals are given the opportunity to introduce themselves; this is a valuable moment, allowing them to be briefly in the limelight. The introduction can be done in a variety of ways – for instance, a draw is made and participants put into pairs, and each individual introduces the other to the rest of the group. To do this, they have to get to know each other a little. There are many ways of setting up an introduction; but the fundamental thing is that it does occur.

For the exercises themselves, the participants may be organized in groups or pairs, and one should always try to match individuals, both on a personal or professional basis, bearing in mind the desired result of the test. When testing a textual description of a species, for example, in a group or pair including both a botanist and someone who has never identified plants before, the botanist will be the only one to provide an answer. This will result in an unrealistic evaluation of the text and whether or not it serves to identify a plant: the non-botanist will let the botanist answer so that the evaluation process is pointless. A way of avoiding this situation would be to organize the participants into pairs without experience of identification, and to put the botanists together in a control group so that they can assess the material and check that the information contained in the text is correct, or discuss among themselves whether any other information could be added to aid the identification process.

If at all possible, the tests should involve activities in the field. It is best to plan such activities for the morning sessions, and participants should be divided into small groups, each with a group leader and someone to record the observations, comments, questions and problems that come up during the exercise.

Team members and workshop leaders must have well-defined roles. A workshop leader or coordinator will always present the activities to the whole group, keep track of time, explain how to do the exercises and use the materials, and keep an eye on the work of the team conducting the tests. For each small group or pair, there should be an observer to accompany them during the activities, observe participants' reactions, record the difficulties experienced and the positive aspects of the exercise, and provide guidance, if necessary.

A general meeting or feedback session may be organized, either at the end of each activity or in the form of a general debate at the conclusion of the workshop. This is an opportunity for all members of the group – participants and team – to share opinions and doubts relating to the test material. People often have very different questions and opinions, and each individual may have a very personal and specific point to make on the activities and test material. During the exercises, the observers will record these comments, which can then form the basis for debate. The debate can also be used for testing and checking preferences for particular guide formats, layouts, colours, fonts, textual matters, etc.

Evaluating the workshop

At the end of the workshop, some form of assessment on the part of the participants is a good idea, and this should include an evaluation of the venue and its facilities, the organization of the project, the type of material used, the work of the project team, the activities themselves, and any other questions for which feedback would be useful if holding another workshop in the future. The team can be involved in this process, but it is not strictly necessary. The evaluation may take the form of a general meeting at which everyone can express their opinions, answer evaluation questionnaires or just mark positive and negative points on a coloured form. During the evaluation meeting, questions can either be suggested by the team, raising precisely those points that are judged to require assessment, or the session can take a freer form, with short presentations by participants on any area that they like.

PREPARING MATERIALS FOR TESTING

Each test has its own objective, and both the test material itself and the material which will serve as the methodological basis for the test must be prepared accordingly.

Preparing printed pages

If you are testing illustrations, the quality of the paper, ink and printing process is extremely important. Fuzzy photos do not help anyone to decide what illustrations to include, unless you plan for the final version to also have fuzzy photos! This can be expensive, so think about numbers needed. A set of photos will be required for each plant, including images of those features to be tested (a flower in its entirety; habit (e.g. whether tree, shrub or herb); a flower enlarged; a leaf; a branch in flower; etc.). Producing a set of illustrations for every participant in the test is very expensive, and it is useful to set up a system where each person present can analyse a set at a time, and each set can be passed around all participants, in turn. It is also very costly to print all of the pages of a guide to a publishable quality (including good-quality paper, colour photographs, drawings, etc.), although this is important if the material is to be tested in the form in which it will be published. To save resources, one optimized version can be produced, and the others done to a lower-quality specification. The most important point is that all participants have access to material that depicts the quality of the published guide so that they can express their opinions about it.

With regard to checking texts with descriptions of the plants, it is best, if possible, to test all pages of the guide relating to the plants included and to prepare them in a format as similar as possible to the eventual published guide. This is often hard because of time pressures or the lack of resources for printing the pages; but even so, some pages can be tested in this way.

The quality of printing and the type of paper used is a relevant factor in the test material, and if there are different options regarding this, the materials (whether individual pages or the whole guide) can be prepared accordingly. For example, the paper type could be tested by producing samples on matt black and gloss *couche* paper, and on recycled paper, in white or beige. This would allow users to express their views on the most appropriate options.

When preparing the material, it is also important to try to test different groups of plants or animals so that the participants do not become bored. Another reason to do this is that once the plant has been identified, the participants may, in the next exercise, choose it again on the basis of familiarity, and not because they identified it using the data provided. When a test is carried out using photographs of a plant, followed by another with drawings of the same plant, the participants simply choose the right species because they already know the plant, not because the drawing helped them to identify it. In this case, the test is a waste of time since it is impossible to conclude whether the drawing was useful in the identification process.

Preparing specimens

For testing characters, keys or usability, the testers will need to examine real plants, either whole in the field, or cut specimens brought to the workshop. If specimens are cut, they must obviously be the freshest possible – it is no good asking people to identify specimens that were collected the day before and have since wilted. Above all, the specimens must actually include the features that are necessary for identification. If your field guide relies strongly on bark characters and you cannot bring a sample of the bark to the testing workshop, you must go to the field to test your guide.

Preparing a mock-up

Probably the commonest misjudgement made by field guide writers is to produce a final draft only during the last days of the project. Be safe and aim to produce a working draft – perhaps missing the odd item, but otherwise complete with respect to number of pages, illustrations and indexes – at the latest 75 per cent of the way through the project life span, leaving the last quarter of the project to correct problems that are apparent only when everything is in place.

The main issues for those producing the mock-up are:

- *The quality of the reproduction.* A general rule of thumb is that the illustrations should be as close as possible in size and colour to the final product.
- *The extent to which all text, illustrations and access systems need to be included to make the usability test useful.* You may be able to leave out some information or some species, as long as the overall structure of the guide is there and none of your tests involves the missing information.
- *Who should be involved.* The team who have been involved in producing and pre-testing individual aspects of the text, illustrations and access systems need to be involved in producing the mock-up since they are the ones who know what the final product should contain, what it should look like and what its purpose is. However, there are advantages to bringing into the team those individuals (graphic designers, printers, etc.) who will be responsible for the final production of the guide (see Case studies 9.1 and 9.2).

These decisions will depend upon the purpose for which the guide is intended and the amount of time, money, skill and equipment available for producing the mock-up and carrying out the usability test.

Case study 9.1 Using a graphic designer to prepare the mock-up in Brazil

The production of the guide to forage legumes of the Caatinga (Costa et al, 2002, a spiral-bound colour photo guide to 21 species that are useful to farmers in a semi-arid region of northeast Brazil) turned into a major participatory exercise. The authors found themselves very occupied with the consultations and workshops in order to ensure that the guide was suitable for the needs of the farmers and extension workers in the area, and felt that they lacked the time and specialist skills to prepare the page formats. As the testing progressed, they decided to contract a graphic designer to produce the pages of the mock-up to a similar quality as the published guide in order for the tests to provide the most reliable results possible.

Although she did not have experience in producing field guides, the designer was able to work to create the material in a participatory way, listening to the opinions of the team, so that the end product reflected all decisions taken in the workshops and met the needs of the target audience.

The designer was then given all the text, photos and drawings, as well as the guidelines on how the material should be presented according to decisions taken with the target audience in mind. Constant surveillance of the production process was needed to ensure that it met the testing requirements.

Once engaged, the designer spent 30 hours producing the material. In addition, the team had plenty to do: to produce simple pages with printing and photocopying, they needed 12 hours to scan the 105 photographs and illustrations, 5 hours to format the 60 pages of text and set it on the page, 20 hours to set up and edit the test pages, and 3 more hours to print a high-quality original on the laser printer. Five more hours were required for laser photocopying on coated paper. The printing costs for the original involved approximately two black-and-white and two colour cartridges, as well as the cost of the paper. High-quality (laser) photocopies were then made so that the guide could be tested simultaneously with various user groups.

This professional approach came at a cost. The designer cost US$615, producing a layout for the mock-up and revising it for final publication. In addition, to ensure her interaction with the stakeholders, she spent time in the workshops at a cost of US$92 per day, not including board and accommodation. And, finally, the cost of printing, reproduction and binding the mock-ups was US$184.

As the pages were checked during testing, many questions arose regarding form, colours and graphic design possibilities. We realized that the presence of the designer during testing could make the tests more dynamic and more useful for improving visual aspects of the guide. The designer could be present to resolve doubts and suggest specific solutions, keeping in mind the costs of the different options.

The designer also participated during the testing of the page proofs (a prototype for the guide), when plants were identified by using the guide, in order to give her a full grasp of the users' requirements so that the visual presentation would meet the needs of the target audience. This also enabled her to provide technical advice and involvement in discussions on what format to choose for the guide, possible fonts, colours, artwork, the paper to be used and its availability and, of course, the costs of the various options.

Although this appeared to be a luxury, involving the graphic designer during the participatory preparation of the guide made the process run more smoothly, and the end product was published on schedule.

Source: Maria Theresa Stradmann, Ana Paula Ferreira, Teonildes Nunes and Jorge Costa

CASE STUDY 9.2 PREPARING THE MOCK-UP IN THE OFFICE: THE PROS AND CONS OF A MORE ECONOMIC APPROACH IN BOLIVIA

In contrast to Case study 9.1, the editors responsible for producing the mock-up for the guide to the useful plants of Bajo Paraguá (Vargas and Jordán, 2003) decided to carry out all of these tasks in the office. They had access to high-quality printers and an interest in visual presentation; so although it was time consuming, they saw this as a way of avoiding high costs at the testing stage and of developing their own skills.

The first thing to take into consideration at this stage was that the document would have to be printed in the office, without the benefit of a professional outside printer. This required printing the text pages, the illustrated plants, the covers and the inner covers, and all parts of the document in order to put together the samples needed for validation in the field. The editors made four originals of the final draft and four photocopies in black and white, upon which facilitators could take notes of the corrections in the field and the comments overheard during the tests.

Preparing each one of the samples thus took a lot of time; but carrying out this step was more economical in the end and was necessary for ensuring that the users were satisfied with and approved of the guide, and that they felt involved.

Doing this in the office means that you need to programme some time for printing all of the parts and putting them together – binding or sticking them – and making sure that they appear in the correct size (this can be achieved after binding by cutting all of the pages together in a big guillotine to ensure that the edges of the pages are in line with the cover). The product is thus close to the final guide in appearance, although the quality of the cover and the pages of the illustrations are not as good. Furthermore, because it was printed in the office, normal paper was used, which appeared too 'weak' to be part of the field guide. This was commented upon by the testers; but they understood that it was too expensive to print the mock-up on final quality paper.

At the point of printing, you must have all of the information for the complete text available, as well as the illustrations for the species that have been finished; if something is still missing, it should be for a small group of species so that, overall, it is not really noticeable that some pages are incomplete, or lack information or illustrations. Therefore, the validation is practically at the final point, even though you have to be open minded and expect that you will make some changes and important additions at this stage.

In this case study, some plates were still incomplete, lacking photos of the flowers or fruits that had been mentioned as diagnostic characters of some plants. However, the authors made an effort to complete these illustrations; where it was not possible, the users accepted that they would be included later on.

To conclude, if you want to prepare and print a field guide independently, it is important that the project originator or institution should have the basic computer equipment, or is prepared to make the investment at the beginning, with appropriate capacity to store the information, images and all of the software, including word processing, image editing (such as Photoshop or Corel) and desktop publishing (such as PageMaker).

Source: Israel Vargas and Claudia Jordán

DOCUMENTATION: INSTRUCTIONS AND FORMS FOR THE TEST

To ensure that the workshops go as planned and that all members of the team know exactly what to do and record, the forms and instructions must be agreed and printed in advance. Any printed hand-outs must obviously be legible, and there must be sufficient quantity for all participants, with some left over as possible replacements for faulty material. If there are questionnaires or forms to fill in, the questions listed must be clearly worded so that there is no possible confusion for the user which could lead to a wrong answer. It is a good idea to have the material checked by someone outside the production team to make sure that the text and questions are quite clear.

In most situations the following documents will be useful:

- *Workshop programme.* This is to be given out to all participants in the workshop and all members of the team. It is a document containing information on the activities to occur during the workshop, explaining the aims of the activities, how long they will take, and detailing breaks for snacks, lunch and rest. Although the team members will know about the organization of the workshop, they should also receive the same information as the participants.
- *Test timetable for the project team.* This is to be issued to the team only as a guide to the activities for the team members who will organize the workshop and carry out the tests. Similar to a programme, but much more detailed, it is the projected timetable for all the workshop activities. It must contain the following information: the objective of the tests; the desired result; a list of participants and organizations invited to the workshop; the expected number of people attending (participants and team members); how the activities are to be organized; a complete programme for the whole workshop (including dates); transport details for the team and participants (if necessary); details of the pre-workshop methodology and post-workshop evaluation meetings; a programme containing all test activities; details of where each activity is to take place and how long it will take; test material; notes for team members; material for recording information and participants' responses; details of who is to present the activity and who is to conduct the test; and details of the methodology to be used.
- *Recording forms for participants.* With the aim of recording all of the analyses, responses and comments of the testers, questionnaires can be devised to help participants follow the exercises, step by step, and record their own responses and explanations. For each activity and each item to be tested, a specific form is needed.
- *Recording forms for observers.* In addition to forms for testers, the observers need a form to record their own observations of the testers. Bearing in mind that the observer's role is to notice how difficult or easy the participant finds the activities, this form will contain questions and suggestions regarding what to observe during the test, and questions to understand the reasoning processes of the participant. An outsider observing the process may well pick up on unexpected issues that could arise when using the guide outside the test environment. Using this instrument in this situation, questions may be raised that could later be discussed with all participants at the end of the activity or workshop, with the aim of ironing out all doubts and suggestions.
- *Usability forms.* In order to check that all components of the guide are being assessed, the facilitators/observers in usability tests may use forms such as the completed example for a guide to medicinal plants in Paraíba, Brazil (see Table 9.2). In this case, the tester knows the plant and at first looks for it in the index of common names, but does not find the common name and therefore leafs through the

book. Looking at the drawings, the tester finds the species and then checks the description in the text.

USING THE RESULTS OF TESTS AND WORKSHOPS

When a set of tests or a workshop is finished, some time must be devoted to compiling and analysing the results in order to consider what adjustments need to be made to the guide and, if necessary, to prepare material for a second set of tests, as well as to make any methodological changes required in the test.

Finally, of course, the test will only have been a valuable process if you actually make the changes that have been recommended. This may not be an easy decision – no two testers will express the same opinion – and some balanced argument may be needed to decide what to do next. This is where observation of the testers comes in. Testers' *opinions* may differ; but if observers repeatedly notice that no one is using the index, or many testers are confused by the use of colour coding in the species descriptions, these aspects become priorities. Making changes at this stage can be expensive, so prioritize changes that help comprehension rather those which are simply a matter of preference.

10

Publishing the field guide

Anna Lawrence

INTRODUCTION

Although this chapter is the last in the book, make sure that you read it before you have completed everything else in your guide. There are a number of issues you will need to consider and which you should take into account in your budget, including materials, design, layout, editing, proofreading, printing, publicizing and distributing.

To publish means to 'prepare and issue for public distribution and sale'. If your field guide is to be published in book format, you need to print. Websites are not formal publications, although you will still need to think about publicity. Other formats, such as posters and CD-ROMs, can also be published; but this is usually done less formally and you need only consider finding a reliable means of producing the guide. This chapter covers all aspects of this, whether you want your guide to be printed or turned into a website, sold or donated to users.

The steps in publishing your guide are as follows.

Before publication:

- choose a publisher;
- choose a printer (the publisher may do this);
- complete the final edit;
- print the page proofs;
- check the page proofs;
- print and package the guide; and
- finalize all payments.

After publication, focus on:

- publicity;
- distribution; and
- follow-up.

It is a good idea to assign responsibility for these tasks among the team producing the guide.

CHOOSING A PUBLISHER

Whether you choose to work with a commercial publisher or a small private publisher, or to publish your own book will depend upon the size and cost of your field guide, and the number of people you would like it to reach. It will also depend upon whether you have funding available to finance the printing and distribution and, if not, whether the publisher is convinced that it is worth their while to take on these costs, expecting that they will recover them through sufficient sales.

Finding a commercial publisher

If you expect that your guide is commercially viable, you can approach established publishing companies. Every publisher specializes in different types of books and will therefore have different views on what they are looking for in new book proposals. The best way to start is to look for the name and address of the publishers of some of your favourite books – particularly field guides. Make a shortlist of several publishers to approach because not all of them will be interested. Start making enquiries before you go too far with the planning and production of your guide; if you want it to fit into an existing series or style of field guides, the publisher will want to have an input into shaping the design and content of the guide. But before you approach the publishers on your shortlist, gather together the information that they will need to decide whether to work with you and to provisionally accept the guide for publication.

All publishers want to know, at the very minimum:

- the working title of the book;
- the authors and their qualifications for writing the book;
- what the book will include (usually the publishers will want to see an outline showing all of the chapter headings and a short summary of each, as well as a sample chapter);
- why you think the book is necessary and whether it competes with existing books;
- who you expect will buy the book (what kind of people and how many);
- what sort of size and quality of illustrations the book will need.

Many established publishers have a pre-prepared form indicating their information requirements. These may be available on the internet. A good example is the one provided by Earthscan, the publisher of this book and others in the People and Plants Conservation Series (see Box 10.1). Even if your chosen publisher does not provide such a form, it is a good idea to gather together as much of the information as possible before writing to them to help them make an informed decision about whether to accept your guide.

Particular concerns that publishers may have in the case of publishing field guides will be the costs of printing the illustrations. Colour printing costs about ten times more than black and white, and there are additional costs of setting up the plates. However, exactly how much more depends upon the specification of the guide. This is why you must consult with publishers at the planning stages of your field guide.

You and your publisher will need to plan a realistic schedule and formal arrangements to determine who is responsible for checking proofs, distribution and publicity.

DO-IT-YOURSELF PUBLICATION

There is nothing to stop you from publishing your own field guide; but the advantages that known professional publishers have are that they can publicize the book to relevant audiences, they have existing distribution networks, and they have existing relationships with printers, editors and bookshops. In sum, they are good at getting books to the buyer. If you decide to publish your own book, you will be taking on the challenges of editing, laying-out, printing, publicizing and distributing the guide yourself. That may not be too much of a challenge if you know who is likely to use or buy the guide; in fact, conservation organizations are increasingly developing their own series of publications (see, for example, Case study 10.1). The advantages are that you will be in control of all

---

BOX 10.1 EARTHSCAN'S INFORMATION REQUIREMENTS FOR CONSIDERATION IN A NEW BOOK PROPOSAL

- provisional title;
- names of authors/editors/contributors;
- contact details (including telephone and fax numbers, and email address);
- qualifications and careers to date;
- publications;
- a description of the book and 100-word synopsis;
- a draft table of contents;
- chapter summaries (and, if appropriate, authorship);
- sample chapters and/or the introduction (the more material you can send, the better);
- an approximate word count;
- number and type of illustrations;
- time schedule for completion of the final manuscript;
- purpose of the book;
- why the book is needed;
- shelf-life;
- a list of competing titles already available and an explanation of how your book will be different;
- market breakdown (by subject area, profession, academic level, territory);
- secondary markets;
- relevant academic courses (for compulsory and supplementary reading);
- professional reading;
- marketing channels (for example, associations, mailing lists, websites, review media);
- how you can help to promote and market the book;
- any important design specifications;
- if you are able to typeset the book and provide camera-ready copy for the printers;
- further relevant information.

of these activities, which may result in faster publication and a product that fits your own ideas of what is needed.

Checklist of key points

If you choose to publish yourself, allocate responsibilities within your production team for the following tasks:

- Find printers and binders and work very closely with them, with iterative rounds of checking to make sure that everything is as it should be and that quality is maintained throughout. This is especially important in field guides where the illustrations must be reliable, lines must be clear and colours must be reproduced accurately.
- Negotiate a realistic time schedule with the printers.
- Set up a distribution list and copy delivery.
- Consider publicity.

DESKTOP PUBLISHING

During the last 30 years, the publishing process has been shaken up by the development of desktop publishing (DTP) software, such as Aldus PageMaker (the first DTP programme, developed in 1985) or QuarkXPress. These are useful for both self-publishing and preparing camera-ready copy of your book for publishers. DTP software can range from packages aimed at family home use, to those favoured by professionals (such as QuarkXPress). Costs range, accordingly, from around US$50 up to US$20,000. When deciding what to buy, make sure that you have the computing specification needed for your chosen package. The software will list compatibility requirements for its running – for example, Adobe PageMaker 6.5 Plus requires Windows NT 3.51, Windows 95 or Windows 98 to run.

Getting an ISBN number

Most published books have a unique number allocated to them under a system known as the International Standard Book Number (ISBN). This number is a unique machine-readable identification number which means that the book can be identified and ordered by bookshops and buyers anywhere in the world, without confusing it with a different book with the same authors or title. The number has been 10 digits long for most of its history, but is in the process of being converted to 13 digits as this book goes to press (note on our copyright page that both the 10-digit and 13-digit format are given). ISBN appears on the cover and copyright page of the field guide, as well as in publishers' catalogues and advertisements, book reviews, bibliographic databases and library catalogues. It means that publishers, librarians, booksellers and buyers can use this number to order and stock the book. The system was invented in 1966, and to date 159 countries are members.

ISBN numbers are allocated in blocks to each member country, and within that, each publishing house has its own code. If you plan to publish several guides or other books and want them to be known and available internationally, you might consider register-

CASE STUDY 10.1 CREATION OF A PUBLISHING HOUSE SPECIALIZING IN BIODIVERSITY AS A RESULT OF PREPARING A FIELD GUIDE: EXPERIENCES AND LESSONS LEARNED FROM FAN PUBLICATIONS IN BOLIVIA

Pierre L. Ibisch and Silvia Añez

The Fundación Amigos de la Naturaleza (Friends of Nature Foundation, or FAN) is one of the most successful conservation non-governmental organizations (NGOs) in Bolivia. The mission of FAN is 'to conserve biodiversity through protection and the sustainable and equitable use of the natural resources in Bolivia'. The Forest Department of FAN, having begun as an entity that largely worked specifically for the institution or within a framework of projects funded by donors, has turned into a unit which is now able to offer services to third-party institutions and which, in addition, is an important generator of technical/scientific information. Because of the growing need to disseminate specialist information about biodiversity and conservation, and having identified a great gap in Bolivia of professional publishers who will publish on this theme, FAN Publications was created.

It all began with the opportunity to publish the Spanish version of *Neotropical Rainforest Mammals: A Field Guide* (Emmons, 1990), the first FAN publication to be edited with an international market in mind. FAN therefore made a special effort to achieve high quality with this work and to establish a process for successful commercialization.

FAN applied for an ISBN number, and the learning process catalysed the creation of the publishing house. The process of obtaining an ISBN number is standard in most countries, but was only introduced to Bolivia during the year that FAN's first guide was published. In the end, we managed to publish the first Bolivian guide on a biological/ecological theme that fulfilled all of the requirements.

The experience with this first guide stimulated the publication of further works, many of them having, at least partially, the characteristics of a guide: one was on a different family of plants (orchids in Bolivia), while another was the first guide to the trees of the Inter-Andean Valley of the Department of Santa Cruz. Scientific documents were also published, such as a CD-ROM about progress towards a conservation plan for an important region of the country, and various articles in the *Journal of the Bolivian Botanical Society*. The publishing house and its products contributed to the creation of a positive, professional and scientific image for FAN. We have reached the point where third-party institutions, such as the Wildlife Conservation Society, are contracting the services of FAN Publications to publish their guides and books, such as *A Manual for Researching Wildlife*.

The initiative was established with funds destined for the production of the first guide when FAN did not manage to cover all of the indirect costs of translation and editing. Through an agreement with an oil company (Andina SA), which financed the printing of the first work and supported the setting-up of a publications fund through the sale of the guides, we managed to cover real direct and indirect costs. Currently, the project is in the process of becoming self-sufficient. Since FAN is a non-profit-making NGO, whatever profit comes from its activities serves to increase the publications fund that is being reinvested in new publications about the biodiversity of Bolivia and its conservation.

Through practical experience, we have learned the first lessons of the market and commercialization. We have identified electronic mail as a very efficient and cheap medium, and we have also begun to explore the possibilities of the internet, which can be synergistically linked with email and which has already been exploited by big publishers and distributors.

The website of FAN Publications (www.fan-bo.org/editorial/) provides publicity about the guides and about the publishers themselves to users around the world. For example, it outlines the contents pages, sample pages, reviews and prices of the FAN guide list.

ing to have your own ISBN code. To do this you need to contact the ISBN agency in your own country and provide them with information on:

- corporate name, address and publishing imprints;
- the name and telephone number of the person responsible for implementing ISBNs;
- the number of titles published to date;
- the number of titles anticipated for publication over the next ten years.

Publisher prefixes are issued on the basis of this information, along with a manual outlining numbering practices and a logbook listing all ISBNs available to the publisher (International ISBN Agency, 2004).

FINALIZING CONTENT

Make sure that all individuals who have written original parts of the manual are included in the guide's authorship. In the case of guides resulting largely from local knowledge, there may be a large number of authors recognized as having contributed unique knowledge, as well as editors – those who have made major editorial decisions and are responsible for the final product.

Include in the acknowledgements everyone who has helped in any way but is not actually an author. For example, you can include contributors of information, background researchers and taxonomic experts who have identified specimens.

Finally, double-check that you have sought and obtained permission to reproduce any text or images covered by copyright, and acknowledged their source.

PRINTING

Finding a printer

In Chapter 3 we drew attention to the need to have a rough estimate of printing costs before you start, for the various options – paper, binding and ink are all available in different choices of quality and toughness. Now, however, you need precise quotations, and this will be possible with the results of your testing process from Chapter 9. Armed with precise information on the number of pages and the amount of colour needed, you can revisit your printing companies and make a final decision about who will print your field guide most economically and quickly without compromising on the quality.

The entire process of publishing a book should take from four to six months; but this will depend upon the country and publisher. You should estimate another month for the print production and printing process.

Points to raise with the printer before making your final choice include:

- Confirm costs and quality.
- Confirm the time frame (when is the soonest the printer can begin; how long will it take to produce page proofs; how long after the return of page proofs will the book be printed?).
- Confirm the format in which the printer expects to receive the field guide.
- Agree upon the details of the cover design.

Preparing your field guide for the printer

Books are not printed line by line, like a computer printout. Instead, they are printed from plates a page at a time as a single image, and the final copy of your field guide must be supplied, accordingly, as camera-ready copy.

With many publications there is a choice to be made at this stage about how to supply your material to the publisher and then printer. Either the text is supplied as a word-processed document, with illustrations separate, and the whole is formatted by the publisher, or the author supplies camera-ready copy. With a field guide – particularly, of course, a field guide that has been prepared with such close regard for users' needs and thoroughly tested for usability – there is no question that the approved layout and format must be maintained. Producing camera-ready copy is by far the best way to ensure this. If you prepared your page layouts and mock-up using desktop publishing software (see Chapter 8 and 9), all will be straightforward at this stage. If you used word-processed text and pasted in illustrations, you will need to communicate very closely with the publisher or other person preparing the final camera-ready copy to ensure that it remains faithful to the format already chosen. This author once had the surprising experience of receiving copies of the field guide to which she had contributed – fresh off the press and which she opened with great pleasure – with species descriptions inadvertently printed in italics.

In any case, whoever produces the final copy, the authors are responsible for final proofreading – you must be certain that everything is there, nothing is missing, nothing has been repeated, and that there are no spelling mistakes or errors such as 'see page xx'. All of the changes recommended in the final testing should, of course, have been incorporated by now; but it is surprising how many may not.

When everything is ready, it will be printed one page to a sheet on high-quality paper. Again, the authors must check for quality of overall appearance – particularly the illustrations, without which your field guide will not work.

Finally, you can keep costs down by following the tips in Box 10.2.

BOX 10.2 REDUCING PRINTING COSTS

- Compare prices and request samples to get the best deal.
- Ordering larger quantities reduces the cost per individual item.
- If you can avoid colour, black ink is cheaper.
- Print on both sides of the paper to reduce the costs of paper and postage.
- Submit perfect camera-ready copy. Any changes that the printer is required to make will cost extra.
- Avoid large areas of solid black. Good ink coverage on areas such as these is difficult, and the printer may charge extra.
- Use standard paper sizes.
- Avoid printers' 'convenience' services, such as folding, collating and stapling – do these yourself.
- Make a deal – small local printers may give you a discount if you promise to use them exclusively.

Source: adapted from www.howtoadvice.com/Printingcosts

The printing process

Books used to be printed by slotting each individual letter of each individual word into a printing press, rolling ink across it and pressing on the page. The process is now both greatly simplified and much more complex.

You do have some straightforward options if you just want to print a few copies. A simple handwritten or typewritten guide can be photocopied. If you have prepared it in a computer, you can print off multiple copies. But the cost can quickly become enormous, especially with colour pages. Instead, most books are printed from what is called camera-ready copy, where each page is treated as a photograph, or individual image, and stored on a computer disk. The disk goes through a process that turns each page into a separate piece of film negative. Depending upon the country, this can cost up to US$10 per page for black-and-white text and double that for colour pages. The costs are highly variable, depending upon the number of colours; but it is a significant initial cost and one of the main reasons that large print runs are more economical than smaller print runs – the initial costs are distributed over a larger number of books.

The printer then turns the film negative into a page proof for each page, which shows the exact position of everything in the book. These page proofs must be carefully checked by everyone who is responsible for the field guide, and any remaining errors should be reported to the publisher and printer. With luck, a few weeks later your guides will be printed, the publisher will pay for them and they will be delivered to the publisher's door. How do they reach the users from there?

GETTING YOUR GUIDE TO THE USERS

Letting people know that you have published your field guide, and making sure that enough copies reach the relevant societies, bookshops and businesses, is a key step, but one that is often neglected. In preparing this book, we conducted a survey of most of the field guides that had been produced in eastern Bolivia and northeast Brazil. We interviewed the authors and publishers about the decisions they made, particularly about how they published their guides and ensured that they reached the people who needed to use them. This showed up a widespread weakness: production is not always accompanied by strong publicity, and authors themselves reported that they lack opportunities to communicate with each other and share experiences. These are some of the lessons they reported from experience.

Pricing your field guide

Before you try to sell your field guide you will have to set a price that covers your costs and even, perhaps, gives you some profit – to reinvest in further field guides or to provide the authors or contributors with some benefits and compensation for their time and knowledge. However, the book needs to be affordable, too, so setting the price can be a careful balancing act. If the field guide has been produced as part of a project, the production and printing costs may already be covered by the organization funding the project, and you may be able to distribute the field guides free. Otherwise, you may set a price that you know some users can afford, and then distribute a number of copies free to the contributors and others who cannot afford to pay the cover price.

Remember, however, that you are not going to receive the full cover price for every copy sold. Usually, bookshops buy in bulk from the publishers at a discount that can range from 30 to 70 per cent so that they, in turn, make a profit when they sell the book.

Publicity

In planning your guide (see Chapter 3), you will have decided whom the guide is for. When you are ready to print, announce the forthcoming publication of the guide, and make sure that this information reaches those users by employing the information systems they use themselves – for example, through shops, NGOs or schools.

Start doing this at the stage when you are getting estimates for the printing costs. Consider what would be a good way of reaching users and buyers. Whether radio, newspapers, newsletters of relevant organizations, conferences or a formal book launch, the best tactics will depend upon the audience you are trying to reach, their shopping and reading practices, and the cultural practices of the country in question. Think beyond book shops: if your guide will appeal to botanists, make sure it is reviewed in botanical journals by sending review copies to the editors. If your book is just what eco-tourists are looking for, arrange for it to be displayed prominently in their favourite hotels.

Distribution

Successful distribution of a field guide to the people who want to buy and use it depends upon making good use of existing networks. Many of these will be the same ones that you use to publicize the book before it is ready to send out.

Although publishers may publicize your book, it is a good idea to think of ways of doing this yourself to boost distribution and sales, especially since any publicity from the publishers is likely to be short-lived. There are a number of steps that you can take to publicize your book and increase sales. Several guides to successful book marketing exist, such as Appelbaum (1998) and Kremer (2000). These offer practical ideas such as advertising on the internet, radio, TV and other forms of media, and advice on the best ways to achieve this. Sending free samples to newspapers can mean free advertising if reviews are written as a result, and many journals also review relevant books.

Direct mailing can be successful, but you must be careful to target the correct market. You can keep a record of stock for the outlets where your book is being sold, so more copies can be made available once all the shelf copies are gone.

Selling field guides can be a new experience for many authors and institutions, and it may seem initially rather mysterious how and when the books sell. It can be extremely valuable, therefore, to record the numbers of guides distributed to each outlet, and to ask the outlets to keep track of who bought them so that you can carry out an evaluation later on. Large commercial booksellers will not be willing to do this; but many others will and can provide you with important information on who is using your guide.

Under certain circumstances, the authors or contributors to a field guide may, in fact, want to *restrict* distribution rather than maximize it. This was the case, for example, with the production of a field guide to medicinal plants by the Dusun communities around Kinabalu National Park in Sabah, Malaysia, who wanted to make their knowledge available to their own people and descendents, but only to a limited number of trusted outside organizations (Laird, 2002). The resulting protocol developed by the communities (Agama, 2002) documented concerns about loss of traditional knowledge, noted the need to use and document knowledge in order to conserve it, highlighted concerns about possible misuse of published knowledge, and set out the terms under which the medicinal plants manual was to be distributed – only within the village, to other villages on receipt of written request, and to collaborating institutions on condition that they, in turn, respected the restrictions on distribution.

FOLLOW-UP: TRACKING THE SUCCESS OF YOUR FIELD GUIDE

For many authors, producing a field guide will have been a huge learning experience, involving the acquisition and sorting of new information, as well as compromises because you cannot find out all you would like to about every species or include pictures of each diagnostic feature. Finding out how your guide has been used and received will add to that learning experience and will make revisions and second editions possible. Such an evaluation or impact assessment can also help to prove to donors how successfully you have used their money or can highlight ways in which future projects could be improved.

The simple way to tell if your guide is successful is to follow the distribution and sales by keeping a good record of how many copies are sent to each point. But this will only be satisfactory if your only objective is to ensure that people own a copy of the guide. How can you know whether it has achieved your more profound objectives – such as disseminating knowledge and motivating people to use and protect biodiversity?

Evaluation relates to the success of the guide in performing its *function* – that is, in helping to identify and/or find the information the users require about a particular species. Impact assessment, on the other hand, researches the *consequences* of the successful use of the guide – in other words, the changes in people's behaviour or beliefs as a result of identifying the plants or discovering the information. The impact is affected both by the motivation and expectations of authors, as well as by contextual factors, such as agricultural policy, land tenure and the existence of projects to use the guide and implement conservation decisions. Consequently, there are both intended impacts (for example, more environmental awareness, more native tree planting) and unintended impacts (see Chapter 1 for examples, such as the increase in knowledge of tree distribution from readers' feedback to the authors).

Impact assessment can be challenging for several reasons and a profound undertaking. More information is given in Guijt (1998), Modak and Biswas (1999), Morris and Therivel (2001) and Roche (1999). From our own experience researching the impact of field guides in Bolivia and Brazil, we found that, in many cases, the authors had not considered whether their guide had any impact – they were just happy to have finished and published it. This is understandable – what is more surprising is that many authors could not say whether their objectives had been fulfilled because they had never identified objectives in the first place. Others found it difficult to trace their users or even distributors.

The process of identifying indicators of success for a field guide can illustrate how difficult it is to measure such success. The example from Bolivia given in Case study 10.2 shows how scientists and communities producing a guide for eco-tourists in

CASE STUDY 10.2 INDICATORS OF IMPACT FOR *BIODIVERSIDAD DEL PARQUE NACIONAL NOEL KEMPFF MERCADO*

When considering and defining indicators of impact for their *Biodiversidad del Parque Nacional Noel Kempff Mercado: Principales Ecosistemas y Especies* (*Guide for Eco-tourists: Attractive Species of the Principal Ecosystems of the Noel Kempff Mercado National Park*; Vargas and Jordán, 2002), Fundación Amigos de la Naturaleza (Friends of Nature Foundation, or FAN) staff thought about the different stakeholders and their objectives, both short term and long term, in producing and using the field guide. They held a workshop with all of the people involved in producing the guide, including indigenous communities in the buffer zone of the national park, scientists studying the flora of the park, and park guards who accompany eco-tourists.

In order to identify impact indicators for the field guide, FAN staff first reminded themselves of their objectives in producing the guide and the assumed objectives of the eco-tourists in using the guide. From these, they considered ways of measuring the success of those objectives. The process of reflecting upon objectives and indicators had some interesting consequences, as Tables 10.1 and 10.2 show. The team of authors realized that some of their own objectives were short-term low-impact ones that were already achieved by producing the guide – in other words, all of the work required meant

Table 10.1 *Author objectives and indicators of impact for the eco-tourist guide*
Biodiversidad del Parque Nacional Noel Kempff Mercado

Objectives	Indicators
Helps with identification by presenting information about the most distinctive characteristics of the principal useful species.	Number of non-specialists able to identify the species increases.
Motivates eco-tourists to visit different sites of the Parque Nacional Noel Kempff Mercado (PNNKM) and the neighbouring communities.	Number of visitors to different sites in the PNNKM increases.
Transmits conservation values of the plant species to the park's visitors and to the community, in general.	Visitors' appreciation of the value of PNNKM increases. Number of supporters of PNNKM increases.
Compiles information and describes the most outstanding characteristics of the different ecosystems of the park and of the principal plants which it shelters. Disseminates local knowledge about use of the principal plants and complements it with scientific information about them.	These objectives are difficult to measure because they have no measurable effect. The authors realized that this is an 'internal' objective – the mere fact of producing the guide has achieved the purpose of compiling information. The other objectives are more important in terms of achieving a visible impact from the information.
Recovers and values traditional knowledge about the use of the plants, complemented with scientific knowledge of the same.	Villagers could respond about the information, which they thought had been forgotten, and about new information that the guide gives them.

Source: interviews with the authors of the guide

that they now had compiled the information in a useful way. The more profound objectives are those which have an effect on the *users* of the guide. In some cases, those objectives were relatively easy to assess using quantitative indicators; but even in these cases it was difficult to be sure of cause and effect. For example, if the number of visitors to the national park increases, is that because transport has improved or because they are more aware of the park, and if the latter, did the field guide help to raise awareness?

Simple indicators can provide an idea of trends; but if you are serious about trying to understand the impact of your guide, you will need to use more qualitative research methods that explore the reasons why people interact with biodiversity and how your guide has influenced this.

Table 10.2 *Eco-tourist objectives and indicators of impact (as perceived by park guards) for the eco-tourist guide* Biodiversidad del Parque Nacional Noel Kempff Mercado

Objectives	Indicators
Have access to distinctive information about the different ecosystems of the Parque Nacional Noel Kempff Mercado (PNNKM) and the principal plants which it shelters. Increases knowledge about the use and traditional management of some plants as carried out by the neighbouring communities around the park. Able to identify the most common species of each ecosystem.	The guide production team realized that all of these objectives are difficult to track. But the park guards who accompany tourists on their explorations of the park acquire a good understanding of people's knowledge and perceptions, and report back on changes. This aspect of evaluation must therefore rely on *qualitative assessment* – in other words, the impressions that the park guards have of the knowledge of the eco-tourists.
In the longer term, increases awareness of the unique value of PNNKM and the need for protection.	Indicators proved difficult here – what can eco-tourists do to demonstrate their sense of value for a place? More quantitative indicators can be used to assess this: numbers visiting the park; numbers buying the guide before visiting; and numbers buying the guide while visiting.

Source: interviews with park guards

Bolivia (Vargas and Jordán, 2003) struggled to find ways of predicting and measuring impact.

A similar exercise with communities producing a guide for their own use led to intense discussions about the need to conserve traditional knowledge and medicinal practices, and touched on lofty goals such as 'reducing the migration of our children to the cities'. Although these indicators will not be used in a formal impact assessment, the process of discussing and proposing indicators was an important one for the authors and helped all of the primary stakeholders to develop their ideas about the guide and its value to them.

Getting feedback

If you want to evaluate the success of your field guide in helping people to identify plants and find out more about them, you will need feedback from the users. This can be done through including a note in the introduction inviting the users to send their comments and observations to the authors or publishers, or by including a feedback form at the end of the book. Such a form can be quite simple and may request information such as:

- name, occupation and address of the person providing the feedback;
- reason why this person is using the field guide;
- aspects and features of the field guide that the user likes;
- features that the user finds more problematic;
- specific species that the user has found difficult to identify when using the guide and why;
- suggestions for improvement.

More detailed feedback can be obtained by interviewing users of the field guide. This can begin by tracing distribution networks outwards to the users, then interviewing users about how they have employed the guide.

By this stage, if you have followed the scientific and participatory processes we have outlined in this book, you will have an attractive and accurate guide that will be eagerly anticipated by your user group. We wish you much success in the process and look forward to the results.

Acronyms and abbreviations

APG	Angiosperm Phylogeny Group
BMP	Windows bitmap
C	Celsius
CBD	Convention on Biological Diversity
CBR	community biodiversity register
CD	compact disk
CIAT	Centro Internacional de Agricultura Tropical (Centre for Tropical Agricultural Research, Bolivia)
CIBAPA	Central Indígena del Bajo Paraguá
cm	centimetre
DBH	diameter at breast height
DELTA	Description Language for Taxonomy
DFID	UK Department for International Development
DNA	deoxyribonucleic acid
DOF	depth of focus
dpi	dots per inch
DTP	desktop publishing
EMF	enhanced metafile format
EPS	encapsulated postscript format
EU	European Union
FAN	Fundación Amigos de la Naturaleza (Friends of Nature Foundation, Bolivia)
FRP	Forestry Research Programme (UK)
g	gram
GB	gigabyte
GIF	graphic interchange format
GIS	geographical information system
HTML	hypertext markup language
ILDIS	International Legume Database and Information Service
ISBN	International Standard Book Number
JPEG	Joint Photographic Expert Group
km	kilometre
LAWG	Leaf Architecture Working Group
m	metre
MAB	Man and the Biosphere Programme
MB	megabyte
MEK	most efficient key
mm	millimetre

NGO	non-governmental organization
PDA	personal digital assistant
PDF	portable document format
PNG	Portable Network Graphics
PNNKM	Parque Nacional Noel Kempff Mercado (Noel Kempff Mercado National Park, Bolivia)
PRA	participatory rural appraisal
RBG	Royal Botanic Gardens, Kew
RHS	Royal Horticultural Society
SASOP	Serviço de Assessoria às Organizações Populares Rurais
SEPASAL	Survey of Economic Plants for Arid and Semi-Arid Lands
SERBO	Sociedad para el Estudio de Recursos Bióticos de Oaxaca
TIFF	tagged image file format
UK	United Kingdom
UN	United Nations
UNESCO	United Nations Educational, Social and Cultural Organization
US	United States
UV	ultraviolet
VFH	Virtual Field Herbarium
WMF	Windows metafile format
WWF	World Wide Fund for Nature (*formerly* World Wildlife Fund)

References

Abbasi, S., F. Mokhtarian and J. Kittler (1997) 'Reliable classification of chrysanthemum leaves through curvature scale space', *Proceedings of the International Conference on Scale–Space Theory in Computer Vision*, Utrecht, The Netherlands, pp284–295

Agama, A. L. (2002) 'Dusun communities' efforts to control distribution for a medicinal plant manual around Kinabalu National Park', in Laird, S. (ed) *Biodiversity and Traditional Knowledge: Equitable Partnerships in Practice*, Earthscan, London, pp96–97

Agra, M. F. (1996) *Plantas da Medicina Popular dos Cariris Velhos*, PNE, João Pessoa, Brazil

Alexiades, M. N. (1996) 'Conducting ethnobotanical research', in M. N. Alexiades and J. Wood Sheldon (eds) *Selected Guidelines for Ethnobotanical Research: A Field Manual*, New York Botanical Gardens, New York, pp3–94

Allen, D. E. (1984) *The Naturalist in Britain: A Social History*, Princeton University Press, Princeton, NJ

Alvira, D., R. Foster and M. Metz (undated) 'Arboles Pioneros géneros comunes', Chicago Field Museum, example of a Field Museum Natural History Rapid Colour Guide; various authors for single sheet guides (see www.fm2.fieldmuseum.org/plantguides/rcg_intro.asp)

APG (Angiosperm Phylogeny Group) (1998) 'An ordinal classification for the families of flowering plants', *Annals of Missouri Botanic Garden*, vol 85, pp531–553

APG (2003) 'An update of the Angiosperm Phylogeny Group classification for the orders and families of flowering plants: APG II', *Botanical Journal of the Linnaean Society*, vol 141, pp399–436

Appelbaum, J. (1998) *How To Get Happily Published*, HarperCollins Publishers, New York

Arber, A. (1986) *Herbals: Their Origin and Evolution – A Chapter in the History of Botany 1470–1670*, 3rd edition, Cambridge University Press, Cambridge

Arbonnier, M. (2004) *Trees, Shrubs and Lianas of West African Dry Zones*, CIRAD Montpellier, France/Margraf Publishers, Weikersheim, Germany/Muséum national d'histoire naturelle (MNHN), Paris, France

Ashton, M., S. Gunatilleke, N. de Zoysa, M. D. Dassanauake, N. Gunatilleke and S. Wijesundera (1997) *A Field Guide to the Common Trees and Shrubs of Sri Lanka*, WHT Publications Ltd, Sri Lanka

Atran, S. (1990) *Cognitive Foundations of Natural History: Towards an Anthropology of Science*, Cambridge University Press, Cambridge

Aubréville, A. (1959) *La Flore Forestière de la Côte d'Ivoire*, Centre Technique Forestièr Tropical, Nogent sûr Marne, France (three volumes)

Beard, F. S. (1944) 'Key for the identification of the more important trees of Tobago on characters of bark and blaze', *Empire Forestry Journal*, vol 23, pp34–36

Beentje, H. J. (1994) *Kenya Trees, Shrubs and Lianes*, National Museums of Kenya, Nairobi, Kenya

Belin-Depoux, M. (1989) 'Des hydathodes aux nectaires foliaires chez les plantes tropicales', *Bulletin de la Société Botanique de France, Actualites Botaniques*, vol 136, pp151–168

Bell, A. D. (1991) *Plant Form: An Illustrated Guide to Flowering Plant Morphology*, Oxford University Press, London

Berjak, M. and J. Grimsdell (1999) *Botanical Databases for Conservation and Development*, WWF-UK, www.peopleandplants.org/whatweproduce/Books/botanical/Databases.html

Berlin, B. (1992) *Ethnobiological Classification: Principles of Categorization of Plants and Animals in Traditional Societies*, Princeton University Press, Princeton, NJ

Berlin, B., D. Breedlove and P. Raven (1973) 'General principles of classification and nomenclature in folk biology', *American Anthropologist*, vol 74, pp214–242

Bevan, N. (1997) *Usability Testing World Wide Web Sites*, National Physical Laboratory, Teddington, UK, www.acm.org/sigchi/web/chi97testing/bevan.htm

Blamey, M. and C. Grey-Wilson (1989) *The Illustrated Flora of Britain and Northern Europe*, Hodder and Stoughton, London

Blunt, W. and W. T. Stearn (1994) *The Art of Botanical Illustration*, 2nd edition, Antique Collectors' Club, London

Bramwell, D. (2002) 'How many plant species are there?', *Plant Talk*, vol 28, pp32–34

Bridge, P., D. R. Morse, P. Jeffries and P. R. Scott (eds) (1998) *Information Technology, Plant Pathology and Biodiversity*, CAB International, Wallingford, UK

Bridson, D., H. Eremeeva, L. Forman and D. Geltman (1995) *The Herbarium Handbook*, Royal Botanic Gardens, Kew, UK

Brown, D. (1991) *Human Universals*, McGraw Hill, New York

Bubondt, N. (1998) 'The odor of things: Smell and the cultural elaboration of disgust in eastern Indonesia', *Ethnos*, vol 63, no 1, pp48–80

Burtt, B. D. (1953) *A Field Key to the Savanna Genera and Species of Trees, Shrubs and Climbing Plants of Tanganyica*, Government Printer, Dar es Salaam

Caballé, G. (1993) 'Liana structure, function and selection: A comparative study of xylem cylinders of tropical rainforest species in Africa and America', *Botanical Journal of the Linnaean Society*, vol 113, pp41–60

Carlquist, S. (1991) 'Anatomy of vine and liana stems: A review and synthesis', in F. E. Putz and H. A. Mooney (eds) *The Biology of Vines*, Cambridge University Press, Cambridge, pp53–71

Casagrande, D. G. (2000) 'Human taste and cognition in Tzeltal Maya medicinal plant use', *Journal of Ecological Anthropology*, vol 4, pp57–69

Chattaway, M. M. (1953) 'The anatomy of bark: (i) The genus *Eucalyptus*', *Australian Journal of Botany*, vol 1, pp402–433

Christophel D. C. and B. P. M. Hyland (1993) *Leaf Atlas of Australian Tropical Rain Forest Trees*, CSIRO, Australia

Civille, G. V. and B. G. Lyon (1996) *Aroma and Flavor Lexicon for Sensory Evaluation Terms, Definitions, References and Examples*, ASTM Data Series Publication DS 66, West Conshohocken, PA

Classen, C., D. Howes and A. Synnott (1994) *Aroma: The Cultural History of Smell*, Routledge, London

Corner, E. J. H. (1988) *Wayside Trees of Malaya*, 3rd edition, Malayan Nature Society, Kuala Lumpur

Costa, J. A. S., T. S. Nunes, A. P. L. Ferreira, M. T. S. Stradmann and L. P. de Queiroz (2002) *Leguminosas Forrageiras da Caatinga espécies importantes para as comunidades rurais do sertão da Bahía*, Universidade Estadual de Feira de Santana/SASOP, Bahia, Brazil

Cotton, C. M. (1996) *Ethnobotany: Principles and Applications*, John Wiley and Sons, Colchester, UK

Cronquist, A. (1988) *The Evolution and Classification of Flowering Plants*, 2nd edition, New York Botanic Gardens, New York

Cullen, J. (1978) 'A preliminary review of ptyxis (vernation) in the angiosperms', *Notes of the Royal Botanic Gardens, Edinburgh*, vol 37, pp161–214

Cunningham, A. B. (2001) *Applied Ethnobotany: People, Wild Plant Use and Conservation*, Earthscan, London

Dahlgren, R. M. T. (1975) 'A system of classification of the angiosperms to be used to demonstrate the distribution of characters', *Botaniska Notiser*, vol 128, pp119–147

Dale, I. R. and P. J. Greenway (1961) *Kenya Trees and Shrubs*, Buchanan's Kenya Estates and Hatchards, London

Dale, M. B., R. H. Groves, V. J. Hull and J. F. O'Callaghan (1971) 'A new method for describing leaf shape', *New Phytologist*, vol 70, pp437–442

Dallwitz, M. J. (2000) *Comparison of Interactive Identification Programs*, www.biodiversity. uno.edu/delta/www/ comparison.htm

Dallwitz, M. J., Paine, T. A. and Zurcher, E. J. (1998) 'Interactive keys', in Bridge, P., D. R. Morse, P. Jeffries and P. R. Scott (eds) *Information Technology, Plant Pathology and Biodiversity*, CAB International, Wallingford, UK

Davidoff, J., I. Davies and D. Roberson (1999) 'Colour categories in a stone age tribe', *Nature*, vol 298, pp203–204

Dawkins, H. C. (1951) 'Graphical field keys of Uganda trees: 1. Forest trees, Mengo District', *East African Agricultural Journal*, October, pp90–103

de Garine I. (1997) 'Food preferences and taste in an African perspective: A word of caution', in H. Macbeth (ed) *Food Preferences and Taste*, Berghahn Books, Oxford and Providence, RI, pp187–207

de Queiroz, L. P., J. A. S. Costa, T. S. Nunes and M. T. S. Stradmann (forthcoming) *Um Guia de Campo Para: As Leguminosas da Caatinga da Bahia: Espécies com Potencial Forrageiro*, unpublished manuscript awaiting publication

Dickinson, T. A., W. H. Parker and R. E. Strauss (1987) 'Another approach to leaf shape comparisons', *Taxon*, vol 36, pp1–20

Duke, J. A. (1969) 'On tropical tree seedlings: 1. Seeds, seedlings, systems and systematics', *Annals Missouri Botanical Garden*, vol 56, no 2, pp125–161

Dutfield, G. (2000) *Intellectual Property Rights, Trade and Biodiversity*, Earthscan/IUCN, London

Edmonson, A. (1997) 'Plants common on sand dunes', Field Studies Council Fold Out Card Series No OP43, www.field-studies-council.org/publications/publicationsmore.asp?id=8&category =foldout

Edwards, M. and D. R. Morse (1995) 'The potential for computer-aided identification in biodiversity research', *Trends in Ecology and Evolution*, vol 10, pp151–158

Emmons, L. (1990) *Neotropical Rainforest Mammals: A Field Guide*, University of Chicago Press, Chicago, IL

Empire Forestry Association (1953) *British Commonwealth Forest Terminology 1*, Empire Forestry Association, London

Empire Forestry Association (1957) *British Commonwealth Forest Terminology 2*, Empire Forestry Association, London

Evans T. D. (2001) *A Field Guide to the Rattans of Lao PDR*, Kew Publishing, London

Farjon, A., J. A. Perez de la Rosa and B. T. Styles (1997) *A Field Guide to the Pines of Mexico and Central America*, Kew Publishing, London

Foxworthy, F. W. (1927) 'Commercial timber trees of the Malay peninsular', *Malay Forestry Research*, vol 3, p195

Foxworthy, F. W. (1932) 'Commercial timber trees of the Malay peninsular', *Malay Forestry Research*, vol 10, p289

Freeman, H. (1961) 'On the encoding of arbitrary geometric configurations', *Institute of Radio Engineers, Transactions on Electronic Computers*, EC10:260-8, vol 10, p260

Frodin, D. (2001) *Guide to the Standard Floras of the World*, 2nd edition, Cambridge University Press, Cambridge

Gandhi, A. (2003) 'Content based image retrieval: Plant species identification', Oregon State University NSF–ITR/IM project summary, www.cs.oregonstate.edu/~tgd/leaves/ acer-quercus.pdf

Gardner S., P. Sidisunthorn and V. Anusarnsunthorn (2000) *A Field Guide to Forest Trees of Northern Thailand*, Kobfai Publication Project, Bangkok

Geesink, R., A. J. M. Leeuwenberg, C. E. Ridsdale and J. F. Veldkamp (1981) *Thonner's Analytical Key to the Families of Flowering Plants*, Leiden University Press, The Hague, and PUDOC, Wageningen

Gentry, A. H. (1993) *A Field Guide to the Families and Genera of Woody Plants of Northwest South America*, University of Chicago Press, Chicago

Gillison, A. (2002) 'A generic, computer-assisted method for rapid vegetation classification and survey: Tropical and temperate case studies', *Conservation Ecology*, vol 6, no 2, p3, www.consecol.org/vol6/iss2/art3

Givnish, T. J. (1987) 'Comparative studies of leaf form: Assessing the relative roles of selective pressures and phylogenetic constraints', *New Phytologist*, vol 106 (supplement), pp131–160

Govaerts, R., D. G. Frodin and A. Radcliffe-Smith (2000) *World Checklist and Bibliography of Euphorbiaceae*, Royal Botanic Gardens, Kew, UK (four volumes)

Grete Herbal (1526) *The Grete Herbal*, anonymous author, printed by Peter Treveris, London

Guijt, I. (1998) *Participatory Monitoring and Impact Assessment of Sustainable Agriculture Initiatives*, Discussion Paper 1, International Institute for Environment and Development, London

Hall, F. B. and J. M. Lock (1975) 'Use of vegetative characters in the identification of species of *Salacia* (Celastraceae)', *Boissiera*, vol 24, pp331–338

Hallé, F. (1971) 'Architecture and growth of tropical trees exemplified by the Euphorbiaceae', *Biotropica*, vol 3, no 1, pp56–62

Hallé, F. (1995) 'Canopy architecture in tropical trees', in M. D. Lowman and N. M. Nadkarni (eds) *Forest Canopies*, Academic Press, San Diego, CA

Hallé, F., R. A. A. Oldeman and P. B. Tomlinson (1978) *Tropical Trees and Forests: An Architectural Analysis*, Springer Verlag, Berlin

Hallé, N. (1962) 'Monographie des Hippocrateacées d'Afrique occidentale', *Mémoires Institut Française d'Afrique Noire*, vol 64, pp1–245

Hamilton, A. C. (1981) *A Field Guide to Uganda Forest Trees*, Makerere University, Kampala

Hamilton, A. G. (1897) 'Domatia in certain Australian and other plants', *Proceedings of the Linnaean Society of New South Wales*, vol 21, pp758–792

Hansen, B. and K. Rahn (1969) 'Determination of Angiosperm families by means of a punched-card system', *Dansk Botanisk Arkiv*, vol 26, no 1, pp1–44 + 172 cards

Harley, R. and A. M. Giulietti (2004) *Flores Nativas da Chapeda Diamantina [Wild Flowers of the Chapada Diamantina]*, RiMa Editora, São Carlos, Brazil

Harris, J. G. and M. W. Harris (1994) *Plant Identification Terminology: An Illustrated Glossary*, Spring Lake Publishing, Utah

Hartman, R. and B. E. Nelson (2003) *Taxonomic Novelties from North America North of Mexico*, Missouri Botanical Garden Press, Missouri

Hawthorne, W. D. (1990) *Field Guide to the Forest Trees of Ghana*, Natural Resources Institute, Chatham, UK

Hawthorne, W. D. (1995) *Ecological Profiles of Ghanaian Forest Trees*, Tropical Forestry Paper 29, Oxford Forestry Institute, Oxford

Hawthorne, W. D. and N. Gyakari (2006) *Photoguide to the Larger Trees of Ghana's Forests*, Oxford Forestry Institute, Oxford

Hawthorne, W. D. and C. C. H. Jongkind (2006) *The Woody Plants of Western African Forests: A Guide to the Forest Trees, Shrubs and Lianes from Senegal to Ghana*, Royal Botanic Gardens, Kew, UK

Hawthorne, W. D., D. Jules, G. Marcelle and R. Wise (2005) *Caribbean Spice Island Plants. Trees, Shrubs and Climbers of Grenada, Carriacou and Petit Martinique: A Picture Gallery with Notes on Identification, Historical and Other Trivia*, Oxford Forestry Institute and Grenada Forestry Department, Oxford

Hepper, F. N. and R. W. J. Keay (eds) (1954–1972) *Flora of West Tropical Africa*, 2nd edition, HMSO, London

Hewson, H. J. (1988) *Plant Indumentum: A Handbook of Terminology*, Australian Flora and Fauna Series No 9, Bureau of Flora and Fauna, Canberra, Australia

Heywood, V. H. (1993) *Flowering Plants of the World*, Batsford, London

Heywood, V. H. (ed) (1995) *Global Biodiversity Assessment: Summary for Policy-Makers*, Cambridge University Press, Cambridge, UK

Hickey, L. J. (1973) 'Classification of the architecture of dicotyledonous leaves', *American Journal of Botany*, vol 60, no 1, pp17–33

Hickey, L. J. and J. A. Wolfe (1975) 'The bases of Angiosperm phylogeny: Vegetative morphology', *Annals of Missouri Botanic Garden*, vol 62, pp538–589

Hill, R. S. (1980) 'A numerical taxonomic approach to the study of Angiosperm leaves', *Botanical Gazette*, vol 141, pp213–229

Hora, F. B. and P. J. Greenway (1940) *Checklists of the Forest Trees and Shrubs of the British Empire–Tanganyika Territory*, J. Burtt Davy (ed), Imperial Forestry Institute, Oxford

Hort, A. (1916) *Theophrastus: Enquiry into Plants*, William Heinemann, London

Howard, R. A. (1974, 1977, 1979, 1989) *Flora of the Lesser Antilles*, Arnold Arboretum, Harvard University, Cambridge, MA (four volumes)

Hughes, C. E. (1998a) 'Monograph of *Leucaena* (Leguminosae–Mimosoideae)', *Systematic Botany Monographs*, vol 55

Hughes, C. E. (1998b) *The Genus* Leucaena: *A Genetic Resources Handbook*, Tropical Forestry Paper 37, Oxford Forestry Institute, Oxford, UK

Hui-hin Li (1974) 'An archaeological and historical account of cannabis in China', *Economic Botany*, vol 28, pp437–448

Hunn, E. (1977) *Tzeltal Folk Zoology: The Classification of Discontinuities in Nature*, Academic Press, New York

Hutchinson, J. (1973) *The Families of Flowering Plants*, 3rd edition, Clarendon Press, Oxford (two volumes)

Hyland, B. (1982) *A Revised Card Key to Rainforest Trees of North Queensland*, CSIRO, Melbourne

Hyland, B. P. M., T. Whiffin, D. C. Christophel, B. Gray, R. W. Elick and A. J. Ford (1998) *Australian Tropical Rain Forest Trees and Shrubs*, CSIRO, Australia

Hyland, B. P. M., T. Whiffin, D. C. Christophel, B. Gray and R. W. Elick (2002) *Australian Tropical Rain Forest Plants: Trees Shrubs and Vines*, CSIRO, Australia, Interactive CD-ROM (see also www.anbg.gov.au/cpbr/cd-keys/rfk/learn.html)

International Association for Plant Taxonomy (2000) *International Code of Botanical Nomenclature (St Louis Code): Regnum Vegetabile 138*, Koeltz Scientific Books, Königstein (see also www.bgbm.fu-berlin.de/iapt/nomenclature/code/SaintLouis/0000St.Luistitle.htm)

International ISBN Agency (2004) *Frequently Asked Questions about the ISBN System*, www.isbn-international.org/en/faq.html

Jackson, B. D. (1928) *A Glossary of Botanic Terms*, 4th edition, J. B. Lippincott Company, Philadelphia, US

Jacobs, M. (1966) 'On domatia – the viewpoints and some facts', Koninklijke Nederlandse Akademie Van Wteneschappen, *Proceedings Series C*, vol 69, pp275–316

Jensen, R. J. (1990) 'Detecting shape variation in oak leaf morphology: A comparison of rotational-fit methods', *American Journal of Botany*, vol 77, pp1279–1293

Johns, R. J. (1976–1978) *Common Forest Trees of Papua New Guinea*, Forestry Department, PNG University of Technology

Johns, R. J. (1978) 'A new approach to the construction of field keys for the identification of tropical trees', *Australian Journal of Ecology*, vol 3, pp403–409

Junikka, L. (1994) 'Survey of English macroscopic bark terminology', *IAWA Journal*, vol 15, pp3–45

Keating, R. C., D. Cutler and M. Gregory (eds) (2003) *Anatomy of the Monocotyledons: Araceae and Acoraceae*, vol 9, Oxford University Press, Oxford

Keay, R. W. J., D. P. Stanfield and C. F. A. Onochie (1960) *Nigerian Trees, Volume One*, Government Press, Nigeria

Keay, R. W. J., D. P. Stanfield and C. F. A. Onochie (1964) *Nigerian Trees, Volume Two*, Government Press, Nigeria

Keay, R. W. J. (1989) *Trees of Nigeria*, Clarendon Press, Oxford

Keller, R. (1994) 'Neglected vegetative characters in field identification at the supraspecific level: Phyllotaxy, serial buds, syllepsis and architecture', *Botanical Journal of the Linnaean Society*, vol 116, pp33–51

Keller, R. (1996) *Identification of Tropical Woody Plants in the Absence of Flowers and Fruits: A Field Guide*, Birkhäuser Verlag, Berlin

Kremer, J. (2000) *1001 Ways to Market Your Books*, Open Horizons, Fairfield, Iowa

Lack, A. J., C. Whitefoord, P. G. H. Evans and A. James (1998) *Dominica: Nature Island of the Caribbean – Illustrated Flora*, Ministry of Tourism, Dominica

Lack, H. W. (2001) *Garden Eden: Masterpieces of Botanical Illustration*, Taschen, London

Laird, S. (2002) *Biodiversity and Traditional Knowledge: Equitable Partnerships in Practice*, Earthscan, London

LAWG (Leaf Architecture Working Group) (1999) *Manual of Leaf Architecture – Morphological Description and Categorisation of Dicotyledonous and Net-Veined Monocotyledonous Angiosperms by Leaf Architecture*, Smithsonian Institution, Washington, DC

Lebrun, J.-P. and A. L. Stork (1991–1997) *Enumeration des Plants à Fleurs d'Afrique Tropicale*, Conservatoire et Jardin Botanique de la Ville de Genève, Geneva (four volumes)

Ledig, F. T., R. W. Wilson, H. W. Duffield and G. Maxwell (1969) 'A discriminant analysis of introgression between *Quercus prinus* L. & Q. alba L.', *Bulletin of the Torrey Botanical Club*, vol 96, p156

Letouzey, R. (1986) *Manual of Forest Botany: Tropical Africa*, volumes 1–2 (translated by R. Huggett), Centre Technique Forestier Tropical, Nogent-sur-Marne, France

Linnaeus, C. (1753) *Species Plantarum*, Salvius, Stockholm (two volumes) [facsimile edition 1957–1959, Ray Society, London]

Liu, L. and Sclarof, F. (2000) 'Index trees for efficient deformable shape-based retrieval', *Proceedings of the IEEE Workshop on Content-Based Access of Image and Video Libraries (CBAIVL)*, Hilton Head, South Carolina, June

Lock, J. M. (1989) *Legumes of Africa: A Check-List*, Royal Botanic Gardens, Kew, UK

Loncaric, S. (1998) 'A survey of shape analysis techniques', *Pattern Recognition*, vol 31, pp983–1001

Lorenzi, H. (2002) *Árvores Brasileiras: Manual de Identificacao e Cultivo de Plantas Arboreas Nativas do Brasil*, Editora Plantarum, São Paulo, Brazil

Mabberley, D. J. (1997) *The Plant Book*, 2nd edition, Cambridge University Press, Cambridge, UK

Martin, G. J. (1995) *Ethnobotany: A Methods Manual*, Chapman and Hall, London

McCusker, A. (1999) *Flora of Australia Web-Glossary*, www.anbg.gov.au/glossary/webpubl/splitgls.htm

Mears, J. A. (1989) *Plant Taxonomic Literature: Bibliographic Guide*, Chadwyck-Healy, London

Mennega, A. M. W. (1988) 'Wood anatomy of the Hippocrateoideae (Celastraceae)', *IAWA Journal*, vol 18, pp331–368

Metcalfe, C. E. (1988) *Anatomy of the Dicotyledons: Magnoliales, Illiciales and Laurales/Sensu Armen Takhtajan*, Oxford University Press, UK

Metcalfe, C. R. and L. Chalk (1979) *Anatomy of the Dicotyledons. Volume 1: Systematic Anatomy of Leaf and Stem, with a Brief History on the Subject*, 2nd edition, Clarendon Press. Oxford

Modak P. and A. K. Biswas (1999) *Conducting Environmental Impact Assessment in Developing Countries*, United Nations University Press, Tokyo

Monro, A., D. Alexander, J. Reyes, M. Renderos and N. Ventura (2001) *Arboles de los Cafetales de El Salvador*, Natural History Museum, London

Morris P. and R. Therivel (2001) *Methods of Environmental Impact Assessment*, Spon, London

Morse, D. R. and G. M. Tardivel (1996) *A Comparison of the Effectiveness of a Dichotomous Key and a Multi-Access Key to Woodlice*, Report on British Ecological Society Small Ecological Project Grant No 1160, UK

Moskowitz H. (1975) 'Cross-cultural differences in simple taste preferences', *Science*, vol 190, pp1217–1218

O'Callaghan, J. F. (1970) 'An interactive system for leaf shape measurement', *International Journal of Man-Machine Studies*, vol 2, p29

ODA (Overseas Development Administration) (1995) 'Guidance note on how to do stakeholder analysis of aid projects and programmes', available at www.euforic.org/gb/stake1.htm

Pankhurst, R. J. (ed) (1975) *Biological Identification with Computers*, Academic Press, London

Pankhurst, R. J. (1991) *Practical Taxonomic Computing*, Cambridge University Press, Cambridge

Pankhurst, R. J. (1993) 'Principles and problems of identification', in R. Fortuner (ed) *Advances in Computer Methods for Systematic Biology*, Johns Hopkins University Press, Baltimore, pp125–136

Payne, W. W. (1978) 'A glossary of plant hair terminology', *Brittonia*, vol 30, pp239–255

Prance, G. T. (2001) 'Discovering the plant world', *Taxon*, vol 50, pp345–359

Press, M. C. (1999) 'The functional significance of leaf structure: A search for generalizations', *New Phytologist*, vol 143, pp219–231

Pretty J. N., I. Guijt, J. Thompson and I. Scoones (1995) *Participatory Learning and Action: A Trainer's Guide*, IIED, London

Putz, F. E. and H. A. Mooney (eds) (1991) *The Biology of Vines*, Cambridge University Press, Cambridge

Ramey, V. (1995) *Aquatic Plant Identification Deck*, Center for Aquatic Plants, University of Florida, Gainesville, Florida

Raunkiaer, C. (1934) *The Life Forms of Plants*, Oxford University Press, Oxford

Ray, T. S. (1992) 'Landmark eigenshape analysis: Homologous contours – leaf shape in *Syngonium* (Araceae)', *American Journal of Botany*, vol 79, pp69–76

Rejmánek, M. B. and S. W. Brewer (2001) 'Vegetative identification of tropical woody plants: State of the art and annotated bibliography', *Biotropica*, vol 33, no 2, pp214–228

Ribeiro, J. E. L. S., M. J. G. Hopkins, A. Vicentini, C. A. Sothers, J. A. S. Costa, J. M. Brito, M. A. D. Souza, L. H. P. Martins, L. G. Lohmann, P. A. C. L. Assunção, E. C. Pereira, C. F. Silva, M. R. Mesquita and L. C. Procópio (1999) *Flora da Reserva Ducke: Guia de Identificação das Plantas Vasculares de Uma Floresta de Terra-Firme na Amazônia Central*, INPA, Manaus, Amazonas, Brazil

Ripley, B. D. (1996) *Pattern Recognition and Neural Networks*, Cambridge University Press, Cambridge

Roche, C. (1999) *Impact Assessment for Development Agencies: Learning to Value Change*, Oxfam, UK

Rollet, B. (1980–1982) 'Interet de l'etude des ecorces dans la determination des arbes tropicaux sur pied', *Review Bois et Forêts des Tropiques*, vol 194, pp3–28; vol 195, pp31–50

Rosayro, R. A. de (1953) 'Field characters in the identification of tropical forest trees', *Empire Forestry Journal*, vol 32, pp124–141

Schmidt, D. (1999) *A Guide to Field Guides*, Libraries Unlimited, Westport, CT (see also supplement at www.library.uiuc.edu/bix/fieldguides/main.htm)

Schnell, R., G. Cusset and M. Quenum (1963) 'Contributions a l'étude des glandes extraflorales chez quelques groupes de plantes tropicales', *Revue Generales de Botanique*, vol 70, pp269–342

Seddon, S. A. and G. W. Lennox (1980) *Trees of the Caribbean*, Macmillan Education Ltd, London

Serier, J. B. (1986) 'Les secretions d'arbres', *Revue des Bois et Forets des Tropiques*, vol 213, pp33–39

Shanley, P., M. Cymerys and J. Galvão (1998) *Frutíferas da Mata na vida Amazônica*, Editora Supercores, Belem

Shanley, P. and G. R. Gaia (2002) 'Equitable ecology: Collaborative learning for local benefit in Amazonia', *Agricultural Systems*, vol 73, pp83–97

Shanley, P., I. Höhn and A. V. de Silva (1996) *Receitas sem Palavras: Plantas Medicinais da Amazônia*, Editora Supercores, Belem

Simpson, D. R. and D. Jones (1974) 'Punch card key to the families of Dicotyledons of the western hemisphere south of the United States', Field Museum of Natural History, Chicago

Sloane, H. (1707) *A Voyage to the Islands Madera, Barbadoes, Nieves, St. Christophers, and Jamaica with the Natural History of the Herbs and Trees, four-footed beasts, fishes, birds, insects, reptiles &c. of the last of those Islands to which is prefix'd an Introduction, wherein is an account of the inhabitants, Airs, Waters, Diseases, Trade &c. of that place; with some relations concerning the neighbouring continent, and Islands of America Illustrated with the figures of the things described which have not been heretofore engraved in large copper plates as big as the life*, two volumes, privately published for the author, London

Soepadmo, E. and K. M. Wong (eds) (1995–ongoing) *Tree Flora of Sabah and Sarawak*, FRIM, Kuala Lumpur

Spicer, R. A. (1986) 'Pectinal veins: A new concept in terminology for the description of dicotyledonous leaf venation patterns', *Botanical Journal of the Linnaean Society*, vol 93, pp379–388

Stace, C. A. (1965) 'The significance of the leaf epidermis in the taxonomy of the Combretaceae 1: A general review of tribal, generic and specific characters', *Botanical Journal of the Linnaean Society*, vol 59, pp220–252

Stearn, W. T. (1966) *Botanical Latin*, Thomas Nelson and Sons Ltd, London

Stevenson, R. D., W. A. Haber and R. A. Morris (2003) 'Electronic field guides and user communities in the eco-informatics revolution', *Conservation Ecology*, vol 7, no 1, p3, www.consecol.org/vol7/iss1/art3

Symington, C. F. (1943) 'Forester's manual of dipterocarps', *Malay Forestry Research*, vol 16

Systematics Association Committee for Descriptive Terminology (1960) 'I. Preliminary list of works relevant to descriptive biological terminology', *Taxon*, vol 9, no 8, pp245–257

Systematics Association Committee for Descriptive Terminology (1962) 'II. Terminology of simple symmetrical plane shapes', *Taxon*, vol 11, no 5, pp145–156, 245

Tailfer, Y. (1989) *La Foret Dense d'Afrique Tropicale: Identification Pratique des Principaux Arbres*, vol 1, ACCT, Paris

Taylor, C. J. (1960) *Synecology and Silviculture in Ghana*, Nelson, Edinburgh

Theobald, W. L., J. L. Krahulik and R. C. Rollins (1979) 'Trichome description and classification', in C. R. Metcalfe and L. Chalk (eds) *Anatomy of the Dicotyledons*, 4th edition, Clarendon Press, Oxford, pp40–53

Thikakul, S. M. (1985) *Manual of Dendrology*, Forestry Institutional Support Project, Cameroon, National Centre for Forestry Development and Canadian International Development Agency, Groupe Poulin, Quebec, Canada

Thomas, K. (1983) *Man and the Natural World*, Allen Lane, London

Tilling, S. M. (1984) 'Keys in biological identification: Their role and construction', *Journal of Biological Education*, vol 18, pp293–304

Timberlake J., C. Fagg and R. Barnes (1999) *Field Guide to the Acacias of Zimbabwe*, CBC Publishing, Zimbabwe

Trockenbrodt, M. (1990) 'Survey and discussion of the terminology used in bark anatomy', *IAWA Bulletin*, vol 11, pp141–166

Uphof, J. C. (1942) 'The ecological relations of plants with ants and termites', *Botanical Review*, vol 8, pp563–598

van Wyk, A. E. (1985) 'The genus *Eugenia* (Myrtaceae) in Southern Africa: Structure and taxonomic value of bark', *South African Journal of Botany*, vol 51, pp157–180

sVargas, I. G. and C. G. Jordán (eds) (2002) *Biodiversidad del Parque Nacional Noel Kempff Mercado: Principales Ecosistemas y Especies*, Fundación Amigos de la Naturaleza, Santa Cruz, Bolivia

Vargas, I. G. and C. G. Jordán (eds) (2003) *Principales Plantas Utiles del Bajo Paraguá*, Fundación Amigos de la Naturaleza, Santa Cruz, Bolivia

Vargas, I. G., A. Lawrence and M. Eid Otazu (2000) *Arboles y arbustos para sistemas agroforestales en los Valles Interandinos de Santa Cruz, Bolivia*, Fundación Amigos de la Naturaleza, Santa Cruz, Bolivia

Villiers, J. F. (1973) 'Icacinaceae', *Flore du Gabon*, vol 20, pp3–100

van Vliet, G. J. C. M. (1979) 'Wood anatomy of the Combretaceae', *Blumea*, vol 25, pp141–223

Webb, A. (1999) *Statistical Pattern Recognition*, Arnold, London

Westfall, R. H., H. F. Glenn and M. D. Oanagos (1986) 'A new identification aid combining features of a polyclave and an analytical key', *Botanical Journal of the Linnaean Society*, vol 92, pp65–73

Whitmore, T. C. (1962a) 'Studies in systematic bark morphology: I. Bark morphology in Dipterocarpacae', *New Phytologist*, vol 61, pp191–207

Whitmore, T. C. (1962b) 'Studies in systematic bark morphology: II. General features of bark construction in Dipterocarpaceae', *New Phytologist*, vol 61, pp208–220

Whitmore, T.C. (1962c) 'Studies in systematic bark morphology: III. Bark taxonomy in Dipterocarpaceae', *Gardens Bulletin Singapore*, vol 19, pp321–371

Whitmore, T. C. (1963) 'Studies in systematic bark morphology: IV. The bark of beech, oak and sweet chestnut', *New Phytologist*, vol 62, pp161–169

Wierzbicka, A. (1994) 'Semantic universals and primitive thought: The question of the psychic unity of humankind', *Journal of Linguistic Anthropology*, vol 4, no 1, pp23–49

Winston, J. (1999) *Describing Species: Practical Taxonomic Procedure for Biologists*, Columbia University Press, New York

Wise, R. (1998) *A Fragile Eden: Portraits of the Endemic Flowering Plants of the Granitic Seychelles*, Princeton University Press, Princeton, NJ

Witkowski, S. and C. Brown (1978) 'Lexical universals', *Annual Review of Anthropology*, vol 7, pp427–451

Wood, G. H. S. (1952) 'Bark as a means of tree identification', *Journal of Oxford University Forest Society*, vol 6 (III), p15

World Bank (2005) 'Request for proposals: Local language field guide materials for youth in Asia', available at www.cepf.net/ImageCache/cepf/content/pdfs/rfp_2ebnppyouthfield guides_2epdf/v1/rfp.bnppyouthfieldguides.pdf

World Wide Web Consortium (2002) 'Extensible mark-up language (XML)', www.w3.org/XML

Worms, E. A. (1942) 'Sense of smell of the Australian Aborigines: A psychological and linguistic study of the natives of the Kimberley Division', *Oceania*, vol 8, no 2, pp107–130

Wright, J. F., D. R. Morse and G. M. Tardivel (1995) 'An investigation into the use of hypertext as a user interface to taxonomic keys', *Computer Applications in the Biosciences*, vol 11, pp19–27

Wyatt-Smith, J. (1954) 'Suggested definitions of field characters (for use in the identification of tropical forest trees in Malaya)', *Malayan Forester*, vol 17, pp170–183

Yunus, M. and D. Yunus (1990) 'Systematic bark morphology of some tropical trees', *Botanical Journal of the Linnaean Society*, vol 103, pp367–377

Index

Join our
online community
and help us save paper and postage!

www.earthscan.co.uk

By joining the Earthscan website, our readers can benefit from a range of exciting new services and exclusive offers. You can also receive e-alerts and e-newsletters packed with information about our new books, forthcoming events, special offers, invitations to book launches, discussion forums and membership news. Help us to reduce our environmental impact by joining the Earthscan online community!

How? – Become a member in seconds!

>> Simply visit **www.earthscan.co.uk** and add your name and email address to the sign-up box in the top left of the screen – You're now a member!

>> With your new member's page, you can subscribe to our monthly **e-newsletter** and/or choose **e-alerts** in your chosen subjects of interest – you control the amount of mail you receive and can unsubscribe yourself

Why? – Membership benefits

- ✔ Membership is free!
- ✔ 10% discount on all books online
- ✔ Receive invitations to high-profile book launch events at the BT Tower, London Review of Books Bookshop, the Africa Centre and other exciting venues
- ✔ Receive e-newsletters and e-alerts delivered directly to your inbox, keeping you informed but not costing the Earth – you can also forward to friends and colleagues
- ✔ Create your own discussion topics and get engaged in online debates taking place in our new online Forum
- ✔ Receive special offers on our books as well as on products and services from our partners such as _The Ecologist_, _The Civic Trust_ and more
- ✔ Academics – request inspection copies
- ✔ Journalists – subscribe to advance information e-alerts on upcoming titles and reply to receive a press copy upon publication – write to info@earthscan.co.uk for more information about this service
- ✔ Authors – keep up to date with the latest publications in your field
- ✔ NGOs – open an NGO Account with us and qualify for special discounts

Join now?
Join Earthscan now!
name
surname
email address

Earthscan Member

[Your name]

Click to Change

My profile
My forum
My bookmarks
All my pages

www.earthscan.co.uk

THE EARTHSCAN FORESTRY LIBRARY

provides a collection of publications that address the key issues and innovations in policy, practice and theory that are shaping Forestry. Combining a wealth of knowledge and expertise from internationally renowned figures in the field, this Library is an essential resource for forestry practitioners, policy makers, conservationists, researchers and students worldwide.

Browse and buy on-line at **www.earthscan.co.uk**